ER

The Unofficial Guide

Mark Jones

For Lorraine

First published 2003 by Contender Books
Contender Books is a division of
The Contender Entertainment Group
48 Margaret Street
London W1W 8SE

This edition published 2003
1 3 5 7 9 10 8 6 4 2

ISBN 1 84357 035 1

Cover pictures © Getty Images
Plate sections © Retna Pictures (UK and US) Ltd, Getty Images

Printed in the UK by Bath Press, Bath
Cover and plates design by Burville-Riley
Text designed and typeset by Burville-Riley

Table of Contents

The characters

The episodes

Foreword

ER is one of TV's great success stories. Now in its ninth year, millions of viewers the world over regularly tune in to watch the lives of the doctors and nurses at County General Hospital, Chicago.

It's hard to do justice to a show that has thrilled and entertained for so long. In this book, I've tried to capture some of that excitement by focusing on the elements that have made it so popular: the staff of County General. This isn't a book about the medicine of *ER*, or even about the patients – it's about the cast of regular characters, their stories and lives.

The book is broken into two main sections: Characters and Episodes. The Character section has two chapters. The first, on the main cast, features biographies of all those characters past and present who made it to the title sequence: Carter, Benton, Weaver, Greene, etc. The second chapter, on the supporting cast, features short entries on many of those characters that have made repeat appearances over the years. It's not exhaustive – I've only included people we know something about – but it does cover the majority. Apologies to any die-hard Dr Zogoybi fans!

The Episodes section includes chapters on each season. Every episode has a summary. Again, it's not exhaustive – there isn't enough space to include some of the very minor story strands – but it does give a flavour for each show as a whole. Each episode is broken down into story strands, with smaller plots listed under *Other Threads*. I've also included season overviews that identify the key themes running through each year of the show.

For the best stories, the 'ones to watch', there are slightly longer entries and some comment. These aren't just my favourites: the list was compiled by polling subscribers on the *ER* Internet discussion groups in the UK and in the US. Hopefully the shortlist is a bit more representative than it otherwise would be.

Enjoy.

Mark Jones, October 2002

Acknowledgements

Many thanks to John Binns for his advice and guidance, especially in the early stages of this book. Thanks also to the usual suspects: Lisa Brattan, the Jones clan, Lance Parkin and Gareth Wigmore; to those who polled on the Internet newsgroups, notably Tracey Michelle; Michael Colvin; Lorraine P; Lewis; Sara Mitchell; Jonathan Chun; Harper; ZigZag; Adrienne; Brenda; Trig; Liz Batty; Ceindreadh; and to Michèle Brown and Sasha Morton at Contender for their support and enthusiasm for this project from the outset. Mentions must go to Anna Crow, Sam Shadforth and Dave Todd for letting me see the episodes I couldn't find – thanks guys! Lastly, but not least, special thanks goes to Lorraine Mann, the Obi-Wan of accountants, for her unfailing support and constant supply of tea and cake. This one's for you.

Current Main Cast

John Carter, MD *(Noah Wyle)*

Medical Student, 1994–5

Surgical Sub-intern, 1995–6

Surgical Intern, 1996–7

Emergency Medicine Intern, 1997–8

Resident, 1998–2001

Chief Resident, 2001–

John Truman Carter was born in 1970 into one of Chicago's richest families. His father, Roland Carter (called Richard by most), had a net worth of $178 million in the late 1990s. His grandparents, Millicent and Jonathan Truman Carter, lived in the palatial family home in Chicago. Their influential friends include the city's Mayor and Greg Davies, one of County General's key benefactors. The Carter Family Foundation, run by Millicent and her husband, remains a key supporter of local initiatives.

While he had a privileged upbringing, Carter's childhood was not without difficulty. His brother, Bobby, died of leukaemia when John was at school. Their mother, Eleanor, found it difficult to cope with his death. Afraid to risk suffering another loss of this magnitude, Eleanor distanced herself from her surviving son. She and Richard spent most of their time in Europe while John grew up at boarding school and with his grandparents.

Having watched the doctors with Bobby, John decided to pursue a career in medicine. It was a controversial choice: his grandparents wanted him to take over the family business. John refused and entered medical school, provoking a family disagreement that would run for many years. In fact, Bobby's loss also determined the type of doctor John would become. A colleague, Abby Keaton, once suggested that the experience explained Carter's strong empathy with children.

Carter began medical school in Chicago in 1992. He took rotations in psychiatry and dermatology. On 17 March 1994, he was assigned to Peter Benton at County General for trauma and surgical rotations. Benton was a hard taskmaster, dismissive of Carter's previous experience with "the well-dressed specialties", yet he was a key influence on Carter's professional development. Unrelentingly demanding, impatient and domineering, Peter Benton expected only the very best from his student. Carter had to work harder and harder just to keep up.

In his early days, Carter showed his inexperience. He informed the wrong family of a death and let his personal feelings interfere in the case of a transvestite who later committed suicide. He even dated a flirtatious patient and contracted a sexually transmitted disease. From the start, Carter showed a strong competitive streak that would remain throughout his career. But he also showed a natural ease with patients like Mary Kavanagh in stark contrast to his mentor, Peter Benton (1-2 to 1-10).

In these early days, Carter was also helped significantly by Mark Greene, whose more understanding approach contrasted sharply with Benton's style. When Carter complained about excessive scut work, it was Mark who persuaded Benton to let Carter do more procedures. There is a sense in which Carter was torn between two mentors, between the ER and the OR. He toyed briefly with the prospect of a trauma sub-internship and almost lost his place at County. It was only when a last-minute surgical sub-internship became available that Carter was able to return to County for his fourth year (1-22 to 1-24).

Now a surgical sub-intern, Carter was given more responsibility and placed under more pressure. Benton made it clear that Carter's performance reflected on him and brooked no lapses. Carter was assigned his first patient, Ed Menke, in October 1995 (the man died, 2-3). Benton also attached Carter to Carl Vucelich's pioneering "clamp and run" study. Carter identified candidates for the study, including Mrs Rubadoux. The Rubadoux case was a pivotal moment in Carter's career. He learned a hard lesson about being honest with his patients and their families (2-10 to 2-14). He later chastised himself for using his patients as guinea pigs for procedures.

Meanwhile, Carter hoped for a resident's position at County. In February 1996, he received a positive recommendation from Benton and in March he matched as a surgical resident at County. Overjoyed and in celebratory mood, Carter drank on duty and Dr Hicks asked for Carter's expulsion from the surgical service. Instead, Carter was told to work out his penance in the ER, and helped Mark Greene during a busy night shift (2-15 to 2-18).

The rest of Carter's sub-internship did not run smoothly. He competed with Dale Edson for patients and lost his girlfriend, Harper Tracy, in the process. He was also told he had not done enough ambulatory medicine and had to do a last-minute rotation with Doug Ross. It was while caring for one patient on this rotation, T. C. Lucas, that Carter missed his graduation. He also switched his application at the last minute from the surgical blue team to the surgical red team to continue working with Benton (2-18 to 2-22).

In September 1996, Dr John Carter returned to County as a surgical intern – and found Benton worse than ever. Benton put Carter under tremendous pressure. A kindred spirit was resident Dennis Gant, who Benton put under even greater pressure. Carter was not there to support Gant and was shocked when Gant was killed on the El. Although a verdict of accidental death was recorded, there was always the suspicion that Gant committed suicide. Carter felt guilty and was bitter at Benton's apparent lack of feeling. Angry, Carter accepted a place on Dr Hicks' team in January 1997 (3-1 to 3-13).

Meanwhile Carter had a promising relationship with Abby Keaton, a paediatrics surgeon recently transferred from Southside. Carter's desperate attempts to keep their relationship quiet from Peter Benton were ultimately doomed to failure. Carter was disappointed when Abby relocated to Pakistan (3-7 to 3-11).

Towards the summer of 1997, Carter had several run-ins with Donald Anspaugh, the hospital's Chief of Staff. Anspaugh was impressed with Carter's diagnostic skill, but was annoyed when Carter doubted his. The root of their disagreements was actually more fundamental. Carter had become more interested in his patients and trauma work, and requested a transfer to become a trauma resident instead. Anspaugh came to respect Carter's wish and granted the request over the summer, although Carter was told to repeat his internship (3-17 to 3-22).

Carter had several problems as an ER intern. He had foolishly said he would work for free to ensure his transfer. He was told to run all cases past Maggie Doyle, a second-year resident he had taught the previous year. Then he was given a medical student, George Henry, who had no practical experience. On top of all that, his professional relationship with Benton was worse than ever. Benton was offended that Carter had not let him convince him to go into surgery. The truth was that Benton believed Carter would make an exceptional surgeon, and that Carter would have been talked round to becoming one (4-1 to 4-5). Nevertheless, Carter seemed suited to life in the Emergency Room. He showed tremendous maturity when he handled a chemical contamination emergency in the ER and won acclaim from the emergency services (4-15).

Carter also became involved with paediatrician Anna Del Amico, although there was an unhappy catalyst. During Christmas 1997, Carter discovered that his cousin, Chase, was taking heroin. John enlisted Anna's help and together they tried to detox Chase in secret. They were unsuccessful: Chase took an overdose and suffered permanent brain damage. Carter's grandparents were furious that Carter had hidden the truth from them and withdrew financial support. John maintained only limited contact with his family through his grandmother, Millicent (4-10 to 4-16). Carter was also dismayed to lose Anna. She was reunited with her former boyfriend Dr Max Rocher in summer 1998, and together they returned to Philadelphia.

In autumn 1998, Carter became a second-year ER resident and was assigned a new student, Lucy Knight. Carter put Lucy under the same pressure he had received from Peter Benton. Lucy had her limitations, but covered them up. Carter was misled and gave her more responsibility – more than she could deal with. Lucy's mishandling of a Hallowe'en party resulted in Carter being fired from his job as a dorm supervisor. Their relationship worsened until they dealt with a case of a kidnapped girl (5-1 to 5-10). Carter later came to appreciate the pressure he had put on Lucy through his dealings with a prospective medical student, Antoine (5-19 to 5-22).

In fact, Lucy and Carter's tension was partly sexual. Despite a brief clinch, they agreed they were not suited and decided to remain friends. Carter developed a deep respect for Lucy, recognising her significant skills as a psychiatrist.

In autumn 1999, Carter briefly dated Elaine Nichols. Elaine was the former wife of Carter's cousin, Douglas; they had divorced three years previously. During the autumn, Elaine was diagnosed with breast cancer and had a mastectomy. Carter tried to be supportive but was uncomfortable and the relationship suffered. Although Carter got back with Elaine, she decided to move on. She left for Europe in the winter (6-1 to 6-5).

A short time later, tragedy struck. On 14 February 2000, Paul Sobriki, a patient with mental health problems, stabbed Carter and Lucy. It was only the fast, brilliant surgery of Benton and Anspaugh that saved Carter's life. Sadly, Lucy died. Carter felt guilty that he never gave Lucy the credit she deserved. Carter was affected by post-traumatic stress: he suffered insomnia and flashbacks and began overreacting to violent patients. He turned to pain medication and steadily increased his intake, becoming dependent. Carter's colleagues eventually found out and confronted him about his drug use, but offered him a way out. It was Benton who persuaded him to admit his problem and enter a rehabilitation clinic (6-13 to 6-22).

Carter stayed in a rehabilitation centre in Atlanta from May to September 2000. On his return to Chicago, it was clear he had not really admitted his problems to himself. Carter was put on restricted duty but resented the restrictions under which he had to work

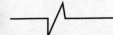

(Romano wanted to know "who's watching the drugstore cowboy"). His first days back were difficult: an array of minor cases, a reliance on others for some procedures, and spot drug tests. More frustrating was the murder of a woman in the ER after Carter had just performed a miraculous save (7-1 and 7-2).

His recovery would take a long time. One night, during a long shift in December, Carter took two pills he found on a patient, although thankfully he did not ingest the drugs. After persuasion from Abby Lockhart, his sponsor at AA, Carter told Kerry Weaver, who put Carter on restricted duty once more. It was a turning point. Carter visited his cousin, Chase, and admitted his problem fully. His recovery began and he soon proved himself under pressure when attending a train wreck (7-1 to 7-13).

It was during Carter's rehabilitation that he started a long flirtation with Abby Lockhart. Abby was a recovering alcoholic and agreed to be his AA sponsor. They grew closer during a Carter Family Foundation fundraising ball when Abby ran into her ex-husband. Clearly Abby had some feelings for John: her concern over John's fling with Rena was not just because she was 19 years old. However, there were many complications, not least Abby's increasing involvement with Luka Kovac. They remained friends, but Carter said he wanted to be more than that (7-22).

Meanwhile, Carter had a shot at becoming Chief Resident, but was disappointed to hear that his recent drugs infraction cost him the post. He heard he was not being considered for any attending positions and began considering his options. Six weeks before his residency was due to run out, a startling opportunity became available. Jing-Mei Chen, who had been made Chief Resident in September 2001, struggled under pressure and killed a patient. She was suspended, and later resigned over problems with Kerry Weaver. His probationary period over, Carter accepted the post.

Carter soon had family issues to deal with. In autumn 2001, his grandfather died. Shortly after, his grandmother Millicent was diagnosed with Shy-Drager syndrome. She became increasingly disorientated and needed private nursing care (8-1 to 8-8).

Meanwhile, John's parents divorced. His mother, Eleanor, came to Chicago and latched on to John as a means of support. John was furious that Eleanor had been so unsupportive throughout his life, a result of her pain over Bobby's death – "Bobby died and I lost a mother" – and was angry when Eleanor played out their past with a young leukaemia patient. However, the case prompted Eleanor to start dealing with Bobby's death. Carter was pleased when she supported the patient through his illness (8-10 to 8-14).

Carter continued to play for Abby. Their prospects were bleak until the autumn, when Abby and Luka broke up. Just then, Susan Lewis returned. Carter had pursued Susan unsuccessfully in 1994 and held a torch for her ever since. They dated over the winter months but the relationship did not work. Susan still saw Carter as the medical student of seven years ago; Carter was still in love with Abby. Abby and Carter finally got together in the summer of 2002, a year after Carter had told Abby his feelings.

At work, Carter suddenly found himself with a higher profile. His mentor, Peter Benton, left County in the winter to join a private practice. Then, in early 2002, came the illness and tragic death of Mark Greene. As the next longest serving ER doctor, Carter had to fill the significant void. Carter succeeded in holding the ER together during news of Mark's death, and soon showed strength mediating between newcomers Michael Gallant and Gregory Pratt. By early summer 2002, Carter had "set the tone", as Mark had said he would.

Trivia: Benton's mother thought the Carter family may once have been slave-owners in Tennessee who owned Benton's ancestors. Carter used to play with Fabergé eggs among his Weebles. He won dressage competitions on his horse, Marigold, and won several rosettes at Temple Farms in 1985. The Carter family commissioned an oil painting to celebrate the win. Carter was at school with the son of Greg Davies, the multi-millionaire benefactor of the hospital. He got two perms while in high school. He and his friend Tony Sirisolo used to steal communion wine when they were children. During high school, Carter would call on Millicent unexpectedly and they would have cocoa and talk. In 1990 he took part in the Whitbread round-the-world yacht race, but his boat capsized during the Sydney to Auckland leg. Carter used to be a junior varsity wrestler, and his first white doctor's coat was tailored.

Carter has Peter Benton's appendix in a jar: it used to grace his mantelpiece, along with several photographs taken during the operation. Carter takes one sugar in coffee, though he used to hate coffee when he was 15. He escaped carol singing by claiming to have "chronic tone deafness and acute stage fright". He can't use a tumble dryer. Carol thinks a beard makes Carter look "mythic". Nuns find Carter irresistible (Haleh: "What is it with you and nuns, Carter?" Chunni: "It's almost kinky."). Carter reckons reality television is one of the four horsemen of the apocalypse.

He has a "thing" for Darla in Radiology ("The one with the collagen lips?" – Susan). Carter lost his virginity aged 11 to the family's 25-year-old housemaid. The weirdest place Carter ever had sex was on a train to Seattle (he may have been on his own…). During sex, Carter delays the inevitable by recalling the instruments in the trauma room, and at the height of passion with Rena, he yelled "Stat!"

Carter's grandfather had a heart attack while driving the lawnmower and crashed into the pond. He has an Uncle Everett who has a hunchback. Carter still gets sick at work after eight years. He now uses Mark Greene's stethoscope.

Jing–Mei ('Deb') Chen, MD *(Ming-Na Wen)*
Medical Student, 1995
Resident, 1999–2001
Chief Resident, September–October 2001
Attending, 2002–

Jing-Mei Chen was born in 1970 to prominent and wealthy parents. Chen's mother became Chief of Surgery at St Bart's. Her father was able to have his daughter given a place at County by making a substantial donation to the hospital's finances. The family house is large and staffed by servants.

In January 1995, Chen, then using her anglicised name Debra, started work in the ER as a second-year medical student. Deb was very inexperienced and caused havoc on her first day. She and Carter were soon in competition. Deb benefited from a photographic memory and could make astonishing diagnoses. She was always alert and prepared; and outclassed Carter at a trauma presentation in February. Deb's ambitions were never in doubt: she eagerly asked Benton for an ER sub-internship placement shortly after she started (1-12 and 1-13).

It was Deb's competitiveness and ambition that led her to make a near fatal error. Carter and Deb had to complete a certain number of procedures to finish the year with high honours. These procedures would also influence the award of the trauma sub-internship. Determined to win, Debra performed a central line on a drug addict. She lost the guide wire and William Swift had to step in to save the patient. The incident was almost fatal and the hospital could have been sued. Deb later confessed that she didn't care about the patient: "I wanted the procedure." Deb admitted that this was the major difference between herself and John Carter. Deb Chen left County, and medicine, in April 1995 (1-20).

But she was not out of medicine for long. In August 1995, she was on a subway when a man suffered a heart attack. Deb was able to save his life. The event made her realise she had a gift for medicine that she should not waste. She joined a medical programme in New York but this fell apart in autumn 1999. Around Christmas, her father made a big donation to County General to buy her a residency mid-year. Although Romano knew her background (he thought the guidewire incident showed her to be "way too much of an over-achiever"), Deb was allowed to return. She started worked as a resident in the ER around New Year 1999, but now used the name Jing-Mei (6-10).

Chen still had her run-ins with Carter, who was surprised at her return. Carter still showed himself to be more interested in the patients, and they disagreed over "soft admits" (6-11). Chen still seemed equally competitive, both with Carter and Dave Malucci (6-13). Jing-Mei was also just as determined: she trapped Romano into signing a petition supporting compulsory testing of babies for a rare genetic disorder (6-20). Romano seemed grudgingly admiring of her tactics! Chen soon set her sights on becoming Chief Resident.

In April 2000, Jing-Mei treated Frank "Rambo" Bacon, a nurse from ICU (6-15). They evidently saw more of each other, because Chen discovered she was pregnant some time in the autumn (7-01). Jing-Mei felt that a baby would injure her career prospects and decided to put the child up for adoption. She tried to keep the pregnancy a secret and only told Frank when she needed his consent for adoption. Kerry found out at 22 weeks, when Chen struggled to cope with the delivery of a premature baby. Jing-Mei's mother did not hear until Thanksgiving 2000. Her shock at discovering that the father was black confirmed to Jing-Mei that her family could never accept the child.

In December 2000, Chen gave birth. Giving up the child to his new parents proved more difficult than she had hoped, but she did so anyway. After, she remained in contact with the parents who named her son Michael Alexander (7-9 and 7-18). Chen took maternity leave but was annoyed some months later to discover that she could not become Chief Resident because the leave had put her behind on procedures. Jing-Mei alleged discrimination and Kerry was forced to reconsider her position (7-21 and 7-22). In September 2001, Chen became Chief Resident (8-1).

Jing-Mei's time as Chief Resident was as brief and tragic as her time as a medical student had been six years previously. Chen struggled with the new demands and frequently asked for Kerry's advice. Kerry was highly critical and urged Jing-Mei to take charge. However, Jing-Mei panicked when faced with a man who'd had a severe heart attack. She paged Weaver but Kerry did not answer. Instead of checking the man's X-ray, Chen administered drugs that collapsed his weak aorta, causing fatal internal bleeding. It was a serious error of judgement. Kerry was highly critical of Chen and later covered her own back during an investigation by Risk Management. Chen was told she was no longer Chief Resident and put on probation for one year and suspension for one month. Angry at Kerry's betrayal, Jing-Mei resigned. Carter was offered her post. Remembering her son, Chen told Carter: "Promise me, John, that whatever sacrifice you make for this place, you just make sure it's worth it." (8-2 to 8-4)

During her months away from County, Chen looked into Kerry's absence on the night of the incident. She discovered that Kerry did not attend because she had left her pager in the bathroom at Doc Magoo's, the diner across the street from the hospital. Early the next year, Chen approached the hospital and demanded to be reinstated. Despite Kerry's opposition, Romano made Jing-Mei an attending and agreed she would not have to report to Weaver (8-11 and 8-12).

Back in the ER, Jing-Mei could now act almost independently of Weaver. Kerry rightly feared discipline problems and soon found Chen flouting her authority. When Kerry stressed her wish to avoid a divided team, Jing-Mei suggested that Kerry could quit (8-13). Though they have broken down their barriers since, there are still unspoken tensions between Weaver and Chen.

Trivia: Carter's peer evaluation of Chen for the position of Chief Resident pushed her over the top on the rankings. Jing-Mei has a photographic memory. She once took LSD in some spiked chocolates. Chen gave her date "hand relief" during the first Harry Potter movie – he wanted to marry her!

Elizabeth Corday, FRCS *(Alex Kingston)*

Holder of Surgical Fellowship, 1997–8
Intern, 1998–9
Cardiothoracic Fellow, 1999–
Associate Chief of Surgery, 1999–

Elizabeth Corday was born in England in 1964, the only child of Isabelle and Charles. After birth, she was given to a nurse while her mother went to Spain for three weeks. Elizabeth was sent to boarding school when she was five. Isabelle continued to work as a noted physicist throughout Elizabeth's childhood. Charles was a surgeon, like his father before him, and a cardiothoracic specialist. Elizabeth decided to follow in his footsteps but once intimated that she also became a doctor to rattle her mother. Charles and Elizabeth stopped speaking at Elizabeth's medical school graduation in 1991 and did not see each other again until Elizabeth's wedding ten years later.

Elizabeth trained in the UK. She completed a medical degree and became a Fellow of the Royal College of Surgeons. In Great Britain, she worked as a surgical lecturer in orthopaedics and trauma, roughly equivalent to a senior surgical resident. She also worked with Donald Anspaugh's former colleague Sir Lyle Sugden ("old Suggie") in his latter days. In September 1997, Corday joined County General through the BTA ("been to America") scheme as a surgical fellow (4-1). Her sponsor was Dr Robert Romano. Charles Corday already had the measure of Romano before Elizabeth moved to Chicago and was never keen on her working with him.

Corday was thrown into a highly competitive environment. Her first few months at County were characterised by a difficult relationship with Peter Benton. Benton felt Corday used his difficulties looking after his son to cherry-pick the procedures she would carry out. He retaliated by encouraging Corday to perform an appendectomy without supervision. Shortly after, the two found themselves working together on Romano's surgical team and reconciled their differences (4-2 to 4-8). They started dating a short time later.

Although Benton's accusations of manipulation were not entirely fair, Corday was driven by a thirst for procedures. In December 1997, she performed a risky fibula transplant on Allison Beaumont. The surgery put Allison into a coma. Corday was mortified that she had ignored what was best for her patient to perform a procedure. Later, she befriended Allison and became a forceful advocate for Allison's care, arranging vocal cord surgery at no cost. Allison was so impressed she became a paramedic. However, in May 1998, Allison was injured during training. Corday saved her life once more, ruefully noting: "You can put them back together, but you can't keep them that way." (4-9 to 4-19).

Romano was highly critical of Corday's approach in his first six-month assessment of her. Apart from maligning her interest in vocal cord surgery, he was highly critical of her actions in the March 1998 case of Leo Leipziger, a man she saved from a collapsing building, where she endangered paramedics (4-15). They also clashed when Corday ran an artificial blood (or haemo A) study in the ER while Romano ran a similar study in the OR. Romano offered Corday a place on his study, but she declined (4-17).

In fact there was more behind Corday's problems with Romano. In early summer 1998, Romano asked Elizabeth out. She declined, saying she does not date colleagues, though still in a relationship with Peter Benton. When Romano discovered her relationship with Peter, he hinted that she might not have a future at County. Sure enough, in June 1998, Romano discontinued his sponsorship (4-20 to 4-22). The matter was later raised as part of a sexual harassment enquiry into Romano. Corday provided a statement then retracted it under pressure from Romano (5-12 and 5-13).

Despite losing her sponsorship, Elizabeth was keen to stay in Chicago, not least for Peter. She was interviewed in Denver and almost gained a sponsorship from Cromley. In autumn 1998, her father tried to recruit Elizabeth to his own practice, but she declined. Elizabeth finally took Kerry Weaver's suggestion and started over as an intern to gain her US licence.

She was assigned to "weasel" Dale Edson, but later transferred to work for Benton. Benton was determined to not show any favours and worked Elizabeth hard. During one very long shift, she almost killed a man by administering the wrong dose of magnesium (5-7). At the hearing, Corday defended herself valiantly, criticising the practice of working interns for 36 hours straight. The hospital agreed Corday was not at fault. Meanwhile Elizabeth was upset by Peter's lukewarm support. He needed to devote more time to his son, Reese, and they had grown apart. Elizabeth ended their relationship in December 1998 (5-9).

Their relationship quickly gave way to rivalry. In April 1999, as Elizabeth's internship was coming to an end, she proposed a new trauma research fellowship at County and was first in line. She was furious when Benton applied for the post and got it. However, Romano quickly gave Elizabeth a five-year cardiothorasic position he had earmarked for Peter. Romano admitted he would do anything to keep Corday in surgery, including making himself scarce (5-18 to 5-22). Meanwhile, Elizabeth grew closer to Mark Greene. They started dating in the summer of 1999.

In September 1999, Corday was dismayed when Romano succeeded Anspaugh as the hospital's Chief of Staff. Elizabeth quickly approached Charles Cameron at Rush Hospital for an alternative cardiothorasic fellowship. However, she was surprised when Romano appointed her as Associate Chief of Surgery. Corday objected to being announced as the new post holder without the matter being discussed first, but Romano knew she would accept! Corday soon found herself doing Romano's dirty work. After two months, she finally insisted she would not blindly follow Romano's instructions and earned herself more of a free hand. She did note of Romano: "You have to admire the method in his madness, no matter how sociopathic." (6-1 to 6-6)

Although now a senior manager at the hospital, Elizabeth was still free to operate as a trauma surgeon. On a paramedic ride along in November 1999, she withheld treatment from Dean Rawlins, a suspected rapist, until he provided information. Over the next months, Corday was exposed to the true horror of the man as he tormented both her and the victim's family. Corday duped Rawlins into confessing to more murders by promising him a lethal dose of morphine. As much as she would have liked to administer a real dose, Corday knew her job, for better or worse, was simply to put Rawlins back together again (6-7 to 6-11).

In January 2000, Elizabeth was surprised to hear her mother was in town. Isabelle was delivering lectures on adaptive optics and wave particle duality, but hadn't told her Elizabeth she was coming. Mark encouraged Elizabeth to meet her mother. They started to make some progress, although Isabelle's brief fling with Mark's father, David, made Elizabeth distinctly uncomfortable. When Isabelle was due to leave, Elizabeth made arrangements to see her one final time. Isabelle took an early flight (6-12 to 6-16).

Elizabeth and Mark became more serious and in autumn 2000 they were engaged. They moved to a house in the suburbs. Shortly after, Elizabeth found out that she was pregnant – the same day that Mark discovered he had a brain tumour (7-7). Elizabeth encouraged Mark to get a second opinion and was present at his operation on 31 December 2000 (7-2 to 7-10).

It was an unhappy time at work also. Elizabeth botched an endoscopic procedure on a patient, Al Patterson, causing paralysis. Patterson filed a malpractice suit. Elizabeth lied in court to protect her career. In January 2001, the hospital reached an out of court settlement for $1.5 million. The case shocked Elizabeth and she began to lose her nerve. It was only Romano's brutal tactics – leaving Corday to panic by herself in surgery – that brought her back to her senses (7-6 to 7-12). Corday quickly proved she was back at the top of her game by operating for several hours while heavily pregnant. She and Mark married in April 2001. Their baby, Ella, was delivered in the summer (7-19).

From autumn 2001, Elizabeth's marriage came under strain with the arrival of Rachel Greene, Mark's daughter from his first marriage. She came at the wrong time: Elizabeth was struggling to cope with motherhood and was being investigated for a series of post-operative deaths at County. Elizabeth accused Alex Babcock of killing her patients, although this was later disproved (8-5 to 8-7).

Meanwhile, Rachel was slowly going off the rails. In spring 2002, Ella ingested two of Rachel's ecstasy tablets and was rushed to the ER. Ella recovered, but the incident was a breaking point for Elizabeth. Mark refused to choose between his daughters, so Elizabeth took Ella and left. Meanwhile, Mark's tumour returned. It was only after she discovered the truth that they were reunited. Elizabeth was instrumental in helping Mark reunite with Rachel and was present in Hawaii when he died (8-13 to 8-21).

Trivia: Before joining County, Elizabeth was involved with Jeremy, "a self-possessed dermatologist". She is a formidable darts player and loves practical jokes – she used to live down the road from a joke shop. Elizabeth was going to marry Tommy Bradshaw, the little freckle-faced boy who lived down the road. He was later indicted for tax fraud. Elizabeth has an uncle who works at Birmingham University. She loves the smell of talcum powder on a man. Both Elizabeth and her mother Isabelle are terrible at ten-pin bowling. Isabelle spoke before the University of Chicago Department of Astrophysics on "Pulsars and Globular Clusters".

Elizabeth is an expert at robotic surgery (she is a certified in AESOP, unlike Romano) and has a reputation for doing a speedy colon dissection. She found Denver "a bit flat". At Hallowe'en 1998, Elizabeth dressed as Heidi. She is a fan of T. S. Elliot and went through a disco phase in December 1998. The family dog was a Bouvier breed.

Michael Gallant *(Sharif Atkins)*
Medical Student, 2001–

Michael Gallant was born into a military family. His father served for 26 years as a non-commissioned officer. Most of Michael's six brothers and sisters serve in the armed services. His brother Gavin is a munitions specialist for the US Air Force, based in Texas. His younger brother Frank is a marine working out of Pendleton. His sister Carol is in the Caro Vincent. The only siblings not in the forces are his youngest brother, Steve, who is 14, and Michael's twin sister, Susan, who teaches in Washington DC and has cerebral palsy.

Michael minored in English Literature at Howard University before joining the US Army reserves. He served for one year on active duty as a Lieutenant. The army put him on their scholarship programme and now pays for his medical education.

Michael joined County in late 2001 as a third-year student. He was assigned to John Carter for his ER rotation. His first day on the job was "a whole different kind of crazy" to active service. He was told he was doing things wrong by a patient who turned out to be a second-year medical student in need of psychological help. He also treated Hilliker, a mall security guard, who injured a boy in a chase. A retired cop who never used his gun during service, Hilliker felt so guilty he tried to commit suicide. Gallant took pity on him and tried to persuade Luka not to inform the police because the guard still had friends on the force. Luka informed them anyway, to Gallant's dismay.

Gallant's army training has given him strength under pressure. In late 2001, he helped Kerry Weaver perform a Caesarean on a woman trapped in a crashed ambulance. Gallant's heroic actions saved a fireman from electrocution and enabled the baby to be brought to the ER safely. Although Kerry took issue with Gallant's gung-ho actions, she gained a lot of respect for the young student. Carter noted Kerry's apparent ease with Gallant later: "Oh, so it's *Michael* now?"

Gallant's working relationships have not all been trouble-free. In spring 2002, Gregory Pratt joined the ER for a three-month internship in trauma medicine. Pratt, Gallant's senior, derided Michael's abilities. Gallant refused to back down and together they ran a procedure that nearly killed their patient. Carter berated Gallant's actions. Michael was keen not to be confused with Pratt. While they were both complicit, Gallant showed the greater remorse and responsibility.

Trivia: One of Gallant's first tasks in the ER was to take a stinking stool sample: "Yeah, those old ladies can surprise you, huh?" Carter quipped. Gallant lost his virginity to Tanya McBride in the balcony of their church after choir practice. Michael was 14 years old and in the ninth grade. He doesn't approve of smoking in public buildings. He is allergic to dogs. According to a psychic, Gallant reminds Frank of his son.

Luka Kovac, MD *(Goran Visnjic)*
Temporary Staff, 1999
ER Attending, 1999–

Luka Kovac was born in Croatia, one of two brothers. He grew up on his grandfather's farm near the coast before moving to Zagreb as a teenager. His father, a talented abstract painter, had a day job as a train driver. Luka went to college and later undertook his compulsory service in the Croatian army.

Luka married Daniella and they had two children, Yasla and Marco. During the war, the family lived in a small apartment in Vukovar. Daniella wanted to move out of the town but Luka was keen to finish his internship. One day, while Luka was at the market for supplies, an artillery shell hit their apartment building. Marco was killed instantly. Daniella was critically injured but Luka could not abandon Yasla to take his wife to safety. Daniella and Yasla both died. Luka, raised as a Catholic, lost his faith.

Luka moved to America, perhaps choosing Chicago because it was home to some distant relatives. He started working as a "moonlighter" – a substitute doctor brought in to cover staff absences (6-1). As such he had a flexible lifestyle: he bought a houseboat and lived in the city during the summer, moving south in the winter. In summer 1999 he started working at County General as a temporary member of ER staff. In November, he was made an attending after the departure of Dr Gabe Lawrence (6-7).

Given his tragic past, it is unsurprising that Luka had an uncompromising moral outlook. Early in his time at County, he provoked an abusive husband into assaulting him so that he could have him arrested and therefore protect the man's wife (6-3). He demanded that Dave Malucci take responsibility for giving a young boy the tragic news that he had inoperable cancer – an incident that also showed Luka's teaching talents (6-10). Luka insisted on selecting the recipients of a donor kidney, rather than give it to the first person on the list (he was so choosy, the nurses joked he would have to take it home with him!)

(6-17). More significantly, Luka refused to treat a seriously injured gunman and chose to help the shooter's less critically injured child victim instead. Benton was furious with him, and Luka's actions contributed to the gunman's death (6-22).

Luka was also vocal in cases involving children. He criticised Kerry Weaver for putting a young boy into care and breaking up a family (6-10). He helped mount a sting operation against an abusive mother (6-12) and showed great skill and sensitivity in breaking news of the death of a young couple to their two children (6-13). In summer 2000, Luka treated Gloria Milton, an 18-year-old who refused to have a Caesarean delivery to save her child. Luka tried to get a court order to overrule her decision, but it came too late. Luka was disgusted by the needless death of the child (6-22).

It was perhaps inevitable that Luka, once a parent, grew closer to nurse Carol Hathaway. When they met, Carol was already heavily pregnant. Luka helped get her to County when she went into labour. After the birth, Luka was a support for Carol and was keen to help out. They started dating in (6-19) but the relationship was short-lived: Carol knew she should be with Doug Ross. She ended her relationship with Luka (6-20) and joined Doug in Seattle a few days later.

Luka was greatly disappointed, but began a promising relationship with Abby Lockhart in autumn 2000. Abby had worked briefly but unsuccessfully as a medical student for much of the year. When her ex-husband stopped paying her fees, she returned to nursing. Luka, ever pragmatic, had great respect for her abilities and gave her more latitude than was permitted, incurring the displeasure of Kerry Weaver (7-3). It was his confidence in Abby that kick-started their relationship.

However, the relationship never had time to develop. A mugger attacked Luka and Abby on an early date. Luka beat the man, killing him (7-3). Luka was remorseful and spent a great deal of time trying to find out more about the mugger. Abby found it difficult to help Luka come to terms with the events. She also had her own problems to deal with when her estranged and troubled mother, Maggie, arrived in Chicago. Luka was uncompromising in his assessment of Maggie's mental health and urged Abby to have her mother admitted to hospital.

Although Luka was vindicated, it was not the news Abby wanted to hear, nor the support she needed. She increasingly found support in John Carter (7-19). Carter and Luka clashed both over Abby and incidents at work where Carter questioned Luka's ability to supervise him (6-20 and 7-18). Abby and Luka grew more distant.

While Luka's relationship with Abby grew colder, he began to revisit his religious beliefs. The trigger was Bishop Stewart, an elderly, sick cleric who needed steroids to be able to continue his ministry. Luka grew to respect Stewart's wishes, though the bishop hid his diabetes from Luka, resulting in the exacerbation of a condition called lupus. As the bishop slowly died, Luka confronted his loss of faith. During a harrowing train wreck that prompted Luka to revisit the death of his family, Luka's faith was restored (7-11 to 7-15).

Abby and Luka continued to date over the summer, but their relationship was long since over. Their break-up in October 2001 was acrimonious. Shortly afterwards, Luka began seeing Nicole, an immigrant waitress working in his local bar. He supported Nicole and found her a job at County, but she was dismissed for stealing. Fearing she would lose Luka, she told him she was pregnant. Abby doubted the claim but later discovered that Nicole had a miscarriage after eight weeks. Nicole told Luka she had lied about being pregnant to protect him. Luka only felt sadness that he could not help Nicole more (8-2 to 8-10).

Following his time with Nicole, Luka returned to Bosnia for two months as part of the Doctors Without Borders initiative. On his return to Chicago in March 2002, his strong feelings for Abby were only too clear. When Abby was violently assaulted, Luka found the culprit and beat him violently, threatening to kill him if he came near Abby again. Although the man would heed Luka's words, the incident stopped the police from pressing charges. Luka offered friendly support to Abby, giving her a room at his apartment, but clashed with Carter when Abby started drinking. Abby moved back to her flat a few weeks later, and went on to become an item with Carter, leaving Luka alone.

Trivia: A movie was shot on Luka's grandfather's farm: he and his brother made money out of running errands. Luka's confirmation name was Michael – the patron saint of the sick. He played Hamlet in a school production. Luka learned to fence when he was in college. Daniella was in labour for 16 hours with their first child. Luka has a photograph of Yasla (taken at her fourth birthday party) but has none of Marco. Herb, his second cousin's wife's brother-in-law, is a used car salesman in Chicago. Luka has a PlayStation and likes killing zombies. He doesn't know the rules of softball, and isn't very good at playing Pictionary.

Susan Lewis, MD *(Sherry Stringfield)*

Resident, 1993–6
Attending/Deputy Chief, 2001–

Susan Lewis was born in October 1965, the younger of two sisters. Her mother, Cookie Lewis, was an alcoholic who smoked 40 cigarettes a day while bringing up her kids. Her father, Henry, was a car mechanic, but has now retired (Susan reckons he's "a test-driver for Barcalounger"). Cookie and Henry are still married, although Susan reckons they shouldn't be. "We have ways of screwing people up in my family," she observed.

Susan entered medicine. During her third and fourth years as a medical student, Susan took rotations at Mercy and Lakeside in Chicago. She joined County in June 1993 as a resident where she and Mark Greene became good friends. Susan had a problem asserting herself with senior faculty members despite her naturally strong personality. In January 1995, after she backed down from Jack Kayson, Susan was told to be "an aggressive advocate" for her patients. Lewis quickly learned her lesson and was able to prove this when she treated Kayson for a heart attack. More significant was the tone this incident set in Susan's relationship with Mark Greene. Mark had appeared supportive of Susan, but had actually raised her lack of assertiveness with Morgenstern. Susan was not impressed. There would always be a tension between their professional and personal relationships (1-11 to 1-13).

In terms of personal relationships, Susan's romances were either unhappy or unrequited. In March 1994, she was busy extracting herself from a relationship with a man called Paul. Soon after, she started dating Div Cvetic, Head of Psychiatrics. Susan and Div had a number of professional run-ins that must have put a strain on their relationship.

However, Div was also going through a breakdown and disappeared from County in late 1994 (1-1 to 1-9). Susan later discovered that he was still living in Chicago but he never returned to County General.

Around the same time, Susan had to care for her older sister, Chloe. Chloe was a loose cannon: "She's 34 years old and she can't even part her hair." In autumn 1994, Chloe became pregnant by Ronnie, a drug user who later abandoned her. Chloe herself had problems: she was arrested for being drunk and disorderly in October 1994 and driving under influence in April 1995. Susan helped Chloe through the pregnancy and delivered baby Suzie on 12 May 1995. Intent on caring for the baby, Chloe started studying a computer course at Midwest Business Academy, but later dropped out. She became a waitress but was fired after an argument with her employer. Failing to pull herself together, Chloe fell into bad company and started drinking and using drugs. In early October 1995 she abandoned Suzie in Susan's flat.

As Susan struggled with Chloe, there were further changes at work. In autumn 1995, Mark Greene was made an attending and Kerry Weaver replaced him as Chief Resident. Susan and Kerry clashed almost immediately when Kerry called time of death on one of Susan's patients. "She's irritating as hell," Susan told Mark. "You'd think on her first day she would at least try to be nice." Susan was not alone – Doug Ross said: "If you're considering violence, count me in." In fact, Kerry had a quiet respect for Susan and later urged her to present a rare case to a conference. Susan declined. Meanwhile, Mark undermined Susan again – this time giving Weaver his full support (2-2 to 2-4).

Kerry could not accept the impact Susan's private life had on her work. From autumn 1995, Susan took care of her niece, Suzie, and later considered formally adopting her. She started proceedings in January 1996 after Chloe had been absent for three months. Susan's father, Henry, helped care for Suzie at night, despite Cookie's misgivings. Kerry became concerned about changing shift patterns while Morgenstern urged Susan to take on more responsibility to improve her chances of promotion. Susan was more interested in supporting Suzie. However, in early March 1996, Chloe returned, claiming to have sorted her life out. Susan was advised that she would not get custody. In April 1996, she returned Suzie to Chloe (2-3 to 2-19).

The experience had a lasting effect on Susan. She rejected the post of Chief Resident in summer 1996 in favour of more personal time. She soon missed Chloe and Suzie and considered a transfer to Phoenix General Hospital to be closer to them. It was unfortunate timing. Over the preceding months, she and Mark Greene had grown closer. There were always rumours about a possible romance, but Mark was struggling with the break-up of his marriage and Susan had Chloe and Suzie to contend with. Their romance in autumn 1996 moved slowly – by the time Mark Greene confessed his love for Susan, she was already on the train to Phoenix and her life was taking her away from Chicago. She left from Union Station in November 1996 (3-8).

For the next five years (1996-2001), Susan lived in Scottsdale, Arizona and worked at Phoenix General Hospital. She met Charlie Dixon ("Dixs"), a cowboy, complete with horse and pick-up truck. They were engaged but the relationship ended badly and the break up was "complicated". She decided to return to Chicago, in part to escape Dixs, and in autumn 2001 attended interviews at NorthWestern, Rush and two private practices. Mark Greene – now happily remarried – offered Susan an attending's position in County

General (without Weaver's approval) and, after some convincing, she accepted. Susan remained a close friend to Mark and was supportive in the early days of his illness when he and Elizabeth were at odds.

Susan's first day back revived the old ER feeling: an ectopic pregnancy, a tragic loss and an encounter with a hired hitman. Susan described the day as "an acid flashback without the good parts" (8-5). Susan's induction was not a smooth one. A short time after she started back, she missed a diagnosis of meningococcus, a highly contagious and dangerous strain of meningitis that spread at the University of Illinois (8-6). She was also irked to find Weaver was still here ("It's worse: she's in charge," noted Haleh). They clashed over the wishes of a murderer on death row in January 2002 (8-12).

Susan also became interested in John Carter. Carter had always held a torch for Susan but his feelings weren't reciprocated (1-6 to 1-10). Susan helped Carter deal with his grandmother's illness and they grew closer (8-5 and 8-8). They started dating before Christmas 2001, but their relationship was still one-sided by (8-16). Susan realised there was no chemistry between them and they agreed to part friends.

In 2002, Susan was saddened to discover Chloe had abandoned Suzie in New York and had returned to drug abuse. Chloe was found three weeks later, and entered rehabilitation once more.

At work, Susan took on new responsibilities when she was made Kerry Weaver's unofficial assistant in the ER (8-13). The role involved some responsibilities usually given to the Chief Resident. Susan took some time to adjust to her new managerial role – and was chastised by Kerry for taking food bribes from a pharmaceutical company (Kerry fell ill from eating the same food!) (8-14). Susan also got into trouble for rummaging through the personal belongings of a kinky prostitute and was ordered to attend a sexual harassment seminar! (8-16). Nevertheless, Susan showed herself to be a capable deputy when she and Carter managed the smallpox outbreak at County in summer 2002.

Trivia: Susan lost her virginity to Floyd Walker when she was 15 – they were behind her father's repair shop. Cookie Lewis drank sangria and smoked 4 packets of Lucky Strikes a day while bringing up Chloe and Susan. Susan speaks Spanish. In High School she was voted student "most likely to marry a convict". Susan's jaw makes a clicking noise when she eats and she sleeps with her eyelids partly open. Susan was scared of flying – when she went on holiday to Hawaii she had to be carried off the plane at Phoenix! She overcame this fear when she had to be taken by helicopter to a car crash. Susan had a lhasa apso dog called Happy, but he was run over when she was ten. While she was at County the first time, Susan had a cat that Mark Greene looked after while she went on holiday. In 1995 she treated Mr Binks, a man who stepped on an electric wire, and his life has been "a static cling hell" since then. Susan attends aerobics workouts that Carter considers "sadistic". She was a bridesmaid at Carol's aborted wedding. The weirdest place Susan has ever had sex was on a ferris wheel.

Abigail 'Abby' Lockhart, RN *(Maura Tierney)*

OB Nurse, 1999–2000
Medical Student, 2000
ER Nurse, 2000–

"Abby is the Obi-Wan of nurses… Learn from her you will."
– John Carter (8-20)

Abby Myczinski was born in Minnesota. Her parents separated when she was seven. Her mother, Maggie, was a keen fashion designer and worked in a department store. She was diagnosed with bipolar disorder before Abby was born. Maggie frequently refused to take her medication because she believed it inhibited her creativity. As a result, Abby's childhood was a whirlwind of emotions, sometimes fun, sometimes dangerous. Maggie once chased the ten-year-old Abby around their house with a knife after the girl had visited her estranged father. Maggie made two serious suicide attempts: pills in 1974 and carbon monoxide poisoning in 1983. On both occasions she was committed. In 1986 Maggie left Minneapolis and eventually moved to Tampa, Florida, to stay with Abby's brother, Eric, an air traffic controller. Later, Eric worked in the Air Force in Saudi Arabia.

Abby studied English at Penn State then joined medical school. Although second in her class, she quit halfway through her third year to pursue a career as a nurse. She married Richard Lockhart, a rich doctor. Abby became pregnant but, fearing the child would be bipolar, had an abortion. She didn't tell Richard and later felt that this was the beginning of the end of their relationship. Richard had an affair – he even bought his mistress an apartment. They divorced in August 2000. Two years later, Richard married Kareen, a 34-year-old with a six-year-old son.

In 1999, Abby Lockhart was working as an OB nurse at County General. She was assigned to Carol Hathaway and helped her through her pregnancy (6-6 to 6-8). However, Abby had evidently changed her mind about her career and returned to medical school. In January 2000 she started a trauma rotation in the ER under Dave Malucci. Carol, who had herself once considered becoming a doctor, was notably cold with Abby.

Abby struggled as a medical student. On her first day, she discharged a hypochondriac who later had a heart attack. Mark Greene told Abby to think more like a doctor (6-12). She was frustrated when she could do nothing to save an elderly patient (6-13). She accidentally killed an old man by perforating his colon during a procedure. Although the man already had a fatal condition, Abby felt tremendous guilt. Abby's problem was the legacy of her time as a nurse. She once remarked that 98 per cent of an OB nurse's job was "pure joy" (6-13) and struggled to adjust to the more tragic cases seen in the ER.

Her experience as a medical student merely served to reaffirm Abby's skills as a nurse. Although she showed great diagnostic skill, she showed the softer skills more readily. Abby healed a family rift to enable a bone marrow donation. She counselled a young woman who wanted an abortion, and overcame her difficulties with Carol Hathaway. Abby fitted more comfortably the requirements of a nurse than a doctor.

It was fortunate that this was the case. In September 2000, Richard stopped paying Abby's medical school fees and she was not allowed to continue her studies. Abby returned to nursing and was transferred to the ER: Weaver thought the experience would help Abby when she returned to medical school. In fact, Abby made up her mind not to return. Luka was still trying to convince her to study again almost a year later.

It was the confidence that Luka showed in Abby that triggered their relationship. It was not a happy one. On an early date, they were attacked. Luka's swift retribution resulted in the mugger's death and a prolonged period of guilt. Abby found it difficult to help Luka. Around the same time, she started helping John Carter overcome his drug addiction. Abby was a recovering alcoholic – she had started attending AA in 1995, and agreed to be Carter's sponsor. Although Abby dated Luka, there was always the hint of a relationship with Carter.

As Abby tried to help Luka, she was surprised by the sudden reappearance of her mother in Chicago. At first, Abby tried to disown Maggie. She later admitted that she could not cope with her mother's illness another time. Abby reluctantly took Maggie under her wing. However, her mother's use of anti-depressants began to exacerbate the manic episodes. After one incident, Maggie insisted she would get better, but disappeared from the hospital without treatment. Abby was distraught (7-6 to 7-8).

Over the following months, Abby's relationship with Carter developed. In December 2000, Carter broke the terms of his employment by taking medication during a busy shift. When Abby angrily insisted he find another sponsor, Carter told Kerry the truth. Slowly, he and Abby grew closer, especially after a brief run-in with Abby's ex-husband Richard at a Carter Family Foundation charity ball. Clearly Abby was interested in Carter: she was playfully watchful of his relationship with Rena Trujilo. Luka observed this too, and clashed with Carter a few weeks later (7-9 to 7-18).

When news of Maggie finally reached Abby, it was Carter, not Luka, who provided emotional support. Maggie had been found holed up in a motel in Tulsa. Luka insisted Maggie should be admitted in Oklahoma but Abby wanted to bring her to Chicago. Carter and Abby brought Maggie back but en route she overdosed on medication. Luka chastised Abby, who admitted that his instincts had been right. In the weeks after, Maggie appealed against being committed. Despite Abby's testimony, a court ordered Maggie be released into her daughter's care. Eventually, the two of them reached a peace. Maggie returned to Minneapolis (7-19 to 7-21).

Maggie's reappearance showed that there was little future for Abby and Luka. In early summer, Carter revealed his true feelings for Abby. Still, Abby and Luka continued to date over the summer, but the relationship had long since died. Their break-up in autumn 2001 was acrimonious. Abby immediately made a play for Carter, but he was hesitant. The reappearance of Susan Lewis, for whom Carter had once held a torch, soon complicated matters. Susan and Carter started seeing each other after Susan guessed rightly that Carter did not want to be Abby's "rebound guy". Carter told a stunned Abby that she had too much history with Luka for them to become involved (7-22 to 8-6).

Carter was partly right that Abby and Luka's former relationship still had some currency. Towards the end of 2001, Abby was protective of Luka when he became involved with Nicole, an immigrant waitress. But Abby was also protective of Carter. She tried unsuccessfully to keep him away from Paul Sobriki, the man who had stabbed him and killed Lucy Knight (8-6 to 8-11).

Early in 2002, Abby became involved in the abusive relationship of her neighbours,

Brian and Joyce. Abby encouraged Joyce to leave Brian, but was unsuccessful. A short while later, Abby harboured Joyce when Brian threatened to beat her and persuaded her to go to a shelter. Brian demanded to know where Joyce had gone and violently beat Abby when she refused to tell him.

This time, it was Luka who came to Abby's aid. In retaliation, he beat Brian and threatened to kill him if he touched Abby again. Still, Abby feared returning home and stayed with Luka instead. The incident prompted Carter's renewed interest in Abby. He broke up with Susan and made a doomed play for Abby. Carter also clashed with Luka over Abby's drinking: on her birthday in January, she started drinking again. Carter eventually helped Abby back to her AA meetings. In early summer, during a lockdown at County, Abby and Carter finally kissed.

Trivia: When Maggie took Abby to Disneyland she became manic on the plane, believing they were flying over a nuclear test site. She had to be restrained when she tried to open the doors. Maggie was so frequently incapacitated that, aged ten, Abby used to crib food from her neighbours. Abby lost her virginity at the age of 16 to Howie Thomas: it lasted 20 seconds. At High School, Abby dated Seth and had a crush on Tim. She started smoking at the Spring Formal at High School. Abby once stole a car to get some tickets to see Wham! After a short high-speed chase she was caught and arrested.

Richard and Abby once owned a house, a condo and two cars. Richard is a left-handed golfer and drives a blue BMW with the licence plate 'MAN O MED'. The best present Richard ever gave Abby was a surprise picnic. Abby was a bridesmaid at Richard's sister's wedding – the dress was pink. Abby once performed the Heimlich Manoeuvre on someone at a zoo. She was called "a real firecracker" by a patient: "That's me, Nurse Firecracker."

Gregory Pratt, MD (Mekhi Phifer)
Resident, 2002–

With arrogance only Peter Benton could match, Gregory Pratt burst into the ER in April 2002. It was not to be a permanent placement: Pratt was required to complete a three-month internship at County prior to becoming a resident in July. He swiftly declared that he hoped not to be matched to County, which did him no favours with the staff. Irked, Carter told him to check out a penile fracture and didn't stop him when he went to the wrong patient! (8-18).

From the outset, Pratt's arrogance was an irritation and a danger. He ignored Mark Greene's instructions to check a patient's chart and consequently missed a case of diabetes. The medication he prescribed put the patient into arrest. Mark angrily told Pratt to pay attention or walk (8-18). A while later, Pratt arrogantly derided Michael Gallant's skills and ran a dangerous procedure without supervision. Carter was furious and called Pratt to order, but Pratt ignored him and returned to work. Pratt later felt vindicated when he heard the patient had survived (8-19).

In fact, Pratt seemed to have a low opinion of his chief resident, John Carter. In July 2002, he clashed with Carter over the treatment of a young girl. Carter insisted Pratt's suggested treatment wouldn't work and made his own decision. The patient died and Pratt automatically assumed his approach would have been effective. Carter angrily corrected Pratt and told Pratt to shut up and follow his lead (8-22).

In fact, Pratt needed to do more than just listen and learn. On his last day in the ER, Mark Greene urged Pratt to develop the softer skills and made him tell a patient that he had inoperable cancer. Pratt's efforts were hesitant and cold. When Mark interceded and explained the case from bitter personal experience, Pratt left upset (8-18). Carter and Kerry were also acutely aware of this failing. When Susan complained she had to lance a cyst, Kerry suggested she "Give it to Pratt, he needs the humility" (8-20).

In July 2002, Pratt received his match – his third choice, County. Dismayed, he asked Carter to put in a good word for him with NorthWestern. Although Carter was hardly pleased either, he stood firm: "For better or worse, we drew you."

Trivia: Pratt is keenly interested in Jing-Mei Chen and was not unhappy to be quarantined with her during the smallpox outbreak. After running a questionnaire on the members of staff, Frank concluded that Pratt's ideal career was somewhere between rock star and lion tamer.

Robert "Rocket" Romano, MD *(Paul McCrane)*
Surgical Attending, 1997–8
Acting Chief of Emergency Medicine, 1999
Chief of Staff, 1999–

Arrogant, manipulative and utterly ruthless, Robert "Rocket" Romano is one of County's most prolific and high profile surgeons. In 1997, he was a legend at County despite spending ten months of the year in Europe. While working in Europe, Romano met Elizabeth Corday and agreed to sponsor her BTA (Been To America). Charles Corday, Elizabeth's father, had a low opinion of Romano and was opposed to his daughter working with him. Nevertheless, Elizabeth joined County in September 1997 as a senior surgical resident. Romano arrived a few weeks later (4-1 to 4-5).

Romano's reputation soon brought Peter Benton knocking on his door. Benton, driven by fierce competition with Corday, sought to muscle in on Romano's team. Romano insisted he see how Corday and Benton work together first. He was annoyed when Peter later refused to obtain research samples from a patient. Despite this, Romano clearly saw something in Peter and let him join his team. Their relationship would rarely be as cordial again!

Meanwhile, Romano's relationship with Corday was strained. They clashed over the case of Allison Beaumont, a fibula transplant patient who Elizabeth had put into a coma. Romano refused to allow vocal cord surgery, but Corday found a way round this (4-9 to 4-19). Romano was also annoyed when Corday endangered the lives of paramedics while trying to save a patient from a collapsed building (4-15). They also clashed over rival artificial blood studies (4-7 to 4-17). Although Romano claimed they were still friends, "a match made in heaven", he gave a critical assessment of her first six months at County.

It is fair to say that Romano's interest in Corday was not entirely platonic. In December 1997 he tried to take Elizabeth to the Surgeon's Society Ball, but she bailed on him. In early summer 1998, he asked her out on a date. Repulsed, Corday claimed to have a policy of not fraternising with work colleagues. When Romano discovered she was dating Peter Benton, he discontinued Elizabeth's sponsorship without explanation (4-20 to 4-22).

This was not the end of the matter. Early in 1999, Maggie Doyle accused Romano of sexual harassment. Weaver conducted an enquiry and soon brought up the withdrawal of Corday's sponsorship. Elizabeth agreed to give a statement but Romano threatened her, and Peter, with redundancy. Corday caved. Romano took rapid retribution on Weaver by becoming Acting Chief of Emergency Medicine. He promptly split the workload between Mark and Kerry: "Delegation – one of the eight hallmarks of effective leadership, or didn't you read that book?" he told Kerry (5-12 and 5-13). It was not the last time Romano and Weaver would clash over issues of sexual harassment.

While Romano was utterly ruthless, he knew the value of his staff. From May 1999, he pressed Benton to accept a five-year cardiothorasic fellowship, but Benton applied for and won a trauma fellowship instead. Furious, Romano immediately gave the cardiothorasic fellowship to Corday. Nevertheless, Romano was disappointed: he knew Peter could be an enormously successful surgeon (5-18 to 5-22).

In autumn 1999, Donald Anspaugh announced that he was resigning as Chief of Staff and Romano was named as his likely replacement. Horrified, Mark and Kerry agreed to oppose Romano's appointment. When Kerry saw the support Romano had garnered, she changed side. Romano recognised the sacrifice and made Kerry the new Chief of Emergency Medicine. Mark was furious but thought "a Romano-Weaver double homicide would be overkill" (6-1).

Now the most powerful man in County General, it was only natural that Romano should abuse that power. He appointed Corday as Associate Chief of Surgery and used her to do his dirty work. It was only with pressure from Anspaugh that Corday stood up to Romano and earned herself a little more freedom to act (6-2 to 6-5).

Romano continued to practice as a surgeon and found a new working relationship with Lucy Knight. Lucy was a fierce advocate for Valerie Page, a 24-year-old in need of a heart transplant. She interrupted Romano's Christmas and demanded he operate. Romano agreed but told Lucy to expect disciplinary action – he had his reputation to think about. Shortly after, Lucy called on him again and again he obliged. Romano clearly had a deep respect for Lucy. When she was stabbed, it was Romano who fought hardest, though in vain, to save her. It was a rare glimpse of his softer side (6-9 to 6-14).

A few months later, Romano deigned to work with "the little people" in the ER for a day and clashed again with Kerry Weaver. He forbade Weaver to perform a central line on a patient in a vegetative state. Kerry performed the procedure anyway. Romano was furious and suspended her as Chief of Emergency Medicine. When Kerry returned a few weeks later she was unrepentant (6-17 and 6-19). Romano would later suggest that "ER" stands for "Everyone's Retarded" (8-15).

More serious was another clash with Peter Benton. In autumn 2000, Corday recommended Peter for tenure, but Romano remembered Peter's betrayal and claimed he was not a "team player". When Peter reported Romano for refusing to treat a patient without insurance, Romano fired him. Peter was irate: "You couldn't pay me enough to work for you again, you arrogant little prick." (Corday added that Romano is "a horrid little turd".) Romano was more vindictive than Peter could have imagined – he rubbished the surgeon's good name, and Peter was forced to grovel for a post. Romano gave him a job with less stature and less pay (7-1 to 7-5). Romano continued to harass Peter for months: berating him for failing to manage the ER, and later making him Director of Diversity without his consent (7-12 to 7-14).

Meanwhile, Romano's relationship with Corday seemed to mature. In the last months of 2000, Corday was accused of malpractice after she botched an endoscopic procedure. Her confidence shattered, Elizabeth began to fail at work. During one operation, Corday, panicking, paged Romano several times but he never arrived. Instead, Romano watched silently as Corday started to regain her composure and saved the patient. Though utterly ruthless, he probably saved Corday's career (7-12). He seemed to become more protective of Elizabeth. After completing lengthy surgery while heavily pregnant, Corday received a pizza and ice cream from Romano with the note "Nice work, Mom" (Mark suggested they have the food tested first). Romano was also kind to her at her wedding in April: "You look beautiful, Elizabeth. Greene's a lucky man." (7-17 and 7-18) Romano had finally accepted that Corday was no longer fair game.

At this time Romano's sexual harassment suit came back to haunt him. Romano disliked Dr Kim Legaspi, probably because she, like Maggie Doyle, was gay. He took the first opportunity he could to fire her. Kerry Weaver, who had dated Kim, berated Romano for his history of sexual discrimination. She threatened to resign unless Kim was reinstated – and told Romano to pick his battles very carefully (7-16 to 7-22). Romano showed the political sense to back down but couldn't resist later appointing Kerry as County's spokesperson for lesbian health issues (8-19). Romano also clashed with Kerry over the case of Jing-Mei Chen and forced her reinstatement. He also appointed Susan Lewis as Kerry's assistant, without her agreement (8-4 to 8-13).

Towards the summer of 2002, the ER heard of the tragic illness of Mark Greene. Romano showed almost uncharacteristic sensitivity at this time, as he had almost a year earlier at Corday's wedding. It was Romano who convinced Elizabeth to return to Mark's side in his dying days (8-17 to 8-19). Romano, too, was not without emotion when he heard of Mark's death (8-20).

Trivia: After being nagged by a deaf relative in the ER, Romano noted: "That's why I prefer my patients anaesthetised." He has a gardener whose head was run over by an ice-cream truck as a kid. Romano has knocked himself out, been operated on by Benton and was once manhandled by acrobats. He is known as the best colon dissector after Elizabeth Corday. Romano's niece outgrew Sesame Street aged eight. In his spare time, Romano is a sumo wrestler and plays golf. He likes the doughnuts with the little sprinkles on top. Romano is a member of the Polar Bear club. He drives a jaguar, which "some moron from Radiology" backed into. In late 2000 he was dating Micky, a blonde beauty with a penchant for fur coats. Romano does not perform head or neck surgery but still managed to attend a conference on the subject in the Caribbean over the Christmas holidays. Romano was recruited by the Marshall Hillberg sperm bank, an elite gene pool: "Can't have too many extra Romanos running around, spicing up the gene pool, can we?" He knows some sign language: he once told Reese to take care of his father, while Peter wasn't looking. His stethoscope appears to be gold-plated.

Kerry Weaver, MD *(Laura Innes)*

Chief Resident, 1994–5

Attending, 1995–6

Acting Chief of Emergency Medicine, 1997–9

Chief of Emergency Medicine, 1999–

Kerry Weaver was born in 1963, and was immediately put up for adoption. She never knew her real parents. Her adopted mother died in 1997. Her adopted father may have owned a game reserve in Africa – certainly she once had a farm in Africa where she met Mlungusi, a friend who visited Chicago in Christmas 1995. In December 1998, she put out a request on the Internet to find her birth mother, but to date she has not found her.

Kerry attended medical school in Chicago where Dr Gabriel Lawrence taught her. In her third and fourth years, Kerry took rotations at Mercy and Lakeside hospitals: she impressed during her third year when she handled multiple traumas from a double-decker bus accident. During her rotations, she briefly worked alongside Doug Ross. Kerry then became a resident in the trauma room at Mount Sinai, where she stayed for three years. In 1995, she left Mount Sinai to join County General as Chief Resident.

News of Weaver's appointment was received apprehensively at County by all except Peter Benton. Kerry already had a reputation for discipline and managerial efficiency: she was hired because these were precisely the qualities Mark Greene lacked. Kerry did not disappoint. In her first weeks, she stopped the cherry-picking of cases and made residents clean up after procedures. While these practices met the approval of Carol Hathaway, the residents objected. Kerry made an enemy of Susan Lewis (2-2). Susan and Kerry found working together difficult (see *Susan Lewis*). Susan would later decide that having Weaver breathing down her neck was too high a price to pay for being Chief Resident!

While Kerry and Susan came to stomach working together, Kerry found it impossible to deal with Doug Ross. From her first day, Kerry disagreed with Doug over the psychiatric care of a young boy (2-2). Their relationship did not improve over the next four years. Kerry maligned Doug for his relationship with Nadine Wilks, and insisted he be tested for alcohol and cocaine (3-4). She refused to underwrite his paediatrics fellowship from October 1997 (4-4) and fervently opposed his appointment as Paediatrics Attending. Kerry also challenged his research into patient-controlled anaesthesia (4-16). When Doug resigned in 1999, Kerry was all too pleased to see him go.

Kerry's most important professional relationship was with Mark Greene. Although Kerry was Mark's opposite in almost every way, Mark gave her strong support, even against his friend Susan Lewis (2-4). More often than not, he was happy to let Kerry take the glory – and the additional work. In summer 1996, Mark agreed to support Kerry's application to become an attending in the ER on the condition that she offered the Chief Resident post to Susan. However, he was frustrated when Kerry implemented more new measures in the ER: codes for the admissions board, formal chart reviews and regular staff meetings. It was all too much for Mark, who revoked the new procedures to cheers from the staff (3-1).

As an attending, Kerry showed her better qualities. She was a sympathetic and supportive friend to Jeanie Boulet, who was diagnosed with HIV in July 1996. Kerry was instrumental in guiding the hospital-wide assessment of policy on HIV+ workers. She also allowed Jeanie to continue working, albeit with conditions, and became Jeanie's personal supervisor (3-3 to 3-9). Although their relationship would flounder, Kerry and Jeanie became close friends.

Ever ambitious, Kerry started chasing a tenure position after only six months as an attending. In late December 1996, she and Mark competed during tenure review week. Ultimately the matter was settled on their skill with colleagues. Mark and Kerry were asked to show prospective interns around the ER: all of Mark's applied, none of Kerry's did. Kerry was put out when Anspaugh recommended that Mark take a teaching position at County as soon as possible (3-11 to 3-13).

The incident merely showed that Kerry's career would run along a different line to Mark's. In October 1997, Kerry eagerly covered for David Morgenstern to become Acting Chief of Emergency Medicine (4-2). Mark was more than happy for Kerry to take the extra paperwork. However, Kerry inherited a budget deficit of $1.7m. She immediately cut spending, pulled Doug's ER funding, and fired Jeanie. Kerry made some progress in putting the department back in the black, but it was not enough. In November 1997, Anspaugh hired Synergix Physicians Group (SPG), an ER consultancy, to balance the ER budget. Although sceptical at first, Kerry was swayed when she became personally involved with SPG's Dr Ellis West. Their relationship did not last long: Kerry discovered that SPG had closed many of their trauma departments in the Midwest, threatening patient care. Kerry withdrew all support and the SPG deal fell through.

From September 1998 it became apparent that Morgenstern would not return and a new Chief of Emergency Medicine had to be found. Kerry was eager but was not on Anspaugh's list of contenders. She was interviewed but the post was offered to Dr Dan Litvak, a high-flyer from New York. When Litvak turned down the offer, Kerry was hopeful, but the hospital decided to reopen the search for someone with a national reputation. Infuriated, Weaver resigned as Interim Chief and refused to resubmit her name. Anspaugh filled in (5-3 to 5-7).

Although an attending once more, Kerry was still roped into personnel issues. Early in 1999, she conducted an investigation into charges of sexual harassment and discrimination brought by Maggie Doyle against Robert Romano. Though Romano's guilt was clear, the case fell apart. However, Kerry forced Romano to give Maggie a fair evaluation. Her victory was short-lived. A few weeks later, Romano volunteered to take over as Interim Chief – and divided the workload between Mark and Kerry (5-12 to 5-14).

Kerry's difficulties with Romano did not end there. In September 1999 Romano was rumoured to be the likely replacement for Anspaugh as Chief of Staff. Kerry and Mark agreed to oppose Romano's appointment, but Kerry realised Romano's candidacy was widely supported and backed down. Mark was furious. Kerry was rewarded with the job of Chief of Emergency Medicine, although she now had to suffer Romano as her immediate boss (6-1).

As Chief, one of Kerry's first acts was to hire her former teacher Dr Gabriel Lawrence as an attending. Gabe had inspired Kerry to pursue a career in trauma medicine. However, Mark felt he was a bad choice: "He doesn't know how to operate in an inner city ER." In fact, the problem was Gabe's health: he was in the early stages of Alzheimer's. The news broke Kerry, who couldn't let him continue to practice and was distraught. Mark was barely sympathetic: "You jumped at the chance to impress him – student hires teacher" (6-3 to 6-7).

The year 2000 proved to be notably difficult for Kerry. On St Valentine's Day, the ER had to deal with the stabbing of John Carter and Lucy Knight. When Lucy died, Kerry and Romano silently prepared her body. It was a brief moment of agreement between the two: a few weeks later they clashed over the care of a woman in a persistent vegetative state. Romano suspended Kerry but she returned unrepentant (6-15 to 6-19). Into the summer, Kerry had to contend with Carter's drug abuse. On his return, she and Mark had to keep Carter under close supervision (6-22 to 7-3).

It was around this time, autumn 2000, that Kerry was introduced to Dr Kim Legaspi, a psychiatric consult to the ER. It was a difficult period for Kerry as she came to understand her sexuality and balance it with her career. Kim was frustrated that Kerry wanted no one to know she was gay. Kerry was frustrated: "I've been on the outside my whole life fighting for acceptance and respect, and now you're asking me to do this all over again?"

Early in 2001, Kim was accused of sexual harassment by a former patient. Romano concluded that Kim's sexuality was the problem. Kerry hid her own sexuality and her defence of Kim was lukewarm. Furious, Kim refused to see Kerry any more. Luka encouraged Kerry to tell Kim how she felt but nothing had changed between them. Later, Romano fired Legaspi over a small infraction but alluded to "that other matter". It was the final straw: Kerry angrily revealed she too was gay and, outlining Romano's history of discrimination, warned him to pick his battles wisely (7-4 to 7-22).

Kerry feared that her sexuality would become common knowledge but Romano kept it quiet. In late 2001, Kerry started seeing Sandy Lopez, a firefighter. Taking matters into her own hands, Sandy kissed Kerry in the ER, causing great consternation. Kerry was furious, but Sandy insisted she had done Kerry a favour. Romano quickly capitalised on the revelation by turning County into a Centre for Lesbian Excellence and making Kerry its official spokesperson (8-19).

Meanwhile, Kerry had serious personnel issues. She promoted Jing-Mei Chen to Chief Resident in September 2001 but Chen seemed overly reliant on Kerry's advice. Kerry lost her pager leaving Chen to fend for herself. Chen's patient died. Kerry covered her own back during the investigation. Chen resigned but later discovered the truth about Kerry's pager and demanded to be reinstated as an attending and to have no reporting line to Kerry. The result was a free agent operating within Kerry's ER, immune to her rules and regulations. Kerry was slowly able to regain Chen's trust, but the whole matter had proved divisive (8-1 to 8-13).

The second personnel problem was Dave Malucci. Ever since he started, Kerry had a serious issue with "Dr Dave" (6-2). She regarded him as sloppy, undisciplined and less than thorough. When he considered buying a BMW, she commented on his "misguided sense of job security". It was Dave who suggested the procedure that Chen permitted and that killed a man. Kerry was livid: "In a perfect world, Dr Malucci, I wouldn't submit any patients to your care. If you knew your ass from your elbow, or even gave a damn... this man might still be alive." Shortly after, Kerry found Dave having sex with a paramedic in the ambulance bay and fired him immediately. Dave did not go quietly: "You're a sad cold-hearted bitch... You know why this stupid ER is so important to you lately? ... Because it's the only thing you've got in your life. Nazi dyke." (8-2 and 8-3)

As 2002 progressed, Kerry, like all her colleagues, had to deal with the sad news of

Mark Greene's terminal cancer. Mark left the ER quietly in the summer, and simply told Kerry to "live a little". She surprised herself with the depth of her dismay at the news of his death: "Mark and I always butted heads," she told Sandy. "I knew this was coming for a while, and I never imagined I would feel like this." Remembering Mark's final words to her, Kerry decided she would no longer hide her sexuality.

Trivia: Kerry walks with a crutch, although no one knows why. Kerry reckons two gallons of water is enough to give you a solid flush. Kerry once took a day off to attend a chrysanthemum show ("Great. The day I need her she's off playing Martha Stewart" – Romano). According to Abby's mother, Kerry has exquisite bone structure. Kerry's adopted mother thanked Dr Gabe Lawrence for inspiring Kerry to go into emergency medicine. Kerry is likely to have written a lurid romance novel set in an ER that featured a sexual encounter between the Weaver character and "Martin Bean". Maggie Doyle described the author as "an incurable romantic who is very warped".

Kerry loaded her own voice on to the staff room computer so it gave error messages in her tones. The computer became known as Hal. Kerry reads Cosmo for power-dressing tips. She has an eclectic music collection, including Grace Jones' version of *Ring of Fire*. Kerry is a season ticket holder at the Chicago Symphony. She produced badges for all staff outlining the ER's core values: creativity, accountability, respect and excellence – CARE. Gabe Lawrence noted: "That's a lot to live up to", while Mark wanted more respect: "See, it's even on your stupid badge!" As a resident, Kerry always left her house early during inclement weather to avoid being late. Corday once described Kerry as an "easily threatened minor demi-god". Kerry loved a puppet show as a child that featured "Mr Whiskers". She later inherited Mr Whiskers, but a "furry" masturbated with it! According to Sandy, Kerry snores like a truck driver. Kerry inherited Stinky the dog when his owner died.

Former Main Cast

Peter Benjamin Benton, MD *(Eriq la Salle)*

Surgical Resident, 1994–8
ER Trauma Fellow, 1998–2001
Director of Diversity, 2000–2001

Peter Benton was born in 1966. His father, a car mechanic, died when Peter was a child. Peter's only sister, Jackie, married Walter who inherited the repair business. At High School, Peter was frequently in trouble. He credited his turnaround to Mr Ferris, his science teacher, who inspired him to go into medicine.

Peter took the medical school admissions tests in 1988. Although he did not know it, his results were low for the year and he was given his place as part of a quota scheme for black students. Ironically, Peter worked harder to ensure that no one would think that he had gained his place in this way. While at medical school he took an obstetrics rotation at Lakeside and briefly worked with Mark Greene. He graduated in June 1993 and worked with Kerry Weaver at Mount Sinai before joining County General as a surgical resident.

Benton's surgical ability was never in doubt. David Morgenstern once noted that Benton's students came out of rotations stronger than any other tutor's (1-6). In May 1994, he was assigned a new medical student, John Carter. Benton was a profound influence on Carter, shaping his development into one of County's most capable doctors. But the path was not smooth. Benton was frequently frustrated by Carter's interest in his parents and his lack of focus on surgery. Carter resented Benton's lack of encouragement. Nevertheless, John came to respect Benton and thanked him for setting the bar high.

Benton's relationship with Carter highlighted a bigger problem – Peter's supreme arrogance and overconfidence. As a second-year resident, Benton was so confident that he applied for the Starzl fellowship, a position usually given to a more senior resident. Ultimately he lost out to experience: the fellowship was awarded to Sarah Langworthy, one year his senior, in November 1994 (1-3 to 1-7).

Peter's overconfidence soon had more tragic consequences. In 1994, Peter's mother was in failing health. He hired Jeanie Boulet, a physical therapist at County, to provide nursing care for his mother and started swapping shifts to spend more time at home. During one 48-hour shift, Benton ignored Hicks' instructions to get some sleep and continued operating, performing remarkably well. He returned home smug but was asleep when his mother fell down the stairs and broke her hip (1-13 to 1-17). After the accident, Peter was forced to accept the need for full-time nursing care. Mrs Benton was admitted to the Melville Care Home in March 1995 and died two months later.

During these events, Peter grew closer to Jeanie Boulet. Jeanie was unhappily married and Peter latched on to her for support. They began a clandestine affair that continued throughout the summer. In autumn 1995, Peter asked Jeanie to leave her husband. She refused and she and Peter split up. Peter was hurt and reacted badly when Jeanie started training at County as a Physician's Assistant (1-13 to 2-6). A year later, Jeanie was diagnosed with HIV. Peter did not contract the disease and was critical of Jeanie's decision to keep her illness from the hospital (2-21 to 3-3). Their bitterness lasted some time but eventually gave way to a lasting friendship.

Shortly after his relationship with Jeanie ended, Peter joined Dr Carl Vucelich's "clamp and run" study. Vucelich was impressed and Peter delighted: Vucelich was a respected senior member of staff who could exercise significant patronage. However, Peter suspected Vucelich of manipulating his research and was removed from the study when he raised his doubts. Peter was torn between protecting his career and revealing Vucelich's dubious practices. Peter wrote to the ethics committee and Vucelich published the complete unadulterated research. The incident only served to enhance Peter's career – Vucelich nominated Peter for Resident of the Year in May 1996 (2-6 to 2-16).

In October 1996, Peter joined Dr Abby Keaton for a three-month elective in paediatric surgery. However, Keaton raised doubts over his ability to deal with the emotional concerns of his patients. Again, Peter's overconfidence became an issue. He jeopardised the life of baby Megan Herlihy and needed Keaton's urgent assistance. Keaton berated Peter for failing to admit his limitations. Peter took note, but Keaton refused to recommend him for a second rotation (3-3 to 3-11).

Meanwhile, Peter undertook the training of several surgical interns, including John Carter and Dennis Gant. He was particularly hard on Gant, a black surgeon who Peter thought had to work twice as hard to prove he wasn't hired to fill a quota. Gant was given long shifts, took few breaks and was often assigned more patients than his colleagues. Unsurprisingly, he started to suffer from Peter's unrelenting pressure. Gant was later struck by an El train and died in the ER. The coroner recorded a verdict of accidental death but there was always the suspicion that Gant had jumped (3-1 to 3-11).

The combination of Benton's failure at paediatric surgery and the death of Dennis Gant took its toll. Benton withdrew from surgery. Hicks expressed concern and had Carter join her own surgical team. Peter eventually came to terms with his actions and returned to work. He also joined Hicks' team in spring 1997 (3-11 to 3-17).

Around this time, Peter heard he was going to be a father. In September 1996, he had met up again with an old girlfriend, Carla Reese. They met several times over the next few months (3-1 to 3-8). Peter initially ignored his parental responsibility but became more enamoured with the idea when Carla and child were endangered in a car accident (3-13 to 3-16). Reese was born two months early, but was critically ill. It was several weeks before he was taken off a ventilator (3-21 to 4-2).

Meanwhile, Benton clashed with two work colleagues. First was John Carter who had transferred from surgery to emergency medicine during the summer. Benton was annoyed that he had wasted his time teaching Carter (4-1 to 4-5). Second was Elizabeth Corday, a new senior surgical resident from Great Britain, who raised the standard in the OR. Benton thought Corday took advantage of his family problems to cherry-pick procedures. They reconciled their differences and both joined Romano's surgical team. Shortly after, they started dating (4-2 to 4-8).

Benton's relationship with Corday was never entirely promising. Peter had issues with dating a white woman. There was also the added pressure of Romano's romantic interest in Corday. But more importantly, Peter needed to give more attention to Reese. When

Corday came under criticism at work in autumn 1998, Peter was not supportive. Elizabeth quickly ended the relationship but they remained friends (4-8 to 5-9).

Benton was placed in a difficult situation with David Morgenstern. Morgenstern returned in spring 1998 after suffering a heart attack, but was not confident at work. Benton had to intercede in surgery when Morgenstern made a critical error. Peter was suspended but Morgenstern later recognised his error. He reinstated Peter then resigned as ER Chief. Benton was sad to have lost his mentor (4-17 and 4-18).

In autumn 1998, Reese was diagnosed as profoundly deaf. Peter looked into corrective surgery but eventually decided to raise his son to live with the condition. Peter took a brief posting in a rural hospital to raise money for Reese's sign language lessons (5-1 to 5-16).

Meanwhile, Peter's need to spend more time with Reese necessitated a change in his schedule. Unhappy at the idea of spending five years tied to a cardiothoracic specialty, Benton applied for a new trauma fellowship. Romano was furious – as was Corday who had expected to get the post. Benton went on to win the trauma fellowship and Corday took cardiothoracic (5-18 to 5-21).

Ironically, no sooner had Peter made arrangements to see more of Reese than Carla announced her intention to move overseas with her new partner. Peter refused to let her take Reese. From autumn 1999, Peter and Carla attended court-ordered mediation to reach a settlement. Peter was incredulous when Carla claimed he was not Reese's father. Peter made a heart-rending appeal to Carla not to take his son away. Carla agreed to his request (5-22 to 6-6).

As the holder of a trauma fellowship, Benton spent more time working in the ER. He met and started dating paediatrician Cleo Finch. Their work relationship was fiery and Peter's sister Jackie believed Cleo was not serious about him. Nevertheless, the couple grew closer (6-10 to 6-19).

Peter also found himself working with Carter again at a critical point in Carter's life. On 14 February 2000, a psychotic patient stabbed Carter. It was only Peter's skill and determination that saved Carter's life. Carter suffered emotional problems following the attack and became dependent on painkillers. Benton forced Carter to admit his problem and took him to a rehabilitation clinic. Benton was fiercely protective of Carter on his return (6-13 to 7-1).

The move back to the ER made more of an enemy out of Romano, who was angry that Peter had misled him over the cardiothoracic post and took every opportunity to be disruptive. In autumn 2000 Corday recommended Benton for a faculty position, but Romano refused, questioning Peter's loyalty. When Peter reported Romano to the authorities for another matter, Romano fired him. Peter tried to find another job in Chicago but found that Romano had rubbished his reputation. He was forced to grovel to Romano and accept a *per diem* position on a lower salary (7-1 to 7-4).

A few weeks later, Peter's nephew Jesse was shot dead by a gang. Peter helped Jesse's girlfriend, Kynesha, who was threatened after she named Jesse's killers. However, Kynesha was unruly and later ransacked Cleo's home. Through the incident, Peter realised his feelings for Cleo: "I'm not easy. I haven't been there for you, like you've been there for me. I've never worked at being with someone. I've never even wanted to. But I want to with you." (7-6 to 7-11)

Meanwhile, Romano cynically appointed Peter as Director of Diversity in early 2001.

Peter upheld the appeal for William White who was later accepted to medical school. When William thanked him, Peter said, typically: "Don't thank me, just work your ass off." During this period, Peter checked his own file and discovered he had been hired to fill a quota. It was something he had fought to disprove all these long years (7-12 to 7-19).

In autumn 2001, Carla died in a car accident and Peter became locked in a custody battle with her partner, Roger, for Reese. Peter was backed into a corner and agreed to take the DNA test he had resisted two years ago. It proved that Reese was not his son. Nevertheless, Peter fought. When he realised his work schedule was hurting his case, he appealed to Romano for flexibility but was refused. Instead, Peter found work with Cleo's new hospital. Peter was granted custody and left County on Christmas Eve, 2001.

Trivia: Peter is a vegetarian and hasn't eaten meat since 1992 (although he once ordered a chicken sandwich at County). His favourite meal is sweet potato pie. At high school, Peter got in trouble for filling a condom with gas from a Bunsen burner and blowing it up. When Peter was ten he stayed at boys' club camp and reported another boy for stealing money from the equipment fund. The boy in question broke Peter's nose and they didn't speak all summer. Peter doesn't smoke.

His mother applauded when he graduated medical school – although he once told Carter he missed his graduation because he was in surgery. In medical school he delivered a 700g baby – it died of a brain bleed. Peter has a nephew nicknamed "Peanut". He has a "soft spot" behind his left ear. Peter hadn't had alcohol for years before he started dating Corday – she got him drunk on two glasses of Pimm's. When Kerry Weaver treated a patient with a bleeper stuck up his ass, Benton noted: "Never underestimate the elasticity of the anal sphincter." Peter is ambidextrous and can operate with both hands.

Jeanie Boulet, PA *(Gloria Reuben)*
Physical Trainer (part-time), 1994–5
Physician's Assistant in the ER, 1995–8
Physician's Assistant in the Paediatrics ER, 1998–9

Jeanie Murdoch was born 1966, the older of two sisters. Her mother gave Jeanie's younger sister preferential treatment. Her father's family was from LaVerne, Mississippi. Jeanie trained as a physical therapist and worked for some time in rehabilitation and private nursing care. She married Al Boulet on 17 April 1988 but the marriage was not a happy one. Jeanie was alone in her desire for children, while Al had a string of affairs. Their relationship was already under considerable strain when she started working at County General in 1995.

It was while working as a part-time physical therapist at County that Jeanie met Peter Benton. He hired her to provide private nursing care for his mother. After Mrs Benton's death, Peter and Jeanie grew closer. They had an affair, but it ended sourly when Jeanie could not bring herself to leave Al. Shortly after, Jeanie applied to several Chicago hospitals to train to become a physician's assistant. She started at County on 30 November 1995, a few weeks after she and Benton had split up. In December 1995, she and Al separated.

Jeanie's early months at County were characterised by clashes with Peter Benton (2-6 to 2-19). Jeanie also had difficulties with Carol Hathaway. In December 1995, Carol wrote an assessment of Jeanie which criticised her lack of assertiveness and said she needed to be more proactive. Jeanie took the points on board and won Carol's approval some time later (2-11 to 2-14). Nevertheless, Jeanie was always uncomfortable with the "treat and street" necessities of the ER, which were a far cry from the long-term relationships built up in physical therapy.

In June 1996, Al Boulet tested positive for HIV. He may have had the disease for as long as ten years. Jeanie also tested positive on 3 July (she still hadn't told her family three years later). For many months, Jeanie could find nothing but hate for Al. She was also concerned about losing her job. She kept her illness secret and attended a clinic at Highland Park. Benton, who tested negative, was critical of her deception. However, Kerry Weaver guessed and agreed to keep the matter quiet. When Mark Greene discovered the truth after treating Al Boulet the revelation sparked a hospital-wide assessment of policy on HIV+ workers. In the end, each department made its own policy. Jeanie was allowed to work as long as she did not operate in deep-penetrating, poorly visualised cavities (3-9).

Jeanie's divorce came through in December 1996. She had a brief relationship with Dr Greg Fischer, but found it difficult to adjust to life with her illness (3-12 to 3-18). Their relationship suffered and came to a surprising end when Jeanie rediscovered feelings for Al after treating a woman dying of an AIDS-related illness. Jeanie resolved no longer to hate Al (3-18). But Jeanie and Al did not find happiness. Al was dismissed from his construction job when his colleagues discovered his HIV status. He found it difficult to get work in Chicago and got a six-month contract in Atlanta. The couple finally parted in December 1997 (4-2 to 4-9).

In October 1997, almost one year after she had been put under restricted terms of work, Jeanie broke the rules to help a patient. Weaver was furious and in November fired Jeanie as part of her cost-cutting measures. Jeanie was persuaded to fight her dismissal on grounds of discrimination. Donald Anspaugh soon reinstated her. Weaver was annoyed that Jeanie used her HIV status to her advantage, but Jeanie may have had good grounds (4-6 to 4-9). Later, Jeanie and Kerry were to become close friends.

The wrongful dismissal claim made Jeanie unpopular, but she soon regained the confidence of Donald Anspaugh when she treated his son, twelve-year-old Scott, for a recurrence of cancer from January 1998. Jeanie quickly bonded with Scott and was hired as Scott's private duty caregiver. Over the four months, their relationship became very strong. Though Jeanie never revealed her HIV status to Scott, Anspaugh felt sure his son sensed this and treated Jeanie as a kindred spirit. Jeanie's relationship with Scott was one of the most touching and evocative points of her career. Scott died in May 1998 (4-11 to 4-18).

In autumn 1998, Jeanie built on her a natural ability to work with children and joined the Paediatrics ER as Doug Ross's full time Physician's Assistant. A few months later, she met Reggie, a Chicago cop, and Dr Baker, a plastic surgeon at County. For a time, she dated both, but called off the relationships when she was diagnosed with Hepatitis C (5-15). Jeanie angrily suspected Al, but had in fact contracted the disease from a patient. Jeanie's confidence was shattered again. It was not until a preacher showed his faith in her that she was able to deal with her illness (5-19). In the summer, she reunited with Reggie and their relationship blossomed (5-22).

In October 1999, Jeanie sought to adopt an HIV+ baby, Carlos, whose mother had died from an AIDS-related illness. Jeanie feared she would not become a foster mother because she was unmarried. Reggie proposed, but Jeanie feared he did so for the wrong reasons. When social services heard that she had illegally tested the baby for HIV, Jeanie was refused adoption rights. The incident proved to her that she loved Reggie in his own right and she accepted his proposal. As they were married in a civil ceremony at the City Hall, Jeanie and Reggie received news that they could foster after all and were given temporary custody. Jeanie left the ER to become a full-time mother (6-1 to 6-6).

Trivia: Jeanie loves gospel music and holidayed at a Laurentian wilderness in summer 1998, jamming all night and singing gospel music into the early hours. Al regarded Jeanie as an over-achiever. During High School, Jeanie worked at a veterinary practice and learned "mouth to mouse" resuscitation. Jeanie's father was so delighted when she graduated college that he danced on a table. Jeanie always wanted a remote controlled garage door. Jeanie's "porn star name" is Nibbles McGee – Nibbles was her first pet, McGee was her mother's maiden name. Jeanie is a fan of the Blackhog Islanders hockey team. She is an avid viewer of *Days of Our Lives* and likes John Woo movies. In spring 1999, Jeanie's family still did not know her HIV status.

Anna Del Amico, MD *(Maria Bello)*
Paediatrics Resident, 1997–8

Anna Del Amico was born in South Philadelphia into an Italian-American family. She had seven brothers, one called Hank. All married. Her mother and father separated; her father remarried.

Anna completed four years undergraduate study and four years at medical school where she took rotations in paediatrics and emergency medicine. In 1996 she became a paediatrics resident in Philadelphia and started dating her attending, Dr Max Rocher. Rocher was a Percodan addict and Anna tried repeatedly to help him overcome his addiction: "I've done the detox dance more times than I can remember."

In June 1997 she joined County for an emergency paediatrics elective. She became a second-year paediatrics resident a month later. Her paediatrics supervisor was Doug Ross; her emergency medicine supervisor was Mark Greene. Anna's arrival in the ER was a baptism of fire: her first case was Greene, who was violently attacked by an unknown assailant. A few weeks later, she assisted Janet Coburn in delivering Peter Benton's son, Reese. Benton put Anna under significant pressure, but she more than proved herself (3-20 to 3-22).

More tempestuous was her relationship with her paediatrics supervisor and Doug Ross. Ross felt Anna could be overly thorough and in July 1997 he intervened in some of her cases. Anna's response was to act more independently and keep Doug out of the loop – actions that would jeopardise patient care. Anna was also frustrated that returning patients only wanted to see Ross. It was only when Anna made a patient uncomfortable by insisting she examine him that she and Doug started to overcome their differences.

They were soon working together effectively (3-21 to 4-5).

During her time at County, Anna dated John Carter. Anna knew nothing of Carter's family background: she believed he was struggling by on a resident's salary and even paid his bail when he was arrested for obstruction of justice. Carter did nothing to dissuade Anna of this perception and she was annoyed when she saw Carter's palatial family mansion. They also had some run-ins at work, notably over Carter's decision to give a serial rapist a more risky form of care. Nevertheless, they grew closer and Anna proved a great support when Carter tried to help his cousin Chase get off heroin. Anna's experience with Rocher proved invaluable and Carter was grateful for her help (4-10 to 4-16).

Anna was often frustrated by the realities of life in the ER. In March 1998 she was annoyed when a hospital transferred a critically ill patient to County because he had no medical insurance. When the hospital discovered the man had a good policy, they took him back, endangering him again. Furious, Anna said: "I knew it was a dump, but this is gross negligence." (4-16) In May, she treated the victims of a bomb attack on an abortion clinic. One patient was halfway through an abortion but Anna refused to finish the procedure. Later, she insisted she had no moral objection to abortion but Weaver pointed out that "something happened in there" (4-19).

In spring 1998, her former boyfriend, Dr Max Rocher, arrived in the ER to write a feasibility study on a Paediatrics ER at County. He recommended its creation and considered applying to run it but wanted to know where he and Anna stood. Evidently, Anna and Max had a future together as she moved back to Philadelphia over the summer to work in the Paediatrics ER (4-20 to 5-1).

Trivia: Brought up with so many brothers, Anna "wraps a mean diaper". She has an Aunt Tessa who regards her as the family freak! She has delivered more than 200 babies. When she moved to Chicago she lived in a motel but her next-door neighbours kept her awake: Anna reckoned the tenacious lovers were "working on some kind of record". A good breakfast for Anna consists of scrambled eggs, wheat toast, blueberry pancakes and orange juice. She once spent a day in the ER looking after a patient's Tamagotchi but it died.

Margaret 'Maggie' Doyle, MD *(Jorja Fox)*
Intern, 1996–7
Resident, 1997–9

Maggie Doyle was born in Chicago and grew up on the West Side in the same neighbourhood as Carol Hathaway. Her mother was a nurse and her father a policeman – the third generation of the family to enter the force. Maggie also had an older sister, who went to school with Carol Hathaway, and a brother, Jimmy, who has Down's Syndrome.

Maggie studied at St Monica's school and took her pre-med night school course at Malcolm X Community College. She was thrown out of nursing college for an infraction: "I was never very good at following orders." In summer 1996, she completed medical school and joined Southside as an ER intern. A few months later, Southside was closed and some staff moved to County General. Maggie, like Abby Keaton and Donald Anspaugh, was one of those kept on.

In her first few months, Doyle befriended Carol Hathaway, but the feeling was not mutual. Hathaway was frustrated that she had grown up in the same neighbourhood, and gone to the same school, as Maggie Doyle but now had to help train and take orders from her. Carol decided to take a pre-med course and apply for medical school. Although she passed, Carol later abandoned these ambitions (3-3 to 3-18).

Maggie soon proved to be an outspoken member of staff. Early in her time at County, she had the police arrest a woman who tried to abort her baby by drinking. Mark and Kerry were critical but Maggie was indignant: "Tell you what, if I get to testify against the bitch, I'll do it on my own time." Doug Ross was impressed: "I think we're gonna like her." (3-8) Maggie also helped a domestic abuse victim escape from her husband by giving her money from the staff's Christmas fund (3-10). Maggie was also reprimanded for her fierce outbursts in the case of Louise Cupertino, a young girl who was refused surgery because she had Down's Syndrome. Maggie brought her brother Jimmy in to talk to Louise (3-16).

A forceful personality, Maggie was highly competitive and clashed with John Carter. Doyle was at first a little intimidated by Carter: she felt that surgery was too cut-throat and claimed she wouldn't like to do it. Tragically, one of the patients they competed for turned out to be their colleague, Dennis Gant. A few weeks later they competed over an AIDS patient with a gunshot wound. It was only Maggie's knowledge of firearms that prevented Carter from infecting himself. Carter made a play for Maggie but hadn't realised she was gay (3-14).

Maggie's difficulties with Carter did not end there. Over summer 1997, Carter changed specialty from surgery to trauma medicine but was forced to re-sit his internship. Maggie, now technically a year senior, became Carter's immediate supervisor, much to his chagrin (4-2). When Maggie gave one of Carter's cases to Anna Del Amico, he suggested she had a thing for Anna. In fact, it was Carter who pursued Del Amico, ultimately without success (4-3).

Doyle was driven by a great sense of injustice, perhaps stemming from the discrimination she had suffered during her life. In autumn 1997, she urged Jeanie Boulet to fight her dismissal on grounds of discrimination. Jeanie took Doyle's advice and was reinstated. However, almost a year later, Maggie faced similar treatment. Robert Romano had a problem with homosexual members of staff, so much so that he would use the mildest incident to dismiss them. In January, he was angered when Doyle let a patient eat before surgery and maligned Maggie to Corday and Anspaugh. Corday was surprised – Maggie was spoken highly of and was being considered for Chief Resident in the ER. Maggie complained to Romano, hoping he would ease off, but instead he wrote a highly critical evaluation of her. Maggie later reasoned that Romano felt "anything goes with the gay chick".

Maggie made a formal complaint to Weaver, who launched a sexual harassment investigation. Corday agreed to support the case, but was then scared off by Romano. Doyle was furious that Elizabeth protected her "own place in the food chain". Although the case collapsed, Weaver forced Romano to retract his evaluation of Maggie. Despite this, Maggie did not stay at County for much longer. As she once said to Corday: "Self-respect's a bitch."

Trivia: Doyle's father was the third generation of the family to serve in the police force.

She also had a cousin in the Chicago PD and another who was convicted for breaking and entering, but went on to become a locksmith. Her ex-girlfriend was Amy Elliott, a policewoman who was "jealous as hell". Maggie has a wide knowledge of firearms and owned a stun gun and mace spray. She hid a .357 Magnum under the driver's seat of her car and once scared a mugger at a drive-thru. She drives a red BMW and on her first day parked it in Carol Hathaway's space. Maggie is a smoker and hid beer behind the fridge in the staff room.

Cleo Finch, MD *(Michael Michelle)*
Paediatrics Resident, 1999-2001

Cleo Finch was born in Indianapolis, the only daughter of a white mother and black father. Two of her three brothers went on to work with their father in insurance. Cleo was also offered the opportunity, but found working with family "stifling".

Cleo entered medicine and joined County General as a Paediatrics Resident in 1999. During her time there, she was a fierce defender of children's care and took a very dim view of parental failings. She quickly branded as "irresponsible" an HIV+ mother who decided to have a child, unwittingly annoying Jeanie Boulet. But Cleo was equally critical of her own failings. She was devastated when she missed a case of iron poisoning, believing instead that it was a case of food poisoning. The child later died, nevertheless Weaver confirmed that Cleo had done all she could.(6-1 to 6-4).

Cleo's dogged pursuit of the child's needs could sometimes blind her to the wider issues. She clashed with John Carter over the treatment of Eddie Bernero, an obese, diabetic 12-year-old. Mr Bernero had started a new job but was not yet covered by the company's medical insurance. He asked that his son's diabetes be hidden so he could claim for it later. Cleo was unrelenting, but Carter falsified the chart on the condition that Bernero made all efforts to care for his son. Cleo was furious, and vindicated when Eddie returned early in the next year in a more serious condition. Later she had a drunk boy, Chad Kottmeier, separated from his alcoholic mother at Christmas and admitted into a treatment programme (6-7 and 6-9).

Towards the end of 1999, Cleo started dating Peter Benton. It was not an easy relationship. Cleo was uncomfortable that Peter's previous girlfriends, Elizabeth Corday and Carla Rees, were still on the scene. Corday once accused Cleo of using her relationship with Peter to secure surgery for her patients. But Cleo also clashed with Peter. He was highly critical of Cleo when she failed to check the label on medication she had prescribed for one of his patients: "They teach you that on the first day." Despite this, they stayed together, although the relationship was often strained. Jackie, Benton's sister, once suggested that Cleo was not serious about Peter and just wanted to have fun.

In fact, Cleo was serious about Peter but felt her feelings were not reciprocated. When Peter was sacked in autumn 2000, Cleo urged Peter to fight the case. She was also supportive when Peter's nephew, Jesse, was killed in a gang shooting. The incident had the added complication of Kynesha, Jesse's girlfriend, who Peter and Cleo protected for some weeks. Eventually Peter threw Kynesha out. Kynesha blamed ransacked Cleo's apartment. The incident prompted Peter to reveal his deepest feelings for Cleo; although Cleo appeared unmoved (7-6 to 7-11).

Things between Cleo and Peter were to get worse before they got better. They had to come up with a convincing story to cover their malpractice in the case of an elderly patient who became altered and was killed by police. Peter was annoyed when Cleo failed to care for Reese when he trapped his hand under a piano lid and was unable to communicate by signing. They also clashed at work when Cleo refused to co-sign surgery on a man dying of AIDS. During their argument, Cleo accidentally contaminated herself. Worried, Peter immediately put Cleo on the "triple cocktail" drug treatment and ordered blood tests. For the summer and early autumn 2001, Cleo lived under the shadow of her blood test results. However, the initial results proved negative and these were confirmed a few months later.

The end of 2001 proved to be a time of change for Peter and Cleo. Peter started fighting a custody battle for Reese – who, he discovered, was not his biological son. Cleo was a pillar of support, although her negligence when caring for Reese in early summer was brought up during the hearings. Cleo left County to set up the Paediatrics Urgent Care facility at Chamburgh. Peter joined her at the same practice a few weeks later to secure custody of Reese. All three were united at Christmas 2001, now a family.

Trivia: Cleo always jogged four miles to work each day: "Makes you wanna dislike her, doesn't it?" Kerry told Lucy Knight. Cleo's grandmother could predict through dreams – she knew instinctively when her cat would be ill.

Mark Greene, MD *(Anthony Edwards)*

Resident, 1991–4
Chief Resident, 1994–5
Senior Attending, 1995–2002

Mark Greene was born in 1964, the only child of David and Catherine ("Ruth"). One was an agnostic Jew, the other a lapsed Catholic. David was an officer in the Navy and did more than one tour in Vietnam. Every few years, the family moved with David's job. Mark's childhood had no certainty: they lived in Jacksonville, Norfolk, Corpus Christi, Washington DC and New York. Nevertheless, Mark considered Hawaii to be his childhood home: their three years at the naval base there was the longest they ever spent in any one place.

Mark was not a model pupil. He was high for most of the eighth grade, and was bullied (probably by Jerry Walker in the tenth grade). David turned down a promotion to Admiral and took a desk job so he could be at home to look after his troublesome son. Mark and David did not get along: "I hated everything he stood for and I made sure he knew it." (8-21) Mark felt he came between his mother and father, and rashly suggested that Doug Ross had missed nothing by having an absentee father. Doug bitterly noted that at least David had always been there for Mark (4-7).

In 1980, at the age of 16, Mark met Jennifer, who was to become his first wife. After they married, Jen worked through the day and studied law at night to allow Mark to go to medical school. Their daughter, Rachel, was born on 16 February 1989.

Mark Greene left medical school in 1991 and joined County General to specialise in emergency medicine. One of his new colleagues was a former classmate, Peter Benton. In the second year of his residency, Mark was accepted for the NASA space programme, but abandoned his ambitions to support his wife and daughter (5-11). When Mark was a third-year resident, Dr Susan Lewis joined County. Susan was to become one of his closest friends.

In 1994, Mark was appointed Chief Resident in the ER under Dr David Morgenstern. He quickly showed the people skills necessary when he helped the staff through Carol Hathaway's attempted suicide. He was headhunted by a Chicago private practice, but turned down the substantial offer to continue working in the ER. However, he was not above using more underhand methods to avoid conflict at work: his treatment of Susan Lewis during her conflicts with Kayson (1-11 to 1-14) left much to be desired. The same capacity was shown during his investigation into Jeanie Boulet's HIV status (3-9 to 3-10) two years later.

Yet, Mark was torn between home and work. Once Mark became Chief Resident, Jen was keen to push her career and passed her Bar exams in May 1994 (they celebrated by making out in the ER). However, the pressure of their careers soon took its toll. Jen took a job in Milwaukee and left Mark in February/March 1995. They started divorce proceedings in December 1995. Jen remarried (Craig Simon) in September 1996 and was made a partner in her law firm in December 1998. The separation had a significant effect on Rachel who started to misbehave to get attention.

It was a difficult time for Mark, made worse by a failure of his medical judgement in the Jodi O'Brien case (1-18). The tragic case haunted Mark throughout his career. It also put his promotion to an attending physician into serious doubt. It was only after much consideration that William Swift approved, with reservations, Morgenstern's recommendation that Mark be made an attending. The O'Brien malpractice case was settled out of court in February 1996 (2-10 to 2-13). Soon after, Mark was able to win back the respect of obstetrician Janet Coburn (2-15) and proved himself to be vastly capable under pressure (2-18).

As an attending from 4 September 1995, Mark had to help the ER adjust to the managerial fervour of new Chief Resident, Kerry Weaver. In particular, he had to mediate between Weaver and Susan Lewis (2-1 to 3-8), a relationship that showed only small signs of improvement when Lewis returned to the ER some years later. Mark, meanwhile, had his own clashes with Weaver. Although rivals for a tenure from October 1996 (3-5), Mark never sought the competition. He was all too happy for Kerry to take on the extra work that goes with Chief of Emergency Medicine, preferring instead to focus on patients. He was more annoyed when Kerry later failed to support his opposition to Robert Romano's promotion to Hospital Chief of Staff some years later (6-1).

At this time, Mark was free and single. He had a string of short-term relationships with patients (Iris, Heather Morgan, Polly Mackenzie) and colleagues alike (Chuny Marquez, Nina Pomerantz). His longest relationship was with receptionist Cynthia Hooper (4-4 to 4-16), but this ended unhappily when Mark confessed he did not love her. His strangest relationship was with Amanda Lee, the impostor Chief of Emergency Medicine, who had an unhealthy obsession with Mark. Mark later noted: "there's something about me that brings out the worst in people... I'm like a magnet for negativity" (5-10). Perhaps Mark's greatest error was his reluctance to act on his feelings for his long-time friend, Dr Susan

Lewis. By the time he confessed his love for her on the platform of Union Station (3-8) it was too late. By the time Susan returned to County five years later, Mark had remarried. Nevertheless, they remained close friends and she was a major support in his last days.

Mark's key professional relationship was with Doug Ross. Mark and Doug were more like brothers, with Mark the older, protective sibling. Throughout their time at County, Mark showed an almost overbearing concern for Doug's self-destructive tendencies. Doug was often frustrated by Mark's refusal to see him as an equal and by Mark's air of infallibility: "It's like there's you and the Pope." (2-13) At times, Mark threatened to cancel Doug's paediatrics fellowship (2-5 to 2-8) and almost had him sacked (Josh McNeil case, 4-20 to 4-22). In the end, a severe professional disagreement over the euthanasia of Ricky Abbot (5-12 to 5-15) led to Doug leaving County. Remarkably, their friendship, although bruised, remained intact.

Mark was a particularly effective mentor. Though regarded as Weaver's "intellectual inferior", Mark proved himself to be an inspiring teacher and was urged to seek a teaching position from 1996 (3-5). In September 1998, he was offered the post of District Medical Director for EMS, a part-time position to oversee the medical education of paramedics. However, Mark rejected the post, and an offer of a position at NASA, to focus on patient care (5-12). In fact, throughout his career Mark tried to avoid the associated paperwork ("publish or perish", 3-18) to get back to patients. His care for prostitute Loretta Sweet and her children between September 1995 and July 1996 is particularly noteworthy (2-1 to 2-22), as was his care for Al, a homeless man, throughout his time at County (8-20). It was this side of Mark Greene that made him such a positive role model for John Carter – the man who was to step into Mark's shoes.

In summer 1997, Mark was brutally attacked at work (3-20). In the months after, he suffered post-traumatic stress and underwent significant personality changes. His relationship with his friends and family deteriorated to the point where his daughter Rachel was kept away from him. It was only after helping Doug Ross deal with the death of his father (4-7) that Mark was able to start to come to terms with his illness. Mark still had flashbacks to the incident years later (5-7). He was able to put the matter to some form of rest when helping Mobolage Ekabo, a Nigerian immigrant who suffered post-traumatic stress years after being tortured (5-13 to 5-19). And yet, Mark never again took threats to himself or others lightly. When an abusive parent sought revenge against Mark and his family, Mark withheld treatment and let the man die (7-21 to 8-01).

Mark also had his own family problems to deal with. In retirement, David and Ruth Greene had settled near a naval base in San Diego. Mark rarely visited, but on an impromptu call in November 1997 he discovered their health was fading. David needed oxygen to help live with emphysema, and Ruth was on medication for high blood pressure. In spring 1998, Ruth suffered a series of small strokes that induced dementia. She was confined to a wheelchair and required constant care. She died of a heart attack in September 1999.

During 1999, Mark began a tempered romance with British surgeon Elizabeth Corday. It was only after Corday had concluded a long-running rivalry with ex-boyfriend Peter Benton that she and Mark got together (5-22). Elizabeth supported Mark as he rebuilt his relationship with his father. David moved to Chicago to live with Mark and had a brief fling with Elizabeth's mother, Isabelle. David also developed a strong friendship with

Elizabeth. Sadly, Mark discovered that David had lung cancer (6-15). David had tried to keep the matter quiet – it was an action that Mark himself would later repeat. On his deathbed, David confessed that the day Mark became a doctor was the proudest of his life. David died in summer 2000 (6-20).

Elizabeth and Mark were engaged in September 2000 and moved to a new house in the suburbs. A short while later they learned that Elizabeth was pregnant, but their happiness was short lived. Mark was diagnosed with a brain tumour and given eight weeks to live. However, Dr Burke in New York suggested a treatment that could buy Mark two more years. On 31 December 2000, Mark had a 3.5cm mass removed from his frontal lobe. Returning to work, Mark suffered mild aphasia and was ordered to undertake competency testing. He passed, but joked that he had been assessed "somewhere between serial killer and talk show host" (7-15). Elizabeth and Mark married in April 2001 and Elizabeth gave birth to their daughter, Ella, shortly after (7-18 and 7-19).

The marriage, did not run smoothly. Rachel Greene, now a troublesome teenager, moved back to Chicago in autumn 2001. Mark's apparent inability to control Rachel came to a head when Ella swallowed some of Rachel's ecstasy pills (8-13). Ella made a full recovery but the incident divided Mark and Elizabeth and she moved out with their baby. Just as this happened, Mark discovered that his tumour had returned – this time it was inoperable (8-15).

In his last few months, Mark continued to work and to hide the truth from his colleagues, and even his wife: "the moment you tell them, they look at you differently," he noted, mirroring his father's words two years previously (6-15). Finally, the illness became too much and Mark made a quiet departure from the ER (8-18). He spent his last days trying to "fix" his daughter, Rachel, taking her to his childhood home in Hawaii. Elizabeth and daughter Ella then joined them. Mark died in summer 2002.

Trivia: Mark once admitted that a helicopter ride was the high point of his residency, although this was probably not true of his time as an attending when he was almost killed in a helicopter crash. Mark is an expert at making his mother's rhubarb pie. He learned to dance the tango for his first wedding; otherwise he would never have learned. He used to play hockey at college, second line. Before his first tumour operation, Mark had never been a patient in the OR. His grandfather was called Matthew and he had an uncle who was a closet ballerina. His father taught him to ice skate at Madison Square when they lived in New York for two months. Mark rates *Attack of the Killer Tomatoes* as "a classic". He used to receive a crate of live lobsters every Memorial Day in thanks for a pericardiocentesis. He worked for the stroke team and promoted the use of t-PA at County. Mark's most unusual medical case was a man with a live bullfrog in his ass.

Carol Hathaway, RN *(Julianna Margulies)*

Charge Nurse, 1994–2000
Clinic Manager, 1996–9

Carol Hathaway was born in Chicago in 1967, one of three sisters. Her family were Eastern Orthodox Catholics originally from the Ukraine. Her father died when she was very young. She was brought up by her mother, Helen, who was supported by Carol's uncles, Michel and Ted. Michel was to give Carol away at her wedding.

Carol studied at St Monica's (the same school as Maggie Doyle) before training to become a nurse. She joined County in 1990 where she met Doug Ross. Carol and Doug dated for two years but the romance ended when Doug, fearing commitment, "replaced" her. Carol began dating John "Tag" Taglieri, an orthopaedic physician at County. Carol still held a torch for Doug and she slept with him while dating Tag during the winter of 1993–4. Nevertheless, Carol and Tag were engaged.

On 17 March 1994, Carol took an overdose of barbiturates and was admitted to the ER. She miraculously recovered. Carol never truly revealed her reasons for attempting suicide. Doug Ross felt enormously guilty but she insisted there were "more depressing events" in her life than their failed relationship. Much later, she rationalised that she "just got wrapped up in everyone else's expectations of me... I forgot who I was". Whatever the case, Carol's attempted suicide made her take stock of her life. She moved out of Tag's and back with her mother. Carol returned to work on 12 May 1994 and took counselling for nine months. She also drew strength from the example of some of her patients, notably Mrs Packer (1-2) and Mr Gasner (1-4).

Carol became enormously thankful that her attempted suicide did not succeed, but her personal life was still in turmoil. While Tag tried to reassure Carol, Ross pursued her. Carol decided to stay with Tag but their relationship was strained from February 1995 when Carol sought to adopt an orphaned Russian girl, Tatiana. Carol also contemplated returning to Doug at the time. On the day of their wedding, 18 May 1995, Carol had to admit she did not love Tag as much as he loved her. Tag left and never returned (1-24).

Carol did not run back to Doug and instead started a relationship with paramedic "Shep" Shepherd, whom she met in September 1995. Carol grew in confidence and bought a run-down house of her own by the elevated train line (2-5). The relationship became more serious (2-10) but the death of Shep's partner, Raul, in the spring, brought a change to his character. Shep became violent and almost assaulted Carol but refused to take counselling. Eventually, Carol told Shep she had just got her life together and couldn't help him recover his (2-16). For the next year, Carol focused on her career.

Carol drew on her painful personal relationships to help her patients. She had learned to deal with problems directly and encouraged her patients to do the same (1-7). Carol helped an abusive father, Mr Krosset, into a successful rehabilitation (2-1 and 2-12). Carol was also keenly responsive to the emotional needs of individual patients, and respected nurse-patient confidentiality above all (6-15). However, Carol was not scared to involve social services or the police when there was clear evidence of wrongdoing (4-17). Above all, Carol was monumentally compassionate: she once helped a dying man smoke cannabis to relieve the pain of the last stages of his illness (5-12).

Carol was determined that hospital regulations should not get in the way of patient care, and clashed with hospital management. In July 1996, she resigned over the hospital's "treat and street" attitude and readiness to pander to the insurance companies (2-22). She couldn't stay away, though, and returned a few weeks later – to the amusement of her colleagues (3-1). Nevertheless, Carol now took more interest in hospital policy. In autumn 1996, she objected to hospital plans to "float" nurses to other departments and had the policy changed (3-6 to 3-9). In return, Carol had to sit on the hospital-wide re-engineering committee. However, she soon found herself regarded as "management" by her fellow nurses, and was increasingly excluded. Matters came to a head when, during an unofficial nursing strike, Carol killed a patient. She went to the press, to prevent either the nurses or the hospital making capital from the story. Carol was immediately suspended (3-12 to 3-16).

Carol also distanced herself from her fellow nurses by deciding to become a doctor. A key factor in this was Maggie Doyle. Doyle had grown up in the same neighbourhood, had studied at St Monica's (her older sister was in Carol's history class) but had become a doctor. Carol was resentful: "I'm a nurse and I gotta take orders from her all day long and I hate it." (3-18)

In October 1996, Carol started a pre-medical school course at Malcolm X Community College and passed the entrance examinations. She passed in the top 15 per cent and Weaver nicknamed her "Doctor Einstein". However, Carol came to see that as a nurse she could impact many more lives in a more individual way. The key events were a bungled store robbery while she was suspended (3-15) and later the treatment of young mother, Andrea (3-19), when she had been reinstated from February 1997. Given her experience, Carol was cool with Abby Lockhart, her OB nurse, who became a med student in the ER from January 2000 (6-12).

While Carol focused on work, Doug Ross hit rock bottom (3-4). He started a slow rehabilitation. In summer 1997, they revived their relationship and succeeded in keeping it quiet until the end of the year, when they were engaged. However, in February 1998, Carol had a brief clinch with paramedic Greg Powell (4-12) that threatened their relationship. Doug agreed to give Carol time to adjust. From the autumn, they began trying for a child.

Shortly after Carol and Doug were reunited she hit on the idea of a service to treat those patients who "slipped through the cracks" in the system (4-1 to 4-4). In autumn 1997, Carol formed a free health-care clinic that used the ER premises two or three times each week. She secured $75,000 funding from the Carter Family Foundation to set up and received a further $150,000 on Christmas Eve 1997. The clinic continued to grow and, almost a year after it was set up, Carol received funding to hire a permanent member of staff. She hired Nurse Practitioner Lynette Evans with whom she had a fiery relationship. However, early in 1999 Doug's treatment of Ricky Abbott brought calamity to the clinic. He obtained a PCA machine from Carol that was later used in the mercy killing of Ricky. The clinic was closed on the orders of Donald Anspaugh and Doug Ross resigned. Doug asked Carol to join him in Seattle but Carol insisted her life, work and family were all in Chicago. They broke up (5-12 to 5-15).

Shortly after Carol and Doug broke up, Carol discovered she was pregnant with twins. She decided to keep the babies and was inspired by the example of a schizophrenic mother, Coco (5-5 to 5-19). Carol eventually told Doug about the babies, and he respected her wishes to stay away (5-20 to 5-22). Meanwhile, Carol had to adjust her workload. She tried to help Meg, a pregnant waitress at Doc Magoo's. Meg was a drug addict and Carol finally had her arrested to protect the unborn child. The events with Meg were traumatic and came shortly before Carol's labour (6-4 to 6-7). On Thanksgiving 1999, Carol gave birth to twins Kate and Tess. Carol almost died during the births but was saved by the swift actions of Janet Coburn and Mark Greene (6-8). Carol later revealed her children's surname is Ross (6-18).

Now a single mother, Carol grew closer to Luka Kovac (6-1 to 6-21). Although there was a potential for romance, Luka's feelings were never requited. Carol missed Doug. She left County in the summer to join her "soul mate", Doug, in Seattle (6-21).

Trivia: In her childhood, Carol climbed television poles to heights of 200 to 300 feet. Carol and Doug "closed the deal" on their first date, on the kitchen floor. Of the twins, Kate is the troublemaker. Carol's engagement ring from Taglieri cost an estimated $12,000. Carol was "stuck" by a needle five times but never contracted a disease. Carol speaks some Russian, is phenomenally gifted at simple mathematics and has expressed a low opinion of democracy. She is allergic to some flavours of edible massage oil. Her "Provocation to Assault Interval" is 21 seconds. At Carol's Christmas party in 1996, her Ukrainian relatives re-enacted the purges in her front room. At another, Carol's Uncle Ted wanted Doug Ross to play *Silent Night* on a tambourine. For Carol, Dr Bernstein will always be known as "the epidural man".

Lucy Knight *(Kellie Martin)*
Medical Student, 1998–2000

Lucy Knight was born and raised by her "capable self-sufficient single mom", Barbara. Lucy decided on a career in medicine and joined medical school, taking her first rotation in trauma medicine as a third-year medical student at County General. Chicago was not her first choice – she had hoped to study in San Francisco, which she had visited as a child.

Lucy started work in the ER in September 1998 and was assigned to John Carter. Lucy was remarkably dizzy. On her first day, she took a message for a dead patient on his mobile phone. A few weeks later she spent much of her day trying to track down a corpse she had left in the hall! Yet she was very knowledgeable. While Carter suspected she was reliant on a palmtop computer for answers, Doug Ross recognised her abilities on her first day (5-1).

Although keen to impress, Lucy had little experience of procedures. She soon came to rely too heavily on the nurses and started to take credit for their procedures. Unsurprisingly, she rapidly came into conflict with Carol Hathaway. However, Lucy's ploy backfired when she couldn't assist Carter in a trauma situation. Lucy confessed all, but Carter was firm: "Rule number one down there is it's not about you." He warned Lucy that if she lied to him again, she would be thrown off the rotation. Their relationship went from bad to worse when Lucy let a dorm party run riot – resulting in Carter losing his job as an RA (5-1 to 5-5).

This was an unpromising start to Lucy's relationship with Carter, a relationship that proved to be critical both professionally and personally. Carter was intent on winning the Chief Resident's position and knew the best way to get it was to prove himself as a tutor. He expected a high standard from Lucy: after all, he was a former student of Peter Benton. But Carter was learning too. Lucy became highly critical of his failure to explain situations, notably after a soft admit to manipulate an insurance claim (5-6). When Carter insisted she write her own evaluation, Mark Greene was determined to make them resolve their differences. It was not easy. It took the case of Corinna, and the search for her fugitive father, to build some form of rapprochement. This was reinforced at Christmas when together they performed their own Christmas miracles (5-1 to 5-10).

In fact, part of the tension between Lucy and Carter was sexual. Carter's girlfriend, Roxanne, suspected he had something going on with Lucy before they had resolved their differences (5-8). Carter certainly reacted negatively to Lucy's burgeoning relationship with Dale Edson in early 1999. It was around this time that Lucy moved on to a surgical rotation with Peter Benton and ceased being Carter's student. Almost inevitably, they got together (in one of the exam rooms) but decided they were unsuited. Carter still had a look out for Lucy who he grew to respect fondly. He tried to get her to stop taking Ritalin, a drug she was prescribed in the eighth grade but which she was unable to stop taking. There was always the suggestion that Lucy held a torch for Carter (5-21 to 5-22).

Following her surgical rotation (a relatively quiet period, marked only by the interesting case of Mrs Fong (5-17), Lucy moved on to the psychiatric department under Dr Myers. It quickly became apparent that Lucy was a natural. In summer 1999 she treated Seth, an aggressive foster child, and realised he had been over-medicated. Lucy recommended psychotherapy and rationalised medication. The diagnosis impressed Carl DeRaad, Head of Psychiatrics, who told Myers he could learn from his student (5-19). Lucy certainly learned well and applied her knowledge during a second trauma rotation with Carter, which started a few weeks later (5-21).

Lucy's confidence grew in later months. In autumn 1999, she angrily competed with Carol Hathaway for a rehab space for a patient (6-5). At Christmas she treated Valerie Page, a 24-year-old in need of a heart transplant. Lucy researched an unusual procedure and harassed Robert Romano to operate on Christmas Eve. Despite, or because of Lucy's impertinence, Romano warmed to her. Sadly, Valerie later died but the case showed Lucy to be a forceful advocate for her patients and a physician of increasing stature (6-9 to 6-11).

On 14 February 2000, Carter and Lucy treated Paul Sobriki. Carter thought Sobriki's altered state was a result of meningitis. Lucy discovered Sobriki's problems were psychological too late. Sobriki found a knife and stabbed Lucy four times. Though operated on by Corday and Romano, the hospital's two most senior surgeons, Lucy's injuries were fatal. She died later that day. Ironically, a few months later, Lucy was matched for a resident's position in Psychiatrics at County (6-14 to 6-18).

Trivia: Lucy's grandparents have been married for 56 years and still have great sex. She wanted to become Chief Resident. She didn't drink coffee ("can you imagine me on caffeine?"). When a patient was admitted with a carrot in his ass, Lucy was amazed "he swallowed it whole"! Lucy was keen to learn kickboxing. She wore thongs.

Dave Malucci, MD *(Erik Palladino)*
ER Resident, 1999–2001

David "Dr Dave" Malucci joined County in autumn 1999 as a second-year resident. His record was hardly promising. Dave had not been a diligent student: he "had fun" in college, his grades "sucked" and his MCATs were poor ("a long story", he claimed). Dave studied medicine on Grenada in "the Harvard of the Caribbean". The name of the school, however, did not impress his colleagues, especially Carter. Dave was indignant, and pointing to the name on his white coat, said "It still says MD, Carter. See?"

From the start, Dave's ability was in question. He didn't follow Carter's orders, gave incomplete instructions to his students and readily accepted the diagnoses of nurses rather than seeing his patients. Dave was angrily chastised by Dr Gabriel Lawrence after he was derogatory about a patient, upsetting a relative: "One thing you've still got to learn is that every patient is somebody's boyfriend, girlfriend, father, mother, son," noted Lawrence. "They don't exist simply for you to learn new and interesting procedures... Next time open your eyes before you open your mouth." Unsurprisingly, he soon made an enemy of Kerry Weaver and incurred her wrath when he saved a man trapped on a building site. Malucci was not covered by insurance to work in the field. Kerry berated him for his cavalier attitude (6-2 to 6-4). Romano also had a low opinion of "Malatucci".

In truth, Dave cared about his patients but had great difficulty dealing with the raw emotions of the ER. Early in his time at County, he was asked to read a final message to a man who had died. Dave's conscience got the better of him and he eventually read the message to the body. In January 2000, he treated Jason, an 11-year-old with lymphoma. Dave tried to pass the patient to Oncology, but Luka persuaded him to break the tragic news (6-4 and 6-10). Dave also had difficulty when treating Jeff, a young man who was trying to contract HIV from his partner. Dave was incredulous but eventually spoke calmly and rationally with the man. Jeff didn't take Dave's advice (7-13).

Dave also had a keen sense of injustice. When he heard of a backroom clinic prescribing illegally imported medication, Dave confronted the dealers and gained a black eye. He also got enough evidence to have the clinic closed down (6-11). Dave violently assaulted a father who had sexually abused his daughter. He was told to suture the man, but deliberately used insufficient pain medication (6-20). Later, Dave took issue with Mark Greene over his dispassionate treatment of a young boy who Dave thought was a victim of domestic abuse. Dave baited the father to have him separated from his son. Mark suspended Dave for a week (7-16).

However, Dave was not a diligent doctor. In early 2000, he was assigned Abby Lockhart as a student but Dave was nowhere to be seen (it was Carter who taught her how to intubate). Dave readily accepted the diagnoses of others. In early summer 2002, he took Abby's opinion and missed an ovarian abscess. Corday, who had to operate on the woman, pulled no punches: "Do you want to know the staff's opinion of you? You're lazy, sloppy and your careless attitude towards your responsibilities as a physician endangers patients' lives, as witnessed today. In other words, none of us think you're much of a doctor." (6-11 to 6-21)

Clearly, Dave could not afford to overstep the mark, but soon did. In autumn 2001, he treated Paul, a 27-year-old who had suffered a heart attack. Dave suspected cocaine abuse and asked Jing-Mei Chen for permission to administer drugs to prevent blood clots. It was a fatal misdiagnosis: the man had a weak aorta that collapsed and caused massive internal bleeding. Weaver was furious: "In a perfect world, Dr Malucci, I wouldn't submit any patients to your care. If you knew your ass from your elbow, or even gave a damn... this man might still be alive." A few days later, Kerry caught Dave in a clinch with a paramedic in the ambulance bay. It was the final straw: Kerry listed his five letters for unprofessional behaviour, the counselling taken after each and two failed rotations. Berating his "cowboy" attitude, she fired him. Dave left, but not before forcefully giving his own opinion of Kerry Weaver.

Trivia: Dave's parents are Catholics but went through a "charismatic" phase. His Uncle Al has his tumour on his mantelpiece. Romano referred to Dave as "Malatucci". Dave can repair cars and spent a long time working on Weaver's. He once considered buying a BMW in topaz blue: Kerry noted his "misguided sense of job security". Dave got sick on a chopper ride: "Hey, hey! I told you – I had the flu." He had an ambition to work through every medical student and had mother-daughter fantasies about Abby and Maggie. He also fantasised about Kim and her girlfriend, not realising that her girlfriend was Kerry Weaver. In late 2000 he spent a day avoiding Stephanie and the previous day avoiding a different girl. Dave is not into wedding lists. He had a fascination with Weaver's leg but was unable to uncover the truth about it. Dave once removed a screw from a patient's leg by using a screwdriver. The man refused pain medication and screamed the ER down. Dave has a crippling fear of clowns.

Douglas Ross, MD *(George Clooney)*
Paediatrics Fellow, 1994–8
Paediatrics Attending, 1998–9

Born in February 1962, Douglas Ross was the only child of Ray and Sarah. Ray Ross was an inveterate gambler and womaniser who abandoned his wife and son. Ray would periodically arrive from nowhere and whisk Doug away in his Cadillac for days on end. Doug grew up deeply resentful of his father, and highly protective of his mother. Only later would Doug realise how much his father had influenced his personal relationships. Doug's mother later remarried.

Doug decided to go into medicine. He showed a natural aptitude for the subject, but a notable disinclination for hard work. In his third and fourth years as a medical student he undertook trauma and paediatrics rotations, including a paeds rotation at Southside Hospital under Dr Donald Anspaugh. He worked for four years as a resident, including one year at Mount Sinai with Kerry Weaver.

At County, he met Carol Hathaway. They dated for two years (1992–4). It was Doug's only serious relationship yet it ended sadly. Scared to commit, Doug "replaced" Carol with someone else. Throughout Carol's engagement to John Taglieri, Doug feared he had done the wrong thing and tried to get her back. Carol was convinced Doug merely wanted what he could not have and was resistant. The result was a string of short-term relationships with beautiful, available women. For little over a year, Doug dated pharmaceuticals representative Linda Farrell, though not exclusively (1-5 to 2-7). His most serious relationship was with Diane Leeds from County's Risk Management department. The affair ended in disaster when Diane became serious (1-23). He then dated a Finnish air stewardess and later his father's girlfriend, Karen Hines.

At work, Doug proved himself to be a gifted doctor, especially with children. He won a paediatrics fellowship, which he would hold for four years. However, his career at County was patchy at best. Doug was more than ready to mete out punishment in cases of abuse. In February 1995, he assaulted an abusive father (1-16) and was ordered to attend counselling sessions with hospital psychiatrist Dr Alan Murphy. Murphy's diagnosis, that Doug was a "a reasonably normal guy with sloppy impulse control" (1-21), was echoed three years later when Weaver objected to Doug's promotion on the grounds of "ongoing problems with impulse control" (5-3). Doug's readiness to jump to conclusions sometimes caused problems with patients: he once accused a father of inflicting cigarette burns on his son, only to discover they were self-inflicted (4-16).

Although a Paediatrics Fellow, Doug spent most of his time in the ER. In September 1995, the Head of Paediatrics, Dr Neil Bernstein, bitterly complained that Ross rarely worked in Paediatrics and that he undermined his authority. The friction was exacerbated by Doug's handling of the Chia-Chia Loh case in October–November 1995 (2-3 to 2-5). Doug felt that Bernstein's clinic had failed the boy and decided to treat the boy himself. As a result, Bernstein refused to support Doug's position from the end of the year (2-6). Doug was told to seek another position, and soon found one at a private children's hospital. However, soon afterwards Doug dramatically saved a young boy, Ben Larkin, in front of live TV news cameras (2-7). Doug's fellowship was reinstated and he reluctantly accepted an award for heroism (2-8).

The incident did little to quell Doug's fervent belief in the patient's concerns over those of the hospital. He once told Weaver: "I just want to make sure that this boy gets a decent shot at a normal life. I don't care about your rules or regulations." But he was less happy when he failed his patients himself. When he missed a case of cancer, he was mortified and paid for the chemotherapy (2-17). Throughout 1996–7, he tried numerous measures to help Charlie, a young homeless girl he met while working on the health-mobile, but with no success.

The Ben Larkin incident also brought about an unexpected turn of events. Ray Ross saw Doug's efforts to save Ben on live television and came to Chicago. They had not seen each other in 22 years. Although resistant at first, Doug mellowed and started to rebuild their relationship (2-15). However, Ray soon left without any warning and Doug did not see him again. In November 1997, Ray Ross died in a car crash. He had been drinking and killed himself, his partner, Sheri Fox, and a father of six.

Clearly much of Doug's behaviour can be drawn from his father's influence. Doug's aggressive attitude to bad parents was perhaps a reaction to Ray's abandonment. When Ray visited, Doug was keen to get back at him by sleeping with his girlfriend. Later, Doug chastised himself for doing a "good impression" of his father when he clashed with Mark Greene over his heroism award (2-8). Doug once told Ray that he had learnt his lesson well from his father and never committed to anything in his life: "no fuss, no messy details" (2-16). Sadly, Doug also had a son (born 1987) whom he never met (1-12).

From autumn 1996, shortly after he broke up with Ray's girlfriend Karen, Doug's behaviour became increasingly self-destructive. It reached a climax during his one-night stand with Nadine Wilks, an epileptic who killed herself with tequila and cocaine. Doug tested positive for alcohol but not drugs. The incident was the last call for Doug (3-4) and he slowly started to turn his life around. After a long period on his own, Doug renewed his interest in Carol Hathaway. They started dating again in the summer of 1997, but kept their relationship quiet until November when Mark Greene helped Doug deal with the death of his father (4-7). By the time Carol made the official announcement on Christmas Eve 1997, the staff had taken bets on how long it would take her to come clean. At that moment, Doug proposed. However, scared to commit, in February 1998, Carol had a brief clinch with paramedic Greg Powell (4-12). Doug backed off to let Carol come round in her own time.

It was just as Doug and Carol started dating again that Doug was introduced to Dr Anna Del Amico. Anna was a paediatrics resident he supervised for one year. Surprisingly, Doug clashed bitterly with Anna over her fierce independence – a characteristic usually attributed to Ross (3-21 to 4-5). In fact, Anna raised the standard against which Doug was judged: on showing Anna around the ER, he asked Kerry to take her back: "I'm intimidated enough already." (3-20) Doug and Anna soon resolved their differences and gained each other's trust (4-5).

Funding for Doug's post again came under scrutiny in October 1997 when Kerry Weaver, now acting Chief of Emergency Medicine, refused to underwrite his salary from the ER budget (4-4). Doug was told to undertake research and find independent funding but his project, patient-controlled anaesthesia (PCA), came under heavy criticism from Weaver and Anspaugh (4-16). In response to the funding crisis, Doug refused to complete fellowship renewal forms and persuaded the Dean to consider creating a Paediatrics Attending position in the ER (4-17 and 4-18). Doug also encouraged a study by Dr Max Rocher into the possibilities of a Paediatrics ER at County (see *Anna del Amico*).

However, Doug did not find support. Kerry Weaver fervently opposed his proposed appointment as Paediatrics Attending, although he had more success with Mark Greene. Mark was perhaps impressed with Doug's restrained treatment of incendiary cases like Jad Houston (4-16) and Zoe (4-19) and was won over after watching Doug in action on the day of the ER annual banquet (4-18). However, Mark's trust was quickly undermined when Doug rashly put Josh McNeil, a crack baby, through rapid detoxification in June 1998 (4-20 to 4-22). Although the senior staff later endorsed Doug's actions, the case marked a turning point in Doug's relationship with Mark and Kerry.

After a short period on probation, Doug was made a Paediatrics Attending, much to the annoyance of Weaver (5-3). He was immediately in trouble when he discussed treatment options with a girl without her parents' consent (5-3). However, he showed uncharacteristic diligence in trying to sign off all paediatrics trauma cases (the initiative lasted less than one day (5-5).

Despite failing to obtain research funding, Doug continued to show an interest in PCA. From early 1999, he began treating Ricky Abbott, a young boy with the painful terminal condition ALD. Doug raised the ire of Mark Greene when appropriating experimental pain medication for Ricky. Later, he falsified documents to obtain a PCA machine. When the pain became too much for Ricky, Doug told the mother, Joi Abbott, how to increase the dose. Ricky was brought to the ER in arrest; and died. Doug was suspended by Weaver and became the subject of a criminal investigation. Although no charges were brought, the incident forced the closure of Carol's clinic and brought an end to Doug's career. In February 1999, he resigned from the ER and decided to move away. He asked Carol to join him but she knew her work, family and friends were in Chicago. A few days later, Carol discovered she was pregnant with twins. She gave birth to Tess and Kate in December 1999 and moved to Seattle to be with Doug in summer 2000.

Trivia: Doug's birthday is in early February; his star sign is Aquarius. Whenever Doug went to the store for Carol, he bought a box of animal crackers. Kerry's report into Doug's behaviour after the Josh McNeil incident cited "complete disregard for hospital policies and procedures... disrupting workplace behaviour... ongoing problems with impulse control". Doug merely noted: "That's right, Kerry. I'm a psycho." Doug was the hospital's biggest gossip and was affectionately known as "Doctor Intercom". Doug is not a trained anaesthesiologist. He used to race TR7s when he was young. Doug has a "three-date rule" – Doug and Carol closed the deal on the first date! Doug once told a mother that her son had died but she was so shocked she asked if his arm was broken. Doug's pain medication thesis was ahead of its time, but was proven by someone else. When Doug was knocked down by a single punch, Carol remarked she never knew he had such a glass jaw. Doug played varsity basketball (Augusta 20). Ray once left Doug in a hallway in Atlantic City while he screwed the hat-check girl. Doug's favourite Winnie-the-Pooh character is Eeyore.

Supporting Cast

Haleh Adams *(Yvette Freeman)*
Senior Nurse, 1994–

One of County's most experienced nurses, Haleh has worked in emergency medicine for more than 20 years. She trained most members of the ER staff at County, once noting that Mark Greene was "the best scut puppy I ever had". Such familiarity is a core part of Haleh's working relationships, as is her commitment to compassionate care.

As the second most senior nurse in the ER, Haleh took temporary charge in March 1994 following Carol Hathaway's suicide attempt. Haleh was a key member of the nurses' union and organised an unofficial strike in spring 1997 over the floating of ER nurses to other departments. During Carol's suspension, Haleh took charge once more, but was clearly unsuited to the task. She was grateful when Carol returned to work.

Haleh was also a friend of Mookie James and arranged for his work placement in the ER. A rather more unwanted frequent visitor was Pablo, a homeless man, who only attended Carol's clinic on a Thursday because he knew Haleh would be on duty!

Donald Anspaugh *(John Aylward)*
Chief of Staff, 1996–9
Senior Surgeon, 1999–

An accomplished surgeon and hospital Chief of Staff, Donald Anspaugh learnt his trade in the US Army. He once shared billets at West Point with Norman Schwarzkopf and in

1974 worked with British surgeons, including Corday's former colleague Sir Lyle Sugden, on joint NATO exercises. Back in Chicago, Anspaugh rose to Chief of Staff at Southside hospital where he had a reputation as a maverick ("completely lumpy", according to Morgenstern) and pioneered the "health-mobile" project. When Southside was closed in 1996, he was made Chief of Staff at County. Anspaugh soon lived up to his reputation when he made the slowest working ER doctors wax his car – a jet black Cadillac Seville with burgundy interior.

Nevertheless, Anspaugh proved himself to be a capable hospital manager. He headed several internal investigations, including that into the tragic death of Dennis Gant and Doug Ross' treatment of baby Josh McNeil. Anspaugh also showed great prudence: he allowed Jeanie Boulet to return to work amid claims of wrongful dismissal, and allowed John Carter to change his sub-internship specialty. Anspaugh also allowed Carol's clinic to continue under the management of Lynette Evans, a nurse he had recommended to Carol. On the other hand, he was responsible for the appointment of psychotic impostor Amanda Lee as Chief of Emergency Medicine in December 1998! He paid his penance by having to take on the post in the interim.

Anspaugh's private life was less happy. His wife died of cancer in 1997. His son, Scott, also died of cancer in May 1998 following a long fight with the illness. Anspaugh was particularly grateful to Jeanie Boulet, who cared for Scott in his last months. Donald Anspaugh has one daughter, Yvette.

Anspaugh stepped down as Chief of Staff in autumn 1999 lamenting "the mind-numbing day to day detritus of this job". He returned to surgery and operated on Carter after his stabbing. Anspaugh attended Mark Greene's funeral in 2002.

Trivia: Anspaugh once expressed a fondness for dinosaur pencils. He once had a patient who thought he had hypnotised him so he could drink his blood. He is a member of the prestigious Fair Oaks golf club and mixes with some of Chicago's high and mighty.

Alex Babcock *(David Brisbin)*
Paediatric Anaesthesiologist, 1998–2001

Alex Babcock worked at County from 1998, often assisting during operations as an anaesthetist. He assisted Dr Kotlowitz on pioneering cochlea transplant surgery. Babcock was also the anaesthetist during Carol Hathaway's labour: he earned her lifelong gratitude as "the epidural man". Babcock had a more difficult relationship with Elizabeth Corday. In autumn 2000 he claimed that Corday botched an endoscopic procedure. Corday was sued for malpractice but the hospital agreed an out-of-court settlement. A year later, Corday was investigated when several of her patients died from post-operative complications. Corday discovered that Babcock had assisted on each case and claimed he was the culprit, even at one point searching his lab and claiming he was a supporter of euthanasia. "I can't think of a humane doctor who isn't," he noted. Their bickering prompted Romano to suspend both from active service until the matter was investigated. Although the final report dismissed Corday's claims, and they were both reinstated, Elizabeth still refused to let Babcock near Ella when she was critically ill.

Graham Baker *(Carl Lumbly)*
Plastic Surgeon, 1999

Graham Baker, a widower, first met Jeanie Boulet when he was called as a plastics consult to the ER. They dated for a few months. However, Jeanie also continued to see Reggie, a cop. When Jeanie discovered she had contracted Hepatitis C from a patient, she stopped dating both men.

Neil Bernstein *(David Spielberg)*
Head of Paediatrics, 1995–6

Bernstein was Head of Paediatrics during a turbulent period in the career of Doug Ross. In autumn 1995, he complained to David Morgenstern that Ross was almost always on duty in the ER. Ross regarded Bernstein as an idiot and was dismissive of his authority and rude to his physicians. When the two clashed over the case of Chia-Chia Loh in November 1995, Bernstein refused to renew Doug's fellowship. It was only Doug's remarkable save of Ben Larkin, covered live on TV, that saved his job. The hospital board supported Doug's reinstatement and gave him an award for heroism. Bernstein wrote a new contract for Doug, underwritten by the ER.

E. Ray Bozman *(Charles Noland)*
Reception Clerk/Trainee Nurse, 1995–7

E. Ray Bozman was one of County's most versatile members of staff. When he joined in November 1995, he had already worked as a rodeo clown, UPS delivery man, short order cook and licensed day care worker. Deeply spiritual, he had joined the "human potential" movement in the 1980s as a leader and trainer. He supplemented his meagre nurse's salary by teaching an evening yoga class at Malcolm X Community College and working on the reception. E. Ray Bozman seems to have given up his career at County around summer 1997, no doubt to move on to something completely different.

Janet Coburn *(Amy Aquino)*
Attending Physician, Obstetrics Department, 1994–c. 2000
Head of Obstetrics, c. 2000–

One of County's most experienced doctors, Janet Coburn was an intimidating and abrasive presence. She was vociferously opposed to the non-renewal of Doug Ross' fellowship (2-1). When a colleague, Dr Anna Castigliano, was due to deliver in the ER, she specifically requested that Coburn not be called to supervise!

Coburn's most serious run-in was with Mark Greene. In 1995, Greene missed eclampsia in the case of Jodi O'Brien. His decision to press on with the delivery saved the baby but resulted in the death of the mother. Coburn insisted she had "never seen such a chain of errors of judgement" and advocated severe action be taken against Mark (1-18 to 1-20). However, Coburn later came to respect Mark's abilities when he had to deliver nine babies during a frantic night in the ER (2-15). Still, the incident continued to haunt their professional relationship. When Carol Hathaway went into labour, Mark Greene fought successfully to prevent Coburn performing a hysterectomy. OB Nurse Abby Lockhart noted that Carol had Mark to thank for her future unborn children. Coburn also supervised the delivery of Reese Benton and was Jing-Mei Chen's personal physician during her pregnancy.

By 2000, Coburn had risen higher in the ranks of the hospital and sat on the interview panel for prospective students with Peter Benton and Robert Romano (7-14).

Div Cvetic *(John Terry)*
Head of Psychiatrics. Left November 1994

A talented psychiatrist of 15 years and County's Head of Psychiatrics, Div Cvetic showed signs of clinical depression towards the end of 1994. His partner of six months, Susan Lewis, found Div increasingly distant and difficult to talk to. In fact, the day-to-day was taking its toll: "After 15 years, not one week has gone by without being bitten, spat, puked or peed on," he noted. From September he showed an increasingly harsh attitude towards his patients and clashed with Susan: "You try to find ways not to hate them," he recorded into a Dictaphone. "You feel nothing." In November 1994, he left his job and his apartment without informing anyone. No news was heard for several months until Susan discovered Div was safe – and living with a woman who owned a chain of mortuaries.

Carl DeRaad *(John Doman)*
Head of Psychiatrics, 1999–

Carl DeRaad was Head of Psychiatrics when Lucy Knight undertook a successful psych rotation. DeRaad was impressed with Lucy's diagnostic abilities and her determination to treat through psychotherapy rather than medicine. He referred one of his residents, Dr Myers, to learn from Lucy's example (5-19). It may have been DeRaad's recommendation that resulted in Lucy being matched to County's Psychiatrics department as a resident in July, tragically a short while after she had been murdered in the ER. DeRaad offered counselling to members of staff in the aftermath of the Sobriki incident. He persuaded John Carter to talk to him and forced Carter to recognise that the incident was not an "accident" but a brutal attack. He advised Carter that his recovery would take some time (6-19).

As could be anticipated, DeRaad came into conflict with colleagues in the course of his work. In autumn 1999, Luka Kovac was annoyed when DeRaad could not hold a violent and abusive husband. Luka eventually provoked the man to assaulting him so he could have him arrested. Some months later, DeRaad could not hold a young woman with suspected anorexia and bulimia, angering Corday. Nevertheless, a short time later, DeRaad and Luka tried to convince an 18-year-old stabbing victim to save her unborn child. Their efforts were unsuccessful and the child died.

Dale Edson *(Matthew Glave)*
Medical Student, 1996
Surgical Resident, 1996–

Arrogant and manipulative, Dale Edson was hardly County's model surgical resident. He studied medicine at Harvard and took a six-week thoracic elective at Hopkins. He joined County in June 1996 for a trauma surgery sub-internship. Carter was deeply envious: Dale had performed an appendectomy even before starting at County and had a history with Harper Tracy. For the next few months the two men competed for procedures – it was this that ultimately led to Carter and Harper's break up.

In late 1996 Dale and Carter clashed over the case of Mr Percy, a surgical patient who Carter thought needed a psych consult. Carter was reluctant to challenge Anspaugh's decision to operate and the patient died. Dale was quick to ridicule Carter for not going with his instincts. Carter slammed him into a locker (3-7). They again clashed when Dale administered antibiotics that nearly killed a patient. Carter guessed immediately that Dale falsified the chart to cover himself: "If you do anything like this again, I'll bury you." Nevertheless, Dale still felt he could cross Carter and was quick to ridicule him when he changed from surgery to emergency medicine. Benton regarded Dale as a weasel and thought Carter would have become twice the surgeon Dale could ever be.

Dale matched to County and became a surgical resident. When Corday was forced to work as an intern during 1998–9 she was annoyed to be assigned to Dale. Dale was quick to treat Corday like any other student and gave her excessive scut work. She eventually transferred to Benton. Romano was surprisingly sympathetic, noting he "couldn't handle taking orders from a weasel like Dale". Shortly after, Dale again clashed with Carter when he had a brief relationship with Lucy Knight (and discovered she wore thongs).

Lynette Evans *(Penny Johnson)*
Nurse Practitioner, 1998–9
Clinic Manager, 1999–

When Carol Hathaway was looking for a permanent nurse for her clinic, Donald Anspaugh warmly recommended Lynette Evans. Lynette was one of County's Nurse Practitioners. Carol was impressed when Lynette showed a no-nonsense approach with a troublesome youth, and hired her on the spot.

However, Lynette and Carol did not always see eye-to-eye. In October 1998, Lynette wanted to sedate a violent patient but Carol was critical and ordered that Lynette work only in the clinic from then on. Lynette took issue when Carol refused treatment until a young girl went on the birth-control pill. Carol also objected to Lynette running an antenatal clinic for black mothers only.

Despite this, the two grew to be supportive of each other. Lynette was a comfort when

Carol had trouble conceiving. When Anspaugh threatened to close the clinic following Carol's support for Doug Ross, Carol convinced him to let the clinic carry on with Lynette as manager.

Greg Fischer *(Harry J Lennix)*
Virologist, Infectious Diseases Department, 1997

Before joining County, Greg Fischer ran his own private practice. His business partner died of an AIDS-related illness and Greg turned to hospital medicine. At County he ran the AIDS programme and oversaw a new treatment study. From early 1997, he served as virology consult to the ER.

When Jeanie Boulet was looking for a personal physician, Kerry Weaver immediately recommended Greg – "one of the most eligible bachelors in Chicago". Greg and Jeanie soon started dating – stargazing and picnics in sub-zero temperatures! As Greg became more serious, Jeanie felt more uncomfortable with her illness. Struggling to cope, she grew closer to her ex-husband Al. Greg ended his relationship with Jeanie when he discovered she was still seeing Al.

Steve Flint *(Scott Jaeck)*
Head of Radiology, 1994–

Dr Steve Flint, Head of Radiology, has been a regular presence in the ER for many years. The department had a poor reputation for keeping on top of things and Mark Greene knew a good relationship with Flint was the key to success. Flint was present when Mark Greene discovered his father had lung cancer. Mark was later diagnosed with a brain tumour and was also treated in Radiology. Flint has walked the line of acceptable behaviour before: he refused to permit an X-ray on a patient with no insurance, riling Carol Hathaway who ended up paying for the film. Romano is often in a race with Radiology to get to a patient and treat them first!

Frank *(Troy Evans)*
Reception Clerk, 2000–

Frank was a Chicago cop for 21 years before he replaced Jerry Markovic on the reception desk. His only experience with medicine prior to joining County in summer 2000 was a knee replacement he had six months earlier! It was almost impossible for Frank to break free of his time as a cop. He looked at wanted posters and in autumn 2000 spotted a wanted murder suspect receiving treatment and called the police. Frank also wanted to use a baton on the homeless!

It's fair to say that Frank is not the most understanding of people: he labelled Luka a "freakin' liberal foreigner," and told Kerry Weaver she was going to hell for being gay. Frank has also a mine of useless scientific information: he can name each of Jupiter's eight moons and reckons the second ice age is almost upon us.

Randi Fronczak *(Kristin Minter)*
Reception Clerk, 1995–

Randi may not have led a blameless life, but certainly has the experience to deal with the demands of an inner-city ER. She has a criminal record for "malicious mischief, assault, battery, carrying a concealed weapon and aggravated maim". When she discovered a man had started a fire alarm for some attention, she punched him out! Inventive and bright, Randi suggested an immediate solution to Carol's nursing budget problems – although it resulted in unofficial strike action. Her knowledge of finance probably comes from an accountancy course she took to prepare for the launch of her own range of clothes, "Randi-wear". She certainly had a talent for fashion: she helped Kerry Weaver prepare for her interview for ER Chief by providing a leather jacket and appropriate accessories. Randi held a torch for Jerry Markovic and Raul Melendez, and described Gabe Lawrence as "the attractive older guy", but instantly dismissed the advances of Doug Ross. She was a witness at Jeanie Boulet's marriage to Roger.

Trivia: Randi once broke past security guards and made it through the front door of the White House. She is well connected in the criminal underworld and knows a couple of guys who can track down a repo guy instantly!

Dennis Gant *(Omar Epps)*
Surgical Intern, 1996–7. Died January 1997

Dennis Gant studied at LSU medical school before joining County as a surgical intern in 1996. He and John Carter were assigned to Peter Benton. Together, they quickly found Benton to be "an intern's worst nightmare": they worked extremely long shifts, were ordered to complete excessive paperwork and given limited time in the OR. Gant's first evaluation was mediocre: Benton criticised his speed, lack of preparation and attitude. Gant was irked, but Benton insisted his evaluation was fair.

Carter and Gant soon came to suspect rightly that they were being treated more harshly that Benton's other interns. Benton was determined that Carter should not get preferential treatment just because he was Peter's former student. More importantly, he insisted that Gant – a fellow black doctor – had to work twice as hard and be twice as good just to be accepted. It was not a sentiment Gant shared: "You're a real prick, you know that?"

Nevertheless, he was determined not to get another poor evaluation. "Benton wants me to pull my weight, I'm damn well gonna pull it," he told Carter. "I'm not letting him get another shot at me." The result was a gruelling schedule. Over the Christmas period he was running 20 charts at once. He completed one 34-hour shift, only to find he was on duty the next day too. The schedule started to play havoc with his social life: his girlfriend, Monique, decided she wouldn't visit at Christmas as Gant would have no time to see her. Gant requested two days leave to sort out their differences, but Benton refused. Meanwhile, Carter was too engrossed with Abby Keaton to be a support for Gant. When Benton and Anspaugh were highly critical of Gant after a long shift, Carter did not back up his colleague.

In early January, Gant was brought in to County after being hit by an El train, and died in the ER. Although the coroner recorded a verdict of accidental death, the staff could not be sure that he hadn't jumped. Carter suspected suicide and was sure that Benton's harsh teaching methods – and his lack of support for Dennis – were at the root of it. "You can be sure that he never received any encouraging or supporting word from you," he told Benton. "All he ever got from you was harping and criticism. And now he's dead and you're going to have to face it."

Wendy Goldman *(Vanessa Marquez)*
Junior Nurse, 1994–7

Wendy started her nursing career as a junior nurse at County. Active in the day-to-day life of the hospital, she was a writer for County's *Hospital News* and wrote a cover story about Mark Greene (2-3). From 1996, Wendy was more likely to be seen on night shift, and Kerry Weaver put her on an exercise bike for a study of the effect of the circadian rhythms on night-shift workers.

Lydia Grabarsky *(Ellen Crawford)*
Senior Nurse, 1994–

A core member of the ER team, Lydia has been one of the regular staff since before 1994. She has been married twice. Her first husband was unpromising: the most romantic gift he gave her was a vacuum cleaner. She met her second husband, Chicago cop Al Grabarsky, on Valentine's Day 1995. They were engaged on 24 October 1996, but Lydia became frustrated that Al kept putting off the big day. They married in November 1997 in an impromptu ceremony at the hospital chapel. In 1999, Lydia was trained to cover Carol Hathaway as Charge Nurse. She may have taken on more responsibilities since Carol's departure. She is only a few years away from retirement.

Trivia: Lydia once had a poem published in *Good Housekeeping*. Her Hallowe'en costume is a ghoulish maid's outfit. She has been accidentally stuck by a needle nine times, but has never been infected. She is a master of the "blood alcohol level" game and can always predict the right amount. She has a sister with children.

George Henry *(Chad Lowe)*
Medical Student, 1997

Medical student George Henry undertook a four-year research degree (MD PhD) before being assigned to John Carter to undertake his compulsory trauma medicine rotation. Henry had no practical medical training of any kind: the only time he was able to assist Carter was when one of the patients showed signs of "happy puppet disease", the condition Henry had researched at med school. Henry also suffered from a wide range of allergies that prevented him from seeing patients! During one severe allergic reaction to his latex gloves, Henry had an out-of-body experience. Given his track record, Carter had to give Henry a number of U/Es ("Unable to Evaluate"). He was disappointed when Henry returned in December 1997 to re-take his trauma rotation. Carter finally approved Henry when he intubated a dead man – Carter didn't want to risk inflicting Henry on live patients!

Angela Hicks *(C. C. H. Pounder)*
ER Attending Physician, 1994
Senior Surgical Attending, 1994–

Angela Hicks joined County in 1994 as an ER Attending: Doug Ross mistook her for a nurse and put her on bedpan duty! In fact, Hicks was one of County's most capable physicians and a remarkably talented surgeon. She took responsibility for training surgical residents and medical students, including Peter Benton. Hicks became a key influence on Benton: she constantly questioned his single-minded pursuit of procedures (1-10) and urged him to consider his patients more. "It's not about ambition," she once told him. "It's about healing people." Nevertheless, Hicks regarded Benton's skills highly and was keen to find him a place on her surgical Red Team from 1997.

Hicks had a more tempestuous relationship with John Carter. She disciplined him after he manipulated the system to admit a patient to the OR. On one occasion she pressed for his expulsion from the surgical programme (Anspaugh refused). In the end, however, she also respected Carter's abilities. She was highly critical when Benton appeared to be wasting Carter's skills and poached him for her own surgical team. She also mediated between Carter and Benton on several occasions, not least when Carter wrote a highly critical assessment of Benton's abilities as a teacher. Hicks also had a mischievous sense of humour: she couldn't resist telling Carter about Benton's errors as a young surgeon and rescheduled surgery so that Carter could perform Benton's appendectomy.

Cynthia Hooper *(Mariska Hargitay)*
Reception Clerk, 1997–1998

Cynthia Hooper grew up in Joliet and Virginia before moving to Chicago in 1997. Before joining County, Cynthia had worked as a cold caller selling vitamins – she was sacked when she refused to sell to old people on the grounds that it was "too late for them". She had also worked as a cashier at a Ford dealership. In October 1997, Mark Greene hired her, despite an appalling interview: Carol Hathaway was firmly against the appointment.

Mark may have had an ulterior motive, as he and Cynthia started dating soon after. However, Cynthia was a little "needy" and hoped Mark would let her move in with him when the tenancy ran out on her apartment. Mark missed the obvious cue, largely because he wasn't that serious about her. Mark was frustrated when Cynthia joined him on a visit to his parents in San Diego. It was too much, and Mark admitted he didn't love her. Cynthia left immediately and was not seen again. She moved on to work as an administrative assistant in a law firm (4-2 to 4-16).

Trivia: At school, Cynthia won a role in 'Death of a Salesman' so her teacher could see her in her pants. Both her parents are dead and she has no brothers or sisters. She has a son, Jason, who was raised on a trailer park by her estranged partner's parents until he was two.

Lily Jarvik *(Lily Mariye)*
Nurse, 1994–

Lily is one of the ER's longest serving nurses. She was a great support to Carol Hathaway and was always ready to cover for her (3-1). A key organiser of the social life of the ER, Lily eagerly prepared Jerry's birthday celebration in 1998 (5-1). She was trapped outside the ER during the Lockdown (8-22).

Jack Kayson *(Sam Anderson)*
Head of Cardiology, 1994–

Jack Kayson is one of the longest serving members of staff at County. In 1994 he had a series of clashes with Susan Lewis over her treatment of cardiology patients in the ER. Lewis was intimidated by Kayson and did not question his decision to discharge a patient for fear she was wrong. The patient later returned in full arrest. The resulting enquiry found Kayson's assessment to have been inadequate. Shortly after the results of the enquiry, Kayson suffered a heart attack. Lewis forcefully advocated a course of tPA, with which Kayson weakly concurred. The incident rebuilt their relationship. Indeed, Kayson later asked Lewis out, claiming the heart attack had given him a whole new perspective on life! (1-2 to 1-13)

Kayson was also involved in the case of Louise Cupertino and argued for her right to receive a heart transplant (3-16). He was the leader of the enquiry into the death of Dr Lyle Swanson in May 1998 (4-19). He clashed with Jeanie Boulet in October 1998 over the treatment of illegal immigrants (5-4).

Abby Keaton *(Glenne Headly)*
Paediatric Surgeon 1996–7

Holder of the Paediatrics Surgeon of the Year award (1995) and the Price award (1996), Abby Keaton was already a renowned surgeon when she joined County on the closure of Southside in autumn 1996. Benton was keen to work with Keaton and to try his hand at the challenging field of paediatrics surgery. His assessment of Keaton was harsh: "She doesn't say what she wants. She's soft. She doesn't act like a surgeon." In fact, she had all the qualities that Benton lacked, the precise qualities he needed to succeed as a paediatrics surgeon.

When his rotation with Keaton finished at the end of three months, Keaton refused to recommend Benton for another, citing his inability to deal with the emotional needs of his patients. Meanwhile, Carter was dealing with her emotional needs. Carter was disappointed when Abby left in January 1997 to practise in Pakistan. Susan Lewis recalled Carter's infatuation with Abby when she returned to County in 2001.

Trivia: Abby likes deep-pan pepperoni pizza with anchovies. She wears size 7 surgical gloves with no powder.

David Kotlowitz *(Dennis Boutsikaris)*
Visiting ENT Surgeon, 1998

Dr Kotlowitz was Chicago's foremost surgeon in the field of cochlear implants. Corday recommended that Benton speak to him after his son, Reese, was diagnosed with profound deafness. Kotlowitz's work to restore hearing in young patients had attracted significant criticism from deaf groups who claimed he wanted to wipe out deafness. In fact, they were very near to the mark: Kotlowitz could see no reason why any child should not have their hearing restored. It was Kotlowitz's harsh attitude, and the more positive influence of Dr Parks, that convinced Peter to abandon a surgical solution to Reese's deafness (5-7).

Sarah Langworthy *(Tyra Ferrell)*
Surgical Resident, 1994–5

Sarah Langworthy competed with Peter Benton for the Starzl Fellowship in autumn 1994. Despite Benton putting up a strong fight, and performing amazing surgery, Langworthy was awarded the fellowship due to seniority. Sarah intimated that she would have liked to go out with Peter Benton, but he immediately told her that any sexual chemistry was only in her head.

Gabriel Lawrence *(Alan Alda)*
ER Attending, 1999

"One of the founding fathers of emergency medicine," Dr Gabriel Lawrence was a legend before he stepped through the doors at County. He served in the army for many years and pioneered a form of medical superglue that took 30 years to be approved for civilian use. He was Kerry Weaver's tutor at medical school and her inspiration for becoming an ER doctor. They became close friends. Gabe was in no doubt of Kerry's skill and her rapacious appetite for knowledge: "There were times when you drove me nuts!"

Gabe was a flighty character. Ever creative, he was quick to invent new solutions in crisis situations. A mine of information, he knew everything from the story of the first stethoscope to the little-known Radavicci test for mental incapacity. Unlike Kerry, Gabe was not a keen administrator and preferred to see patients: "Paperwork!" he once lamented. "You can run, but you can't hide." Socially, Gabe also had a rollercoaster background. Divorced several times over - "all my ex-wives are alive and living well" – he had an estranged son whom he had pushed into medicine. Gabe freely admitted he was not good in relationships: "I can diagnose a million diseases, but I still can't figure out women. I guess that's what makes them so damned irresistible."

Despite his inventiveness and immense knowledge, Gabe did not convince Mark Greene of his fitness to work at County. Mark was critical of Kerry's desire to impress her old teacher, and insisted: "He doesn't know how to function in an inner city ER." He was right: Gabe showed forgetfulness, ordered the wrong tests, got names confused and eventually went into meltdown during a multiple trauma. But it was more than an inability to work in the hectic trauma room environment. A year previously, Gabe had started to exhibit mental problems; a friend of his, a Boston neurologist, diagnosed Alzheimer's. Gabe continued to work, but couldn't hide the symptoms for long: his employer at New Western, Renee Spielman, suspected a problem but Gabe quit when she asked for a neurological exam. It was then that he joined County.

For Kerry Weaver it was a heartbreaking and harrowing moment – her mentor and friend slowly reducing to "a veteran in diapers". He left in late 1999 but not before completing one last miraculous save: "Score one for the absent-minded professor, huh?"

Amanda Lee *(Mare Winningham)*
Chief of Emergency Medicine, 1998–9

Amanda Lee was hired in autumn 1998 as David Morgenstern's permanent replacement. Nicknamed "General Lee" by Jerry, she soon took charge of the ER. Amanda had a colourful past. She had been engaged once, but her fiancé was killed when his horse spooked at a bridge. Her brother committed suicide in Christmas 1997. Her grandfather was a pitcher for the Cincinnati Reds.

Amanda worked for one year in Alaska and, as a third-year medical student, wrote a research paper on phobias, *Fearing Fear*, which was published in the *Cornell Medical Journal*. She later claimed the article was "poorly written psycho-babble". In December, Amanda started dating Mark Greene and became more and more obsessed with him: she even created Christmas tree decorations from photographs of Mark!

In fact, Amanda Lee was an impostor who had stolen the real A. W. Lee's medical school transcripts to get into a residency programme! "Amanda" was also known as Barbara Harden and Janice Angelheart and had posed as an architect and lawyer. Anspaugh had never taken up her references. Unsurprisingly, she was fired when the hospital found out.

Kim Legaspi *(Elizabeth Mitchell)*
Psychiatric Consultant. Dismissed 2001

Dr Kim Legaspi met Kerry Weaver when she worked as a psych consult to the ER. Kim and Kerry hit it off and Kerry slowly found herself falling into a relationship. However, Kim insisted that they were in different places emotionally and stopped seeing her. Kerry became reluctant to call Kim as a consult. Kim confronted Kerry and the incident triggered Kerry into realising she wanted to be with her. They continued seeing each other in secret for several weeks. However, Kerry feared she did not want to "adopt a lifestyle" and they broke up.

In spring 2001, Kim was called to consult on Shannon, a young girl who caused a train wreck by driving her car on to the tracks. Shannon was confused about her sexuality and had attempted suicide. Kim explained her own sexuality, hoping to help, but was accused of sexual harassment. Kerry was highly critical of Kim's actions but defended her to the police and to Romano, who insinuated that Kim's homosexuality was the problem. Hearing this, Kerry decided to play down her own sexuality and was lukewarm in her defence of Kim at the hearing. Kim was furious. Kerry later made an appeal to get back with Kim but was unsuccessful.

A few months after the sexual harassment hearing, Kim was fired by Romano after she refused to let psych nurses take responsibility for post-operative complications. Romano later insinuated that he had fired Kim over her sexuality. Kerry was furious and, revealing her own sexuality, told Romano to pick his battles wisely. Romano backed off, but Kim refused to work with him or Kerry again. She moved to California and got a job in San Francisco. Kerry may have visited her during summer 2001.

Jerry Anthony Markovic *(Abraham Benrubi)*
Supervising Emergency Service Co-ordinator/Unit Service Co-ordinator
(aka Desk Clerk), 1990–

Jerry Markovic started working in the ER in 1990. He grew up in West Chicago and for some time lived with his Swedish mother in Cortez Street. He took an IT course at Midwest Business Academy in 1993 and graduated with merit. In October 1995, he was promoted to the position of "supervising": although the post involved no extra money, benefits or additional responsibility, Jerry now had to wear a tie.

Although the ER seems to have been Jerry's primary job, he had plenty of money-making schemes to supplement his income. He tried to interest his colleagues in an elaborate pyramid scam but without success. He tried to capture a genetically engineered mouse that escaped a lab. He eventually had to split the $5,000 reward with Jeanie and Wendy who discovered the rodent and revived it using "mouth to mouse" resuscitation. His interest in an escaped kangaroo was no doubt similarly motivated by money. Jerry tried to sell his sperm to Cryogen Labs by posing as a doctor with an IQ of 145. Weaver forced him to take the test: Jerry got 15 – less than you would if you answered the questions at random!

In October 1997, during a budget crisis in the ER, Jerry accidentally fired a grenade launcher and destroyed the ambulance bay. Weaver immediately put him on night shifts for four months as a punishment. Jerry returned to day shifts, but was still up to mischief. He stole medical supplies for his cousin Lloyd for a fancy dress competition: Weaver deducted the cost from his wages. When he was ill, he made three crank calls to the ER. However, it was Jerry who first raised suspicions about Amanda Lee when he caught her taking things from Mark Greene's locker. He was vindicated when Lee was found to be an impostor and fired.

A year later, Jerry retired from the ER. He broke his retirement in 2002 to do a little temping and was immediately annoyed to find his place usurped by "psycho-fascist" Frank. Almost polar opposites, Jerry and Frank instantly clashed and started a fight in the ER. Although Frank insisted "it's him or me", both were almost suspended by Kerry Weaver for fighting.

Trivia: Jerry's birthday is in September. He's a fan of pro-wrestling and persistently hassled Kornberg. The first time Jerry touched a horse was when one was brought to the ER in autumn 1998. It was not a good experience: he was soon covered in manure after the horse had an enema. Jerry's "porn star name" is Rex Voytec (first pet's name plus mother's maiden name); his "romantic novelist name" is Anthony Broadway (middle name plus home street name). He has cats. He reckons David Bowie's *Space Oddity* is the ultimate expression of freedom. His sister has started her own pastry business. Jerry was once the cause of a staphylococcus outbreak – a disease spread by not washing his hands after going to the bathroom!

Chuny Marquez *(Laura Ceron)*
Nurse, 1994–

Mexican by birth, and a native Spanish speaker, Chuny has been an invaluable aid in the ER, not least as a translator. She has five brothers, one of whom, Julio, packs a .45. Her cousin Enrico had a crush on firefighter Sandy Lopez at school. In early 1997, she had a brief fling with Mark Greene. The relationship never had much promise: Mark was nursing a broken heart after the departure of Susan Lewis, while Chuny's last ten relationships had told her she shouldn't plan for the future. E. Ray Bozman reckoned it was "astrologically doomed" and was proved right: they broke up but remained good friends.

Trivia: Chuny's "porn star name" is Fluffy Flores (her mother's maiden name was Flores and her first pet was called Fluffy). She regards herself as a "motorbike chick". She and Mark Greene had sex in the time it took to burn fried eggs!

Malik McGrath *(Deezer D)*
Nurse, 1994–

Malik is one of the ER's most familiar faces. An excellent all-round nurse, he was keen to assist Lucy Knight in her early days in the ER. Malik has been quick to highlight racist behaviour. In 1997, he asserted that Mark Greene had shown a racist attitude during the Kenny Law case. Mark admitted that he had made racist assumptions but had tried not to act on them. Malik also clashed with paramedic "Shep" Shepherd in 1996 over statements made about the quality of black parenting. In his spare time, Malik is an amateur rapper and DJ and would have loved a Gameboy – if Carter hadn't swapped it for guns with local children! He also loves pro-wrestling and hockey – he once attended a winter hockey game with Susan Lewis after they found tickets on a deceased tramp they called "Icicle Andy".

Trivia: Malik's "porn star name" is Satan Monroe (his mother's maiden name was Monroe and his first pet was called Satan!).

Raul Melendez *(Carlos Gomez)*
Paramedic/EMT, 1995. Died 1996

Chicago Paramedic Raul Melendez was partnered with "Shep" Shepherd in Unit 47. In September 1995, they were joined briefly by Carol Hathaway who started seeing Shep. A few months later, Raul was seriously injured when he followed Shep into a burning building to rescue some children. Raul suffered more than 90 per cent third-degree burns and died in the ER, with Shep at his side.

David Morgenstern *(William H. Macy)*
Chief of Emergency Medicine, 1994–8

If we are to believe him, David Morgenstern had one of the most peculiar upbringings of anyone at County General. His father was a tanner who came from a long line of Russian Jews; his mother was a Highland Scot who worked as a taxidermist. David grew up in North Dakota and decided to go into medicine as a boy after he attempted to save the life of a baby mole. As a medical student, Dr Lyle Swanson taught him histology, and inspired him to become a surgeon. It was a career he relished: "Give me a good sick body that needs a little slicing and I'm a happy man."

Morgenstern rose through the ranks to become Chief of Emergency Medicine at County General. He was a prolific teacher and supervised many of County's residents, including Mark Greene, whom he regarded as the finest resident he'd ever seen. He eagerly supported Greene's promotion to attending. Morgenstern also had tremendous regard for Benton and remarked that Benton's students were often the most capable and prepared. Benton in turn regarded Morgenstern as his mentor. Morgenstern also developed a strong relationship with Kerry Weaver, whom he appointed as Chief Resident in 1995.

Despite his quirkiness, Morgenstern could be a firm leader. He took a dim view of Susan Lewis' failure to stand up to Jack Kayson in 1994, and urged her to become "an aggressive advocate" for her patients. He had Doug Ross suspended over the Chia-Chia Loh incident. After Ross' dramatic save of Ben Larkin on live television, Morgenstern felt bound to reinstate him (Ross berated Morgenstern's sycophancy). Morgenstern was sufficiently well respected to be seconded to Harvard for six months to establish a trauma medicine training program at Brigham. He was disappointed when the program didn't pass the committee stage, and returned to County in September 1995.

It was a period of change for the hospital. In autumn 1996, cutbacks forced the closure of Southside hospital and its amalgamation with County General. Morgenstern was concerned by the appointment of the Southside Chief, Donald Anspaugh, as County's new Hospital Chief of Staff. Morgenstern regarded Anspaugh as being "completely lumpy".

In September 1997, Morgenstern suffered a heart attack during the filming of a documentary about County's ER. He was stabilised and moved to cardiology. Doped up on morphine, he told Weaver: "I don't mind telling you, sometimes I've felt like a sheriff with no posse, like a general with no grunts in the field, like a lone shepherd high up on a hill with no sheepdog... Everywhere you look there's sheep, sheep, sheep..." Perhaps Morgenstern had been under more pressure than people realised: when Kerry replaced him as Interim Chief she discovered the ER was $1.7 million over last year's budget. Anspaugh noted that financial stringency was not Morgenstern's strong point, and hinted that some would like to see him replaced permanently.

When Morgenstern returned after an absence of 197 days, all was not well. He now had a greater interest in the individual stories of each patient and spent long periods of time with them. In surgery, he appeared shaky and unsure – the newly arrived Elizabeth Corday was astonished to discover that the unimpressive surgeon was the Chief of Emergency Medicine.

In May 1998, Morgenstern operated on Dr Lyle Swanson, his mentor, and accidentally cut the gastric artery. Benton pushed Morgenstern aside and tried to save Swanson but was unsuccessful. The incident sparked a bitter argument between the two surgeons that resulted in Benton's suspension. However, Morgenstern later consulted a tape of the operation and accepted he had made a mistake. "I've let this situation get completely out of hand," he admitted. "I was covering my own ass."

His last two actions were to reinstate Benton and resign. Suddenly free of the pressure, Morgenstern seemed reinvigorated: "Smell that – the smell of spring. All green and full of possibilities." By contrast, Peter Benton was dismayed: "I lost my mentor today, and the hospital... lost a great surgeon."

Trivia: The Morgensterns celebrate Burns Night. On one such occasion in 1995, Morgenstern tried tossing the caber and injured himself: "I conked myself, the buffet table and Great Aunt Jean Ferguson." Carol mistook his kilt for a Catholic schoolgirl's outfit. Morgenstern was invited to present at a conference in Miami but left his slides on the plane. He once asked Weaver out for dinner and a movie: "Have you ever seen *Caligula*?" Carter received a basket of muffins from Morgenstern when he was matched to County as a resident.

Dr Myers *(Michael Buchman Silver)*
Psychiatrics Resident, 1995–

Myers is a general psychiatrist. In Autumn 1995 he was asked by Kerry Weaver to consult on one of Doug Ross' paediatrics cases, but Doug insisted on a specialist paediatrics psychiatrist instead (2-2). Later, Myers was Lucy Knight's supervisor on her psych rotation. He was annoyed that Lucy had not prepped all his patients, but Mark Greene insisted Lucy was on her rotation to learn to talk to patients, not chase after her resident. Lucy was commended by Carl DeRaad, Head of Psychiatrics, for recommending psychotherapy over medication. DeRaad told Myers he could learn from his student (5-19).

Adele Neuman *(Erica Gimpel)*
Social Worker, 1998–

Adele has long served as County's social worker and has been involved in a number of important cases. In autumn 1998, she mediated in the case of Carlos, a young baby with HIV. It was Adele who arranged for Jeanie Boulet and Reggie to adopt Carlos. A few months later, she assisted Cleo Finch with the case of Chad Kottmeier, a drunk teenager: Adele put Chad on an alcohol treatment programme. In early 2000, she assisted Peter Benton in naming Kynesha a ward of the state, following the young girl's fight at a half-way house.

More significant and traumatic was the treatment of Ben Fossen, a seven-year-old boy who was beaten by his father. Adele arranged for Ben to be taken into care. Shortly after, Mr Fossen became violent and went on the rampage, attacking individuals who had separated him from his son. He hunted down Adele and shot her in the back. Although stabilised, Adele had no sensation in her legs. Adele has been in a wheelchair since, and has been undergoing treatment to be able to walk again.

Conni Oligario *(Conni Marie Brazleton)*
Nurse, 1994–

Conni is a mother of three. Her third child, born February 1996, was a little reluctant and had to be induced: she tried the famed beet soup at Doc Magoo's, but it was a set up for a baby shower from her colleagues. Conni helped Susan Lewis care for her niece Suzie during Chloe's absence. Connie briefly clashed with Doug Ross over racist assumptions he may have made in the case of Kanesha Freeman (1-5).

Doris Pickman *(Emily Wagner)*
Paramedic/EMT, 1994–

Doris Pickman became a paramedic in autumn 1991. She was injury free until September

1998 when she was shot while helping a gunshot victim. She soon recovered and was back on active duty. It was around this time that Mark Greene was offered the post of District Medical Director for EMS (Emergency Medical Services). Doris advised him that no one in the post had ever achieved anything. In January 1999, she was one of several paramedics to be posted to fire engines. During one incident, she was unable to help a patient because she had to be rushed to a fire. Doris feared for her post but Mark Greene talked to her chief to explain the situation. Doris returned to duty. A few months later, one of her partners on the rigs, Lars, was shot dead in retaliation for Carter's injury of a member of the public.

Nina Pomerantz *(Jami Gertz)*
Psychiatric Consult/Counsellor, 1996–7

A trained psychiatrist, Pomerantz worked as a hospital counsellor during the autumn of 1996. She helped Dennis Gant when he had troubles settling in at County and later counselled John Carter following Gant's death. Nina started dating Mark Greene in spring 1997 and frequently worked in the ER as a psych consult. She clashed with Maggie Doyle, Jack Kayson and Mark Greene over her decision to refuse Louise Cupertino, a patient with Down's Syndrome, a heart transplant. Mark Greene persuaded her to approve the application (3-16). She was still dating Mark when he was violently assaulted in the ER. Although she tried to be supportive, Mark struggled to cope with the aftermath of the attack and they broke up soon afterwards.

Trivia: Nina was divorced and had a daughter, Emma, aged six. She claimed to have used electric shock therapy to prevent Emma wetting the bed. Nina boasted she was good at ten-pin bowling. She was at school with Polly Mackenzie, who Greene foolishly tried to date simultaneously!

Bogdanalivetsky 'Bob' Romansky *(Malgoscha Gebel)*
Reception Clerk, 1994–5

Although hired as an aide to the ER, Bogdanalivetsky – or "Bob", as Doug soon nicknamed her – was once a vascular surgeon in Poland. This fact was only discovered when Bob intervened to save a patient when no other medical staff were available. Bob was concerned that her actions – practising without licence or insurance – might prevent her from taking the exams to practise in the US. Bob was last seen working as an ER aide in 1995.

Ray "Shep" Shepherd *(Ron Eldard)*
Paramedic/EMT, 1995–6

Chicago Paramedic Ray "Shep" Shepherd partnered Raul Melendez in Unit 47. In

September 1995, they were joined briefly by Carol Hathaway. Shep and Carol started dating and the relationship became more serious towards the end of the year. However, in early 1996 Raul died after Shep led him into a burning building to rescue some children. Shep was devastated and, feeling guilty and embittered, started to become more violent. He was highly critical of his new partner, Reilly, a rookie who he thought had been forced on him as punishment for killing Raul. He became increasingly intolerant of patients and during one violent episode, almost assaulted Carol.

Carol covered for Shep during the investigation into his conduct but their relationship was long since over. "I can't do this, Shep. I have finally gotten my life together. It's taken me a long time… I love you, but you need help. And if you can't get it together to get that help, I can't be with you." Shepherd was last seen with a new girlfriend at a Paramedics vs ER ball game on 4 July 1996.

William "Wild Willie" Swift *(Michael Ironside)*
Temporary Chief of Emergency Medicine, February – September 1995

William Swift went to Ohio State with John Taglieri where he acquired the nickname "Wild Willie". In February 1995, Swift was appointed as Chief of Emergency Medicine to stand in for David Morgenstern, then on a six-month secondment to Harvard in 1995. A bit of a loose cannon, Swift enjoyed scaring drunks in the waiting area by waking them while wearing a tribal mask! Almost his first action was to call a fire drill to test response time and assemble the duty staff for a meeting. He was unimpressed by Greene's failure to show (Mark was in Doc Magoo's, and was christened "Dr Bagel" by Swift).

Swift and Mark had a turbulent relationship. Swift was critical of Greene's behaviour in the aftermath of the Jodi O'Brien case (1-18), a form of depression exacerbated by the collapse of his marriage to Jen. As a result, Swift was unsure whether to approve Morgenstern's recommendation that Mark be made an ER attending. Swift finally saw Mark's potential when Mark stood up to him during a trauma. Swift backed the application and Mark was made an attending. On Morgenstern's return, Swift left but visited briefly in his new capacity as an attending for Synergix Physician Group (4-11). He confided to Mark that he was having the time of his life. Swift also attended Mark's funeral in 2002.

Dr Tabash *(Ted Rooney)*
Paediatrics Resident, PICU, 1997–8

Tabash oversaw the care of Reese Benton in the Paediatrics ICU over summer 1997. He suggested an experimental treatment to help Reese's lungs develop. Tabash also had to break the sad news that Reese could have brain damage from oxygen starvation. He extubated Reese after a summer in PICU in autumn 1997 (3-21 to 4-2). A year later, Tabash told Peter that Reese was profoundly deaf and would need a digital hearing aid (5-2).

John "Tag" Taglieri *(Rick Rossovich)*
Orthopaedic Surgeon, 1994–5

John Taglieri went to Ohio State where he played football with William Swift. He became a professional footballer then entered medicine, training to become a surgeon. He joined County as an orthopaedic surgeon; Benton reckoned he looked like King Kong. He started dating Carol Hathaway in 1993. Carol still held a torch for Doug Ross and cheated on Tag with Doug over the winter of 1993–4, although Tag did not find out until much later.

Early in 1994, they were engaged to be married but Carol's attempted suicide in March forced her to take stock. Though she moved back with her mother, and was pursued by Doug Ross, Carol decided to stay with Tag. Their relationship was strained, however, when Carol pursued the adoption of Tatiana, an abandoned Russian girl, in February 1995. On their wedding day, 18 May 1995, Carol admitted to Tag that she did not love him as much as he loved her. Tag accepted her decision and left. He never returned.

Yosh Takada *(Gedde Watanabe)*
Nurse, 1997–

Kerry Weaver hired Yosh during the supposed budget freeze of winter 1997–8. His appointment prompted Jeanie to press a case of wrongful dismissal. A year later he found himself on the receiving end of homophobic comments made by paramedic Morales. Yosh helped Cleo Finch treat a young girl with iron poisoning: the case was the subject of an internal investigation by Kerry Weaver. He and Malik set up the practical joke that resulted in Malucci being injected with Haldol! Yosh's favourite poet is Octavio Pall – he spotted that Amanda Lee had plagiarised one verse!

Harper Tracy *(Christine Elise)*
Medical Student, 1995–6

Harper Tracey was a high-flyer from an early age – in more ways that one. As a child she used a lot of drugs, but still came 15th in her year of 2,000 students. She went to college, where she studied (and had a one night stand) with Dale Edson. She decided she wanted to become either a doctor or a fighter pilot and was recruited by the US Air Force. She was put on their scholarship programme: the USAF agreed to pay her medical school fees on condition that she served for four years after her residency.

In 1995, Harper joined County as a third-year medical student. Her medical school professors warned her that County was full of burn-outs who didn't care. They couldn't have been proved more wrong than in the case of Chia-Chia Loh, a young boy whom Doug Ross helped to the detriment of his career. Harper was devastated by the incident and slept with Ross. Mark Greene threatened to report their fling, but the matter went unpunished.

Harper built a closer relationship with John Carter who helped her through her studies. However, Carter's constant "sucking up" to the surgical staff and rivalry with Dale Edson frustrated her. She unceremoniously dumped him. Harper left County on 2 May 1996 to take an OB rotation at Parkland Hospital, Dallas.

Trivia: Harper's favourite Winnie-the-Pooh character is Tigger. She may have a pierced navel, and wants to be an astronaut.

Carmen Turino *(Salli Saffioti)*
Infection Control, 2001

Dogged, persistent and pedantic, Carmen Turino was the irritating jobsworth appointed to supervise Elizabeth Corday in late 2001. Carmen's investigation revealed no evidence that Corday had an infection she was passing on to her patients, giving rise to suspicions that Corday was on a mercy-killing spree.

Dr Upton *(Megan Cole)*
Pathology, 2000–

A regular face in County, Upton is the hospital's senior pathologist and performs most autopsies. Ever eager to get a fresh corpse, she talked Abby Lockhart through a procedure to drain the abdomen of a patient – little realising the man had been killed on Abby's first attempt (6-17). Upton was highly critical of the hospital-wide rumours that motherhood was interfering with Corday's work: "It's sexist crap," she told Elizabeth (8-6).

Carl Vucelich *(Ron Rifkin)*
Senior Cardiovascular Surgeon, 1995–6

Carl Vucelich was one of County's most senior and influential members of staff. His reputation alone was enough to secure County millions of dollars in research grants. In autumn 1995, he launched a study of the surgical "clamp and run" technique to repair aortic aneurysms. A rival study was undertaken in Norway: "We don't want the Vikings to steal our thunder." Part of the County study involved the use of a new life-saving drug that Vucelich rather theatrically called Lazarol. Vucelich assembled a senior team, including many of County's shining lights.

In December 1995, Peter Benton approached Vucelich for a place on the research team. Impressed by Benton's forthright approach – "You're arrogant as hell… I like that" – Vucelich let Peter join the study and later promoted him to Research Associate. Vucelich's team soon came to regard Benton as "Carl's chosen one", although Vucelich was suspicious when Benton refused port and a cigar at a party and accused him of contributing to the downfall of civilised society! Vucelich also approved of John Carter in whom he saw much promise.

However, the project did not run smoothly. Peter became concerned that Vucelich was manipulating his results. Confronted, Vucelich removed Peter from his team and threatened him with redundancy. Peter was torn but eventually wrote to the hospital Ethics Committee. Vucelich finally published the research in early summer 1996 with an addendum covering the excluded cases. Peter's letter to the Ethics Committee was returned without further action.

Although defeated, Vucelich clearly respected Peter for standing up to him. In May 1996, Benton was made Resident of the Year – it was Carl Vucelich's nomination that secured Benton the award.

Zadro White *(Monté Russell)*
Paramedic/EMT, 1995–

Zadro is a paramedic who lives for the "rush part" of the job. He recounted how he once had to find and transport an anaphylactic headbanger in an audience of 10,000 at a Metallica concert. Instructions were relayed over a cell phone! In spring 1999, Zadro was injured when called to deal with an injury at the site of some rioting tenants. With Zadro unable to drive, Carter took the wheel and accidentally ran over a member of the public. Zadro later recovered but Lars, his fellow paramedic, was shot by a member of the crowd who believed him to be Carter. Lars died in surgery and Carter had to break the tragic news to Zadro.

Season One
1994 – 5

Themes

Carol Hathaway recovers from her attempted suicide and starts to plan her future with John Taglieri, but is pursued by ex-boyfriend Doug Ross. Although Carol resists his advances, Doug is convinced that Carol still thinks about him. As her wedding day to Taglieri approaches, Carol appears to get cold feet.

Mark Greene's relationship with his wife, Jen, deteriorates as their careers take them in separate directions. When Mark is offered an attending position in the ER, Jen is not convinced that Mark will leave his work for her and threatens to leave him. Meanwhile, Susan Lewis seems a likely rival for Mark's attentions.

Surgical student John Carter has a difficult relationship with his tutor, Peter Benton. As Carter starts spending more time with his patients, Benton and fellow student Deb Chen wonder if he is suited to a career in surgery. When a sub-internship in trauma medicine becomes available, Carter is torn.

Peter Benton takes every opportunity to show his skills as a surgeon and puts his career before his family. As he becomes more determined to prove his abilities, Peter's arrogance gets the better of him and he fails his sister and mother. He enlists the help of Jeanie Boulet to care for his mother and they grow closer.

Susan Lewis faces criticism of her competence at work. At home, she must contend with her wayward sister, Chloe.

Ones to Watch

1 – 0: *24 Hours* – The glorious double-length pilot episode where it all began. The ER staff are astonished when Carol Hathaway is rushed in after taking an overdose.

1 – 9: *Blizzard* – A quiet night in the ER turns to chaos as the staff deal with the victims of a multi-vehicle pile up. An adrenalin rush from start to finish.

1 – 18: *Love's Labor Lost* – Mark makes a critical misdiagnosis that puts a mother and child in danger. A key storyline that resonates throughout the series.

1 - 24 *Everything Old is New Again* – The season finale. Carol's wedding takes a dramatic twist. Meanwhile, Carter risks losing his place at County.

One to Watch

"24 Hours"

1 – 0: First transmitted 19 September 1994
Written by Michael Crichton; Directed by Rod Holcomb

24 hours in the ER brings a surprise patient

17 March 1994, 05.00: Mark Greene is woken by Lydia to deal with a patient who has arrived in the ER drunk and disorderly. Mark is reticent, but Lydia tells him the patient is their colleague Doug Ross. Barely able to stand, Doug drunkenly waxes lyrical about a woman he has been with that night. Wendy Goldman asks Mark if Doug always behaves this way – he replies: "Only on his nights off."

Once Ross has sobered up, he is pleased to find his new med student is an attractive young woman called Tracy Young. Turning on the charm, Ross tells her they will be working closely together. Tracy insists not *that* closely. Knocked back, Doug flirts with Carol Hathaway. He wants to renew their relationship, but Carol is going out with another doctor, John "Tag" Taglieri. Doug missed his chance.

Later, a patient is rushed into the ER in arrest: Carol has overdosed on pills. Distraught, Doug can't understand why this has happened, but Mark insists that they don't ask this question of any case. Mark works feverishly to save Carol but she has taken a combination of fast-acting medications – she knew what she was doing.

Upset, Doug struggles to treat a baby boy brought in by his childminder. The boy has cuts after supposedly falling from his cot, but Doug also notes burn marks on the baby's legs. Convinced that this is a case of child abuse, Doug severely berates the mother. He is also short with Tracy when she loses a chart. Despite this, Tracy asks him out for coffee.

That night, Greene and Morgenstern watch over Carol. She is not expected to live, but the doctors hope for a miracle. The clock reads 05.00 and an exhausted Mark takes the opportunity for a quick sleep. No sooner has he closed his eyes than he is woken for another hectic shift.

Mark Greene's work life is causing difficulties at home

Mark tells Doug he and his wife Jennifer are having difficulties: with Jen studying for her Bar exams, and Mark working shifts, they hardly see each other. Later, Mark meets Jen and their seven-year-old daughter Rachel in the canteen. Jen persuades Mark to speak to Dr Harris, who runs a private practice in Chicago. Mark muses on this as he works, but clearly gets a buzz from delivering a baby with Carter's help. When he sees Harris he is offered a job with a vastly increased salary, better working hours and bonuses. Despite this, Mark seems reticent and, enjoying his work in the ER, decides that he doesn't want to leave County.

Medical Student John Carter starts his ER rotation

Anxious third-year surgical student John Carter arrives for his ER rotation. He is assigned

to arrogant surgical resident Peter Benton. Benton gives Carter a rapid tour, pointing out the trauma room "where most of the action is" and showing a barely disguised dislike for ER "pill-pushers". David Morgenstern, Head of the ER, advises Carter to learn all he can from Benton "except attitude". Despite being told by Benton that he is a trainee surgeon and not part of the medical service, Carter helps Mark deliver a baby and clearly enjoys the experience.

Later, Carter feels sick when he helps Benton perform emergency surgery on a knife-wound victim. Mark finds Carter outside getting some air and offers some advice: there are two kinds of doctors – those who keep their feelings, and those who get rid of them. "If you're going to keep your feelings, you're going to get sick from time to time," he notes. Mark cheekily adds that Benton got sick all the time as a student! It is advice that will stay with Carter for a long time (8-20).

Arrogant surgical resident Peter Benton proves his skill

The ER staff watch a news report that shows a building has collapsed and 12 people are injured. As they prepare for casualties, Benton reckons it's a "good day for us surgeons". However, Benton is angry to be told he is too inexperienced to perform some of the operations. Frustrated, he snaps at Carol when he finds that the nurses have drunk all the coffee and laments his 90-hour week and pitiful salary. Unimpressed, Carol sarcastically says her heart bleeds for him!

With the other surgeons busy treating the victims of the building accident, Benton is left alone to treat Mr Harvey who has a ruptured aneurysm and is bleeding into his stomach. The surgery is complex and Peter struggles, but keeps his head until another doctor arrives. Together they stabilise the patient. Morgenstern notes Benton was "lucky as hell", but concedes he was right to operate. He congratulates Peter on saving the man's life. Benton is pleased.

Other threads

Resident Susan Lewis treats Mr Parker and discovers the 40-year-old may have cancer. Lewis braces herself and gives Parker the news. He is scared and worries about letting down his wife and children. Susan explains the risks he faces, but admits that nothing in this life is certain.

Mark Greene treats Liz, a flirty college student, but resists her advances.

The pilot episode – also known as *The Beginning, ER – The Movie*, or *24 Hours*, as here – is an engrossing introduction to the series. Michael Crichton succinctly establishes the main characters of Greene, Ross, Carter and Benton while neatly setting the template for the series to come. It sets the tone and is worth watching again with *The Letter* (8-20) to appreciate the parallels the later episode draws.

Nevertheless, there are a few noticeable differences between the pilot and the regular show. Benton shows a glimmer of camaraderie and even joviality that is quickly ironed out. Most significantly, Carol Hathaway is killed off. It was the overwhelmingly positive audience reaction to the character that gave rise to her miraculous recovery.

"Day One"

1 – 1: First transmitted 22 September 1994
Written by John Wells; Directed by Mimi Leder

The ER staff treat the victims of a car accident

A family is freed from a car wreck and flown to County. The driver that caused the accident is brought with them. Doug and Mark treat the daughter and send her for a splenectomy. Benton treats the mother, but her injuries are more serious. Meanwhile, Susan assesses the dangerous driver. As the man bitterly complains about his minor abrasions, Nurse Malik McGrath mutters "there's no justice".

Later, Benton tells the father that his daughter will be OK but his wife has a spinal fracture and internal bleeding and will not survive. Tactless, Benton asks about organ donation and the husband breaks down. Uncomfortable, Peter warily offers an arm around the man's shoulders.

The weaknesses show in Mark and Jen's relationship

Jen arrives to tell Mark she has passed her Bar exam. They celebrate by making out in an exam room, but accidentally press an emergency button and are soon found out! Later, Mark treats two newlyweds and their wedding guests who have food poisoning. Next, he helps an old man to accept his wife's decision to refuse a respirator: as the wedding reception continues in the ER, the man sings to his wife as she slips away. That night, Mark returns home but is too tired to spend time with Jen. Sad, Jen realises that Mark will never leave his job.

Benton's diagnostic skills are called into question

Carter and Benton treat Ivan, a liquor store owner shot during a hold-up, and a patient with abdominal pain. Benton insists the latter has thrombosis, but the man's own doctor claims it is no more than a urinary infection and tells Peter to stop showing off. Carter is embarrassed but Benton is dismissive. Later, Benton discovers that his patient had a ruptured bowel – his diagnosis was right after all.

Doug feels responsible for Carol's suicide attempt

It has been eight weeks since Carol's attempted suicide, but Doug has not yet spoken to her. He tells Mark that he has driven to Carol's mother's house, but hasn't got out. Mark insists that Doug can't blame himself but Doug is unconvinced. That night Doug goes to see Carol. The atmosphere is tense and Carol bluntly insists she is fine. Doug doesn't know what else to say.

Other threads

Carter is dismayed when he has to give rectal exams to a group of tourists with food poisoning. His day improves when he treats Liz, a flirty college student (1-0) with a rash

on her bottom! Later, Liz suggests they go back to her place and Carter readily agrees.

Lewis tries to admit a patient with senile dementia but psych consult Div Cvetic refuses. The man is discharged but later returns having walked the streets naked. Lewis admits the man herself and argues with Cvetic. That night she heads home exhausted – and gets into bed with Div Cvetic.

"Going Home"

1 – 2: First transmitted 29 September 1994
Written by Lydia Woodward; Directed by Mark Tinker

Carol Hathaway returns to work

Carol's mother insists her daughter isn't ready to return to work but Carol is determined to go. That day, the staff anticipate Carol's return, but Ross urges them to be sensitive around her. In fact, Carol quickly makes jokes at her own expense. Despite this, Carol is struck by the thought she was a patient not so long ago. Mark sees her concerns but insists no one else is worried. Later, Carol treats Mrs Packer, an elderly woman with leukaemia who has fallen at home. Although she is anaemic, Mrs Packer refuses a transfusion so she can attend her granddaughter's christening. However, she collapses and has to accept the procedure. Determined to leave straight afterwards for the christening, Mrs Packer tells Carol that life may be giving up on her, but she is not giving up on life. The words are not lost on Carol.

Doug tries to get back with Carol

Doug invites Carol to lunch but she spends time with her fiancé, orthopaedic surgeon John Taglieri instead. Nevertheless, Doug is persistent and, getting Carol alone later, tells her he wants to go out with her again. Carol insists he is just feeling guilty. She is happy with Tag, who has been there for her both before and after her overdose. Doug hopes what they had is worth another chance. Carol drily remarks that Doug had thought that what they had didn't work.

Susan clashes with cardiologist Dr Jack Kayson

Susan Lewis treats Mr Flannagan, a man who has suffered a heart attack. She waits for cardiologist Jack Kayson but he does not arrive and so administers tPA, a drug therapy, instead. Kayson arrives and is infuriated by Susan's actions. Irked, Susan complains to Mark who expresses his sympathy. Later, she is called on to present her case to senior staff in the hospital. The senior staff all agree that Kayson's treatment is the preferred option in such cases. Susan looks to Mark for support but is angry when he, too, agrees with Kayson. However, Susan is pleased when she hears her patient survived with the drug therapy – and that surgery was unnecessary.

Other threads

Chicago PD bring in a disturbed woman (Rosemary Clooney) who is constantly singing. Carter tries to assess her mental state, but without success. It is only when Div Cvetic asks about her music that the woman claims it is 1948 and that she is a child. Cvetic diagnoses Alzheimer's. Later, a patient recognises the woman as Mary Kavanagh, a famous singer. Carter contacts Mary's daughter, who arrives to collect her.

Benton is surprised to see Ivan the liquor store owner (1-1) is back in the ER. Once again, Ivan has been shot during a hold-up. Benton expresses his dismay as he patches up Ivan again.

"Hit and Run"

1 – 3: First transmitted 6 October 1994
Written by Lydia Woodward; Directed by Mark Tinker

Benton puts work before family

Peter is asked to take care of his mother that evening while his sister Jackie and her husband Walter celebrate their wedding anniversary. Peter promises to do so, but at work gets engrossed in competition with rival surgeon Sarah Langworthy for the prestigious Starzl Fellowship. Their competitiveness comes to a head when both go to extreme lengths to try to save a gunshot victim who is almost dead on arrival. Peter forgets about his mother and is berated by Walter for his selfishness. Later, Benton hears that he misdiagnosed a patient who now needs an appendectomy. Morgenstern suggests that Benton – unlike good surgeons – did not listen to his patient. Benton's chances of getting the Starzl Fellowship may have taken a blow.

Ross raises a boy's hopes rather than face a scene

A young mother complains that her son has partial deafness, but Ross finds that the boy's hearing is fine. Instead, he discovers that the woman is a schizophrenic off her medication – she hears voices her son can't. The boy, aware of his mother's illness, is concerned that they will be split up but Ross assures him they won't. However, Cvetic has the mother admitted and the boy is put into care. Carol chastises Ross for giving the boy false hope rather than face a big emotional scene – something he did when they dated. That night, Ross goes to talk to Carol but finds Tag at her flat. Carol chases after Doug and insists she will not let him tear her life apart again.

Carter is disillusioned after receiving his first assessment

Benton tells Carter to identify a deceased patient and notify their family. Carter identifies the man in a High School yearbook and steels himself to make the call. The upset parents arrive – but the deceased isn't their son. Distraught, Carter finds the right parents but has to break the bad news again. Later, Carter tells Jerry that he is a little disillusioned after Benton said he is doing "a generally adequate job". His mood is restored, however, when he delivers a baby in a car with Susan's help. Carter is elated with his success.

Other threads

With Jen out of town for five days, Ross wonders if Mark will make a play for Susan Lewis. Mark insists that they are just friends, although he seems uncomfortable when he hears

of her relationship with Cvetic. Later, Mark treats a man who has had a heart attack while handcuffed to his partner! He is bemused to discover the woman is the man's secretary.

Susan treats Harry Stopac, a stressed businessman who makes calls on his cell phone during her examination. Susan diagnoses irritable bowel syndrome and urges Stopac to rest. Later, Carter finds an electric wheelchair running amok: it is being controlled by Stopac's mobile. Irritated, Mark forces Harry to rest.

"Into That Good Night"

1 – 4: First transmitted 13 October 1994
Written by Robert Nathan; Directed by Charles Haid

Carol and Mark treat a man in need of a heart transplant

Mark and Carol treat Sam Gasner, a man with persistent heart troubles who needs a heart transplant urgently. Gasner knows he will die, but worries about leaving his family. Carol and Mark leave Gasner with his wife and daughter to share their last moments together. The scene makes Carol realise she is glad to be alive. Mark, however, is thinking about supporting his own family. After, Gasner dies, Mark has to break the news to his family. Upset and angry, Gasner's daughter, Sarah, wonders why the doctors couldn't fix her father. Mark admits that they can't fix everything.

Mark contemplates moving for Jen's career

Jen has been offered a job in Milwaukee as clerk to a federal judge, and has decided to take it. Milwaukee is two hours away by train and Mark tries to hide his concern about the stress that this will put on their relationship. He agrees to look for work in Milwaukee, but Jen senses his reluctance. Mark's thoughts are influenced by the death of Gasner. Back home, he agrees to move if that's what Jen wants. Jen knows that he will hate it, but Mark insists that it's not a big deal. Rachel, however, senses that something is wrong between her parents.

Ross and Lewis treat the victim of a car crash

Ross and Lewis take charge of two victims of a car crash. One patient is a teenage girl who is suspected of stealing the car she was driving. Benton guesses that she is on drugs. The other driver is seven months pregnant and goes into premature labour. Ross and Lewis are forced to deliver the baby. The child's lungs have not formed and it has breathing difficulties. After tense moments, the baby is stabilised and Ross assures the mother that the child will be well. The teenage driver dies after surgery.

Other threads

Lewis hears she must face a review board to continue at County General. She is anxious when she hears that Kayson (1-2) is on her panel.

An anxious Carter asks Ross about sexually transmitted diseases. Amused, Ross correctly guesses that Carter has caught something from Liz (1-1) and warns him not to "dip his pen in the company ink". Later, as Carter receives his test results, he sees Liz asking to see a doctor – and receiving interest from Jack Kayson!

Benton is amazed to see Ivan the liquor store owner (1-2) back in the ER again. This time, however, Ivan has shot himself in the foot with his new gun. Dismayed, Benton patches him up for the third time.

"Chicago Heat"

1 – 5: First transmitted 20 October 1994
Teleplay by John Wells; Story by Neil Baer; Directed by Elodie Keene

Rachel Greene visits the ER on a busy day

Despite it being October, it is blisteringly hot in Chicago. The ER is under pressure: Mercy Hospital is closed to trauma and Lakeside has a power cut, meaning that all trauma cases are being diverted to County. The day soon gets worse when a pizza delivery man crashes his car through the ambulance bay doors in panic: his supposed stab wound turns out to be a scratch!

Another surprise visitor is Rachel Greene, who picks a manic day to visit County for the first time. Rachel is shocked to see a gunshot victim brought to the ER. Later, she asks Benton if the patient survived. He didn't. Rachel wonders if Mark would be able to save her if she was sick. Mark tries to comfort his daughter.

Ross makes assumptions about a drugs case

Ross and Greene are puzzled by the condition of Kanesha Freeman, a five-year-old girl in respiratory distress. At first they suspect a heart condition, but Doug realises Kanesha has taken cocaine. The girl's condition is serious but she is stabilised. Kanesha's father arrives and Ross berates him for leaving his drugs where they could be found. The father insists he does not use drugs. Although Conni suggests they give Mr Freeman the benefit of the doubt, Ross orders a drugs test. Freeman is clean – the drugs belong to Kanesha's older sister. Ross awkwardly apologises.

Susan's sister Chloe arrives at the ER in trouble

Susan is disappointed when her sister, Chloe, arrives at the ER short of money. Despite Susan's loan of $500, Chloe has been thrown out of her apartment. Susan reluctantly agrees to let Chloe stay at her home for a couple of days. Later, she realises that Chloe has taken money and credit cards from her locker. Concerned, Susan asks Cvetic to counsel Chloe, but Div doesn't think that is a good idea. When Susan returns home, she finds Chloe has ransacked the place.

Benton treats another victim from the liquor store

Benton hears of another shooting at a liquor store and prepares to patch up Ivan. He is taken aback to find the victim is a 14-year-old boy in a critical condition. Ivan claims that

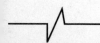

the boy has attacked him before, but police note the boy was unarmed and shot in the back. The boy dies. Ivan is distraught and tells Benton he is sorry. Unimpressed, Benton tells a detective that Ivan confessed to the shooting.

Other threads

Tag is uncomfortable around Doug. Carol assures Tag that Doug only wants what he can't have – she is with Tag now. Pleased, Tag asks her to move back in with him. Meanwhile, Ross hits it off with Linda Farrell, an attractive representative of Novell Pharmaceuticals who is in the ER to drum up business.

"Another Perfect Day"

1 – 6: First transmitted 3 November 1994
Teleplay by Lydia Woodward; Story by Lance A. Gentile; Directed by Vern Gillum

Susan Lewis finds it difficult to celebrate her birthday

It is Susan's birthday and the ER is awash with talk of the little black dress she is wearing for Div tonight. Susan is surprised to discover her relationship with Div is common knowledge, and quickly realises the culprit is Doug Ross, County General's very own "Doctor Intercom". Later, as the staff hold a party for Susan in the ER, Chloe arrives drunk. Susan is concerned, but her sister dismisses her for acting like their mother. The two row and Chloe smashes her hand into a glass partition. Cvetic offers to listen to Chloe while Benton sutures her hand. Frustrated, Susan slips away to the roof where she and Carter share a bottle of champagne Carter received from Mark for performing his first spinal tap.

Carol seems torn between Doug and Tag

Tag is anxious that Carol has not moved back in with him. Carol insists that she just wants to be sure that she is doing the right thing. During the day she helps Doug save a child and surprises herself when she kisses Doug. Later, Mark hears that Doug's date with Linda Farrell has been called off, but Doug isn't bothered – he hints he has been attracted to the sullen and withdrawn type recently. Mark jokes that Doug should go out with him! Later, Carol tells Doug that she is moving in with Tag, citing their clinch as an accident. Doug insists that it was no such thing.

Benton is interviewed for the Starzl Fellowship

Benton is due to be interviewed for the Starzl Fellowship, but can't hide his anxiety. When Carter advises Peter to "play it cool", Benton's response is suitably curt. Later, Mookie James is brought to the ER with cuts from a gang fight. Haleh asks Peter to talk to him and help put his life back on track. Peter is too preoccupied to help. Nevertheless, Haleh finds Mookie a voluntary job in the ER and makes Benton his supervisor. That afternoon, Morgenstern and Bradley interview Peter. It does not go well for him – things look much more promising for Sarah Langworthy.

Other threads

Ross is surprised to find Patrick, a large, happy man, behind the admit desk. Carol quickly befriends Patrick, who has an injured elbow. Patrick is delighted to be given his own X-ray.

Carter is keen to move out of his father's house and is looking for an apartment. Jerry suggests that he should find a flat left vacant by a recently deceased patient! Lydia, however, knows of a couple of spare flats in her apartment block. Meanwhile, Lydia takes a fancy to Chicago cop, Al Grabarsky.

Mark speaks to Jen but she is busy with work. It is unlikely that they will be able to spend much time together.

"9½ Hours"

1 – 7: First transmitted 10 November 1994
Written by Robert Nathan; Directed by James Hayman

Benton hears the results of the Starzl Fellowship interviews

Benton, awaiting the announcement of the Starzl Fellowship, takes his frustration out on Mookie (1-6) among others. As he waits, he is surprised to see his mother brought in with a sprained ankle. Mrs Benton is confused and quickly befriends Carter. Irritated, Benton leaves. Carter fumes that Peter abandoned his mother.

Later, Benton hears that Sarah Langworthy has been given the Starzl Fellowship. Peter claims not to have expected to win it. Sarah suggests that their problem is that Peter is attracted to her. Peter acidly comments that he's never even fantasised about it – although she clearly has.

Annoyed, Peter goes into overdrive and performs an emergency tracheotomy on one of Doug's patients. Doug is furious and accuses Benton of trying to prove something. Benton concedes the case, annoyed that he made a fool of himself in the interview. Doug softens and points out that Benton just saved two lives in five minutes – that should be enough. That night, Benton admits to Walter that he finds it hard to lose. Walter reckons that most people are used to it.

Susan is irritated by Div's bad mood at work

Cvetic is in a bad mood and snaps at Jerry and Susan during the day. When a drunk driver takes a swing at Div, he has him committed for 72 hours. Susan objects and releases the man but knows something is wrong with Div. Meanwhile, Susan's car breaks down and Carter offers to pay the large repair bill. The mechanic hopes that Susan is "worth it". Carter protests that they aren't an item, but the mechanic doesn't believe him.

Carol helps a rape victim

Carol treats Jamie, a young woman who claims that her partner's friend raped her. Tests reveal she had sex with her boyfriend and two other men. Jamie reveals that her boyfriend doubts her story and suspects she didn't resist. Carol insists that Jamie said no and that should have been enough. Carol persuades Jamie to give evidence against her attackers to the police.

Other threads

Mark Greene calls in sick, leaving Ross to struggle as Chief Resident. Ross asks Mark to come in but the noises on the phone reveal Mark is actually spending the day with Jen. In between lovemaking, Jen asks Mark if he has the seven-year itch, implying that Lewis may be more than just a friend. Mark dismisses the idea, suggesting that Jen may be the one with the itch.

Benton saves a wrestler by inserting a catheter into the man's heart. Carter realises that the man is trying to control his weight to make the team and has a form of anorexia. Carter offers to help, but the man seems determined to risk his life.

The ER welcomes a new aide, a Pole called Bogdanalivetsky Romansky. Ross decides she will have to be known as "Bob".

"ER Confidential"

1 – 8: First transmitted 17 November 1994
Written by Paul Manning; Directed by Daniel Sackheim

Susan is concerned by Div's mental state

In the middle of the night, Susan finds Div talking about his woes into his Dictaphone. Cvetic claims to be working on a patient's file. At work, Susan tells Mark of her fear that Div is suffering from depression. Mark is not as sympathetic as she might expect and seems more concerned with Div's ability to treat patients. That evening, Susan waits anxiously for Div to arrive for a meal with Chloe and her new boyfriend. Concerned, she calls Div's home but he isn't in. Somewhere in the city, Div stands in the middle of the road in pouring rain as cars race past…

Carter lets his personal feelings interfere with patient care

Benton is incredulous when Carter decides to take up Mrs Benton's offer of Thanksgiving dinner and refuses to let him attend. Later, Carter and Benton treat Miss Carlton, whose car smashed into a bridge. Carter is uncomfortable to find Miss Carlton is a male transvestite. Disconcerted, Carter sutures in silence as Miss Carlton talks, clearly depressed. After getting stitched up, she goes missing and Carter finds her about to jump from the hospital roof. Cvetic can say nothing before Miss Carlton jumps. Carter realises the car accident was a failed suicide attempt, and is distraught. Benton invites him to his family's Thanksgiving after all.

Carol tells Tag the truth about her and Doug

The ER staff treat Larry and Andy, who were injured in a car accident. Larry dies in the ER.

Andy confides to Carol that he was driving, but later he tells Larry's mother that Larry was behind the wheel. Lydia urges Carol tell the police, but she is reluctant to divulge information told to her in confidence. However, Carol is struck when Larry's mother tells her she is angry with Larry for causing the crash. Carol tells Andy that she has kept things from other people and hates herself for it. Andy takes note. Later, Carol tells Tag that she slept with Doug while they were going out and that she and Doug kissed two weeks previously. Angry, Tag wonders if she wants him to treat her like garbage, like Doug Ross did. Carol tries to explain herself, but Tag is angry and tells her to go to hell.

Other threads

An animal rights campaigner arrives in the ER wounded by a turkey he tried to save from the Thanksgiving dinner table. The turkey died in the process and Tag plucks it for the staff dinner. Later, the injured man confesses that he enjoyed killing the bird – and tucks in to the meal.

Benton and Langworthy work on a man who urgently needs a heart operation. Sarah lets Peter take charge, but he makes a critical error and she has to intercede to save the patient. Peter thanks her for her assistance but Sarah points out that County is a teaching hospital after all. She tells Peter that she is leaving tomorrow. Peter says an uncomfortable goodbye.

One to Watch

"Blizzard"

1 – 9: First transmitted 8 December 1994
Teleplay by Lance A. Gentile; Story by Neal Baer & Paul Manning;
Directed by Mimi Leder

The ER deals with the victims of a 32 car pile-up

Chicago is under nine inches of snow. It's a slow night and the staff make the most of it. Wendy rollerblades through the ER; Malik raps over the PA; there are snowball fights in the ambulance bay and improvised hockey matches inside. Susan and Mark set Carter's leg in plaster, then page him to Trauma One. They watch amused as he careers out into the hallway and falls on his face.

Carol announces that she and Tag are engaged. The nurses are ecstatic and crowd to see the diamond engagement ring. All fall silent as Doug arrives with Linda Farrell, fresh from a weekend in the Bahamas. At first, Doug is unsure how to react to the news, but then quietly offers his congratulations. Asked about their weekend, Linda bemoans Doug's laziness but Carol thinks relaxing in a deckchair sounds pretty appealing. Later, Linda admires the engagement ring and guesses it is worth $12,000.

The ER receives a call: there has been a 32-vehicle pile-up on the Kennedy Expressway. There could be as many as 100 people injured. The caller notes that the rescue vehicles and communications are being hampered by the blizzard conditions and that power is out at Mercy. All the victims are en route to County General.

Although the staff make preparations, the number of wounded quickly overwhelms them. Injuries range from missing thumbs and limbs to people in full arrest. Each patient is graded and tagged on arrival: green for non-urgent cases, yellow for urgent, red for critical, and black for dead on arrival.

Everyone is needed; even Linda Farrell is seen on the phones. Benton gets Mookie to hold a tourniquet as he operates on a patient's leg. Peter insists that he will make a surgeon out of Mookie yet. Patrick (1-6) arrives to see Carol and helps out by adjusting the Christmas decorations. Dr Morgenstern arrives and takes charge, freeing Mark to deal with urgent cases.

In the midst of the chaos, Ross spots a new member of staff and puts her on bedpan duty, thinking she's a nurse. The woman quickly introduces herself as Dr Angela Hicks, the new ER attending. Hicks helps Peter with Dex, whose leg was severed in the pile-up. Hicks decides that they can reattach the limb in the ER to Peter's grim satisfaction.

Susan's patient needs urgent heart surgery, but Peter and Hicks are busy with the amputee. As Susan looks around for help, her patient suffers an attack. Lydia and Wendy panic but Bob intervenes and performs the necessary procedure herself. As the patient stabilises, Susan returns and is astonished. Bob runs from the room. Morgenstern later compliments Susan on her good work! Later, Carter finds Bob crying outside. Bob reveals that she was a vascular surgeon in Poland and fears she will not be allowed to practise in the States now that she has operated without a licence. Carter insists she will be alright and promises to help her out. For now, though, he is still stuck in his cast!

Mark, Benton and Hicks attempt to reattach their patient's leg. During the procedure, Mark receives a call from Mr Blinker, a plumber who called earlier to say his wife was in labour and that they intended to deliver at home. Still operating, Mark talks Mr Blinker through the delivery. Soon the baby's cries can be heard on the line and Mark congratulates Mr Blinker on a great job.

Next door, Doug tries to resuscitate a man who has suffered a heart attack, but to no avail. Doug feels guilty after he green-tagged the man on arrival, but Mark is supportive. Doug also complains that Cvetic has not been down to see a patient claiming to have an alien implant up her nose. Cvetic has not been in all day.

Linda talks to Carol about "perfect love" and speculates about whether there is one true love for everyone. Carol is unsure and wonders why Linda asks. Linda suggests that for Doug Ross, it is Carol Hathaway.

The emergency over, Mark is about to leave when he meets Mr Blinker, his wife and their newborn baby son. They thank Mark for his help.

Adrenalin-pumping from start to finish, *Blizzard* was the first of ER's hallmark high-octane single incident episodes. After the humour of the opening scenes, comes the frantic activity of the car crash and the influx of wounded. This episode, more than any other, shows that ER doctors can only do so much. Plus there are some small notes to continuing threads: the disappearance of Cvetic, the return of Mookie, Patrick and Linda Farrell and a tantalising prospect of romance for Doug and Carol.

Amid it all, we get a sense of the relationship between Benton and new attending Dr Angela Hicks. The incident with Bob was astonishing as the time, but is a little frustrating now: the storyline was never followed up and Bob disappeared from the series early in the second season!

"The Gift"

1-10: First transmitted 15 December 1994
Written by Neal Baer; Directed by Felix Enriquez Alcalá

Mark abandons Christmas shopping to treat a young boy

Christmas Eve. Susan agrees to cover for Mark while he buys a present for Jen. On his way out, he treats Murray, a young boy who fell into water while ice fishing. Mark and Doug try to raise Murray's body temperature, but fear he needs a bypass operation. As Murray is taken to the OR, Linda offers to shop for Mark and later returns with some sexy lingerie! After his operation, Murray recovers consciousness but Mark fears permanent brain damage. Miraculously, at midnight, Murray regains normal brain function. The father thanks Mark for saving Murray – the best Christmas present he could wish for.

Benton promises organ donation without consent

Carter and Benton treat Teddy Powell, a 25-year-old who crashed his snowmobile. Carter notices spinal fluid coming from the man's ear: Teddy is brain dead. Benton decides to use the organs for transplant and is told by Hicks to keep Teddy's heart beating until they get consent from Mrs Powell. Benton tells local hospitals to expect donor organs soon. However, when Mrs Powell arrives, she won't accept Teddy's condition. Hicks lambasts Benton for offering the organs before getting consent. Teddy deteriorates and, just as Benton gives up hope, Mrs Powell relents. Benton sends Teddy's organs to other hospitals and allows himself a small smile.

Doug tries one last attempt to win Carol back

Doug has not been invited to Carol's engagement party. During the day, he treats a depressed old woman who is reminded of a lost love. The case prompts Doug to tell Mark that he thinks about Carol all the time. When he reveals he hasn't told Carol, Mark points out that she isn't married yet. Doug goes to Carol's party but is thrown out by a furious Carol and Tag. Doug insists he loves Carol. Fuming, Carol quietly tells Doug to stay out of her life.

Div's absence is explained and Chloe returns with news

Susan is surprised to hear that Cvetic has quit. Carter takes her to Div's apartment and they find it empty. He takes Susan home and moves in for a kiss. Susan stops him, saying it isn't a good idea. Carter is disappointed but agrees and leaves. Susan heads inside and is shocked to find Chloe there: she is pregnant and intends to call the baby Susan.

Other threads

Carter wakes a Santa Claus sleeping in the waiting area ("chairs"). The man was dizzy but now claims to be better and leaves, worried that he will be late. Later, he is brought back in respiratory arrest and dies. Unable to find any identification, Carter can only conclude that he has killed the real Santa.

Patrick (1-9) and Mary Kavanagh (1-2) return and sing carols to Murray. Carter finds that Mary has been left with her cousin, while Carol knows Patrick is staying with neighbours. Sadly, both have been abandoned for the holidays.

"Happy New Year"

1 – 11: First transmitted 5 January 1995
Written by Lydia Woodward; Directed by Charles Haid

Carter clashes with Benton over scut work

Carter finds a gunshot victim on the street outside County. Mark lets Carter stay in the trauma and talks him through his first intubation. Carter is successful but is frustrated when Benton then hijacks the man for surgery. Carter protests that it is his patient and he wants to stay with him, but Benton is dismissive. Later, Carter hears that the man died in surgery. He angrily tells Benton that he is supposed to be doing his surgical rotation, not scut work. Benton insists that Carter's job is to make his own easier. Carter tells Mark that he thinks Benton is not interested in supervising him. Mark tells him to get used to it.

Later, a car-crash victim with abdominal pain is airlifted to the hospital. Mark lets Carter lead. Benton arrives ready to take over, but Mark encourages him to let Carter work. Morgenstern is impressed with Carter. Afterwards, Benton lets Carter scrub in on an operation. However, Carter contaminates himself in the ER and is made to stand in the corner!

Susan clashes with Kayson

Lewis needs Kayson's signature before she can discharge one of her patients. When she finds Kayson, he insists she should have tried harder. Just then, Chloe arrives and embarrasses Susan. Chloe reveals she is moving to Texas with Ronnie, her boyfriend and the father of her child. Susan objects but is powerless to stop her.

Later, Susan needs Kayson again to review a patient's chart. Kayson doesn't listen to Susan and impatiently gives the man, Mr Vennerbeck, the all clear. Vennerbeck is discharged but suffers a heart attack and is brought back. Fuming, Kayson rushes Vennerbeck to the OR, but the man dies in surgery. Kayson berates Susan for not highlighting the patient's history of back pain – an indicator of the seriousness of the case. Susan protests that it was on the chart and Kayson didn't hear her out. Furious, Kayson insists that he will take the case to Morgenstern for review.

Benton refuses to put his mother in a nursing home

Over lunch, Peter talks to Jackie about their mother. Mrs Benton had a stroke eight months previously and has needed constant care ever since. Jackie insists that looking after their mother is too much: she and Walter have two children and full-time jobs. She suggests putting their mother in a nursing home, but Peter objects. He suggests that Jackie's neighbour, Mrs Luki, could look after their mother.

Other threads

An elderly couple are brought in to the ER suffering the effects of carbon monoxide poisoning. They have been married for a long time and are deeply caring. That night, Ross tells Linda about the couple but she fails to see a comparison with them. Linda thinks Doug will forget her name and that their relationship won't last.

"Luck of the Draw"

1 – 12: First transmitted 12 January 1995
Written by Paul Manning; Directed by Rod Holcomb

Carol takes the plunge

As she undresses a homeless man with HIV, Carol is stuck with a needle. The chances of infection are 1 in 250. While Carol awaits test results, Lydia pesters her for the wedding date. Carol and Tag haven't set it – and Carol isn't sure she wants to get married. Later, Susan and Carol treat Alan, an emotionally disturbed man obsessed with colours. He carries his medical reports in colour-coded files and seems to have an aversion to the colour green. Susan and Carol discover that Alan has cancer. Alan already knows – the information is in the green section of his folder. Carol encourages Alan to face his fears and he decides to move in with a friend who has a green bathroom. Carol is buoyed by Alan's example and announces the big day. Ross proposes a warm toast.

Susan discovers her competency is in question

Susan is anxious about her case review that afternoon. Mark insists Kayson is just covering his ass – just as Kayson walks past! At the review, Morgenstern reveals he cares less about the facts of the case than Susan's failure to be assertive with Kayson. Later, Susan is angry to discover that Mark first raised concerns about Susan's assertiveness to Morgenstern. Shaken, she struggles when Kayson questions her competence during a trauma. Carol finds Susan crying. Later, Mark apologises for not talking to her directly about his concerns. Bitter, Susan refuses his apology.

Ross deals with a stressed carer and his son

Ross treats Ben Gather, a young boy who needs a ventilator. Ben's father explains that Ben suffered brain damage in a car crash two years ago and needs constant care. The boy wakes but Mr Gather has made Ben a DNR (do not resuscitate). Doug angrily tells the father that Ben could die, but Gather goes off to a job interview. Later, the father admits he thought how much easier things would be without Ben and can't believe his callousness. He breaks down, but Ross remains silent.

Other threads

Carter gives new student Debra Chen a whirlwind tour of the ER. He puts her to work on a rectal exam, but Chen doesn't use lubricant! Later, she shocks Carter with the defibrillation paddles. When Carter recovers, Deb and Haleh pretend that they examined him while he was out. Carter is horrified.

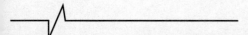

Benton hears that his mother has gone missing. He rails against everyone but himself. Jackie presses for him to agree to put their mother in a nursing home and Peter considers. Later, he finds his mother walking in the city. He suggests she should move into a nursing home, but she pleads not to go.

Carol treats a sociologist who has been assaulted. He is testing the hostility level of people by insulting them! Carol turns out to be in the top percentile! Irked, Carol puts a heavyweight boxer in with the sociologist – and the man is knocked unconscious in seconds.

"Long Day's Journey"

1 – 13: First transmitted 19 January 1995
Written by Robert Nathan; Directed by Anita W. Addison

Susan faces the review board

Susan is angry with Mark as she awaits the review board (1-11). Although Kayson is highly critical of Susan, the board accepts she should have considered the back pain more seriously and agrees to let the matter rest. Later, Lewis is surprised to treat Kayson who is having a heart attack. She orders tPA, a drug therapy which Kayson approves, but surgeon Dr Steinman argues for alternative treatment. Lewis stands her ground and threatens Steinman with a review committee unless he does what she wants.

Benton approaches Jeanie Boulet to help his mother

Benton wants part-time home nursing care for his mother and Haleh suggests Jeanie Boulet, a physical therapist at County. Jeanie feels overqualified, but agrees; Peter is grateful. Later, Peter meets Jackie who is still set on a nursing home. Peter insists he will look after their mother for two days, while Jeanie does three. Peter doesn't want his mother's savings spent on fees, but Jackie points out that some went on Peter's medical education. Peter, though, is in debt.

Carol treats an attempted suicide

Carol helps Mark treat a pregnant woman who has attempted suicide. Carol is struck when the husband sadly reads his wife's suicide note. Afterwards, Carol tells Haleh she tries not to think about her suicide. She didn't leave a note because she couldn't think what to say. Later, Carol and Tag set off for a weekend break. Tag is shocked to realise he has left his goody bag of erotic items under the ER admit desk!

Doug is rattled by Carol's relationship with Tag

Ross treats Zach, a young boy with an open leg fracture, but is reluctant to call for Tag. Tag comes anyway and insists that their differences are personal not professional. Doug discovers that Zach may have a cancerous tumour in his leg but Zach's parents are reluctant to tell their son. Doug convinces them and stays with Zach as Tag performs a biopsy. Later, Doug meets Diane Leeds from County's Risk Management. He tries to chat her up, but she knows his reputation. Doug is disappointed: there was a definite spark between them.

Other threads

Competition between Carter and Deb Chen grows. He is annoyed when she diagnoses a rare allergic reaction: Chen has a photographic memory. Carter presents Deb's diagnosis as his own, but Benton sees through him and gives the patient to Deb.

Mark treats Mrs Chang, a pregnant woman who has taken a herbal drink to induce labour. The Changs want their child to be born now and not in the Year of the Pig. Sceptical, Mark refuses to induce but Dr Noble eventually helps the couple.

Mrs Horne is brought to the ER after falling from a ladder. Her daughter, Mandy, is treated for a hand injury. Carol suspects domestic abuse. Ross questions the son about his father, but discovers that Mandy is the culprit.

"Feb 5, '95"

1 – 14: First transmitted 2 February 1995
Written by John Wells; Directed by James Hayman

Mark builds bridges with Susan as he and Jen have troubles

Mark disagrees with Susan's diagnosis during a trauma. Bitter, Susan demands more respect from Mark and asks that he stop questioning her instructions. Mark tries to talk to Susan and confesses he misses their friendship but she is unrelenting. During the day, Mark treats Grace, who is in the latter stages of breast cancer. She is in great pain and wants Mark to help her end it. Mark is torn but can't do what she asks.

Later, Susan finds Mark depressed about Grace. Softening, she invites him to dinner but Mark is meeting with Jen and Rachel. Meanwhile, Morgenstern invites Mark to stay on at County as an attending. Mark eagerly tells Jen, but she wants her own career too: she wants to continue her job in Milwaukee next year.

Benton returns home late to care for his mother

Benton takes issue when Haleh suggests a course of treatment for his patient. Irked, Haleh insists on only accepting his written instructions for the rest of the day! Benton complains to Carol but she tells him to step off his pedestal and appreciate the role of the nurses. Later, Benton and Carter fight to save a 12-year-old who has been shot in a gang fight. As they work, another boy enters and levels a gun at them. Benton announces that he is too late – the boy is dead. The boy runs out, leaving Carter stunned: "It's madness..."

Later, Peter returns home two hours late. Jeanie is annoyed but has clearly made friends with Mrs Benton. She fears that Peter's mother is in declining health and will soon need more care than either of them can offer at home.

Carter and Deb compete for presentations

Carter and Chen are due to present traumas later, but both complain they have not had enough time to prepare. Peter is unsympathetic. Later, Carter manages to find half an hour to fine-tune his presentation and expects to show up Chen. However, Chen's presentation is an elaborate slide show with graphics! Chen knocks his confidence further by suggesting he doesn't seem the type to be a surgeon – and revealing that her mother is chief of surgery at St Bart's!

Other threads

Ross makes another attempt to approach Diane Leeds by asking her son, Jake, to play hoops with him. Ross learns that Diane and Jake's father split up a long time ago.

Work in the ER stalls when a patient's tree snake goes missing. Carter is startled to find it at eye-level in a wall cupboard. Also, one of the ER's new crash carts is appropriated by Cardiology. Doug, Carol, Lydia, Bob, Conni and Carter mount a raid to get it back.

"Make of Two Hearts"

1 – 15: First transmitted 9 February 1995
Written by Lydia Woodward; Directed by Mimi Leder

Valentine's Day brings its share of "nutcases"

Carter admires his large collection of Valentine's cards while Susan is pleased with a meagre one or two. Ross finds Benton storing flowers and chocolates in the lounge and refuses to believe they are for Peter's mother. Doug has taken the night shift so he can avoid double-booking. It appears to have happened once before and Doug learned his lesson the hard way.

Meanwhile, Mark deals with a group of cheerleaders who ate chocolates spiked with LSD. Deb is unaware and pilfers a few for herself. Later, the staff are bemused to find her wandering the halls in a daze.

Carol treats an abandoned Russian girl

Mrs Hall brings Tatiana, her adopted Russian daughter, to the ER. Tatiana has a fever. Mrs Hall makes her excuses and goes, leaving the ER staff with a false contact number. Carol is able to befriend Tatiana with the few Russian words she has learnt from her mother. Tatiana has pneumonia and AIDS. Carol is frustrated that the girl has been abandoned and that the hospital can do nothing for her.

However, Mrs Hall returns. Carol tells her that Tatiana is seriously ill and she may never return home, but Mrs Hall did not intend to take her home. Mrs Hall found out that Tatiana had AIDS after adopting her in St Petersburg ten days ago. She fears that she will become too close to the girl and will be hurt by her death. Carol is incredulous when Mrs Hall leaves without saying goodbye to Tatiana.

Susan receives unwanted attention

Susan is surprised when Kayson tells her that his near-death experience has given him a

new perspective and offers to mentor her if she wants to go into cardiology. Susan is pleased but worried when Kayson invites her to dinner! Susan claims she is seeing Mark that night and leaves Kayson crestfallen. By chance, Mark asks Susan out and she readily agrees. They go ice-skating and Mark explains his problems: his turbulent relationship with Jen, Morgenstern's job offer and their clash of careers. Nevertheless, they still have fun as Mark singularly fails to skate.

Other threads

Al Grabarsky (1-6) rushes into the ER with a stray dog he hit with his squad car. The dog is saved when Carter performs mouth to mouth! Al thanks Mark, Susan and the assembled nurses enthusiastically – and gives Lydia a big kiss to her surprise and delight. Al decides to keep the dog, whom he calls Bill.

Jake Leeds arrives in the ER complaining of stomach pains. Ross calls Diane but realises Jake is faking the symptoms. Evidently, Jake wants to matchmake Diane and Doug. Doug asks Diane how they should deal with Jake. Diane jokes that they should "cut him open!"

"The Birthday Party"

1–16: First transmitted 16 February 1995
Written by John Wells; Directed by Elodie Keene

Benton misses his mother's birthday party

It is Mrs Benton's birthday and Jackie is planning a party. Benton tries to swap shifts but Hicks is irked that he has swapped shifts four times recently and wants to discourage the practice. She suggests he take a year out if he needs to care for his mother, but Peter insists that won't be necessary. Meanwhile, Carter overhears Benton talking about the party and, assuming it is Peter's birthday, hatches a plan. Peter is called to two patients – only for them to be revealed as belly dancers. Benton is confused and embarrassed as the dancers make him the centre of attention.

Later, Benton treats a stabbing victim and finds racist tattoos on the white man's arms. A policeman tells him that the man was beating a black child with a crowbar when someone came over and stabbed him. Benton hides his anger and stabilises the man before taking him to the OR. He saves him but runs late and arrives after the party has finished. Peter angrily tells Jeanie he "had to save a man with 'Die, Nigger, Die' tattooed on his forearm". She is sympathetic but has to leave when her husband, Al, arrives to take her home.

Carter and Chen compete for an ER elective

Chen asks about Carter's sub-internship next year. Carter has not yet applied for his electives. Chen points out that the competition is stiff: there have been twelve requests for an ER placement. She reckons she has already got it as she asked Benton early on. Despite this, Carter asks Benton what his chances would be if he applied. Peter drily notes they would be the same as anybody else's.

Ross strikes a man suspected of domestic abuse

Ross wakes next to a woman he barely recognises. At work, he examines a young girl who fell from a balcony and discovers bruising on her back: she was kicked. Doug suspects the father and, finding him in chairs, punches him repeatedly. Mark has to pull Doug away. Later, Mark tells Doug that the father is too busy with the police to press charges. Nevertheless, Doug has to go before the review committee for his behaviour. Later, Doug avoids Diane Leeds, who is waiting for him at reception.

Carol considers adopting Tatiana

A tired Carol waits for the hospice to pick up Tatiana. Doug offers to look after her while Carol grabs some sleep. Later, Carol is short with Tag but apologises – she is thinking about adopting Tatiana. Stunned, Tag does not want to watch a young girl die. Later, Carol visits Tatiana in the hospice. She is pleased to see Carol and is lonely without other Russian speakers.

Other threads

It is Rachel Greene's birthday but Mark is unable to leave in time to attend her party.

"Sleepless in Chicago"

1 – 17: First transmitted 23 February 1995
Written by Paul Manning; Directed by Christopher Chulack

Benton's overconfidence endangers his mother

Benton pulls a 48-hour shift to make up for his shift changes. Hicks chastises Peter and berates his single-minded pursuit of procedures. She orders him to get two hours' sleep. Peter relents but tells Carter to wake him for surgical cases. Minutes later he is working on one of Mark's patients. Next, he saves a 16-year-old who has been shot in the neck. Hicks is pleased that the rest did Peter some good; Peter allows himself a wry smile. Peter returns home and falls asleep instantly. He doesn't wake when he must give his mother her medicine. Mrs Benton tries to come downstairs but falls, breaking her hip. Peter wakes and rushes her to the ER. Mark and Susan ask what happened but Peter can't say – he is racked with guilt.

Carter defends the value of compassionate patient care

Carter treats Joseph, an elderly man in congestive heart failure. Joseph can't speak and can't refuse treatment. Later, Carter learns that Joseph has terminal cancer and is a DNR. Carter tries to find Joseph's nearest relative but is unsuccessful. Carter stays with Joseph through the night, reading to him. Benton chastises Carter for wasting time, but Carter acidly notes there is more to patient care than cutting them open. Later, Joseph dies but Carter insists he considers his time well spent. Benton suggests that Carter is wasting his time going into surgery.

Carol is approved to adopt Tatiana

Carol is pleased when she passes the preliminary adoption test. Later, she and Ross treat a young girl with burnt hands. The girl's mother branded her daughter when she caught her masturbating – as her mother had done to her years earlier. Carol calls the police. Carol tells Doug about adopting Tatiana and finds him warmly supportive. Later, she is told she cannot adopt because she attempted suicide. Distraught, she goes to Doug – the only person who believed she should adopt – and breaks down. She asks if she can stay the night, but Doug decides to drive her home.

Mark compromises for Jen but loses out

Morgenstern is leaving County for Harvard but has recommended Mark for an attending position. Mark suggests to Jen that they move halfway between Milwaukee and Chicago to make commuting easier. However, Jen is tired of making sacrifices for Mark and insists he has never given anything up for her. She is leaving him.

Other threads

Mark and Susan meet Dr John Koch, who is writing a study on "re-conceptualising the hospital". He impresses Susan with innovative ideas on hospital reform. Later, the warders take him back to his mental home!

Diane Leeds has written a report on Doug after he assaulted a patient's father (1-16). Doug asks her to dinner but she refuses. Later, she relents and Doug agrees: "if it means that much to you."

One to Watch

"Love's Labor Lost"

1–18: First transmitted 9 March 1995
Written by Lance A. Gentile; Directed by Mimi Leder

Mark tragically misdiagnoses a case of eclampsia

A car squeals past the ambulance bay of County General and a gunshot victim is thrown from the car at Mark and Doug's feet. They take the man inside and manage to get a pulse. Next door, Peter Benton runs procedures on his mother with a senior orthopaedic surgeon. He insists on only the best treatment for her. As she is taken to the OR, Peter tries to stay with her but is told to stay outside.

Carter congratulates Mark on being made an attending. They are joined by Deb and together see a pregnant woman. Jodi O'Brien is almost full term and complains of stomach pain. She constantly feels the need to urinate. Mark diagnoses cystitis and discharges her with antibiotics. Jodi and Sean (Bradley Whitford) thank him. Meanwhile, a boy is brought in with insecticide poisoning, and Jackie arrives with her children. To Peter's surprise, Jackie does not seem interested in blaming him for their mother's fall.

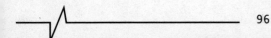

On call: The principal cast at the start of the second season, minus Kerry. Weaver would take more time to make it to the family photo.

Behind the scenes with Julianna Margulies,
ER's Carol Hathaway, who walked the corridors
of County General for six seasons.

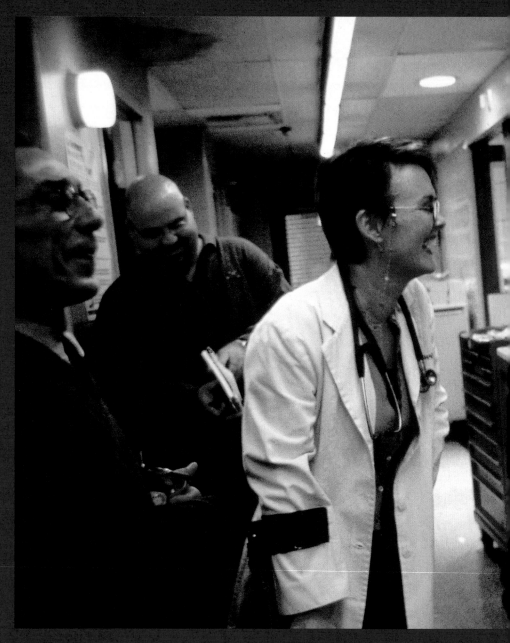

A break from the norm: Laura Innes, Anthony Edwards and George Clooney make the most of time out during the filming of the third season.

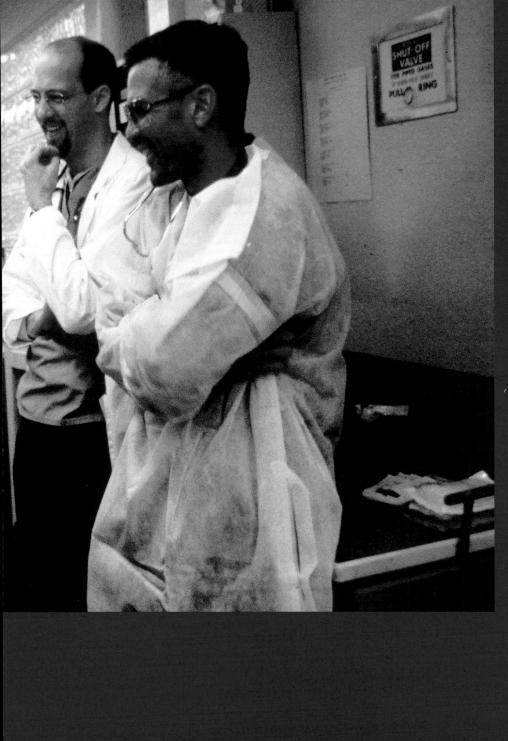

Ready for action: George Clooney waits for the crew
to set up and filming to begin.

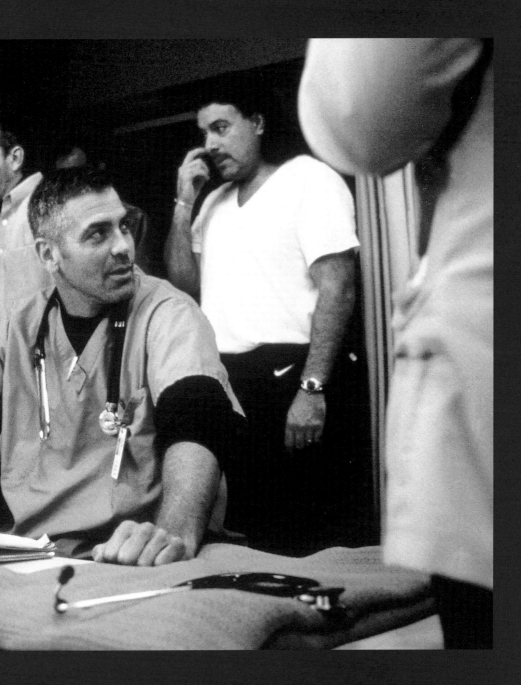

George Clooney, whose departure from the show
in 1999 threatened to break the ER success story.
In fact, the show continued to attract enormous
viewing figures.

7.15pm. Sean O'Brien returns to the ER in panic. Jodi is unconscious in his car and is having a seizure. Mark examines Jodi and quickly reappraises the situation. She has eclampsia, a rare condition where the blood vessels spasm and starve the brain of oxygen. Thankfully the baby's heartbeat is strong. Susan offers to take over, but Mark feels guilty for missing the eclampsia and stays. Jodi's high blood pressure and protein in her urine should have told him something.

9.00pm. Mark tells the O'Briens that they need to deliver their baby tonight. The OB is busy, so Mark suggests they induce in the ER. OB attending Janet Coburn questions Mark's experience but he insists he has delivered about 200 babies. Jodi goes into labour but the baby's heart rate falls. At 2.30am Mark decides to take Jodi to OB and pages Coburn, but they are still waiting at 3.15am. The baby's heart rate falls to 90 and they need to deliver. Feeling out of his depth, Mark sends Carter to get OB resident Dr Drake and not to return without him.

4.13am. With no support from OB, Mark begins a forceps delivery but the baby's shoulders are jammed into Jodi's pelvic bone. He pushes the baby back into the uterine canal. He tells Sean that they need to perform a Caesarean – and that he has never done one. Sean is torn but Mark points out that the baby will be brain-dead if they wait. Sean consents. Susan advises Mark to wait until OB arrive but Jodi's blood pressure is critically high. He calls OB again and makes the incision. Soon, Jodi has two litres of blood in her uterus from a placental abruption. Both mother and child are in grave danger. Mark gets the baby boy out but his blood pressure is too high and he is not breathing.

Carter has his hand on Jodi's heart as Mark and Susan take care of the baby. Mark tries an umbilical line and the baby starts to pink up but Jodi seizes. Coburn arrives and looks in horror at the scene, telling Mark he should have told her he was in over his head. Jodi is stabilised for now.

5.30am. Mark tells Sean that the baby will be fine. Coburn angrily berates Mark and claims never to have seen such a chain of errors of judgement. Just then, Jodi crashes. Mark tries desperately to replace her lost blood but loses her pulse. He shocks her, then tries external heart massage. After 30 minutes, Susan tells him that Jodi is dead. Coburn calls the time of death: 6.46am. Mark immediately heads to the NICU to break the news to Sean.

Later, Carter finds Mark next to Jodi's body. He tells Mark that he did "a heroic thing" but Mark doesn't respond. He refuses Susan's offer of company and gets on the El. Alone, he stares out of the window and begins to cry.

This is a harrowing episode and one that has a rightful claim to being the best of the show's history. The apparent calm of the opening sequences gives way to a gory, bloody mess as Mark struggles desperately to save mother and child. Anthony Edwards' performance is magnificent, charting every second of Greene's failure – from his almost casual misdiagnosis to his near panic at the end. So significant is the story in character terms that echoes of it have resonated ever since, with references in future seasons. It is a pivotal moment in the life of Mark Greene and in the history of the show: an utterly horrendous moment that lingers in the memory.

"Full Moon, Saturday Night"

1 – 19: First transmitted 30 March 1995
Written by Neal Baer; Directed by Donna Deitch

Mark gets off on the wrong foot with new chief Dr Swift

Mark is haunted by the death of Jodi O'Brien. Susan offers to cover for him and encourages him to go home, but Mark heads to Doc Magoo's instead. As he eats a bagel, Mark ignores a talkative stranger, not realising it is Dr William Swift, Morgenstern's replacement as ER Chief. Swift is later mistaken for a junior doctor by Susan but seems to take to her. He also gets a warm welcome from Tag: they were at college together, although back then Swift was better known as "Wild Willie".

Later, the ER is warned to expect 15 to 20 cases from a disaster. The staff are paged, but Mark is playing loud video games and doesn't hear. In fact, the alert is a drill called by Swift to hold a staff meeting! Mark arrives late and Swift sarcastically calls him "Doctor Bagel". Later, Swift tells Susan he is impressed by her and hopes she will apply to become chief resident. Susan reveals she is only a second year, to Swift's surprise. Susan is, however, pleased by the compliment.

At the end of their shift, Doug offers to listen to Mark's problems but Mark prefers to wait for Jen at the train station. Jen insists he did his best for Jodi, but Mark knows he could have done more.

Benton comes to terms with his mother's special needs

Peter confronts Tag over his decision to discharge his mother. Tag insists that Mrs Benton will need special nursing help for the rest of her life. Peter vehemently disagrees. He returns to his mother to find Jeanie has strapped her to the bed for her own safety. Angry, Benton tells Jeanie to leave and not come back.

Later, Peter is paged to the ER for Swift's drill. On his return he finds his mother has fallen out of bed. Her hip is not damaged but she is bruised. Benton apologises to Jeanie: "I can't do this by myself," he tells her. He asks her to help him find a good nursing home for his mother.

The full moon brings a spate of weird cases

Susan tells Carter that a full moon on a Saturday night usually brings its fair share of strange cases. It isn't long before Carter sees a 22-year-old drug user walking with a gurney strapped to his back. Later, he treats some skinny-dippers with frostbite to their nether regions. Finally, Carol treats a man with scratches over his face. He advises her to put him in restraints – he is a werewolf!

Other threads

Chen asks Carter if he has done enough procedures to get high honours. Carter isn't sure, but is determined to make the effort. Soon, they are competing over patients – the first to complete suturing one patient can add the procedure to their tally!

"House of Cards"

1 – 20: First transmitted 6 April 1995
Written by Tracey Stern; Directed by Fred Gerber

Mark presents the Jodi O'Brien case

When Swift disagrees with Mark's diagnosis of a patient, Mark tells Susan that he fears Swift may not make him an attending. Swift is certainly concerned about Mark when he sees him direct a pregnant patient to Susan Lewis. Swift talks to Mark about Jodi O'Brien and tells him to present the case before a conference later.

The pressure of presenting gets to Mark. He treats Mrs Salizar, whom he suspects has tuberculosis, and urges her to have her children tested. Salizar refuses: the tests may alert the authorities to their status as illegal immigrants. When Mrs Salizar's condition is confirmed, Mark angrily insists on the tests. Susan urges Mark to stay calm but Mark is pensive. There is a lot riding on his presentation.

During the presentation, Mark accepts he was wrong to assume he could handle the delivery. He faces stiff criticism from Coburn but is surprised to receive support from Swift. Nevertheless, Mark is annoyed to have been made to present in the first instance. That night, he calls Jen to arrange to see her in Milwaukee the next day, but she can't see him until the weekend. Meanwhile, Mrs Salizar returns to County with her children.

Chen makes a serious error

Benton asks Chen and Carter for their procedure books so he can begin evaluating them for their sub-internships. Chen, who is newer than Carter, has completed fewer procedures and persuades the nurses to pass suitable candidates her way. A case soon arrives but Chen and Wendy can't find a suitable vein for an IV. Chen decides to run a central line. However, during the procedure she loses the guide wire and panics. It is only the action of Dr Swift that saves the man, although the hospital could still be sued. That night, Carter is taken aback when Chen announces she has decided to quit. Chen admits she neglected her patient in favour of the procedure. She sadly notes that this is the difference between herself and Carter – John cares for his patients as people.

Susan has a surprise visitor

Susan arrives home to find Chloe, dejected and heavily pregnant, sitting on her doorstep. Ronnie has stolen Chloe's belongings and left her. Susan comforts Chloe, insisting that they will be OK, but isn't so sure herself.

Other threads

Jeanie has found Mrs Benton a place at the Melville Care Home. Peter tells his mother.

Upset, she asks him if she has to go. Sad, Peter says that she does.

Diane Leeds is annoyed when Doug gives her son Jake a bicycle. Doug insists that Jake wanted it but Diane would have preferred him to ask her. She tells him that he can't get to her through her son, even if Jake hopes that he will.

"Men Plan, God Laughs"

1 – 21: First transmitted 27 April 1995
Written by Robert Nathan; Directed by Christopher Chulack

Benton is frustrated about being unable to cure his mother

At the Melville Home, Peter is annoyed that he can't help his mother more and heads to work frustrated. He treats Samantha, a schoolgirl with low blood pressure, but is unsure of a diagnosis. She arrests and he has to shock her back. Benton realises she is in a diabetic coma; her teacher is horrified, because Sam was eating cake and ice cream. Later, Sam tells Benton she is tired of her illness. Peter is understanding but insists she can't ignore it. She seems to respond to his words.

Next, Benton and Ross treat Charlie, a teenager who has trouble moving one side of his body. An X-ray reveals that Charlie has a brain aneurysm that could blow at any moment. Radiologist Dr Steve Flint notes that only Mercy Hospital has the equipment to perform the surgery. Benton takes Charlie to Mercy in person and finds the relevant surgeon. Carter notes that Benton has been compensating for failing to treat his own mother by curing everyone else.

Doug builds his relationship with Jake

Doug is told he must see the hospital psychiatrist for assaulting an abusive father (1-16). Meanwhile, Doug agrees to coach Jake's baseball team. Linda Farrell arrives and asks Doug out to dinner. Jake picks up on the tension between the two, but Doug brushes it off as flirting. Later, psychiatrist Alan Murphy diagnoses Doug as "a reasonably normal guy, with sloppy impulse control". Doug is surprised by the mild diagnosis but Murphy himself seems a little stressed out and tells Doug not to do it again! That night, Diane asks Doug how serious they are, for Jake's sake. Doug hopes they will be together for a long time.

Mark decides he won't stay at County

Swift asks Mark to attend an important meeting but Mark is due to visit Jen and Rachel in Milwaukee. Swift is irked but Mark is adamant. Later, Rachel is pleased to see Mark, but Jen is cold towards him. Mark tells her that he will take a job in Milwaukee rather than risk losing his family. Jen is too tired to talk.

Other threads

Jeanie wants to become a physician's assistant and invites Peter to dinner. Peter is hesitant but she insists it is just dinner. Later, Peter confesses he has needed Jeanie's help and thanks her. Jeanie thought he could get through anything alone. Peter confesses he used to think so too.

Susan recommends that Carter pursue the ER as well as the surgical sub-internship. Mark agrees to sponsor Carter's application, but isn't sure that his backing counts for much.

Susan takes Chloe to her first ultrasound. The baby is a girl. Chloe is moved by the image on the screen and Susan senses a change in her. Later, she is shocked to discover Chloe has spent hundreds of dollars on shopping for the baby with Susan's credit card.

"Love Among the Ruins"

1-22: First transmitted 4 May 1995
Written by Paul Manning; Directed by Fred Gerber

As the wedding approaches, Carol gets cold feet

Tag invites Diane Leeds to the wedding but Carol is concerned she will bring Doug. Later, Tag is annoyed when Carol can't find the time to go through their vows. Meanwhile, the ER treats a nuns' netball team who may have meningitis. Carol has to test the nuns for pregnancy and is surprised when the coach, Sister Elizabeth, admits she may be pregnant. The test is negative but Elizabeth had hoped otherwise: she is torn between her boyfriend and her vocation. Later, Tag reads Carol his marriage vows: she is the only woman he has ever loved. He asks if Carol feels as deeply, anxious that she has seemed distant lately. Carol insists that she loves Tag and wants to marry him.

Distance grows between Benton and Carter

Swift notes Carter's application for the ER sub-internship does not include Benton's recommendation. Carter asks for Benton's support, but realises he will not get it and rips up his papers. Later, Peter is bemused to see Carter eagerly helping a man with a cut hand. It is Howard Davies, one of the hospital's benefactors, whose son was at school with Carter. Swift calls plastics and hand surgery to please Davies. Peter guesses that Carter's family are rich and Jerry confirms this by finding John's father in *Chicago Magazine*'s "rich list" – with a net worth of $178 million. Benton can't even meet his student loan repayments.

Susan makes a decision about Chloe

Susan treats Donny, a young man who has attempted suicide. Donny's girlfriend, Amy, can't handle the responsibility and leaves. However, Susan later sees that Amy has returned. Meanwhile, Susan is annoyed to discover that Chloe didn't stay for her check-up because the queue was too long. Frustrated, she tells Chloe that she won't be guilt-tripped into caring for her again.

Other threads

It is a surreal day. Swift wakes drunks while wearing an aboriginal mask, while Jerry practices for his opening night in a theatre group production of Romeo and Juliet. Lewis, meanwhile, treats a cab driver who runs a dating service. His catalogue of unattached men includes Cvetic! Carter gets his photo put in for free and is surprised when a beautiful woman from Radiology later asks him out.

Mark complains that Swift is treading on his toes but Doug urges caution. Nevertheless, Mark tells Swift he resents being treated like a med student. Swift tells Mark to adjust his attitude. Later, Mark tries to get close to Jen but Rachel interrupts.

Benton agrees to help Jeanie with her studies. Walter asks if Peter is right to get involved with a married woman. Peter denies it but Walter insists that Peter sounds like Barry White every time Jeanie is around. Peter is amused.

Ross umpires Jake's baseball game and allows him a home run. Jake is embarrassed but Doug insists Jake's "old man" would have done exactly the same.

"Motherhood"

1–23: First transmitted 11 May 1995
Written by Lydia Woodward; Directed by Quentin Tarantino

Chloe gives birth

It is Mother's Day and, appropriately, Chloe goes into labour. She wakes Susan when her contractions are two minutes apart. They race to County with a tape player and music to help Chloe relax. In labour, Chloe demands the Beatles' *White Album* but they can't find it. Instead, Susan sings Chloe's favourite, *Blackbird*, as she delivers little Suzie. Later, Cookie Lewis, Susan and Chloe's mother, arrives to see her granddaughter. Susan expects Chloe will stay at County one more night, then go home with Cookie. Cookie refuses to take Chloe back and chastises Susan for the suggestion. Meanwhile, Chloe carries her daughter around the ER where she sees only doom and gloom. Ross urges her to return to the nursery. Dismayed by what she has seen, Chloe fears she doesn't know how she will cope and asks how she can stop the bad things happening.

Peter's mother dies

Benton is called by the Melville Nursing Home: his mother has suffered a heart attack and died. The on-site doctor explains that they used all their capabilities but to no avail. Stunned, Peter enters his mother's room where Jackie sits crying. They hug, before Jackie leaves Peter alone with their mother. Later, Jeanie finds Peter at the home. This is the first time he has heard "all of our capabilities", although he has said the words many times over. He thought he would be more prepared but Jeanie insists no one ever is. She holds him gently as he starts to cry.

Doug wrecks his relationship with Diane

Diane and Jake have been asked to move out of their apartment and are looking for a bigger place. She suggests that Doug could move in, if he wanted. Scared to commit, Doug agrees only to look at the place they have in mind. Later, Linda Farrell arrives and asks if he has plans but Doug is not interested.

Playing basketball, Mark asks Doug if Carol's wedding has anything to do with his refusal to commit to Diane. Doug doesn't answer. Later, Diane arrives at Ross' flat and sees him leaving with Linda Farrell. Doug protests that he was scared and apologises. Diane simply says: "That's it. Bye," and drives away.

Other threads

Mark offers Carter the ER sub-internship but wants a decision by the end of the day. Carter decides to hold out for the surgical sub-I and rejects the offer, but then hears that the surgical sub-I went to another candidate. Carter tries to backtrack but another candidate has already accepted the ER position.

One to Watch

"Everything Old is New Again"

1–24: First transmitted 18 May 1995
Written by John Wells; Directed by Mimi Leder

Carol's wedding day takes a dramatic turn

The ER staff gather for Carol's wedding. All are present but for the groom. Carol finds Tag sitting outside the church. He thinks that Carol doesn't want him enough. Trying to explain how deeply he loves her, he asks if she feels as strongly. Carol admits that she doesn't, but she does love him and wants to marry him. Tag smiles and says "Thank you" – but his fears have been confirmed and the wedding is off. At the reception, Mark and Malik break the ice by tucking into the food.

Meanwhile, Doug joins Carol in the church. She just wants to be happy, but fears she never will be. Doug insists she will. They go back to the reception, which is now in full swing. Despite the occasion, Carol is called on to make a speech. She is unsure what to say but, looking around the room, she reflects that she is happy to be alive and grateful for so many good friends. "It's been a wonderful year because of all of you," and the crowd cheer. As Carol dances with her friends, Doug looks on wistfully.

It is Carter's last day in the ER

It is Carter's last day. Unsupervised, he tends to a young boy who has shot himself in the head. Unable to intubate, Carter decides to open the boy's throat. Benton arrives in time and Carter asks if he made the wrong decision. Benton says he didn't – but reminds Carter to leave his coat and ID when he leaves. Irked, Carter spots his chance of revenge when he gets to assess Benton as a tutor. He happily hands Hicks an assessment of 16 out of 40. However, Peter later offers Carter the surgical sub-I as their first choice has backed out. Carter eagerly accepts, then rushes to Hicks to retrieve his evaluation of Benton. Hicks has read it, and contrasts it with Benton's glowing recommendation that Carter receive high honours. She lets Carter have another go at Peter's assessment.

Ross and Carter treat Caleb, a young boy with leukaemia who is mean to his sister, Sarah. Though Caleb is irritable, Carter befriends the boy and urges him to be kinder to his sister. He reveals that his brother, Bobby, had leukaemia and took it out on him. Caleb asks if Bobby survived but Carter explains that Bobby's cancer was harder to beat and he died. Caleb remains brave. Later, Sarah thanks Carter. She hopes that one day she will make a difference to someone's life as Carter has done that day. Carter is flushed with success as he leaves the hospital.

Mark is offered the attending position

When Mark and Swift disagree over a patient, Mark becomes irritated and orders his tests anyway. Later, Mark's tests prove he is right and Swift offers a curt "good work". His success is short-lived as Swift reveals the hospital is being sued for malpractice over the Jodi O'Brien case (1-18). He asks Mark to see him later. However, Mark is stunned when Swift offers him the attending position: he had decided to take a chance on Mark. Mark wants to talk to Jen before making a decision. Swift agrees but wants Mark's final word the next day.

Benton comes to terms with his mother's death

Susan and Peter treat Thomas Allison, an end-stage AIDS patient. Thomas' partner, Warner, cannot sign consent for surgery as power of attorney rests with Thomas' mother. Meanwhile, Peter has lunch with Jeanie. Jeanie is not sure whether their relationship should develop, as she fears it is about his mother. Peter wonders if Jeanie finds it easier to think that. Peter returns to County to find Allison's mother with Thomas. She has refused consent. Warner reveals that Thomas wanted to die when he reached this stage. He gave his mother power of attorney because he knew Warner could never let him die. Warner reckons we are never ready to accept the death of a loved one. Later, Peter sits with Thomas and cries.

Other threads

Susan arrives home to change for the wedding. Chloe has gone and left Suzie.

Jake is worried that he did something to come between his mother and Doug. Doug admits it was his fault. Jake realises it was something to do with Linda Farrell, "the one with the nice clothes, and all the hair".

Although without the adrenalin rush of *Blizzard* or *Love's Labor Lost*, *Everything Old is New Again* is one of the high points of the first season. Carter's last-minute panic over his assessment of Benton provides plenty of anxiety and humour. By contrast, the case of Thomas Allison brings out all the heart-rending emotion of Benton's loss. Plus there are import set-ups for the future: Chloe's abandonment of Suzie; Mark's future as an attending; and Carter's family background.

But it's really Carol's wedding that wins the day. Having Tag walk away is a brilliant touch, played against the flow of the story, while we don't go so far as to have Doug and Carol reunited. The wonderful lingering look that Doug has at the end of the episode is enough to more than set up the second season.

Season Two 1995-6

Themes

Eager to achieve, Carter works hard to achieve a resident's position. However, he starts to put procedures ahead of patients, notably in the case of Mrs Rubadoux. His casual disregard for patients almost results in his expulsion. Meanwhile his competitiveness takes its toll on his personal life when he runs into difficulty with Harper Tracy.

Carol starts to find some independence and momentarily finds happiness with paramedic "Shep" Shepherd. However, a traumatic incident changes Shep and threatens to turn Carol's life to chaos.

Doug has numerous run-ins with colleagues and puts his career on the line. Only his miraculous rescue of a boy on live television keeps him at County. Meanwhile, Doug is reunited with his estranged father.

Kerry Weaver joins the ER and soon clashes with many of her colleagues, most notably Susan Lewis. Their power relationship is in a state of flux until Kerry makes a bid for an attending position.

Susan confronts Chloe's abandonment of Suzie by seeking to adopt her niece. However, she soon finds herself in line for the Chief Resident position and is unable to balance family life and work. As the pressure builds, Chloe makes a last-minute reappearance and a bid for custody of her daughter.

Benton's relationship with Jeanie Boulet comes to an abrupt end and he is thrown back into single-minded pursuit of his career. Meanwhile, he finds his place on a high-profile research study is not all it could be and is soon faced with an ethical conflict that threatens to wreck his career.

Ones to Watch

2 – 7: *Hell and High Water* – Doug narrowly averts career suicide when he fights to save the life of a young boy on live TV.

2 – 16: *The Healers* – The ER staff treat the victims of a house fire while Carol awaits news of paramedics Shep and Raul.

2 – 18: *A Shift in the Night* – Mark Greene is put under pressure when he manages a busy night at the ER almost single-handedly.

"Welcome Back Carter!"

2 – 1: First transmitted 21 September 1995
Written by John Wells; Directed by Mimi Leder

Carter begins as a surgical sub-intern

Two hours late for his shift, Carter arrives at County still in his holiday garb. He quickly helps Benton operate on a pregnant woman caught in a drive-by shooting. Already annoyed by Carter's tardiness, Benton angrily notes Carter's lack of preparation and warns that Carter's performance now reflects on him. The rest of the day does not go well. After flirting with new student Harper Tracy, Carter fails to answer Hicks' questions in surgery and faints when a rib-spreader is used.

Mark begins as an attending physician

Morgenstern returns from Harvard and introduces Mark to the demanding life of an attending physician: meetings, appointing a Chief Resident, supervising more students. Mark quickly gives his new med students large textbooks to read and forgets about them until the end of the day! At his first staff meeting, Mark hears Dr Bernstein, head of paediatrics, condemn Doug for working too often in the ER and challenging his authority. Bernstein threatens not to renew Ross' fellowship.

The group then discuss appointing Mark's replacement as chief resident. Susan and Mark have backed Jane Pratt, Susan's former room mate, but Morgenstern suggests Kerry Weaver from Mount Sinai would be a better foil to Mark. Later, Kerry almost appoints herself by bluntly asking Mark when she can start! Lewis and Ross are not amused. Mark has to leave urgently to catch his train back home to Milwaukee.

Carol meets paramedic "Shep" Shepherd

Carol treats a drunk whose son, Noah, called 911. Noah has called the ambulance before; he explains that his parents are separated. Carol angrily tells the father to get himself sorted out but the man is derisory. Meanwhile, Carol hears that she must complete a ride-along. She arranges to ride with Unit 47 and paramedics Raul and Shepherd. Doug notes that "Shep" seems have a keen interest in Carol.

Other threads

Susan has been looking after baby Suzie. She hands her back to Chloe who has been at school. Susan is still disappointed in Chloe.

At midnight, Jeanie Boulet wakes Peter Benton. She has to go home as her husband, Al, is due home. Peter asks her to stay but Jeanie must leave.

Mark treats Loretta Sweet, a prostitute with two children, who has contact dermatitis. Loretta quickly trusts Mark. Meanwhile, Doug takes a keen interest in Holda, a Scandinavian air-stewardess.

"Summer Run"

2 – 2: First transmitted 28 September 1995
Written by Lydia Woodward; Directed by Eric Laneauville

Kerry Weaver begins work in the ER

Kerry Weaver starts as Chief Resident and soon irritates most of the staff. Having worked with her before, Benton and Ross know what to expect, although Doug is still annoyed when Kerry instigates new regulations including "no food runs." It is Susan who really clashes with Kerry, especially when Kerry calls time of death on a patient she was trying to save. Kerry tries to make an effort but Susan is too irritated and lets Mark know.

Meanwhile, Doug treats Byron Fields, a young arsonist. He calls for a child psychiatrist but Kerry cancels and orders a general psychiatrist, Dr Myers, instead. As Ross and Myers argue, Byron sets his room alight. Ross blames Weaver for the incident. Kerry curtly reminds him that he shouldn't have left the child alone.

Later, Mark is called to help a youth who has a bruised chest and is hyperventilating. Weaver realises that the boy has a pocket of blood around his heart and proceeds, with considerable skill, to insert a needle and drain the blood. Mark and Carter are impressed.

Carol begins her paramedic ride-along

Carol is on her ride-along with Unit 47 and hits it off with Shep. Their first case is a fourteen-year-old boy who later dies in the ER. Weaver asks Shep to notify the mother but he flounders and Carol has to help. Carol returns later with a bag lady covered in maple syrup. Their day ends at a funfair and a ride on the ferris wheel.

Jeanie and Peter try to hide their relationship

Jeanie and Peter arrange secret liaisons at work in an effort to keep their relationship under wraps. Jeanie lies to Al so she can see Peter but her car breaks down and Al has to come to fix it. Eventually, Jeanie meets up with Peter – but Peter is having more problems with their sneaking around. He tells Jeanie that she must tell Al. Jeanie is surprised.

Other threads

Carter has overslept so Benton punishes him by making him hold a man's arm aloft throughout surgery! Carter makes amends, however, by finding Peter a hernia case. Morgenstern is also impressed with Carter. Meanwhile, Carter tries to get to know Harper a little better by letting her practise tests on him. Benton does not approve.

Susan is called to the nursery where Suzie has a fever. They try to notify Chloe at her school but discover she dropped out three weeks earlier. At home, Susan confronts Chloe and gets a feeble excuse. Susan's irritation with her sister grows.

Mark treats Loretta Sweet (2-1) who returns doing the "PID shuffle" – Loretta has pelvic inflammatory disease. Mark lets med students Harper and Berenky order the tests, but Loretta knows the score and orders them faster!

"Do One, Teach One, Kill One"

2 – 3: First transmitted 5 October 1995

Written by Paul Manning; Directed by Felix Enrique Alcalá

Carter is given his first patient

Carter complains that he does not have patients of his own, so Benton gives him Ed Menke, who needs a spinal tap. Carter performs the procedure but accidentally biopsies Ed's liver. Carter apologises to Hicks but she reveals Benton once cut off an appendix by accident! Later, Carter and Benton save Menke's liver but he crashes and dies. Hicks asserts that the man would have died without surgery anyway. Carter is dismayed by the death of his first patient. Later, Harper and Carter take Ed's liver to a bar and give him a send off.

Carol gets closer to Shep

It is "crazy fat guy day" for Carol and Unit 47. First, they are called to the flat of Mitchell, an obese rabbit lover whose house is infested with the creatures! Carol insists on bringing Mitchell to County. In the ER, they discover that Mitchell may suffer a cerebral haemorrhage, but he seems more concerned about his pets. However, animal control has already removed the rabbits save one that Shep rescues. Later, Carol and Shep talk an angry fat man off their ambulance roof. Shep asks Carol out for a drink. She demurs but finally accepts.

Susan and Kerry clash

Susan treats Mr Holdhouse, a spiritualist with a Tibetan singing bowl. Susan orders a head CT but Weaver demands other tests first. Irked, Susan tells Mark to get Kerry to cut her some slack. Mark tries to talk to Kerry but she interrupts and complains about Susan! Later, Kerry and Susan clash over an attempted suicide. Mark adjudicates and annoys Susan by agreeing with Kerry. Susan is then annoyed to discover Kerry has put her own voice on the staff computer! It is too much for Susan who retreats to the toilet with her patient's singing bowl.

Doug treats Chia-Chia, a four-year-old boy

Doug treats Chia-Chia Loh, a four-year-old who has overdosed on AIDS pills. Doug confronts the mother for giving her son twice the dose, but discovers she was given two prescriptions. Doug angrily berates Bernstein's clinic. Later, Bernstein warns Doug his job is on the line. Ross is dismissive. He returns to Mrs Loh, who is disconsolate.

Other threads

Jeanie meets up with Peter and tells him she is not ready to leave her husband. Peter is hurt and abruptly ends their relationship.

Chloe heads to County's daycare but is keen to avoid Susan. Later, Susan finds Chloe is high and ready to abandon Suzie to go out with her friend Ruth. Susan urges Chloe not to abandon Suzie but Chloe and Ruth drive off.

The ER gains a new receptionist in the form of sassy admit clerk Randi Fronczak. Doug immediately makes a move, but Randi is not interested.

"What Life?"

2 – 4: First transmitted 12 October 1995
Written by Carol Flint; Directed by Dean Parisot

Susan considers adopting her niece

Infuriated by Chloe's negligence, Susan considers adopting baby Suzie. Her attorney tells her that she must wait three months before she can claim abandonment. Susan tells Doug, who misunderstands and suggests that Dr Haloran and his wife might wish to adopt Suzie. Meanwhile, Susan struggles to find a babysitter who can match her timetable. Susan considers Doug's words and contacts Dr Haloran.

Kerry and Susan reach breaking point

Susan is annoyed when Kerry casually points out her deficiencies. Ross tells Susan that if she's considering violence, "count me in!" Susan is relieved: "It's not just *me*!" Kerry later accuses Susan of neglecting a patient with breathing difficulties. The two begin to argue and Mark has to intercede. He agrees to back Kerry as long as her rules do not prevent residents from doing their best work. Nevertheless he reprimands them both and tells them to get along. Later, Susan and Kerry apologise to each other, but it is clear they still have their problems. Frustrated, Mark looks forward to beer and TV at Doug's that night – but Doug has a date.

Carol is concerned for Shep's safety

Doug sees Carol dropped at work by Shep and bitterly notes he had a dog with that name. During the day, Shep talks to Carol over his rig's radio. During one call, Carol hears a round of gunfire then silence. As she waits pensively, Shep and Raul arrive with a young girl who was shot. The girl's uncle arrives but is more concerned for the kilo of cocaine hidden on his niece. Carol is anxious as Shep chases the man through the ER and tackles him. Shep is pleased to hear Carol was worried for him.

Other threads

Benton has a scuffle with a man selling artificial limbs and dislocates his index finger. He has to pass all his procedures to Carter, delighting John, who gets to scrub in on Hicks' gastroplasty. Benton is reduced to watching, although Hicks notes he can still learn a lot from that. Benton is unimpressed when he is asked to change the music during surgery!

Mark treats an unconscious elderly woman who was collected by a taxi driver from a pick-up point. Mark and Harper fight to have the woman admitted and eventually find a spare room. Later, they are surprised to meet the woman's husband. Tearful, he admits he dumped her with the taxi because he can't care for her any more, but had to come in because he missed her so much.

Chia-Chia, (2-2) returns to the ER. Sympathetic, Doug secretly puts the boy in a quiet room. Later, Kerry tries to put a boy with contagious chickenpox in the same room. Doug intercedes but is reprimanded for not putting his case on the board.

"And Baby Makes Two"

2 – 5: First transmitted 19 October 1995
Written by Anne Kenney; Directed by Lesli Linka Glatter

Susan looks into adoption

The Halorans cannot adopt Suzie for another three months, but would like to take Suzie earlier to let her settle in. They agree to let Susan remain a part of Suzie's life. Susan is still torn and asks Mark about continuing her residency part-time to look after Suzie. She also speaks to her parents. Cookie is unhelpful, but her father offers to take Suzie three days a week, allowing her to adopt and continue her work. Later, Mark tells Susan that Morgenstern was not pleased with her request, but has agreed to raise it at the resident review committee.

Peter treats a domestic abuse case

Benton, his finger injured, is reduced to removing a chip from a child's nose. Annoyed by the restriction, he removes his splint and promptly injures his finger again. He then treats Vicky Madison, a young woman who has been beaten. Peter urges her to talk to the police about her violent husband, but she is hesitant.

Later, he sees Vicky talking to a policeman, but discovers the officer is her partner. Peter ridicules the policeman, who tries to lash out. Another cop insists he needs Vicky's testimony to act. Peter is dismayed. Later, Officer Madison is brought back to the ER badly beaten. The policeman explains that Madison "fell".

Doug and Mark clash over Chia-Chia

Chia-Chia has flu symptoms and Doug needs a spinal tap. Harper is distressed by the procedure and anxious when another is needed due to a lab error. The test reveals meningitis that will kill Chia-Chia. Ross persuades the mother, Mei-Sun, that highly concentrated drugs injected into the spine might save her son.

However, Mark tells Mei-Sun it may be better to let her boy die at home in peace rather than put him through a painful treatment. Mei-Sun follows Mark's suggestion to Doug's annoyance. Upset, Harper goes for a drink with Doug.

Other threads

With Kerry Weaver taking a day's leave, the ER staff celebrate with cake, popcorn and music. They are joined by a new desk clerk, E. Ray Bozman – former rodeo clown, child-minder, and short-order cook.

Benton relieves his frustration by making Carter do several boring procedures.

While suturing, Carter notices a malignant mole and eagerly tells Harper that he will perform a lymph node biopsy. Harper sarcastically congratulates Carter on finding that a man has cancer.

Carol shows Harper the "Turkey File", a list of drug-users who fake illnesses to get narcotics. She comforts Carrie, whose husband had his arm cut off in a hit and run. Later, she finds her in the bathroom high on morphine. Delusional, Carrie reveals she cut off her husband's arm with an axe to claim the insurance. Carol didn't spot that both husband and wife are in the Turkey File.

"Days Like This"

2 – 6: First transmitted 2 November 1995
Written by Lydia Woodward; Directed by Mimi Leder

Mark finds out about Doug and Harper

Mark arrives at Doug's house to find Harper and Ross have spent the night together. Mark is annoyed that Doug has broken hospital rules and throughout the day condemns Doug for his cowboy attitude. Meanwhile, Harper tries to convince Carter that she was feeling vulnerable. Ross apologises to Carter, claiming not to have known about his relationship with Harper. Bitter, Carter sarcastically asks if he can have more time to come to terms with the news.

Peter works with Jeanie and hears about a drug study

Benton tries to earmark one of Susan's patients for Dr Vucelich's aortic aneurysm study, but Susan insists that the patient does not need surgery. Vucelich comes down anyway and convinces the patient to consent to the operation. Benton is later embarrassed when Carter seems to know more about the study than Peter. Benton is cautious about the claimed effectiveness of the drug being studied, Lazarol, but Vucelich is confident that it works.

Benton is unnerved to see Jeanie Boulet working as a physician's assistant in the ER. He ignores her and even tells Carter not to talk to her. When Weaver asks him to show Jeanie how to suture, he barks a few instructions and leaves. Jeanie's day goes from bad to worse: attacked in the corridor, treating an incontinent old man and unceremoniously puked on! Later, she quietly asks Peter if he could be more civil. Peter agrees, but his tone is not promising.

Benton pushes Bernstein too far

Doug treats a young boy who lost consciousness when he fell from his bike. Doug admits the boy anyway, riling Bernstein, who tells Doug his fellowship will end on 31 December. Mark tries to defend Doug but Bernstein insists they will be better off without him. Mark asks Doug why he has pushed him and Bernstein recently. Ross says he doesn't know, but has already told Carol he thinks it's time he left County.

Other threads

The ER treat the victims of a gang fight. When one patient knocks Weaver to the floor, Randi picks up her crutch and knocks the man unconscious. She asks Kerry not to tell her parole officer revealing she has a conviction for "malicious mischief, assault, battery, carrying a concealed weapon, and aggravated mayhem." Her colleagues are speechless.

Carol is buying a house, but can't find time to sign the papers with her notary, Mr Zimble. As the deadline approaches for exchange of contracts, Zimble collapses. Carol quickly signs the last remaining papers, puts the rubber stamp in Zimble's hand and presses down just as the man dies. Later, Carol shows Shep her purchase – a run-down, rickety house directly under the elevated train line!

One to Watch

"Hell and High Water"

2 - 7: First transmitted 9 November 1995
Written by Neal Baer; Directed by Christopher Chulack

Doug makes a dramatic save live on TV

Doug has been offered a job at a private practice. Carol can tell he is not enamoured with the prospect but, with his fellowship ending, Doug has little choice but to take it.

That night, Doug meets up with Linda Farrell. As they drive to a ball in torrential rain, Doug's car has a flat tyre and he gets out to check it. Suddenly, a young boy, Joey, calls for help. He and his brother Ben were playing in an outlet tunnel when Ben trapped his foot in the railings. With freezing cold rainwater washing into the tunnel and the levels rising fast, Ben could drown.

Doug tells Joey to raise help while he tries to free Ben. The boy is behind a locked iron grate. He is cold and Doug tells him to curl up to save heat. Doug can't free Ben's leg and tries to find another way into the outlet pipe. Unsuccessful, Doug heads back to the car to get a jack and crowbar to prise open the railings.

Doug helps Joey find a telephone then returns to Ben who is feeling the effects of the cold. Doug needs to keep Ben awake. He talks to him about baseball as he tries to break open the railings. Ben starts to fall asleep and Doug has to stop several times to reach through the grate and keep Ben's head above water. Finally, he releases Ben's foot, but still can't free the lock.

Suddenly, Ben falls unconscious and disappears under the water. Doug can't reach him and starts smashing at the lock with the crowbar. The lock breaks and the force of water washes Doug and Ben out of the tunnel. As a TV news helicopter circles overhead, Doug dives under the water and after a few tense moments finds him. Ben has arrested and is not breathing. Doug performs CPR and an emergency tracheotomy with his penknife. Finally, Ben starts breathing again.

The news helicopter lands just as an ambulance arrives. The reporter and cameraman eagerly cover the story. The paramedics want to take Ben to Mercy Hospital, but Ross insists the boy needs the hypothermic care unit at County. He suggests they commandeer the news helicopter and fly Ben to County. The paramedics are concerned the helicopter has no emergency medical equipment. Doug insists he will take full responsibility. The reporter is only too keen to offer the helicopter and convinces the pilot to help.

Back in the ER, Mark Greene is pulled away from his game of networked *Doom* to watch Doug's rescue live on Channel 5. Mark and Doug speak over the radio. Mark orders the ER to be prepped for Ben's arrival. Meanwhile, Ben's heart starts to beat erratically. The staff watch as Doug tries to stabilise the rhythm but the boy arrests. Doug ropes the reporter in to help. Suddenly, the picture is lost.

Reporters inundate the ER. Mark defends Doug's decision to bring the boy to County. He races up to the roof where the news helicopter is landing. The news team again start relaying pictures. Mark uses the defibrillator to shock Ben, but after five attempts they still do not have a rhythm. Doug and Mark take Ben inside and try again. In the trauma room, they regain a pulse and begin to warm Ben. The process is taking too long, so Doug calls a cardiac surgeon and profusionist to warm Ben's blood. Doug tells Ben to hold on. The effort works and Ben is saved.

Leaving the trauma room, Ross is thanked by Joey and his parents. Mark sutures Doug's cuts. As they leave County, Doug is swamped by news teams.

Other threads
Benton and Harper stabilise Molly Phillips, a ten-year-old victim of a hit and run. Molly takes to Harper who stays with her while they wait for the girl's parents. On their arrival it becomes clear that the parents are separated and they begin to argue.

Later, Molly takes a turn for the worse. Benton realises she has a ruptured mesenteric artery and has massive internal bleeding. She arrests. Harper watches on haunted as the staff try to save Molly, but their efforts are in vain.

Everyone says it, but it's hard to beat *Hell and High Water*. The pace is unrelenting. From Doug's desperate attempts to keep Ben alive, to losing him under the water, to commandeering the chopper and putting himself on the line – it's an episode where you are with the main character every step of the way. The clever intercutting of the main plot with Benton's attempts to save Molly works neatly: there is a moment where Molly's grieving parents are mistaken for those of Ben and Joey. It's a fantastic episode and rightly "top five" material – you'll never tire of it.

"The Secret Sharer"

2 – 8: First transmitted 16 November 1995
Written by Paul Manning; Directed by Thomas Schlamme

Doug is offered his job at County
Doug's heroic save is big news (2-7) and Greene, Morgenstern and a reluctant Bernstein ask Doug to stay at County. The hospital also plans to present Doug with an award that night. Doug is unimpressed. Later, Doug treats Alan, a young asthmatic, and falsifies his chart to prevent him being transferred. Mark spots a discrepancy and tells Doug that if he

wants to work at County "this cowboy crap has got to stop". Doug is determined to be difficult and they clash in a trauma room. Angry, Mark orders Doug to leave and insists he will make a formal report.

Later, Doug receives a surprise call from his estranged father, his first contact in 20 years. He saw Doug on TV. That evening, an angry Doug gives Mark a preview of his speech which condemns Morgenstern, Bernstein and Mark. However, when the award is presented, Doug takes the award and simply walks away. Mark sees Doug throw it from the roof. Doug admits he was acting like his father – scared to commit. He sheepishly asks Mark if the job is still on offer. Mark says it's his if he wants it.

Carol treats a teenager who attempted suicide

Shep arrives with Julia Kasler, a teenager who has overdosed on pills. Julia is taken aback to learn Carol attempted suicide also. Carol discovers that Julia's mother died recently and her father can't cope. Julia is pregnant by her brother Kyle: she'd only meant to hold him until their crying stopped. Kyle fears his father will shoot him.

Later, Mr Kasler arrives and overhears Carol discussing the case. Carol calls security but finds Kasler in the cafeteria. He hands over his gun so he can't do something he will regret. Later, Shep tells Carol he is glad her suicide attempt did not succeed. So is she.

Carter gets closer to Harper

Carter treats Wilbur, a boy with Bell's Palsy, but is annoyed when the mother wants a second opinion. Carter's view is endorsed and the boy is discharged. However, Doug later realises that Carter did not check for a more serious illness. Guilty, Carter orders extra tests on his next patient and finds a candidate for Vucelich's study, annoying Benton. Later, Carter and Harper visit Wilbur and confirm he is not ill but the mother is not impressed. As they leave, Harper and Carter kiss.

Other threads

Mark tells Susan to stop disrupting the schedules and get a babysitter. By chance, Susan treats Mrs Ransom, an English child-minder. Ransom has a terminal blood disease but would rather refuse treatment and hope for the best. Later, Susan's father offers to cover the night shift with Suzie.

Jeanie finds she has to work with Peter but the two seem to get on. Carter hears that Jeanie has divorced and suggests Peter make a move. Jeanie reveals she and Al have just separated They had other problems that were nothing to do with Peter.

"Home"

2 – 9: First transmitted 7 December 1995
Written by Tracey Stern; Directed by Donna Deitch

Carol treats a psychiatric patient with an artistic talent

Carol and Jeanie treat Josh, a psychiatric patient who insists he is an architect. Josh has run away from his home for the third time and is sleeping rough. As they try to trace Josh's

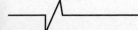

mother, Carol talks to him about his sketches of Sullivan's Arch and then about her house. Josh reckons she will have an original fireplace behind one wall.

Josh's mother arrives and explains that Josh was studying architecture but had a nervous breakdown. Josh is discharged and Jeanie is concerned they can't treat patients more fully. Carol goes to Sullivan's Arch at night and checks that Josh is OK. She returns home and discovers that Josh was right about the hidden fireplace.

Susan is urged to take on more responsibility

Susan treats Rebo, a young woman who had a seizure after sustaining a head injury. The woman has a second violent seizure in trauma. Susan makes an unusual diagnosis, lidocaine toxicity, but this is confirmed when the woman's case history is faxed over from St Anne's.

Weaver urges Susan to present the case at a conference. Morgenstern agrees that it will be a great opportunity to further her career by taking on more responsibility. Thinking of Suzie, Susan reckons she has already done that. At home, Susan finds a Christmas card for Suzie from Chloe containing $3,000.

Jen and Rachel are involved in a car accident

Mark receives a call from a Milwaukee hospital saying that Rachel and Jen have been in a car accident. On arrival, he finds Rachel is unhurt but Jen has a tib-fib fracture. As they are treated, Mark meets Greg Simon and his daughter Amanda, who were also in the car. Later, Mark tells Jen that her operation was a success. She starts to explain about Greg, but Mark has already guessed that they are lovers. Mark asks if she has fallen in love with Greg. Jen has, but says she didn't mean to.

Other threads

Benton hears that Vucelich is recruiting residents for a research project but suspects third-year residents are not candidates. Carter, who spends most of his day in clinches with Harper, tells Vucelich that Benton is interested and arranges a meeting for him. Benton attends and Vucelich confirms that third years do not have the necessary skills. Benton reckons he has. Vucelich responds to Benton's arrogance and invites him to scrub in.

Over dinner, Doug tells his mother (Piper Laurie) that his father, Ray, has been in contact. Ross' mother reckons he just wants money and insists Ray is up to something. Doug assures her that Ray can't touch them – "Never again".

"A Miracle Happens Here"

2 – 10: First transmitted 14 December 1995
Written by Carol Flint; Directed by Mimi Leder

Mark prays for a Christmas miracle

The Jodi O'Brien (1-18) case is reaching a settlement and Mark gives a deposition. He worries that it will taint his record, but is assured it is the best solution. Mark's Christmas looks to be an unhappy one: he is working Christmas Eve and Christmas Day while Jen keeps Rachel for a skating party.

During the day, Mark treats Hannah Steiner, a concentration camp survivor who was pulled from her car at a red light. Her granddaughter, Tiersa, was on the back seat and is now missing. As the police search for the car, Mark urges Hannah to have hope. She has prayed for the first time in many years for Tiersa's safe return and asks Mark to do the same. Thankfully, Tiersa is found safe and well. Mark joins the Steiner family for their Hanukah celebration at Hannah's bedside. Later, Mark and Rachel arrange their "first annual Rachel and Dad post-Christmas, post-Hanukah, pre-New Years celebration".

Carter persuades patients to join Vucelich's study

Benton scrubs in for a "clamp and run" procedure but is told that the patient, Mr Chamberlain, has changed his mind. Vucelich asks Benton to convince the man otherwise, and Benton discovers he was chosen because Chamberlain is black. Meanwhile, Carter convinces Mrs Chamberlain that the surgery is the best option. Eventually they get consent and Carter is invited to scrub in, to Benton's chagrin. Benton tries to finish the procedure in record time, but misses by a few seconds.

Benton sees Mrs Rubadoux, a high-risk candidate for the "clamp and run" study, and tells Carter to get consent for the surgery. Carter explains the range of options to Mr Rubadoux. "Ruby" trusts Carter and asks his advice. Although hesitant, Carter recommends the "clamp and run" procedure. Mr Rubadoux agrees.

Carol brings a little festive cheer to the ER

Despite having a house that is falling down around her, Carol is determined to enjoy Christmas. She is disappointed when her ER carol concert idea fails to get support. Later, Carol treats Stan Calus, an elderly bearded gentleman, who urges her not to rely on others for holiday cheer. Carol agrees and launches into her own tone-deaf version of *The Twelve Days of Christmas*. Slowly, the ER staff join in. Later, everyone meets at Carol's house for a party. Carter congratulates Benton on completing Rubadoux's "clamp and run" in record time. Benton looks forward to Christmas with Jeanie. Meanwhile, Shep tells Carol that he loves her and they kiss passionately.

Other threads

A gang bring in a priest who has been shot by a rival group. The priest is sure he will die and urges one boy not to take revenge. Despite Susan's efforts, the priest dies. Jeanie overhears the boy planning revenge and reminds him bluntly of the priest's words. She seems to get through to him.

Loretta Sweet (2-1) arrives in the ER and announces that she has got a job. Mark is pleased for her.

"Dead of Winter"

2 – 11: First transmitted 4 January 1996
Written by John Wells; Directed by Whitney Ransick

Benton queries Vucelich's study as Carter cares for Rubadoux

Mrs Rubadoux has partial paraplegia, congestive heart failure and kidney problems. Although Vucelich is sure her condition cannot be linked to the "clamp and run" surgery, Peter isn't so sure. They agree to transfer her but can only do so when her condition improves, so they pass her to Carter.

Later, Peter argues with Vucelich over whether the "clamp and run" was the cause. Vucelich insists Mrs Rubadoux was not a suitable candidate and will be removed from the study. Despite their terse exchange, Vucelich makes Benton a Research Associate, complete with perks.

Meanwhile, "Ruby" tells Carter he is not ready to lose his wife. Vucelich tells Carter to hook her to a drip and transfer her. Carter resists but Vucelich bluntly notes that she is dying. Carter can't bring himself to tell Ruby the truth. He gives him his pager number. Ruby praises Carter as the only person who gives a damn. Carter feels guilty.

The ER deal with several victims of abusive parenting

Shep and Raul bring several malnourished black children to the ER. Shep blames the parenting and Benton snaps that his comments are racist. Child services reveal that their crack-dealing parents abused the children and custody was granted to their grandmother.

As they wait for the grandmother, Susan notices a non-reducible mass on one boy. Benton, fuming from earlier, is blunt with the boy and refuses to operate. Jeanie berates his lack of compassion. Shamed, Peter assures the boy about his operation. Later, the grandmother explains she had passed the children back to their mother thinking she had changed. Susan and Haleh are unsympathetic.

Mark is sued for divorce

Mark receives a summons: Jen is suing for divorce. Doug is stunned: if Mark can't hold down a marriage, he has no chance! Mark turns down Susan's offer of a night out and spends the rest of the day in gloom. Later, he treats Loretta's son, Jimmy, who has a fever. Loretta complains of recent vaginal bleeding and Mark examines her. Tests reveal Loretta has cervical cancer, and he asks Lydia to call her back. That night, Mark decides he has to move on in his personal life – and calls on Susan.

Jeanie receives a critical evaluation

Jeanie and Peter treat Mrs Saunders, an obese woman who complains of stomach cramps. She turns out to be pregnant with twins. Later, Jeanie receives her first evaluation. She needs to be more assertive and may not be suited to work in the ER. Jeanie is surprised to discover the author is Carol. Carol explains that Jeanie needs more grit to survive in the ER. Meanwhile, Al tries to patch up their relationship. Taking a firm line, Jeanie says: "No more playing around, no more lies."

"True Lies"

2 – 12: First transmitted 25 January 1996
Written by Lance A. Gentile; Directed by Lesli Linka Glatter

Carter tells Ruby the truth about his wife's chances

Carter is overjoyed when he transfers Mrs Rubadoux, but dismayed when she is brought back in relapse. Ruby insists that Carter care for her. During the day, Carter tries to avoid Ruby. Jeanie is angry when Carter gives Ruby false hope by admitting Mrs Rubadoux into a nerve stimulation study. The neurologist tells Ruby that his wife will never leave the hospital. Angry, Ruby berates Carter and demands the truth. Annoyed, Carter shouts back that Mrs Rubadoux will die. Tearful, Ruby bitterly thanks Carter for finally being honest and leaves.

Benton's ambition jeopardises patient care

Vucelich invites Benton to dinner and tells him to bring a guest. He asks Jeanie, who accepts. Meanwhile, a candidate for the "clamp and run" procedure comes in to the ER while Vucelich is away. Peter convinces Hicks he can run the operation and begins. However, the surgery is difficult and Vucelich arrives in time to stabilise the patient. Hicks apologises for letting Peter's enthusiasm get the better of her. Downcast, Peter tries to cancel the dinner but is needed to make up numbers!

Jeanie and Benton feel uncomfortable among the eminent surgeons and share a joke. Later, Vucelich tells Peter he was disappointed in the surgery but admires Peter's ambition. "I was beginning to fear that I see something in you that you don't see in yourself," Vucelich explains.

Rachel is troubled by her parents' divorce

Mark realises Rachel is not taking the separation well. He takes Rachel, Susan and Suzie ice-skating, but Rachel is difficult with Susan. At work, Mark finally tells Rachel that he and Jen are getting a divorce. Rachel is upset and Mark insists he is there to listen to her. Jen arrives to take Rachel home but she doesn't want to leave. Jen is concerned, as she has to carry Rachel away.

Other threads

Carol is amused when she thinks Morgenstern is wearing a Catholic schoolgirl's outfit. It is actually a kilt: he broke his leg during a pre-Burns Night family "Highland Games". Morgenstern is pleased when his nephews arrive with their bagpipes and the haggis and continue the celebration in the ER.

Susan treats Barbara Dean, a compulsive alcoholic in respiratory distress. Barbara's daughter, Mrs Hardy, is unwilling to talk to her. Meanwhile, Barbara becomes a DNR. As she dies, the daughter has a change of heart. She breaks down as her mother arrests but Susan has to let Barbara die.

Doug's father calls throughout the day but Doug ignores him. Later, he and Carol treat

Noah Crosset (2-1), the son of a drunk father. Doug angrily confronts Crosset about not changing his ways. Carol tells Doug to beat up on his *own* father. Doug tries to call Ray, but hangs up.

"It's Not Easy Being Greene"

2 – 13: First transmitted 1 February 1996
Written by Paul Manning; Directed by Christopher Chulack

Mark is haunted by the O'Brien case

1 February 1996. Mark works on his day off to take his mind off his divorce, the custody battle for Rachel and the Jodi O'Brien settlement (2-12). His day is not a good one: his first patient has a mysterious seizure and dies. The man's wife blames Mark.

Next, Mark hears that the hospital wants to settle the O'Brien case out of court. Mark refuses and vows to fight the case himself if necessary. However, Susan confides that he made an error in the O'Brien case. Mark admits he missed the cause and worries he did the same with his earlier patient. The autopsy results show Mark was not at fault but he is sad that he did all he could and the man still died. Depressed, he reckons he can't win.

Benton suspects Vucelich of manipulating his results

The Vucelich study needs one more patient to be complete. Vucelich asks Peter to become his "clamp and run" ambassador in Europe. Pleased, Peter tells Carter to look out for suitable candidates. Harper finds one and Carter tries to take the credit but is found out. The patient, however, dies of an unknown condition in surgery and is excluded from the study. Benton worries that Vucelich was quick to exclude the patient and checks the rules of the study. Fearing that Vucelich may be manipulating his results, Benton studies the excluded cases.

Susan stands up to Weaver with unexpected results

Morgenstern wants Susan to apply for Chief Resident next year but Susan is worried about caring for Suzie and working with Weaver. Still, she puts herself forward but during the day clashes with Kerry. Irritated, Susan decides that life is too short to have Kerry breathing down her neck and tells Kerry to "stay out of my way". Weaver is impressed she has finally seen Susan act like a Chief Resident and wonders if Morgenstern was right about her after all.

Other threads

Doug treats Ray, an American Football player with dizziness and headaches, but no physiological causes. Doug discovers that Ray is homosexual and frightened about telling his father and brothers. Uncomfortable, Doug calls a psych consult. Haleh accuses him of being homophobic, but Doug denies it. Guilty, Doug later tries to talk to Ray, but Ray's father is with him.

Carol's shifts have been cut back and she is short of money. Later, she treats Mrs Henry who arrives with a $5,000 tub of worms. The woman reveals that the worm manure gives her a six-figure salary. Carol is asked to look after the tub but is later horrified to find it dumped outside the ER and covered in ice. The staff use warming blankets and even a warm water lavage, but it is not enough to save Mrs Henry's worms. Carol has to break the sad news.

"The Right Thing"

2 – 14: First transmitted 8 February 1996
Written by Lydia Woodward; Directed by Richard Thorpe

Benton confronts Vucelich but comes off worse

Benton enquires about the exclusions from the "clamp and run" study and is taken off surgical duty for the day. Mark advises Peter to ensure his claims are correct or his career is over. Later, Benton hears that he "quit" the study and angrily confronts Vucelich. Vucelich insists he decides which subjects are excluded from the study and threatens to have Benton fired. Instead, Benton goes to the Dean of the hospital and has a major row. That night, he tells Walter that he has fought for his career but can't go further. "I'm stupid enough to ruin my career, but I don't even have the courage to do it the right way."

Carter tries to do right by Mr Rubadoux

With Benton off surgical duty, Carter is bored in the ER. He tries stay on Vucelich's study, but is told there is nothing for him to do. During the day he is irritated by patients, branding two cases "losers". Later, Jeanie tells Carter that there is a memorial service for Mrs Rubadoux at 4pm. Carter is agitated and snaps at one of Susan's patients to her annoyance. Susan observes that Carter used to care too much but now hardly cares at all. "What happened to you, Carter?" The words hit home as Carter attends the memorial service. After, he apologises to Ruby for his actions. Ruby politely tells Carter that today is not about him.

Doug receives a visit from his father on his birthday

It is Doug's birthday, and he is stunned when his father arrives. Ray, hoping to renew their relationship, hands Doug a card that contains two tickets to the Bulls game. Ross isn't sure what to make of his father's return. Later, he treats Joseph, a young boy who was bitten at a petting zoo. Doug waits for Joseph's dad to arrive and the two share their disastrous birthday stories.

Other threads

Carter sees Mark and Susan buying tequila for Doug's birthday and assumes they are an item. Mark and Susan are congratulated, but don't know what they have done. When Doug cancels his party, Mark and Susan split the tequila. Slightly drunk, they joke that their purported affair would be as torrid as the staff guessed. Their eyes linger but Susan snaps out of it and gets more tequila.

Susan treats Nathan whose girlfriend, Angel, has AIDS. Susan sees how much Nathan loves Angel and tells him about Angel's status. Susan is pleased when Nathan is supportive but Angel angrily reckons Nathan will only stay if he is also ill.

Jeanie treats T-Ball, an ER regular in the "Turkey File". Jeanie reckons he is not faking his stomach pain and discovers he has blood poisoning. Carol is impressed.

Mark tells Loretta she has cervical cancer. She will require surgery, a hysterectomy and possibly radiation therapy. The five-year survival rate is over 90 per cent, but Loretta can only see the worst case scenario.

"Baby Shower"

2 – 15: First transmitted 15 February 1996
Teleplay by Carol Flint;
Story by Belinda Casas-Wells & Carol Flint; Directed by Barnet Kellmann

The ER becomes Obstetrics for the day

15 February 1996. The OB is closed, so the ER is full to bursting with pregnant women. Coburn is suspicious of Mark's abilities, but is quietly impressed when he realises one woman is having a second set of contractions. Later, Mark and Doug treat Dr Anna Castigliano, who cancelled her breast cancer treatment to save her baby. She only has a few months to live. Her baby girl is delivered safe and well, but Anna is distraught that she will not see her grow up. Later, Coburn congratulates Mark on the nine deliveries. Meanwhile, ER nurse Conni still hasn't delivered her baby and is told to try the beet soup at Doc Magoo's – where the staff surprise her with a baby shower.

Carter is interviewed for a resident's place at County

As Carter prepares for his interview for a resident's position, Harper announces she may be pregnant. Carter is stunned. He is further put on edge when he discovers Benton sent a lukewarm recommendation to the interview panel. Nevertheless, the interview goes well. The panel note Vucelich's standard glowing report, but are more interested in Benton's gushing recommendation. Carter is told that a "solid" from Benton is the highest praise! Carter is buoyed up.

Benton takes bets on his surgical prowess

Benton is dismayed to find he is still off the surgical list. Hicks explains he has been away for so long that it will take time to get back on the board. Spotting his chance, Benton takes a patient to the OR. The man starts to bleed out, but Benton reckons he can save him against the odds. Soon, a large and growing audience crowd to watch Benton "raise the dead". Not content with stabilising the man, Peter fixes his arm too in a "longer than long shot". Afterwards, Carter thanks Benton for setting the bar high. He asks if the man will survive. Benton thinks he will.

Other threads

Susan helps Tina, a pregnant 13-year-old who is about to deliver. While they wait for

Tina's mother, a couple arrive who intend to adopt Tina's baby. With the mother absent, they fear that they can't adopt Tina as well. Tina's mother arrives just after Tina has delivered. They both seem set on keeping the baby.

Having heard his fair share of overbearing new fathers, Doug decides to visit Ray at the Hotel Du Pre. He is surprised to discover that Ray is the owner. Doug tells Ray he is not his father: "A father is someone who's there, and you never were." Ray is apologetic and tries to talk to Doug about old times. Doug softens and they play table football. If Ray wins, they go to the Bulls game together.

One to Watch

"The Healers"

2–16: First transmitted 22 February 1996
Written by John Wells; Directed by Mimi Leder

Paramedic Raul Melendez is seriously injured on a call

Shep and Raul on Unit 47 are called to a burning building. The ground shakes with explosions from inside the house as people flee. A mother tells them that her three children are trapped on the second floor. With no time to wait for support, Shep insists on going in. Raul follows him.

County is alerted and told to prepare for casualties. Carol is horrified to hear that Unit 47 was the first to arrive and that Shep and Raul went inside but have not been seen since. As Mark, Doug and Carter work on the first victims, Carol waits pensively in the ambulance bay. After a long wait, Shep is brought in, suffering from smoke inhalation – but Raul is not with him. Shep, feeling guilty that he led Raul into the building, pleads with Carol to find him.

Jerry receives a call that Raul has been found, but doesn't say how badly burnt he may be. Shep wants Carol to tell Raul that he didn't leave him in there. When Raul arrives, the staff are shocked. Raul has 85 to 90 per cent burns, mostly third degree. Carol breaks the news to Shep, who is distraught.

Carter and Benton set to work on Raul. Carter falls back at the sight and smell of the burnt tissue. He tries to perform one procedure but struggles and lets Benton take over. Later, he apologises to Peter for losing his cool. Benton notes that it doesn't get worse than that. He insists that Carter did well to stay on his feet.

Mark, Susan and Doug hear that the mother that Shep and Raul met on their arrival caused the fire. Her son has mild injuries and her daughter is at another hospital but is stable. Her baby, however, is having trouble breathing. Doug realises that the baby's throat has swollen shut, and is able to intubate. Angry, he tells Mark that if the mother's airway had been blocked, he would have let her suffocate.

Carol hears that Raul is stable but that he won't make it to morning. Raul talks to Carol, who is honest with him. Raul knows he is going to die. He asks about the rescued children and is pleased to hear they are alright. Carol praises Raul, but he reckons it was

Shep's doing. Carol goes to see Shep but he is inconsolable with guilt. She convinces him to see Raul. Slowly, Shep makes his way, but all he can do is cry "I'm sorry" as Raul tries to comfort him.

Other threads

It has been five months since Chloe abandoned Suzie and Susan is making headway with her plans to adopt. However, Chloe arrives at County and makes her way to the nursery for Suzie. Randi lets Susan know, who fears the worst and runs upstairs. Chloe is playing with Suzie as though she had never been away.

Ross goes to meet his father before the Bulls game, but Ray doesn't turn up. He heads to Ray's hotel and finds him flirting with a young woman. Ray tries to apologise. Bitter, Doug tells Ray that he learned his father's lesson well – no commitments or messy details. Ray insists that Doug's actions are his own and not his fault.

Mark buys a motorcycle from a patient. It's part of his plans for sweeping changes of his lifestyle.

This is another event episode and one that captures the camaraderie of the emergency services. Although we only saw Raul briefly in previous episodes, we feel for his well-being through the concern of the staff – and Shep and Carol in particular. Carol's pensive wait in the ambulance bay, while inside the ER struggles with the first victims, is a strong contrast. The relief when Raul is found is immediately replaced by the horror of his condition. Shep's plaintive appeal for forgiveness is made all the more harrowing by Raul's weak but heartfelt attempts to comfort him. Combine this with a wonderful Benton-Carter moment, one that shows the underpinning of their professional relationship, and Doug's disappointment with his father, and you have a very strong episode.

"The Match Game"

2 – 17: First transmitted 28 March 1996
Written by Neal Baer; Directed by Thomas Schlamme

Carter awaits the results of his residency match

Carter is sick with anticipation for his interview result (2-15). Anxious that his competitiveness, selfishness and dispassionate attitude have cost him a place at County, Carter resolves "patients come first". During the day, he treats Mr Leadbetter, a lawyer with anaemia. Unsure of the cause, Carter orders urgent tests. While he waits, he hears he has been made a resident at County. Thrilled, he whisks Harper to a hotel for champagne, leaving Leadbetter with Lewis. When Carter returns, Susan angrily notes that Leadbetter has leukaemia. Hicks chastises him for drinking on duty and threatens his expulsion. Carter feels sick again.

Benton hypocritically accuses Doug of hiding the truth

Benton treats Mr Bowman and his grandson who were hit by a drunk driver. He discovers the grandson has a tumour that Ross missed when the boy came to the ER four months earlier. Mark talks to the hospital attorney, Kathy Schneider, who says that the hospital does not have to tell the family about the error. Guilty, Ross pays for the chemotherapy. However, Peter is furious and tells Bowman the truth.

Doug and Peter have several run-ins during the day. At the end of his shift, Mark angrily tells Peter he is compensating for not standing up to Vucelich. "The truth is a lot easier to tell when it's not your own career on the line," says Mark.

Chloe determines to get Suzie back

Chloe insists she is turning her life around: she is engaged and on a rehab program. Susan refuses to believe her, insisting that Chloe's abandonment was the best thing that happened for Suzie. Chloe tells Susan she wants her daughter back. Fearing Chloe may snatch Suzie, Susan tells the nursery to page her if Chloe arrives.

Later she is paged and races upstairs – but it is Suzie taking her first steps. At home, Susan finds Chloe waiting. They argue bitterly and Susan reveals she is going to adopt Suzie. Incensed, Chloe insists "She's my baby, Susan, and I want her back."

Other threads

Mark has decided to change his style and arrives at work with a goatee beard and blue contact lenses. His day goes well: a bald man eulogises the virility of bald men and Mark is asked to star in an infomercial. It doesn't last: the commercial is for hair-restorer and Doug cancels their trip to a jazz club. Mark goes to the club and bumps into Kathy Schneider, also on the lookout.

Carol is annoyed that Jeanie has been named Employee of the Month and clashes with her during the day over caring for Hugo, a homeless man. Hugo is discharged but brought back minutes later by Shep whose new partner, Reilly, hit him with their ambulance. Shep thinks he has been given a rookie partner as punishment for killing Raul. Carol fails to convince him otherwise.

One to Watch

"A Shift in The Night"

2–18: First transmitted 4 April 1996
Written by Joe Sachs; Directed by Lance A. Gentile

Mark Greene runs a busy shift with a skeleton staff

Mark is asked to cover the ER for the fourth night in a row. Having spent most of the day travelling to and from Milwaukee, he refuses, but relents when he hears that Doug has minor whiplash from a car accident and can't cover for him.

At County, he is frustrated to find Susan and Kerry are on their way out, leaving him with a few residents, a psych intern and Carter who is paying penance in the ER (2-17). There are almost 80 patients waiting, so Mark tries to close County to trauma. Morgenstern disagrees: County management want to close the ER permanently and any hint that they can't cope would give them good reason.

Mark is inundated with minor injuries and troubled relatives. He tells Jerry he will only see individuals with a chart. Mark treats Omar, a young boy who has drunk anti-freeze. There is no ethanol in the ER, so Mark orders an IV of bourbon to stop renal failure. Next is an old woman with the early signs of an MI. Mark refers her to Medicine, but is annoyed to hear that Dr Randall discharged her soon after. He tries to argue the case but Randall refuses to change his mind. Mark also treats Mr Etheridge, an alcoholic suffering from chest pains, who was brought in by his son.

While Mark snatches five minutes to grab a sandwich, he witnesses a car crash only metres in front of him. Shep frees the children from the back seat. The first victims are brought to the ER where Mark and Carter work frantically. Mark reluctantly pages Benton, who is still annoyed over his recent clash with Doug (2-17). Carter accidentally punctures the patient's heart, but Mark is quick to act. Benton arrives late and Mark angrily shouts at him for being slow to answer his page.

Mark checks in on Mr Etheridge and discovers that the man's son Clarky spiked his coffee with a chemical deterrent for alcoholics. Etheridge continued to drink unaware, resulting in the attacks. Stressed, Mark berates the boy, but is stopped by Carol who can see how guilty Clarky feels. Later they discover that Clarky was asked to administer the drug by his mother who has been repeatedly beaten by her drunk husband. Mark informs the police. Clarky remains traumatised.

Chloe makes a brief visit to the ER. She asks Mark to reason with Susan and help her to see that she is turning her life around. Mark makes no promises.

The number of patients waiting to be seen increases and the pressure mounts on Mark. Although having fondly reminisced with Carter about early days with Jen ("Whaddaya gonna do?" he says, dismissing the memory), he snaps at Jen when she calls to ask about Rachel's stomach ache.

Mark finally gets to see a boy with a cut hand who has been waiting hours. The mother is annoyed when Mark notes that the wound has been open for six hours and they should come back in three days for delayed closure. Later, Mark treats Loretta's son and is relieved when she says they didn't have to wait so long.

With the situation getting desperate, Mark decides to treat those in the waiting room from a trolley. Minor injuries are treated on the spot, but procedures cannot be performed without a chart. As Mark rushes between cases, Jerry suspects Mark has lost his mind but Carol realises he is having fun! He and Carter power through the cases, quickly moving from one to the next.

When dawn breaks, and the ER staff arrive, the ER waiting room is almost empty. Susan tells Mark that her lawyer thinks Chloe could have a case. Mark doesn't mention Chloe's visit earlier. Mark finds Benton and tells him that they have to find a way to work together.

Finally, Carter complements Mark on his handling of the situation: it was just what he though medicine would be, just helping people. Mark and Carter ask what each other has planned for their day. Neither has the faintest idea.

Another single-strand episode and a very strong one. But unlike the others, this isn't all doom and gloom – it's a story of survival. As the pressure increases, Mark proves himself to be the most agile, energetic and talented doctor in the ER. His supreme confidence in dealing with all the cases from a trolley is wonderful to watch. And by the end, he's having fun! The delightful moment where Carter and Greene don't know what to do with the rest of their day is a lovely coda.

"Fire in the Belly"

2–19: First transmitted 25 April 1996
Written by Paul Manning; Directed by Felix Enriquez Alcalá

Benton tries to cover a misdiagnosis

Jeanie alerts Peter to a possible appendectomy, Mrs Mendoza. Peter disagrees and later tells Jeanie to discharge the patient. However, Jeanie's suspicions were correct. Peter has to operate when Mendoza's appendix ruptures. The infection spreads and she could die. Peter tells Mr Mendoza that a doctor thought it was food poisoning, but doesn't say that he was the doctor in question.

After surgery, Peter tries to pass the case back to Jeanie but Hicks insists it is his responsibility. She adds that the surgeons already think he betrayed Doug and he should not expect their support now. Chastened, Peter finds Mendoza and tells him the truth. Later, he decides to report Vucelich: "No more excuses."

Carol is concerned when Shep exhibits violent behaviour

During a ride-along with Shep, Carol notices changes in his character. Shep strangles a drunk who attacks Carol and they have to perform CPR to save him. Next, they treat a young boy who caused his mother's death. Shep fears the boy may be "damaged" for life. Later, they witness a violent brawl. As Shep calls for back-up, a brick is thrown at the ambulance. Shep beats the assailant and almost hits Carol when she tries to pull him away.

Carter's competitiveness irritates Harper

Carter competes with new surgical resident Dale Edson, an old flame of Harper Tracy's. Neither has performed an appendectomy and they compete for the next case. Carter finds one candidate, but the pain turns out to be a lodged toothpick!

Meanwhile, Carter hears that interns with the fewest procedures will not be asked back, and determines to take the next case. He excludes Dale from a trauma so he can claim the procedure. Annoyed by Carter's constant attempt to get "suck points" to become a resident, Harper unceremoniously dumps him.

Chloe appeals in court for visitation rights

Susan attends court where Chloe appeals for visitation rights. To Susan's dismay, her father reveals he cannot support Suzie any longer and can't choose between his daughters. The court grants visitation rights. That night, Susan takes Suzie to Chloe. She admits that she has been angry with Chloe and isn't convinced by her change of character. Chloe insists she can be a good mother to Suzie.

Other threads

Morgenstern orders cameras in trauma rooms for teaching purposes. Later, Kerry reviews the tape and hears Mark talking to Doug about his lack of sexual experience! The news gets around but Mark still dates an employee. In bed, Mark's date jokes that they can rewind her tape and critique his technique!

Doug unexpectedly receives $25,000 from Ray. Though the money would cover the cost of Bowman's chemotherapy (2-17), Doug fears it is dirty and decides to hand it back. He goes to his father's place and flirts with Ray's girlfriend, Karen.

"Fevers of Unknown Origin"

2 – 20: First transmitted 2 May 1996
Written by Carol Flint; Directed by Richard Thorpe

Susan is plagued by thoughts of losing Suzie

Susan is called to work on her day off. She treats a pregnant woman with high blood pressure. Susan orders an ultrasound, against Kerry's wishes, and discovers a growth on the adrenal gland. Both mother and baby should be well. The finding is timely as Mark and Kerry are deciding the next Chief Resident that day. Kerry still fears Susan lets her personal life interfere too much. During the day, Susan is plagued by thoughts of being unable to find baby Suzie. Susan later realises that in her daydream she is searching for Suzie's favourite toy, not Suzie. It is the day that Chloe and her new fiancé, policeman Joe, are taking Suzie away from her. Chloe finds Suzie's favourite toy. Susan watches sadly as the family drive away.

Weaver and Benton are up for Resident of the Year

Kerry is hopeful she has won Resident of the Year when she hears the nurses say that the winner clearly wasn't decided on personality! Meanwhile, Peter discovers that Vucelich's published study included an addendum on those cases he had omitted. Benton is relieved. Later, he is paged to Trauma Two and is surprised to find a party. He has won Resident of the Year – Carl Vucelich nominated him.

Shep injures a young boy but tries to cover it up

Shep's temperament continues to worsen. After saving a girl from a collapsed building, he tells Carol that "stupid people shouldn't breed". Later, they treat a boy but are hampered by onlookers. Shep angrily pushes one bystander back, knocking him unconscious. Reilly is angry and files an incident report.

Other threads

Carter is surprised when Hicks tells him he cannot graduate until he has completed an ambulatory medicine rotation. Doug agrees to take Carter on and tells him to "show up, hang out and get an A". However, Carter misdiagnoses his first case. Later, Carter says goodbye to Harper Tracey, who is leaving to join Parkland Hospital, Dallas. They part friends and Carter confesses he will miss her.

Doug has slept with his father's girlfriend, Karen, but the psychology of the situation is not lost on him. Karen is angry that Ray has run off with a large amount of her money. Doug insists that Ray will be back, but it could take years.

Loretta Sweet almost collapses as she arrives at the ER. She has radiation burns but was unaware she should expect them. Angry, Mark confronts oncologist Dr Howard who insists he gave Loretta all the necessary information. Mark is critical and Howard asks if he is a relative. That evening, Mark meets Jen who wants to talk terms and reach a settlement out of court. To their mutual surprise, they end up sleeping together. Both agree it was a bad idea.

"Take these Broken Wings"

2 – 21: First transmitted 9 May 1996
Written by Lydia Woodward; Directed by Anthony Edwards

Susan visits a therapist after losing Suzie

Susan visits a therapist. She reckons that her life is getting back to how it was, but the day's events seem to have unsettled her. Susan listened to the beautiful music of a church choir rehearsing for a christening. Then, after paying for Suzie's daycare ("I love that whole 'insult to injury' thing"), she found one of Suzie's pictures. After that, Susan angrily confronted a mother for shaking her baby. The incident prompted Kerry to resist Mark's calls to appoint Susan as Chief Resident. Susan tells her therapist that she should be able to move on but can't. She fell in love with Suzie: "For the first time in a long time I didn't feel alone."

Jeanie receives shocking news from Al

Al Boulet arrives at the ER with a protracted case of the flu and Kerry orders some tests. Jeanie spots Al and checks his chart. Guessing Kerry's line of thinking from the tests ordered, Jeanie asks the lab to run the tests urgently. She guesses correctly that Al has AIDS. Kerry asks Jeanie if she has been tested. Upset, Jeanie asks how many married people get tested.

Carol lies for Shep at his enquiry

Shep is being investigated following Reilly's complaint (2-20). Carol agrees to support Shep's story, but her testimony is pulled apart by an investigator. Carol is anxious but later hears that Shep has been exonerated. Reilly is still concerned and tells Carol that Shep is dangerous and needs help. Shep, however, is overjoyed and wants to celebrate. Mulling over Reilly's words, Carol makes her excuses.

Doug gives Ray's money to Karen

Karen has heard that Ray is in New Mexico and may never return her money. Doug is dismayed and Karen suspects he is only dating her to hurt his father. Later, Doug scrapes together the $25,000 he was given by Ray and returns it to Karen. He apologetically admits he was taken aback by Ray's gesture. Karen is amused: Ray stole ten times as much, but she has to love Doug for his efforts.

Other threads

Ross and Carter treat T. C. Lucas, a ten-year-old basketball fanatic. Carter is told to stay with T. C. and they cheerily debate the game. Benton decides T. C. urgently needs a liver transplant. Carter breaks the news and tells her she won't be able to play in her tournament. He offers to stay and watch the playoffs, but T. C. is downcast.

Loretta is suffering from abdominal pain as a result of her cancer treatment. She is upset that her two children do not know where she will be from day to day. She may need surgery and doesn't know what to tell them anymore. Al Grabarsky and Lydia look after her children and Mark agrees to take them that evening.

"John Carter, MD"

2 – 22: First transmitted 16 May 1996
Written by John Wells; Directed by Christopher Chulack

Carter graduates from med school

Carter is due to graduate, but must also choose his surgical team for next year. Benton refuses Carter's invitation to his post-graduation party: "You were my assigned med-student, I was your assigned resident. You don't owe me anything, OK?" During the day, Carter visits T. C. Lucas (2-21). T. C. is scared, so Carter stays with her, missing his graduation. Later, Benton admits he also missed his graduation for work and tells Carter to take care of himself.

Later, Carter finds Morgenstern and asks to join the "meat and potatoes" blue surgical team of Peter Benton next year. As Carter is about to leave, E. Ray hands him a parcel from Benton. It is Carter's first coat, embroidered with "John Carter MD" As car crash victims are brought in, Susan calls on Dr Carter to assist.

The new Chief Resident is appointed

Mark reckons he has sold his soul to the devil when he agrees to support Weaver for attending if she lets Susan become Chief Resident. However, Mark is angry when Linda Martins is appointed. Kerry explains that Susan turned down the post.

Susan tells Mark that earlier she treated a 46-year-old man with lung cancer who could not pay for his tests and left. She was reminded of how little time each of them have. She had something with baby Suzie – she wants more than work.

Carol's struggles with Shep take their toll

Carol confronts Shep for missing his psychiatrist's appointment but he simply gets in his car and leaves. Anxious and upset at work, Carol is annoyed when Susan and Kerry discharge a baby before a heart condition could be diagnosed.

Later, Carol is concerned when ordered to transfer a girl with a painful leg fracture. Enraged, Carol quits as Chief Nurse. At home, she finds Shep but tells him their relationship is over. "I love you, but you *need* help," she explains. "If you can't get it together to get that help, I can't be with you."

Other threads

Mark tries to reassure Loretta about her surgery. She is worried for her children and asks Mark to be their guardian should she die. Mark declines but insists she is going to survive. "Damn right I am," she decides.

Al has made a list of all his sexual partners and notes it is not much to be proud of now. Jeanie insists it was never something to be proud of. Later, she tells Peter everything: "Get tested. I'm sorry." Later, her results come back positive.

Doug hears that Karen has acquired 100 Percodan from his prescription rather than 10. He accuses her of changing the dose and she is insulted. Later, Mark tells Doug that Jen is remarrying. Doug admits he was never attracted to Jen – she has skinny legs. Doug tells Mark about Karen. Mark tells him to dump her – but admits she has great legs.

Season Three 1996 – 7

Themes

Carter's life as an intern is not a happy one. The constant jostling for procedures and the harsh treatment of Benton gives way in dramatic fashion with the tragic death of a colleague. Carter also finds himself moving towards the care of the whole patient. As trouble brews with Donald Anspaugh, it's decision time for Carter.

Benton's confidence is rocked when his failure as a paediatrics surgeon is quickly followed by questions over his teaching style after the death of one of his students. Life becomes more complicated when old flame, Carla Reese, announces she is pregnant and decides to keep the baby.

Mark finally decides to make a play for Susan Lewis, but fate is against them. He takes out his bad mood on his colleagues, most notably Jeanie during her time of greatest need. As he finally restores some balance, he is the victim of an apparently random act of violence.

Doug's self-destructive tendencies come to a head and he is forced to reappraise his life. Meanwhile, Carol considers changing her career and finds Doug her only supporter. The two grow closer as the year moves on.

Jeanie Boulet struggles to live with her condition. Her bitterness slowly gives way after she treats a dying AIDS patient. Jeanie and Al grow closer but Jeanie is also seeing virologist Greg Fischer.

Ones to Watch

3 – 8: *Union Station* – As Susan prepares to leave Chicago, Mark finally decides to tell her how he feels. Can he make it to the station in time?

3 – 11: *Night Shift* – As Benton puts pressure on surgical intern Dennis Gant, Carter fails to support his friend.

3 – 22: *One More for the Road* – Carter's career crisis reaches a peak while Carol and Doug grow closer.

"Dr Carter, I Presume"

3 – 1: First transmitted 26 September 1996
Written by John Wells; Directed by Christopher Chulack

New resident John Carter begins work

4 July 1996. Carter joins Doctors Leung, Dixon, Dale and Dennis Gant on Benton's surgical Blue Team. A departing intern describes Benton as "an intern's worst nightmare". He is proved right when Benton tests his interns over breakfast. Carter is ordered to cover the ER and to take the first night shift. Irritated, he clashes with the nurses who quickly subject him to "potty training": constant questions, especially when Carter tries to sleep. Later he is told to cover the surgical wards and SICU too, and the pressure builds.

He is called to see a drunken man who fell through glass, a man with an abdominal aneurysm and a boy burned by fireworks. Panicking, Carter calls for a doctor to help but is reminded that he *is* the doctor. Shortly, Gant arrives and takes some of Carter's cases. Carter buys the nurses some doughnuts by way of an apology. Later, Greene finds Carter outside, exhausted. He gives him a sparkler and assures him that he will make it.

Jeanie and Peter's HIV test results come back

As Peter waits for his HIV test results, Jeanie tells him that her test was positive. She plans to tell Mark that afternoon. Later, Jeanie attends County's HIV clinic and meets a surgical technician from Southside who was pushed out of his job when he was diagnosed as HIV+. Struck, Jeanie tells Weaver that her test results were negative.

Meanwhile, Benton finally receives his tests results: they are negative. Relieved, he tells Jeanie. Jeanie reveals her decision to hide her HIV status but Benton is reluctant to lie for her. Later, Peter goes to his sister's barbecue and meets Carla, an old flame. Carla flirtatiously asks Peter why he doesn't visit her restaurant any more: "It only takes an hour, Peter. Don't you remember?"

Carol is back in the ER

As staff look forward to their Independence Day barbecue and softball game at Grand Park, Carol complains that she has to cover for an ill colleague. Unsympathetic, Malik notes it is tough being the boss, while Haleh teases that she could always quit again. Lily covers for Carol. At the picnic, Carol bumps into Shep, who has a new girlfriend. They exchange a few stilted words.

Other threads

Two Chicago newspapers have reported that the Mayor wants to cut $200 million from the health-care budget and is considering closing County General.

Attending Physician Kerry Weaver annoys the staff by introducing codes on the admit board and twice-weekly meetings for attendings. She also tries to interest Mark in a lecture on "modern architecture for emergency medicine management". It is all too much and Mark reinstates the old system to the cheers of the staff.

Randi complains that a woman called Gretchen has called for Doug all day. Later, Gretchen arrives and arranges a date. When she leaves, Doug calls her answering machine and cancels, saying he is swamped with work.

"Let the Games Begin"

3 – 2: First transmitted 3 October 1996
Written by Lydia Woodward; Directed by Tom Moore

A hospital closure is announced

Morgenstern tells Greene and Weaver that a hospital closure is to be announced at a meeting at 5pm. He has spoken to Donald Anspaugh, the chief at Southside, who fears Southside is the likely candidate. Morgenstern admits that Anspaugh is a crackpot: "The guy's completely lumpy." At the meeting, Southside is announced as the hospital to be closed, but some "staff consolidation" measures are announced – Anspaugh is being made Chief of Staff at County General.

That afternoon, as the staff celebrate, Anspaugh introduces himself to Mark. Weaver confides to Morgenstern that Anspaugh may not be that bad, commenting without irony how people thought she would be bad for the ER. Morgenstern promptly asks her out to dinner, and a screening of *Caligula*!

Jeanie clashes with Benton over her HIV status

Jeanie's doctor prescribes a drug cocktail to fight HIV. The doctor tells Jeanie that if she uses universal precautions and avoids sharp objects she will not endanger her patients or co-workers. Later, Jeanie is angry to receive a bill for Al's medication. His insurance wouldn't cover it, but he admits it is his responsibility. She is annoyed further when Benton excludes her from an operation for fear she will contaminate the patient. He insists he would have quit his job had he tested positive but Jeannie is unconvinced.

Mark and Susan share a blind date

Mark and Susan share their disastrous recent experiences of blind dates but, later that evening, bump into each other on yet more blind dates. The two couples join up, but Mark and Susan's dates hit it off and make their excuses. Mark and Susan are left to enjoy their evening together.

Other threads

Three months behind with her car payments, Carol watches helplessly as her car is repossessed. Carol is in financial trouble and has decided to sell her house. She returns home to see her real estate agent but her mother has insisted the house isn't to be sold. Surveying the general condition, the agent reckons she couldn't have sold the house anyway – and is impressed someone sold it to Carol.

Doug arranges to have dinner with Heather, an attractive young doctor. Heather complains that he never plans more than a few hours in advance.

Carter is woken by Betty, a loud neighbour in his apartment block. As she draws on a cigarette, Betty explains she saw he was a doctor on his mailbox and complains of shortness of breath! Realising he has overslept, Carter barks a few instructions and races off to arrive late for surgery.

Benton is considering a cardiothoracic fellowship with Dr Wayne Lentoff. Dismissive, Morgenstern suggests Peter consider a paediatric fellowship instead.

"Don't Ask, Don't Tell"

3–3: First transmitted 10 October 1996
Teleplay by Jason Cahill;
Story by Paul Manning & Jason Cahill; Directed by Perry Lang

Susan invites Mark to go on holiday with her

Mark is envious when Susan arranges a trip to Hawaii. His day gets worse when Anspaugh announces new measures to speed up cases: the doctor who has seen the least patients in a day must wax Anspaugh's car! Susan tries to cheer up Mark by inviting him to come on holiday with her. Mark is unsure how to take the offer and makes his excuses. Susan hides her disappointment but later tells Carol: "He couldn't wait to get away. I'm such a fool."

Mark's time is tied up with one patient and he is handed the car wax. Finally, he tells Doug he has decided to be spontaneous. He goes to accept Susan's offer but she gives an awkward apology for ever asking. She leaves for Hawaii alone.

Jeanie avoids a procedure for fear of infecting a patient

Jeanie, Benton and Weaver treat a man with large glass shards impaled in his chest. Jeanie excuses herself from assisting and has to cover her reasons to Weaver. Suspecting, Kerry tells Jeanie about one of her friends who is HIV+ and has not told his colleagues. "It's got to be hard to carry that around all day." Jeanie admits it is. Kerry is pleased Jeanie has decided to carry on working: it would be a real loss to the patients if she quit.

Abby Keaton joins the ER

Paediatric surgeon Abby Keaton joins County from Southside. Carter correctly predicts that Benton will ask her for an elective fellowship. Anspaugh tells Benton he will hold his cardiothoracic elective until 6pm, but needs a decision by then. Peter tries to talk to Keaton but she is in surgery all day. At 6pm, Peter makes his way to Anspaugh's office and finds a young woman sitting at Donald's desk, eating pizza. Benton snaps at her but is humbled when she introduces herself. It is Abby Keaton – and she invites him to talk about the fellowship.

Other threads

Carter is woken again by his cigarette-smoking neighbour Betty (3-2). At County, he is frustrated that he and Gant are not scheduled in the OR. They weasel their way in but are found out and assigned to scut work. Gant is not sure he can take this abuse all year. Later, Carter treats Betty for (ironically enough) smoke inhalation: their apartment block has burned down.

Southside intern Maggie Doyle joins and annoys Carol by parking in her space. They treat a retired teacher and discover they attended the same school. The teacher congratulates Carol on becoming a doctor but she awkwardly corrects him. Doyle reveals she wanted to be a nurse but was kicked out of nursing school.

A man arrives after being attacked by a kangaroo. Soon the media are tracking the animal near Jerry's home. Jerry tries to lure the kangaroo unsuccessfully, but Carol finds it rummaging through the dustbins.

"Last Call"

3-4: First transmitted 17 October 1996
Teleplay by Samantha Howard Corbin;
Story by Samantha Howard Corbin & Carol Flint; Directed by Rod Holcomb

Doug's self-destructive behaviour comes to a head

Doug's date is worse for wear. As he drives her home, she has a seizure. In the ER, Carol asks for the woman's name but Doug doesn't know. Doug finds ID in her car – her name is Nadine Wilks – but she is dead when he returns. Nadine tests positive for alcohol and cocaine. Doug wants to stay in the ER, but he is told to be tested for cocaine and alcohol. Doug is irritated when Weaver observes him in Trauma and is curt when the police ask if he prescribed any drugs to Nadine.

Later, Nadine's sister, Claire, arrives looking for Doug. Doug tells her that "a friend" brought Nadine in, but Claire knows what kind of friends Nadine had at 4am. She reveals that Nadine, an epileptic, rarely wore her medical bracelet. Upset, Doug tries to talk to Carol but she refuses. "You're on your own," she says firmly.

Doug returns home and finds Nadine's bracelet in his bathroom. He plays back his answering machine messages – all from women – and erases them all.

Carter and Benton assist Keaton with a young patient

Although anxious about where he's going to live, Carter is more worried about replacing slides for Benton's lecture that burnt with his apartment! Benton starts the lecture before Carter can explain and, embarrassed, has to reschedule.

Later, Keaton asks Carter and Benton to persuade a young girl, Laura, to undergo surgery. Carter succeeds and is invited to scrub in. Benton proves his skill in the OR but fails to reassure Laura's parents. Abby tells him he has great hands but must show some heart. Later, Benton visits Carla's restaurant. She is surprised but pleased to see him, and flirtatiously invites him to stay.

Carol considers a career change

Carol wants to avoid dinner with her mother than night so E. Ray suggests his yoga class at a Community College. Doyle notes it is where she studied her pre-med course. Carol is still uncomfortable around Maggie and is a little put out when Greene tells Carol to help Maggie with a pelvic exam. Maggie has not done an exam in six months and Carol guides her through it.

Later, Carol tells her mother that she is sick of teaching interns to earn more than she does, especially given her financial situation. Carol's mother offers to pay rent so she can stay over on Saturday nights. Carol is not enamoured with the idea but is happier when Carter reminds her that she works Saturday nights. As Carol leaves, she takes details of the pre-med course at the community college.

Other threads

Jeanie is nauseous from the drug cocktail. She treats an attractive dance instructor who teaches her a few steps. Later, he asks her out, but Jeannie awkwardly refuses.

"Ghosts"

3 – 5: First transmitted 31 October 1996
Written by Neal Baer; Directed by Richard Thorpe

Gant is irked to receive a lukewarm evaluation from Benton

It is Hallowe'en, and Chicago is in the midst of a lightning storm. Weaver praises Gant's

care for Frankenstein's monster but Benton is critical and tells Carter to take over. Gant is annoyed by a mediocre evaluation from Benton, but Carter received the same last year. Confronted, Benton tells Gant that he has to do better than the other interns because he is black and people will assume he was hired to fill a quota. He admits Gant's work is not mediocre but tells him to "work twice as hard, stay twice as late, to be twice as good". Gant suggests that Peter should just tell people he was chosen for ability, rather than try to prove it all the time.

Mark takes Susan's advice when he is urged to undertake research
As the staff gossip about a ghost on the fifth floor, Mark is preoccupied with Susan's return from holiday. He is interrupted by Anspaugh who tells him Kerry is on track for tenure and urges Mark to take on one of Weaver's rejected research topics – pus! Susan returns and reveals she was too scared to fly to Hawaii so visited Chloe and Suzie instead. Later, Mark and Susan anxiously go to the fifth floor to pronounce a death, but confuse the corpse for a sleeping staff member! When they find the body, they feel a rush of cold air. That night, at a Jazz Club where Haleh sings, Mark tells Susan his worries about tenure. She insists there's more to life. Mark agrees, and asks her to dance.

Carol is attending a pre-med course
Carol attends her pre-med physics course but her lab partner assumes her nurse's outfit is a Halowe'en costume. Later, she and Doug take a "health-mobile" to the poorer areas of Chicago. They meet Charlie (Kirsten Dunst), a mischievous 15-year-old girl who wants condoms. Later, Carol and Doug treat a stabbing and have to perform surgery on the street. En route back to the ER, Carol tells Doug about her course. He is encouraging.

Other threads
Keaton and Benton treat an eight-year-old girl injured in a hit and run. Carter tells the girl that her father will be alright, aware that the man died in trauma. Benton is critical but Abby admires Carter's tact. Later, Carter has to break the bad news.

Jeanie and Maggie treat an elderly DNR who has overdosed. The husband, Mr Jennings, was asked to administer the drugs but he became frightened and called the ambulance. Mrs Jennings dies and her husband considers he did the wrong thing. Jeanie insists he was there for his wife when it mattered. Later, Jeanie meets Al and bitterly contrasts their marriage with that of the Jennings. "We didn't love, we didn't cherish, we didn't respect. And now you've killed me," she says bitterly.

"Fear of Flying"

3–6: First transmitted 7 November 1996
Written by Lance A. Gentile; Directed by Christopher Chulack

Mark and Susan are flown to a car accident
Susan has to overcome her fear of flying when she and Mark take the air-ambulance to a

car accident. They are the first on the scene and find the driver of the first car is dead. The Herlihy family are trapped in the second car. Mark quickly puts the father, a paediatrician called David, into the helicopter then helps Lewis retrieve son Zach from the car. Zach has facial fractures and his airway is obstructed. The mother, Gail, and baby Megan are left for the paramedics.

At the ER, Mark and Susan revive David but he can't remember the incident. Mark tells the labs to hurry the head CT while Susan retrieves the others from the crash site. David is confused and Mark decides to reunite him with his wife. On seeing Gail, David starts to regain his senses. Mark tells them that Zach will be fine and that Megan is in surgery.

Benton's arrogance endangers a patient

Ross, Gant and Benton examine Megan and find her abdomen is distended. Benton decides Keaton must perform exploratory surgery and gets Gail's consent. In the OR, Benton and Gant help Keaton repair the perforated intestine. Keaton is called away and tells Benton to close. However, Benton spots debris on Megan's liver and it bleeds heavily when he tries to clean it. After several attempts, he calls for Keaton.

Furious, Keaton tells Benton that he has ripped the liver capsule. Keaton tries feverishly to stop the bleeding and eventually succeeds. Megan is taken to the NICU but her lung collapses and she stops breathing. Eventually, she is revived but the prognosis is not good. Keaton berates Benton for ignoring her instructions, arrogantly assuming he knew what to do. She will be responsible if Megan dies but they know it will be Peter's fault.

Gant tries to comfort Benton, but Peter is sarcastic. Gant is angry: "You're a real prick, you know that?" Later, Peter returns to the NICU and recites the Lord's Prayer, but can't seem to remember the words.

Other threads

Rhonda Sterling, a "float" nurse, is covering for Haleh in the ER. Carol is irked when Rhonda keeps a patient waiting and later administers the wrong medication to Zach Herlihy. As a result, Zach is taken to the OR for pancreatic surgery. Angry, Carol tells Rhonda she shouldn't be working the ER. Rhonda is already well aware of the fact.

Jeanie and Maggie are asked to hold a deceased man until a cryogenics company arrive. When the cryogenics representative arrives, he tells them to administer some medicine. Jeanie doubts his qualifications but gives the injections anyway – it's not going to harm the deceased!

"No Brain, No Gain"

3–7: First transmitted 14 November 1996
Written by Paul Manning; Directed by David Nutter

Carter and Edson come to blows

Carter and Gant are asked to find Mr Percy, one of Edson's patients who has a throat tumour. Carter finds Percy and tries to explain the need for surgery but the man can't understand. Carter suggests a psych consult but is scared to press the issue with Anspaugh. The operation goes ahead and Carter impresses. Edson is annoyed when Carter is invited to dinner.

When Carter returns, Dale smugly reveals that Mr Percy had a stroke. He suggests that Carter could have saved him if he had called for a psych consult. Furious, Carter slams Edson against a locker. Keaton breaks them up. Keaton stitches Carter's injured nose and tells him to call her Abby. She moves in forcefully for a kiss.

Peter refuses to accept his failings as a surgeon

Benton has stayed with Megan Herlihy for six days (3-7): they can do nothing to stop the haemorrhaging. Keaton tells Peter he must watch, not operate, to progress as a surgeon. Determined to prove himself, Benton resuscitates a 13-year-old and goes to great lengths in the OR to save him. However, the boy is probably brain-dead. Benton switches off the ventilator and wills the boy to breathe. There is nothing and Benton pronounces time of death. Later, he tells Keaton she was right about him. Keaton tells him to check on Megan. She is showing signs of recovery. Gail Herlihy believes it is a miracle but Benton is dumbstruck.

Mark believes he may have missed his chance with Susan

Carol persuades Mark to ask Susan out but Susan is evasive and insists they need to talk. During the day, Mark treats a researcher of human mating habits who suspects Morgenstern and Susan are an item. Mark tells Carol he may have missed his chance, but Carol is unconvinced. That night, Susan tells Mark that Morgenstern has helped her arrange a transfer: she is moving to Phoenix. Her holiday with Chloe and Suzie has persuaded her that there is nothing to keep her in Chicago any more. Mark is stunned. Susan hugs Mark and admits she will miss him. Mark sadly agrees.

Other threads

Mark and Doug clash over the treatment of a young boy. Doug accuses Mark of being on his "moral high-horse ever since I came in with that OD" (3-4). Doug insists he runs himself down without Mark's help. He is seeing a psychiatrist.

Carol is annoyed when Jerry calls Rhonda to cover the ER. This time, Rhonda hands a detached foot to a patient's wife. Carol threatens an investigation but Rhonda resigns: she believes the hospital have put her in an unfamiliar department to edge her out before she reaches full pension. The nurses are dismissive, until Lydia reveals she is being transferred to neurology for three weeks.

One to Watch

"Union Station"

3 – 8: First transmitted 21 November 1996
Written by Carol Flint; Directed by Tom Moore

Susan Lewis leaves the ER

It is Susan's last day. Mark is irritable and frequently asks for Susan's help. Meanwhile, the staff have organised a party, but Carol notes there is not much time between the end of Susan's shift and her train to Phoenix. Doug tells Mark he must say something to Susan before she leaves, but Mark feels there is no point. Later, Susan takes the flack from Weaver over one of Mark's cases. Susan firmly tells Mark that she can't stand between him and Weaver any more. The atmosphere is awkward.

Meanwhile, Lydia reveals she has called off her engagement to Al Grabarsky because he refused to name the day. Carol tells Al he needs to be bolder and directs him to the hospital chaplain. Later, the staff attend Lydia and Al's impromptu marriage. Mark and Susan catch themselves looking at each other, and smile. Susan catches the bouquet. Afterwards, Mark apologises for using Susan earlier. She apologises for being tetchy, admitting she is no good at goodbyes. She just wants to leave knowing they will always be friends.

As Susan's shift ends, the ER is inundated with eight victims of a road traffic accident. The party over, Susan walks the corridors saying goodbye to Ross and Carol, but Mark is busy with a patient. Later, Mark is annoyed to realise Susan has left. Doug tells Mark he must tell Susan how he feels, or he will spend the rest of his life making everyone else miserable! Mark agrees. He takes a taxi to Susan's flat but she has already left. He races across town to Union Station and thinks the train has gone. A porter directs him to a different platform.

At last, Mark finds Susan getting on the train. She is pleased he came to say goodbye, but Mark wants her to stay. Mark tells Susan he loves her, and berates himself for not saying so earlier. Susan is unfazed: she already knows.

Mark begs her to stay but Susan insists she has a new life that is taking her somewhere else. "I don't want to lose you," he says tearfully. They kiss, but Susan's mind is made up. As the train leaves, Susan leans from the window and says she loves him. Mark doesn't hear. "I love you!" she shouts, before adding a simple "Bye". Mark stands alone as Susan's train leaves Chicago.

Carol is concerned by new nursing schedules

Carol is annoyed when the nurses are yet again scheduled to other departments. She tells Mary Cain in Nurse Management that nurses should cover departments that they are suited to, for example ER staff could cover the ICU. Mary agrees to take up the suggestion if Carol joins the hospital wide re-engineering committee. Carol reluctantly agrees, but the nurses are not impressed. Haleh notes that Carol is beginning to sound like management.

Other threads

Ross and Chuny organise free immunisations as part of a community health project. Charlie arrives with a baby, Ahmed, who she claims is hers. The results of lab tests on Ahmed concern Ross. He tries to contact Charlie at her emergency shelter, but she is not there.

Megan Herlihy is due to be discharged. Benton is awkward when Gail and David thank him and Abby. Abby tells him never to begrudge a good outcome. Later, Benton, Keaton and Carter operate on a baby with a bowel obstruction. Carter and Keaton are surprised when Benton refuses to press on, admitting he does not know what to do next.

Benton is surprised to find Carter in Keaton's office. Covering, Abby explains that Carter is helping her write an article. In fact, most of their efforts do not involve writing. The two agree that what happened between them, on several occasions now, is strictly personal and nothing to do with work.

Meanwhile, Peter is surprised when Carla visits. He gives her a tour of the ER, and introduces her to Carter. When the coast is clear, Carla leads Peter into the suture room for a passionate clinch.

Al hands Jeanie divorce papers. He is prepared to give her everything. He tells her she won't have to worry about him any more.

It's the one we were all waiting for and what an ending to a storyline! After two-and-a-half years of flirtation, Mark finally tells Susan he loves her, but it's too late. *Union Station* is like watching a train wreck in slow-motion, every second a tortuous wait for the next impact. The final race across Chicago to Union Station is classic romantic melodrama – you are willing Mark on with every step. And even in the final exchange, you are kept waiting as Susan's "I love you!" is drowned out by the noise of the train. It's agonising to watch, but we couldn't have it any other way.

"Ask Me No Questions, I'll Tell You No Lies"

3-9: First transmitted 12 December 1996
Teleplay by Barbara Hall; Story by Neal Baer & Lydia Woodward;
Directed by Paris Barclay

Mark discovers Jeanie's HIV status

With Susan gone, Mark has testily thrown himself into work and is sticking to the rules. He treats Al Boulet who has an AIDS-related illness. Mark tells Jeanie, who tells him she tested negative. Jeanie, however, is angry that Al came to the ER. Al admits she is right to be angry but reckons hating him will change nothing.

Meanwhile, Mark checks Jeanie's medical records and discovers she tested positive. He demands to know why Kerry hid the truth, but Kerry is furious that he checked a co-worker's file. Indignant, Mark goes to Anspaugh, who asserts that Jeanie's status is supposition – "and please don't correct me if I'm wrong."

Jeanie discovers that someone checked her file and angrily confronts Mark. Mark insists he should have been told, but Jeanie, furious, reckons she's learnt a lot about Mark that day. Later, Jeanie apologises to Al for blaming him. Al admits he hasn't told any of his co-workers either.

Benton considers Carter's progress, while Gant is swamped

The ER is busy and Gant fields the surgical cases: Benton wants Gant to pull his weight. Carol gives Carter one case, observing that Gant is overworked, but Benton reckons he's just slow. Later, Gant tells Carter he did him no favours by taking Carol's patient and tells him to leave him alone. Later, Benton asks Keaton how she thinks Carter is progressing, but she turns the question on him. Peter reckons Carter is a fast learner and good with children. Keaton says he should tell Carter that, noting how easily discouraged a student can become. Later, Benton does so. Carter is stunned.

Other threads

Carter is disappointed to hear that Abby has decided to work in Pakistan for several months. Abby insists their relationship never had a long-term future and Carter agrees, but clearly thought differently. Later, they drive to a forest and fulfil a Carter family tradition – felling a Douglas Fir for Christmas. Abby asks if they're really allowed to take the tree. Carter reveals his family owns the forest.

At the hospital re-engineering committee, Carol persuades Mary Cain to stop "floating" ER nurses. Haleh is pleased by the news and eagerly starts to tell Mark. Mark assumes she is about to complain about her job. Carol tells Doug to talk to Mark about his behaviour, but when they meet up Mark is already apologetic. He struggles to find a description of his behaviour and Doug offers "a vicious, humourless pain in the ass". Aware of what is going on, Doug tells Mark it's OK to miss Susan.

Carol takes her first exam at pre-med and finds Doug waiting for her outside. He suggests they go for a drink but Carol's lab partner, William, arrives and suggests they all go for ice cream. Doug shrugs and agrees.

"Homeless for the Holidays"

3 – 10: First transmitted 19 December 1996
Written by Samantha Howard Corbin; Directed by David Guggenheim

Charlie is made homeless through Doug's actions

Christmas Eve 1996. Charlie returns with Ahmed, her friend Gloria's baby. Ross finds a tumour in the baby's abdomen and is angry that blood in the baby's nappy was not spotted earlier. Charlie urges him not to rock the boat as Gloria may throw her out. However, when Gloria arrives Doug threatens her with social services. Charlie berates Doug and leaves. That night, Doug finds Charlie outside his house. Gloria has thrown her out. Doug refuses to take her in and takes her to Carol's, where it's "Christmas in the Ukraine". Doug convinces Carol to let Charlie stay.

The ER makes policy on HIV+ employees

Jeanie hopes the hospital won't have to make policy over her but Kerry is unsure. Later, Anspaugh tells Kerry and Mark that the ER must make its own policy governing HIV+ employees. Mark is concerned for patient safety, but Kerry doesn't want everyone knowing Jeanie's HIV status. Meanwhile, rumours spread that someone in the ER has HIV. Kerry reprimands the gossips and says "Employee X" could be anyone. Frustrated, Jeanie tells everyone that she is Employee X.

Jeanie joins the policy discussion. Mark insists that she works within limits, but Jeanie says she would anyway. Kerry volunteers to monitor Jeanie and Mark concedes. Jeanie leaves happier, but notes a change in her colleagues. Carol recounts her attempted suicide and suggests that, if they haven't been friends, perhaps they should be. Later, Al gives Jeanie a star for her Christmas tree. Jeanie puts it on the ER tree. Maggie thinks the star should go on one at home.

Carter discovers Gant is working most of Christmas

Gant has argued with his girlfriend Monique: she isn't coming to Chicago and won't be at Carter's family Christmas party. Abby, however, can attend. Carter tries to rearrange his shifts with Gant. Gant is already doing a 34-hour shift but agrees. They try to make time to get together, but Dennis is working the next night too.

Other threads

Maggie treats beaten wife Mrs Lang and persuades her to leave her husband. When Mr Lang arrives, they tell him that his wife is under observation. Meanwhile, they smuggle Mrs Lang outside and give her a bus ticket to a refuge, paid for by the staff.

Carter has to hide when Benton arrives in Keaton's office. Benton asks to continue his paediatric surgery rotation but Keaton refuses. She notes that Peter doesn't live and breathe for children and is not suited. Benton is disappointed.

Mark finds the perfect gift for Rachel when a homeless man dies, leaving his mangy dog, Nicky. Mark cleans Nicky up – but finds Rachel's stepfather, Craig, has already bought two Labrador puppies. Mark pretends the dog is his and that he just wanted to show Rachel. Mark is pleased when Nicky bites Craig's hand.

One to Watch

"Night Shift"

3 – 11: First transmitted 16 January 1997
Written by Paul Manning; Directed by Jonathan Kaplan

As Weaver races to tenure, Mark clashes with Legal

It is tenure week and Mark is in direct competition with Weaver. He is annoyed to hear he has been written up by the legal department for failing to co-sign charts. Weaver aims for prize tenure with a study of exercise on the circadian rhythms of night shift workers and puts Jeanie and Wendy on exercise bikes.

Meanwhile, Mark treats Shelley, a woman with meningitis who talks in rhyme. He decides to override consent and order a spinal tap, but Legal insist they have to approve the decision. Mark performs the tap anyway, which proves meningitis. Later, he tells Chuny that his chances of making tenure are now zero. He invites her for breakfast, and she agrees. They hit it off and Chuny stays the night with Mark.

Charlie asks Doug's help to pay off her pimp

Doug helps Carol on a maintenance survey of the ER. They are interrupted by Charlie who asks Doug for $100 to pay off a pimp who has threatened to kill her. Doug refuses, noting that Charlie already stole Carol's mother's silverware. Charlie is furious and calls Doug a child molester.

Carol and Doug continue and find a storage room where they used to meet up when they were dating. Carol is reminded of her insecurities. Doug wonders if he was harsh on Charlie, but Carol tells him he was right to refuse. Later, Charlie arrives with a broken arm and jaw. Carol suspects Charlie has also been raped. In confidence, Charlie tells Doug she was, and makes him promise not to tell social services. When she is asleep, however, he makes the call.

Benton angrily berates Gant with horrific consequences

Gant is angry when Benton refuses to grant him two days leave so he can sort things out with Monique. He tries to talk to Carter, but John is tired of hearing about Gant's troubled love life. As Gant persists, Benton arrives and accuses Gant of neglecting a patient, almost resulting in his death. Furious, he tells Gant that if he makes another "lazy mistake" like that, he won't be working at County. Taken aback by Benton's tirade, Carter tries to comfort Gant but is paged.

Gant complains to Anspaugh who calls for Carter's opinion. Torn between his friend and his teacher, Carter says that Peter was harsh but may have had a point. Gant is dismayed when Anspaugh tells him to get a thicker skin. Afterwards, Carter apologises and they agree to still be friends.

Later, Carter and Maggie compete to run the trauma on a man who was hit by an

Elevated train. The patient is badly disfigured and has lost an eye and brain matter. No one is sure if the man jumped or fell. Benton rushes in and tells them to page Gant, berating Gant's laziness. Suddenly, a pager goes off in the room – Maggie realises that the patient is Dennis Gant. Carter and Benton are momentarily stunned – then dive in to work. Gant flatlines.

Other threads

The hospital budget is in crisis and Carol is told she must fire two nurses. Randi suggests that cutting overtime and reducing shifts will save enough money to keep all the staff. Carol is grateful but the nurses are less pleased and threaten to strike.

Benton presses for a second paediatric rotation but is told he needs Keaton's recommendation. Benton arrives at Abby's office and finds her and Carter in a clinch. Carter makes his excuses. Abby wonders if Benton intends to blackmail her. Peter insists he only wants a recommendation based on his skill. Keaton tells him she can't propose him for a second rotation. He will make an excellent surgeon, she says, but not a paediatric surgeon.

This is a pretty solid regular episode, save for the last five minutes. Like *Union Station* it is the culmination of a long-running story. From the start of the third season, Gant's struggles were a quiet undercurrent, never quite taking centre stage. Gant developed as a minor character. His refusal to accept scut work, and frothy relationship with Carter, gave way to anger and confrontation with Benton and finally a single-minded determination to prove Peter wrong. What is harrowing is the way Gant's self-belief takes blow after blow in *Night Shift* – ending with Carter and Anspaugh apparently endorsing Benton's critical view. The revelation in the last minutes is gut-wrenching. The verdict may have been accidental death, but we all know it was suicide.

"Post Mortem"

3 – 12: First transmitted 23 January 1997
Written by Carol Flint; Directed by Jacque Toberen

Benton and Carter struggle to deal with Gant's death

It is the day of Dennis Gant's memorial service. Carter asks Benton to say a few words at the service, but is irritated when Benton refuses, blasé about his role in Gant's death. Later, Carter finds Benton's final evaluation of Gant. It is glowing but Gant never saw it. Angry, Carter tells Benton that Gant only ever received harping criticism from Peter: "And now he's dead and you're going to have to face it."

The police decide Gant's death was an accident, not suicide, but Carter still feels guilty. He talks to hospital counsellor Nina Pomerantz, who reveals that Gant talked fondly of him. After treating a homeless man abandoned by his friends, Carter tells Mark he knew Gant was in trouble but did nothing. Mark tries to console him, but John knows he could have been more of a friend.

Carter leads the memorial service, but Benton arrives late. Carter bitterly introduces Peter to Gant's father who recalls his son's respect for Peter. Benton admits he worked

Dennis too hard and that he would have made an excellent surgeon. Later, Benton confides to Carter he thought that the pressure would make Gant learn, but can't open up more. Carter bitterly notes that they can both pretend nothing happened – "Look what that did for Dennis Gant."

Nurse strike action results in the death of a patient

The nurses organise an unofficial strike and call in sick. Temporary nurses are drafted in but are inexperienced and Carol has to cover for them. Overworked, Carol gives a homeless patient the wrong blood type and he dies. Mark and Kerry insists it was an accident, but Carol demands that the incident be reported. She has to face herself in the mirror knowing what happened.

Doug tries to find a permanent home for Charlie

Charlie is furious that Doug called social services, but softens when he promises not to put her in a home. Doug tries to find Charlie's living relatives but she wants him to adopt her. Meanwhile, social services find Charlie's mother in Chicago. When she admits domestic abuse, social services refuse to release Charlie. Doug denies Charlie's claim that he will adopt her. Doug firmly denies this and Charlie becomes hysterical.

Other threads

Jeanie treats a patient with malaria and meets Dr Greg Fischer from Infectious Diseases. Kerry recommends Greg become Jeanie's HIV doctor as his partner died from AIDS. Jeanie assumes Greg is gay but Kerry later reveals he is one of Chicago's most eligible bachelors – it was his business partner who died. On their date, Greg kisses a hesitant Jeanie. She tells him she is HIV+. An awkward silence descends.

Mark is giving Chuny the full romantic treatment. Carol reckons he is overcompensating for Susan's absence, but Chuny is happy to receive the attention.

"Fortune's Fools"

3 – 13: First transmitted 30 January 1997
Written by Jason Cahill; Directed by Michael Katleman

Benton's difficulties following Gant's death alienate Carter

Carter is annoyed that Peter is not in surgery that day and signs him up for a splenectomy that Benton later cancels. Meanwhile, Peter is stunned when Carla announces she is pregnant and wants to keep the baby. Distracted, Peter forgets to attend a joint presentation with Carter to the surgical team. Carter covers for Benton but faces tough questioning and tries a bad joke to placate the audience. Furious, Carter confronts Benton but gets only a lame apology.

Hicks worries that Benton is wasting Carter's skills and offers him a place on her team. Carter accepts and tells Benton who seems uninterested and distant. Carter fears that Benton doesn't care about his own reputation or career anymore.

Mark and Kerry show prospective interns around the ER

Mark and Kerry show prospective interns around the ER. Kerry's tour is boring: she eagerly shows them "the life of a urine sample". However, Mark's is more interesting – especially when one patient, Heather Morgan, invites him for a drink. Doug compares dating a patient to the Exxon Valdez! Later, Mark's students are thrilled to assist in a trauma.

At the end of the day, Anspaugh announces that none of Kerry's group have applied, but all of Mark's have put County as their first choice! Weaver is irked when Anspaugh suggests Mark seek academic tenure. That night, Mark meets Heather at the bar – only to find his students eagerly observing!

Carol's mistake in the ER goes public

A newspaper has reported the death of an ER patient during the nurse's strike (3-12). Haleh blames a temp for the mistake and is stunned when Carol reveals she made the error. Meanwhile, the revised nursing contracts are leaked. Carol reckons Mary Cain sold her out in the negotiations, but Haleh believes Carol had a hand in the new conditions. Isolated, Carol decides to tell the newspaper that the patient's death was her fault and not a result of the strike. Before she can do anything, Carol is suspended. She tells Haleh to take over the contract negotiations and leaves.

Other threads

Greg has not contacted Jeanie since their date. He is uncomfortable when they treat Mike Patterson, a young husband with a form of syphilis. They tell the couple together and are surprised when Mike's wife, Cindy, is the one who had an affair and contracted the disease. Later, Greg explains he was shocked by Jeanie's revelation. Jeanie bitterly tells him he doesn't have to date a woman with HIV.

Carol and Maggie treat a 58-year-old police officer who was shot by a teenager. Carol sees that the man's hand twitches and realises that the shooter thought he was going for his gun. The officer is close to retirement and doesn't want to be taken off the beat. He only agrees to consider the proposed tests.

"Whose Appy Now?"

3 – 14: First transmitted 6 February 1997
Written by Neal Baer; Directed by Felix Enriquez Alcalá

Carter delights in operating on Benton

Benton is distant at work after Jackie insists he show parental responsibility for Carla's child. He also has a sore stomach. Meanwhile, Maggie and Carter compete for procedures. It is only Maggie's knowledge of firearms that saves Carter from contracting AIDS from a patient. They are annoyed when their GSW is given to another surgeon and they are told to perform an appendectomy.

Carter grins when he realises that the appendectomy patient is Peter Benton: "Oh, there is a God!" Carter orders *Ride of the Valkyries* and *Mack the Knife* played as he goes in to work. He also teaches Maggie a new suturing technique on Benton! When Peter wakes, he mumbles about being too hard on Gant. Carter points out that he's been too hard on him too, but Benton doesn't fall for it.

Benton treats a young boy with cystic fibrosis

Doug treats Jad Houston who has cystic fibrosis. Jad's girlfriend, Katy, says Jad is 19 and a DNR. Doug discovers Jad is actually three weeks from his 18th birthday and needs parental consent for a DNR. Katy reveals they ran away to spend Jad's last three months in Mexico, not in a hospital.

Mrs Houston arrives and refuses to sign a DNR. Doug tries to persuade Mrs Houston. Kerry is concerned that he's taking the matter personally. Eventually, Mrs Houston agrees to sign the DNR, but when Jad arrests she revokes the order. Doug apologises to Jad but must intubate. Jad gives him an obscene gesture.

Mark fouls up his dating logistics

Mark has double-booked dates with Polly MacKenzie and Heather Morgan. Doug warns that women can smell deceit! Mark cancels his date with Polly – but then accepts drinks with Nina Pomerantz. Mark explains his elaborate scheduling to Doug but Doug insists he is too busy healing the sick to talk! Mark is foiled when all three women arrive in the ER and he is unceremoniously dumped by each of them. Back on his own, he asks Chuny out but she refuses. He ends up going out with Doug!

Other threads

Carter makes a move on Maggie and she invites him along to the firing range. Maggie suddenly asks Carter to hide her as a woman walks past. It's her jealous ex-girlfriend. Carter is so stunned by the news he shoots out one of the range's lights!

Jeanie and Greg investigate an outbreak of staphylococcus, caused by poor toilet hygiene. The culprit is Jerry, who is taught how to wash his hands! Greg asks Jeanie out on a date but she wants to keep their relationship professional. However, an AIDS patient convinces her of the need to live her life. She meets Greg for dinner.

Carol arrives to collect her pay cheque and is amused to find the ER in chaos. Haleh has not given out the nursing schedule, ordered too much equipment and forgets to hand out the pay cheques.

"The Long Way Around"

3 – 15: First transmitted 13 February 1997
Written by Neal Baer; Directed by Felix Enriquez Alcalá

Carol is held hostage in a convenience store hold-up

Valentine's Day 1997. Carol goes to a convenience store and finds herself in the middle of a hold-up. An American and a Scot (Ewan McGregor) threaten the shopkeeper, Mrs Novotny, with a gun. Her husband surprises the men and in the confusion a shopper runs for the door. Mr Novotny shoots the American robber, but is then shot twice by the Scot.

Outside, the shopper finds a policeman and soon the store is under siege.

Carol explains she is a nurse and is put to work by the Scot, Duncan, on his injured American cousin, James. Among the other hostages is ten-year-old Robert Potter. Carol is concerned that Robert should not see the injuries, but Duncan is cold. James will bleed to death unless he is taken to hospital, but Duncan refuses to let a doctor into the store. Mr Novotny is critically ill and Carol reminds Duncan that murder is a more serious crime than robbery. She tries CPR but, despite her frantic efforts, Mr Novotny dies.

Taking Robert to the bathroom, Carol finds another boy hiding in a store room. They find a back door but it is locked. As Duncan and James argue about their bungled hold-up, Carol asks Mrs Novotny for the key but is spotted. James, who planned the hold-up, seems blasé but Duncan is upset, especially when Mrs Novotny becomes hysterical. Duncan suddenly remembers Robert and tells Carol to get him. Panicked, Robert scampers into the roof space. Duncan tries to follow but injures himself.

As Carol patches up Duncan, James deteriorates. Carol takes the key. James becomes delirious and talks of Scotland: he could never be content with his father's work. Carol notes her own discontent with her job, but Duncan is surprised, given her skill. He feels guilty about Mr Novotny's death and feels alone, but Carol can empathise, having recently killed a patient (3-13). Suddenly, the boy in the store room makes an unsuccessful bid to disarm Duncan. As Duncan turns to shoot, Carol stands in his way. To placate him, she hands over the door key.

Duncan escapes with Carol through the back door. He thinks he is free when a police car pulls into the alley. Carol tells him to stop, but he runs and is shot.

Duncan and James are rushed into the ER. Carol abruptly takes charge. James is sent to the OR with a perforated spleen but will be alright. Duncan is more seriously injured. As Carol comforts him, they lose his pulse. Duncan dies.

After, another hostage thanks Carol for everything she did, noting no one else could have done what she did. Doug is just happy that she is safe. Kerry admits that they miss her. Carol misses it too: "I love my job, Kerry," she adds and leaves.

"Faith"

3 – 16: First transmitted 20 February 1997
Written by John Wells; Directed by Jonathan Kaplan

Doyle is outraged at the treatment of a patient with Down's Syndrome

Greene and Doyle treat Louise Cupertino, a 35-year-old with Down's Syndrome. Louise needs a heart transplant but is refused a place on the transplant list. Doyle is outraged, but Kayson insists Louise is high-risk. Mark discovers that Nina Pomerantz endorsed Kayson's decision. Although Nina fears Louise would not get the post-operative care she needs, Mark persuades her to see Louise.

They find Louise talking to Jimmy, Maggie's brother, who also has Down's. Nina retracts her objection. However, Mrs Cupertino refuses to allow the surgery. The mother only has a few years left and does not want Louise put in a home after she has gone. She wants them to be together in Heaven.

Carol is reinstated

Carol is unsure about taking her med school admissions test as she is due to hear from County about her job. The Safety Committee decide Carol's error was down to systems problems and not negligence. Pleased, Carol considers taking the exam and is encouraged by Doug. Later, as the nurses celebrate their new contracts, Doug hears that Carol took the afternoon off and goes to see her. Carol took the test but is unsure if she is good enough to get in. Doug insists she is.

Benton starts to come to terms with Gant's death

Benton offers his support to Carla but she refuses, noting Peter always cares about himself first. At work, Peter is put out when Carter shows him photographs of his appendix in a jar! Later, a depressed Peter tells Hicks he felt invincible six months ago but now things aren't working out for him. Hicks reassures Peter that he didn't cause Gant's death, but Peter is aware he was too wrapped up in his career to consider Gant. Hicks tells Peter he is finding his way and will learn from his mistakes: "It takes a lifetime," she notes. "You just have to have faith."

Other threads

Jeanie accuses Greg of being unromantic and is surprised when he arranges a snowy picnic. Greg hopes they can start sleeping together, but Jeanie is uncomfortable. Later, she asks if they can slow down. Greg agrees but is a little hurt.

Jad Houston (3-14), now 18, signs his own DNR. Doug prepares to extubate, but Katy and Mrs Houston have already said goodbye. To Doug's surprise, Jad breathes on his own. He and Katy leave without telling Mrs Houston where they are going.

Carter requests a second opinion and is embarrassed when Anspaugh ridicules Carter's diagnosis in front of some medical students. Carter feels sure he was right and tells Hicks. Anspaugh is taken aback by the accusation, but Carter is proven right. Carter asks to scrub in on the surgery and is surprised to be told he is leading it. Anspaugh reckons Carter is the only one who knows what they are doing today.

"Tribes"

3 – 17: First transmitted 10 April 1997
Written by Lance A. Gentile; Directed by Richard Thorpe

Mark is accused of racism

A white man and a black teenager, Kenny Law, are brought in with gunshot wounds. Mark attends to the more critical white man but annoys Kenny's brother Chris by demanding Kenny be searched for drugs and weapons. Suddenly, Kenny crashes and Mark has to insert a chest tube. Benton takes Kenny to the OR. Mark defends himself against Chris's accusations of racism. Soon, the ER is crowded with Kenny's basketball team. Mark asks Malik to clear the waiting room, but Malik is irked that Mark won't do it himself.

Another victim arrives, this time a white basketball player from a rival team. Mark discovers the shooting was drugs-related, but that Kenny was an innocent bystander. Mark asks Chris not to retaliate but Chris is offended that Mark thinks they were ever involved.

In the OR, Carter saves the white basketball player but Kenny Law dies. Mark asks Malik to help him tell Chris but Malik bitterly tells him to call security if he is scared. Chris breaks down. Later, Mark admits he made racist assumptions but tried not to act on them.

Weaver bargains with a junkie

After treating an attorney with hyper-sexuality, Kerry sees a wheelchair-bound junkie, Brown, who was hit by a car while "jay-wheeling". Kerry trades painkillers in return for Brown's promise to attend detox. Later, she sees Brown leaving and bitterly notes they had a deal. "Yeah, well, never trust a junkie," he says.

Carla is brought to the ER

Jeanie treats Carla, who has a broken ankle from a car accident. The baby is fine but Jeanie needs to know the father's blood type. Jeanie is taken aback when Carla tells her to ask Benton. Peter is concerned for Carla, but Jeanie says he was not requested, nor asked to stay away. Carla starts having contractions but Jeanie is able to convince Carla to have an IV and prevent labour. Later, Peter finds Carla sleeping. He watches a recording of the ultrasound and smiles as he sees his baby boy on the screen.

Other threads

Carol treats Lorri, a College student who may have had unprotected sex but can't remember. She tests positive for a date-rape drug and has been raped. Carol convinces Lorri to talk to the police.

When Hicks notes Benton's busy schedule, he wryly observes that she poached his intern. Later, Hicks offers Benton a place on her team. He is hesitant but she reminds him it is not a matter of ambition. Peter agrees and will be working with Carter again.

As the "young Jedi surgeon so recently humiliated" in a game of hoops, Carter must treat Babs Chenovich, a "crackhead" with abdominal pain. He spends the day tracing her medical records. Babs is impressed by his concern: "Are you sure you're a surgeon?" "Sometimes I wonder," is Carter's wry reply.

"You Bet Your Life"

3−18: First transmitted 17 April 1997
Written by Paul Manning; Directed by Christopher Chulack

Jeanie treats a woman dying of AIDS

It's Al and Jeanie's ninth wedding anniversary. Jeanie is annoyed when Al arrives with roses. She and Kerry treat Suzanne Alner, an AIDS patient who tried to overdose on her medication. Suzanne blames herself for the death of her daughter from an AIDS-related illness. Jeanie is disturbed when Suzanne's husband is pleased that Suzanne is being punished by dying in pain.

Meanwhile, Suzanne, blind from the methanol, mistakes Greg for her husband. She asks for his forgiveness. Jeanie presses Greg but he won't pretend. Suzanne dies. Greg apologises to Jeanie but she is cold and cancels their date. Later, Jeanie visits Al: "I don't want to be angry any more, I don't want to be that kind of person". Al insists he never meant to hurt Jeanie. They have missed each other and embrace.

Mark needs to write up a case to get a teaching position

Mark and Weaver are up for the same teaching position. Anspaugh urges Mark to write up a case. Mark treats Iva Blender, a woman with a history of invasive surgery. Although Mark suspects porphyria, Nina reveals Iva is "a total fruitcake" who likes having surgery. They discover Iva has eaten a tray of instruments.

Playing up to Iva, Mark suggests a painful endoscopy, but is called away to pick up Rachel from school. Rachel has pretended to have leukaemia to get his attention. On his return, Mark finds Kerry has done the procedure and suggests they co-write an article: *The Woman Who Ate the ER*.

Carol is frustrated by her career prospects

Carol fears she has failed her med school exams. During the day, she has a couple of run-ins with Maggie Doyle. She is annoyed when Doug takes Maggie's side. "We grew up in the same neighbourhood," she tells Doug, "and now… I gotta take orders from her all day long and I hate it." Carol is frustrated she can't get through the med school door. Flirtatious, Doug suggests she could get through his door. Carol reckons anything in a bra could do that, but Doug insists he is a reformed character.

Other threads

Doug treats Betty, a teenager who refuses surgery to attend her prom. Doug gives Betty an IV and arranges for an ambulance to pick her up later. She arrives back in time for the operation.

Peter pretends Carla was his patient to find out the chances of gestational diabetes. Later, he tells Carla he wants to be a father to their son. Relenting, Carla lets him help around the house.

When Anspaugh refuses to operate, Carter gets Hicks to perform the surgery. However, the man has gangrene and may die. Anspaugh is furious and Hicks berates Carter's deception. Carter is put on probation – Anspaugh resisted Hicks' calls for Carter's expulsion. "John Carter is not a law unto himself," she reminds him.

"Calling Dr Hathaway"

3–19: First transmitted 24 April 1997
Teleplay by Jason Cahill & Samantha Howard Corbin; Story by Neal Baer;
Directed by Paris Barclay

Carol questions her career choice

Weaver calls Carol "Dr Einstein" – Carol has passed her med school admissions test. Carol and Doug treat baby Joel Thompson but Doug is annoyed when the mother, Andrea, gets in the way. Carol promises to tell Andrea if Joel's condition deteriorates. However, Carol is getting lessons from Kerry when Joel bleeds out. Dismayed, Carol lets Andrea say goodbye to Joel and refuses to let Kerry use the trauma room. Kerry tells Carol to think like a med student, not a nurse, but Carol isn't a student yet. Later, Carol tells Doug she is unsure why she should stop doing a job she is good at. That night, she joins the nurses for beer and pool.

Mark shows his capacity for innovative thinking

Rachel is annoyed when Mark forgets he is to talk to her Brownie troop. During the day, he treats "Mr and Mrs Smythe", one with a button up the nose, the other with a bucket stuck to her bottom. They claim to be studying innovative solutions in emergency medicine, but Mark and Nina are not taken in. Later, Mark shows Rachel's Brownie troop around the ER and Nina congratulates him on his creative problem-solving. They arrange to go bowling.

Carter refuses to sell out Dale after a blunder

Carter arrives unprepared for rounds and is "massacred" by Anspaugh's cross-examination. Later, he impresses Benton with an innovative suggestion but finds Anspaugh unwilling to let him scrub in. Nevertheless, Benton has to leave and Carter is handed the case. Carter has to fight to save the patient when the man has an allergic reaction to an antibiotic: Dale did not take a full case history.

Furious, Carter informs Anspaugh and tells Dale to prepare his alibi. Instead, Dale falsifies the patient's history. Maggie urges Carter to tell Anspaugh, but he resists. Maggie is dismayed. Later, Dale admits he screwed up and thanks Carter. Carter tells him that if he does this again, he will bury him.

Other threads

Jerry hears there is a $5,000 reward for Heidi, a genetically engineered mouse that has escaped from Dr Russell's lab. Wendy finds the rodent and drops a box on it, stunning it. Jeanie and Wendy resuscitate the mouse and decide to claim most of the reward for themselves.

Carla is frustrated that Peter is called away during the day to return to work. Jackie is pleased he is taking his responsibilities more seriously, but anxious that he has not planned days off in the future. That evening, when Peter needs to study, Carla accuses him of not wanting the baby. Peter is indignant and they argue.

"Random Acts"

3–20: First transmitted 1 May 1997
Written by Carol Flint; Directed by Jonathan Kaplan

Mark is brutally attacked in the ER

Chris Law (3-17) angrily confronts Mark over a hospital bill for $19,000 for treatment he believes was racist and negligent. He threatens to "kick some ass" if another bill is received – and will start with Mark. Doug recommends that Mark call security, but Mark thinks Chris was just blowing off steam.

Later, Mark goes to the restroom. As he washes his face, his head is grabbed and banged into the sink. He is pushed into a mirror then punched and kicked into a cubicle. Without his glasses, Mark can barely see. He tries to get up but is beaten again. The figure brutally stamps on his hand and runs. Mark collapses. Later, as Doug shows new starter Anna Del Amico around the ER, he finds Mark. After a frantic few moments, Mark is stabilised, but he doesn't know what happened.

Carter and Benton help a prestigious surgical team

Hicks invites Benton to scrub in with a prestigious team on a kidney transplant. Peter lands Carter a place on the donor team. The donor, Carl, claims to be giving his kidney to sister Jean in return for a stereo and jet ski! Carter promises Jean he will stay with Carl but during surgery he joins the transplant team.

He is horrified when Carl starts to bleed out and he can't rejoin the surgery. Carl is stabilised and Carter slinks away from the post-operative conference to talk to Jean. Benton is concerned that Carter abandoned the accomplished surgeons to attend to the patient. John wonders if that is a problem. Peter isn't sure.

Greg discovers that Jeanie and Al are close again

Jeanie and Al have grown closer. She has had a panic attack over her illness and Al empathises. Al reveals he has become resistant to some of his medication. Jeanie arranges for him to join Greg's trial at County. Greg discovers Al's relationship with Jeanie. He asks if she loves Al, but she doesn't know.

Other threads

Chuny, Carol and Jerry find a lurid romance novel set in the ER. Kerry is unimpressed to read the Weaver character (a bitch with a shrivelled limb) is in love with Dr "Martin Bean"! However, when Carol claims the seduction scene is really hot, Kerry appears proud of the writing!

Doug has taken up golf and tries to get Anspaugh to sponsor his application to Fair Oaks. Later, Carol is dismayed when Doug orders extra tests for the son of a railway tycoon, with sponsorship in mind. Nevertheless, the test reveal the boy has a sight disorder. Carol remarks that Doug is glib, she can't gauge what matters to him any more. Neither can he.

Carla is frustrated when Peter misses an appointment with Coburn. Later, he discovers that Carla has been admitted to prevent premature delivery. Carla is fine and they share a warm reflection on this time together.

"Make a Wish"

3 – 21: First transmitted 8 May 1997
Teleplay by Lydia Woodward; Story by Joe Sachs; Directed by Richard Thorpe

Carla and Peter's baby arrives two months premature

Carla enters labour two months early. Peter is a nuisance in the delivery room and is told simply to comfort Carla. New paediatrics/ER resident Anna Del Amico is called to assist Coburn with the vacuum extraction. The baby is born, but has to be intubated. In the Paediatric ICU, Dr Tabash explains that the boy's lungs are under-developed. Tabash asks the baby's name, but Peter admits he doesn't have one. Jeanie comforts Peter and urges him to speak to Carla.

Later, Tabash suggests an experimental treatment that runs the risk of mental retardation. Peter starts to explain the options to Carla, and tells her they must make a decision. Peter looks helplessly at his son in the PICU.

Mark returns to work

A week after the attack, Kerry is installing security measures when Mark returns to the ER. He is irritable and seems almost manic on the subject of watching patients. Maggie offers Mark some Mace but he refuses (Carter sprays it in his own eye). Mark is dismayed to hear the police can find no reason for the attack.

Mark confides in Kerry that he finds it difficult to accept that he was the victim of a random act of violence. Kerry insists doctors are just like anybody else, and capable of being victims too. Later, Nina asks after Mark, but he is curt with her. As his shift ends, Mark is jumpy when approached by a stranger.

Carter doubts his suitability as a surgeon

Carter is concerned that as a surgeon he does not know enough about his patients as individuals but Benton can't understand his dilemma. Carter treats Mr Lensky, a man with a perforated ulcer who is reluctant to have surgery. Carter discovers Lensky's father died during a straightforward procedure. Kerry suggests a non-operative solution. Carter presents the option to Anspaugh but is told that Lensky must have surgery – the patient's desires are secondary. Angry, Carter notes, "I don't believe I should cut somebody open just because I can." Anspaugh is disappointed that Carter would put his patient at risk rather than operate. Later, Carter sounds Kerry out on changing speciality to emergency medicine.

Other threads

It is Carol's birthday and Doug threatens a surprise party. Carol is dismayed but he reveals he has got her out of it by taking her to dinner. During the day, Carol and Doug work well together placating Russell, an agitated boy with a fractured wrist. Their shift over, Doug takes Carol home so she can change for dinner. She is surprised to find a party for her in her house. Carol insists she hates Doug for it but he is smug, flushed with success. Carol is called on to make a wish and blow out the candles. She looks at Doug before blowing them all out.

One to Watch

"One More for the Road"

3 – 22: First transmitted 15 May 1997
Written by John Wells; Directed by Christopher Chulack

Carter decides to change specialities

Carter talks to Anspaugh about changing from surgery to emergency medicine but gets a

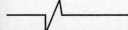

hostile reception. He tries to enlist Mark's support, but Mark suggests Kerry's opinions carry more weight with Anspaugh. Kerry, however, is concerned that they can't pay Carter's salary. He offers to work free of charge for a year. Kerry agrees to approach Anspaugh, but he is unbending.

Meanwhile, Carter and Jeanie look after Burt Kromey, an old man who needs to be put into a care home. When Carter talks to a range of advisors about Kromey's long-term care, Anspaugh criticises him for failing to serve as a surgical consult to the ER. Anspaugh is again angry when Carter tries to find the Kromeys a couple's room at a home, neglecting his rounds. Carter snaps and shouts that he will do his rounds if and when he can. The ER staff stand in stunned silence.

Later, Carter tells Anspaugh that he will make a better doctor than a surgeon. Carter believes he can make a real difference in the ER and asks Anspaugh to support him in that. Anspaugh has had his own doubts about becoming a surgeon over the years and is surprised by Carter's apparent certainty. He asks about the Kromeys and Carter reveals he has been successful. Anspaugh tells Carter to find him the next day and they will arrange matters.

Mark struggles to come to terms with his assault
The aftereffects of the attack are playing heavily on Mark Greene. After a sleepless night, he spends much of his day returning to the scene of the attack. Chicago PD bring photographs of suspects but Mark can't remember anything with certainty. Concerned, the detectives offer a list of help groups, but Mark insists he is fine. When they have gone, Mark injures himself. Doug offers help, but Mark is dismissive. On his way home, Mark is menaced by a gang of youths. As they follow him off the train, Mark pulls a gun on them. As they run, Mark becomes acutely aware of his actions. He runs panicked along a bridge and throws the gun in the water.

Doug is preoccupied with Carol's social life
Anna has a run-in with Doug Ross when she discovers he cancelled many of her tests and discharged one of her patients. Doug, however, is more interested in Carol's mysterious date that evening. Later, a girl is brought to the ER suffering from an overdose. Anna is irked when Carol insists that Doug is called.

Carol reveals the girl is Charlie. Doug stabilises Charlie but she is taking harder drugs and runs when he intends to call a social worker. Anna and Doug chase after Charlie, whom Anna reckons reminds her of herself, but cannot find her. Anna realises that Doug is thinking about Carol. He leaves to find Carol at her home. Carol is surprised to see him, but they soon fall into a passionate kiss.

Other threads
Weaver notes that Al and Jeanie are back together. Jeanie admits she doesn't entirely know how it happened but confirms that she is happy. Kerry asks if that is because of Al. Jeanie insists it is because of her: "I'm not afraid any more," she explains.

Benton is preoccupied during the day and surprises Hicks when he leaves the OR during surgery. Tabash reveals that oxygen starvation may have resulted in brain damage for the boy. Later, Jackie finds Peter in the Hospital Chapel, worried that he can't cope with being a father. He surprises Jackie when he admits that he misses their father. That evening, he rocks his son to sleep as Carla watches.

Again a season finale makes the Ones to Watch list, and for good reason. Carter's battle with Anspaugh, building slowly over the previous episodes, flares up into a startling argument. There is a real feeling that Carter's job is on the line and he could be out of a job. However, one can't help but suspect that Anspaugh's role was originally written for Peter Benton and that a change was needed to accommodate the pregnancy plot. Whatever the case, it is a wonderful chance to see John Aylward in action as the hospital's Chief of Staff. Also, we finally get the payoff to three years of Doug-Carol romance. What's more, it feels right, coming as it does after Doug's fall and rise.

Season Four
1997-8

Themes

When Morgenstern is taken ill, Kerry takes over as interim Chief of Emergency Medicine. She runs into budget problems and enthusiastically supports a team of consultants only to retracts her support later. Kerry also has difficulties with Doug Ross as they both vie for promotion.

Visiting British surgeon Elizabeth Corday finds the professional becomes the personal with Peter Benton. She finds a more unwanted romantic interest coming from another direction. Meanwhile, Elizabeth feels guilty over her treatment of one patient and becomes her personal advocate.

Doug comes through the death of his father more committed to Carol and his career. He garners support for a paediatrics attending position in the ER from Mark, but faces stiff criticism from Kerry. Doug betrays them both when he puts a "crack baby" on a course of rapid detoxification.

Carol begins a clinic in the ER and drums up support from the Carter family. She is also involved in treating the victims of a serial rapist. Meanwhile, her relationship with Doug stalls when she gets cold feet.

Mark struggles through the emotional effects of his assault as he fights the legal case against him. He is forced to face his difficult relationship with his father when his mother is taken ill.

Carter finds his family background causes difficulties as he tries to get closer to Anna Del Amico. He also tackles family issues when his cousin Chase starts fighting his heroin addiction. Anna and Carter grow closer while helping Chase.

Jeanie and Al both suffer the social effects of their HIV status when they lose their jobs. As Jeanie fights for reinstatement, Al gets the chance of a new life in Atlanta. Meanwhile, Jeanie finds support from an unexpected quarter when her immunity deteriorates.

Ones to Watch

4 – 7: *Fathers and Sons* – Doug hears of his father's death and is forced to assess their relationship. Mark is also drawn into considering his problems with his father.

4 – 13: *Carter's Choice* – The serial rapist is found and Carter makes a moral decision in deciding treatment.

4 – 15: *Exodus* – Carter takes the helm when the ER is inundated with mass casualties from a chemical accident.

"Ambush"

4 – 1: First transmitted 25 September 1997
Written by Carol Flint; Directed by Thomas Schlamme

Life in the ER is caught on film

A PBS camera crew has been given exclusive access to County General to make a documentary about the difficulties facing the ER. Benton has been working in the ER for 36 hours to cover staff shortages, notably Carter's move into emergency medicine. Anna Del Amico is particularly resistant to being filmed, but eventually gives consent.

Mark and Doug are unwittingly caught on film as they object to the presence of the film-makers. Doug suggests that Mark's agreement to be filmed is a sign he is recovering from his assault. The film crew probe deeper but Mark refuses to let them present him as a victim.

The crew get plenty of stories during the day. Boz, a 37-year-old cancer patient, is brought to County in respiratory distress. The man is unable to speak and Mark has to intubate. Later, Boz's wife arrives and explains that Boz is a DNR. Mark disagrees with Jeanie's diagnosis of one patient, but is proven wrong when they receive the test results. A teenager called Chico is brought in with injuries from a gang beating. Theo Williams, who interceded, was pushed from a wall and is paralysed.

Meanwhile, Carter is now working full time in the ER. The change has caused difficulties however, not least with Benton who is terse with Carter throughout the day.

Carter is also troubled when Kerry tells him he must resit his internship for abandoning his speciality. Worse still, when Carter is finally interviewed on camera, he is interrupted by a vomiting patient!

Later, Carter treats George, an 82-year-old from a nursing home. George arrests and Carter tries to save him, without requesting extra help. The man dies and the incident is caught on camera. Carter is mortified but Mark offers to give an interview so that the crew don't use the footage of Carter.

Despite allowing the PBS crew to film, Morgenstern looks equally uneasy before the cameras. His flushed appearance soon gives way to chest pains: he is in the early stages of a heart attack. As Weaver quickly takes action, the director wonders if there is one service for doctors and one for patients. Kerry abruptly disagrees.

Finally, Mark stands for interview. He admits that he was assaulted. For Mark, the world's violence has leaked into the ER and he finds it difficult to accept. Reflecting on recent days, Mark admits he is scared of losing control of himself.

Other threads

While Benton deals with the two gang beatings, he is introduced to Dr Elizabeth Corday, a visiting surgical lecturer from England. He is relieved when she takes on some of his workload.

The film crew ask Carol about relationships between staff. Carol insists the old doctor-nurse cliché is an exaggeration – but is later caught on microphone covertly talking to Doug about their relationship!

"Something New"

4 – 2: First transmitted 2 October 1997
Written by Lydia Woodward; Directed by Christopher Chulack

Mark Greene starts behaving erratically

Mark is increasingly tetchy. His mood is not helped by news that the Law family are suing the hospital. Mark objects to tests Carter runs on a drunk, but Carter has correctly diagnosed multiple sclerosis. Mark is also cold with Heather Morgan. Later, Mark and Carol interview for a new desk clerk. Mark is distracted and seems happy to hire a persistent liar. Carol is irked and tells Kerry they should re-advertise the post. Mark is annoyed and immediately offers the job to Cynthia Hooper, a particularly unpromising candidate, when she apologises for giving a bad interview. Carol is further annoyed when Mark "treats and streets" a young girl who has bulimia.

Carter finds his status in the hospital is in question

Carter's good mood is curtailed when he is told to run all procedures past Maggie, who is now more senior. Meanwhile, Carter gets his new student, George Henry, an academic with little practical training. Carter gives Henry a few unpleasant procedures to warm him up. However, Henry proves his worth when he identifies a rare brain disease he has been studying! Later, Henry goes missing and Carter finds him in the labs – where he accidentally irradiates his shoes. Carter is momentarily cheered when he receives a pay cheque. However, the hospital has taken up his offer to work for free and the cheque is an administrative error.

Peter welcomes Reese Benton and Elizabeth Corday

Peter and Carla's baby starts to breathe on his own. Now out of danger, Carla and Peter discuss giving their son a name but disagree over the surname. In the end, they compromise on Reese Benton. During the day, Peter gives Corday the tour. In the OR, Peter realises he has underestimated his new colleague. He is also surprised by her bluntness when she tells a distinguished surgeon he is "remarkably short".

Other threads

Jeanie treats 79-year-old Estelle Webb, who claims her sister pushed her down the stairs. A social worker discovers Estelle's sister died in 1984. Meanwhile, Al is hiding his HIV status at work and is running out of excuses to attend the clinic.

Kerry goes to see Morgenstern, who is high on morphine. David suggests that she fill in for him. Mark is taken aback when Kerry later announces she is Acting Chief of Emergency Medicine.

Carol wakes thinking that Doug has left, but he is making breakfast. She is taken aback when he asks if he can have a drawer to store his things.

Doug annoys Anna by telling her to see more adult cases. He takes over her paediatrics case but fails to spot whooping cough. The boy starts to vomit blood but is stabilised. Doug angrily tells Anna she should have told him she suspected the illness. Anna insists that the boy was her patient.

"Friendly Fire"

4 – 3: First transmitted 9 October 1997
Written by Walon Green; Directed by Felix Enriquez Alcalá

Jerry wrecks Weaver's cost-cutting measures

With the ER running at $1.7 million over last year's budget, acting chief Kerry Weaver devises a plan to restore the balance in six months. Anspaugh is impressed and notes that some would prefer to see her take over the post permanently. He agrees to evaluate her position when Morgenstern returns.

Kerry soon starts to irritate staff when she makes changes to the nurse's clocking-out routine. Next, she tells Doug Ross that his paediatric fellowship will no longer come out of the ER budget and he should find other funding. However, Jerry incurs extra expense when he sets off a Texan's grenade launcher and destroys the ambulance bay! Jerry soon finds himself doing the night shift.

The ER staff deal with an accident at Al's construction site

Al and fellow builder Billy Nelson are injured at work and brought to the ER. Jeanie convinces Al to tell Billy about his HIV status, but Billy reacts badly. Meanwhile, Carol treats Casey, a co-worker who heroically grabbed a cable to keep it from hitting Al and

Billy. The employer is intent on an insurance fraud that, if found out, would lose any benefits for his workers. Carol defends Casey to his employer, but later discovers that Casey was smoking marijuana and caused the accident.

Mark has a day of mistakes

Mark and Carter treat Kirsten, a 27-year-old who has had a stroke and has swelling at the brain stem. They conclude she will never regain consciousness. Carter approaches the husband about organ donation, but is surprised when Kirsten wakes. However, Kirsten has an aneurysm and needs immediate surgery. Given the earlier confusion, the husband is unwilling to consent but later relents.

Meanwhile, a young bulimic girl (4-2) returns to the ER suffering from related illnesses. Doyle is angry that Mark missed the diagnosis, but Carol insists there should be a safety net for these patients. Later, Mark goes on a date with Heather. He is embarrassed to find he is impotent.

Other threads

Carla wants to have Reese circumcised but Peter objects. Instead, Carla approaches an unwitting Anna to perform the procedure. Peter confronts Carla but it is too late. Meanwhile, Peter warms to Corday when she takes on "old tosser" Anspaugh.

Carter is annoyed when Maggie gives his trauma patient to Anna. Suspecting Maggie is after Anna, Carter quickly makes his move and asks Anna out. Their date ends up in a farcical attempt to do Carter's laundry.

Carol is present when Corday asks Doug out. She leaves before she can hear him refuse. Later, Carol apologetically admits she is still unable to trust Doug fully.

"When the Bough Breaks"

4 – 4: First transmitted 16 October 1997
Written by Jack Orman; Directed by Richard Thorpe

Carter confronts Benton over their career choices

Carter throws himself into his internship but finds Benton causing difficulties. Carter treats a motorcyclist who was fleeing police and caused a school bus crash. Benton tells Carter not to call a consult, but the man crashes and Benton is paged. Peter angrily berates Carter as he takes the man to the OR. Irked, Carter tells Anna, who persuades him to confront Benton.

Benton is angry that Carter wasted three years of his tuition and changed speciality without talking to him. Carter feared Peter would change his mind and just wants Benton's respect. Bitter, Peter tells Carter: "You don't want to be treated like my student, stop seeking my approval."

Carol helps deliver a "crack baby"

Carol treats the injured schoolchildren. One girl's arm is hanging off. Another child dies. Carol notices blood leading to the women's bathroom. Inside, she finds Doris, a heroin

addict (4-1) who is in labour. She gives birth but the baby is seriously ill and dies. Doris accuses Carol of dropping her baby and demands a lawyer.

Carol is incredulous when Mark, who was not in the room at the time, can't confirm or deny Doris' accusation. Later, Carol discovers that Mark saw Doris previously and refuses to cover for him. Mark believes they can't help people who can't help themselves. Defiant, Carol insists those are precisely the people they should help.

Jeanie breaks her terms of working in the ER

Al has been sacked from his job and fears he will not get work in Chicago now that his HIV status is known. Jeanie, meanwhile, helps an old man with a collapsed lung. She calls for a doctor but no one arrives. Frantic, she decides to insert a chest tube and breaks her terms of work by reaching into the cavity. Kerry arrives and angrily tells Jeanie to stop. Jeanie checks her hands but she is not bleeding. Later, Jeanie agrees she doesn't want the situation to happen again.

Other threads

Reese is collected by Carla and discharged. Corday oversees, but Peter seems uncomfortable that she knows. During the day, Peter tries frantic efforts to save a "crack baby" but fails. Churned up, he calls Carla and asks after Reese. That evening, Corday covers for Peter so he can see Reese again.

Jen is worried that Mark's moods are having an effect on Rachel and wants to keep her away from him. Mark is more irritable at work and has several spats with Carol. Later, he treats a man who thinks he is an angel and reckons Cynthia is attracted to Mark. After consideration, Mark offers Cynthia a ride home.

Anna treats a young patient whose grandmother insists on seeing Doug. Doug angrily confronts Anna, who later wonders how Carol managed to date him! Meanwhile, Kerry encourages Doug to undertake research work to fund his post.

"Good Touch, Bad Touch"

4 – 5: First transmitted 30 October 1997
Written by David Mills; Directed by Jonathan Kaplan

Mark gives a deposition in the Kenny Law case

It is the day of Mark's deposition in the Kenny Law case. He is short with Benton when asked about parenting and coldly deals with an elderly woman who takes a fancy to him. Mark also deliberately hurts a violent patient until the man agrees to settle down. Cynthia tries to reassure Mark but to no avail. At the deposition, the presence of Chris Law (3-17) and references to the Jodi O'Brien case (1-18) throw Mark. As he becomes angrier, Mark rashly accuses Chris Law of being his attacker.

Carter has second thoughts about leaving surgery

Dale Edson is covering the ER. Amid jibes at Carter's expense, Dale notes that surgeon Robert "Rocket" Romano is letting him scrub in. Later, Carter is dismayed when he makes an excellent save only to watch his patient being taken to the OR by Dale and Romano. Kerry is impressed by Carter's skill, but he wonders if he made the right choice in leaving surgery. Carter is further put out when he sees Edson talking to the patient's wife, and receiving all the attention and thanks. Benton assures Carter that he is twice the surgeon Dale will ever be.

Family life causes difficulties for Benton

Peter is trying to study for a surgery with Anspaugh but is interrupted by Reese. In the OR, he is ill-prepared and Anspaugh angrily tells him to scrub out and catch up on his paperwork. Later, Corday finds Peter asleep on his files. Romano is sponsoring her placement and she could get him a place on Romano's team. Under pressure at home, Benton is not interested.

Later, Peter apologises to Anspaugh but finds Donald is still critical. Anspaugh insists that Corday has raised the standard for surgical residents and risks making them all look bad. Later, Elizabeth introduces Peter to Romano. Romano takes an instant liking to Peter, although his remarks about Chris Rock leave Peter distinctly cold.

Other threads

Carol proposes operating a clinic in the ER to help those patients the system usually fails. Although the project would use volunteers, Kerry fears the clinic would disrupt the nurses. However, she later gives Carol information on finding funds and hopes Carol will press ahead with her idea. Carter suggests the Carter Family Foundation, run by his grandmother, Millicent. Carol decides to approach her.

Anna treats a college athlete who is short of breath. She discovers potential testicular cancer has spread to the lungs and needs to perform a physical. Doug offers but Anna quickly refuses. She is embarrassed when the student gets an erection. Anna is anxious when the student goes missing, but he later returns to finish the examination.

While out drinking, Jeanie and Al are jeered by Billy Nelson (4-3). A fight soon breaks out. Jeanie watches on distraught as Al violently attacks Billy.

"Ground Zero"

4 – 6: First transmitted 6 November 1997
Written by Samantha Howard Corbin; Directed by Darnell Martin

Carol tries to raise funds for her clinic

Carol anxiously prepares her presentation to Millicent Carter for her proposed clinic. Carter hints that "Gamma" loves facts and figures but warns Carol to avoid politics, religion and baseball! Meanwhile, Carter rescues Anna from her cockroach-infested apartment and offers to take her to dinner. She agrees, but Carter later has to cancel, claiming "something came up".

Anna is surprised to hear from Carol that Carter is "real blue blood" and decides to accompany Carol that evening. On arrival at the Carter mansion (and under a portrait of Carter on his prize-winning show horse Marigold), Anna accuses Carter of patronising her.

Although he apologises, Anna is clearly irked. Meanwhile, Millicent is impressed by Carol and offers her $75,000 to start up the clinic.

Benton and Corday become more competitive

Arriving at County, Benton is annoyed to discover that Dr Hicks' schedule has changed and Corday took his gastroplasty. Benton suggests Elizabeth took advantage of his personal circumstances to pick her own surgery, but Corday adamantly insists this is not true and gives him one of hers. Later, he is irked to discover he is missing cutting-edge surgery with Romano that is being televised!

Bitter, Peter suggests that Corday perform an appendectomy and she gets into trouble with Anspaugh. Corday angrily insists she has no agenda, but Peter is disbelieving. Peter asks Romano for a space on his surgical team.

Mark's erratic behaviour reaches a peak

Mark is pleased when the hospital settles out of court with the Law family. However, he is then served directly with a suit for violating Kenny Law's human rights. Mark is short with Doug when he offers help. Carol decides to investigate issues of post-traumatic stress. Meanwhile, Mark presumes an allergy patient is a psych patient and refuses treatment, putting him in severe risk.

Later, he shouts to a hard of hearing woman that her husband will die. The ER falls silent. Doug quickly intervenes, but Mark is already making for the door. Cynthia races after him; he admits he is losing control. Later, Doug visits Mark's apartment. Mark is ready to apologise but sees Ross is upset. Doug's father died in a car crash. Mark decides to take holiday time to make the funeral arrangements with Doug.

Other threads

Anspaugh has hired the Synergix Physicians Group (SPG) to look into the ER's finances. Weaver is irked at the implication and attends the SPG presentation where she asks the speaker, Dr Ellis West, some difficult questions. Nevertheless, West is taken with Kerry and invites her to dinner. Weaver confides she will have to sack eight assistants including Jeanie. West offers advice, but the encounter still goes badly and Jeanie is upset.

Jeanie returns home to find her house filled with candles – Al has found a job in Atlanta and asks her to come with him.

One to Watch

"Fathers and Sons"

4‑7: First transmitted 13 November 1997
Written by John Wells; Directed by Christopher Chulack

Doug and Mark deal with family issues

Mark and Doug drive through the desert to Barstow to identify the body of Ray Ross. Doug discovers that Ray was four times over the legal alcohol limit when he ran a stop sign, killing himself, his girlfriend Sheri Fox and Pedro Lopez, a father of six. Doug is disgusted that his father caused the death of others.

Mark and Doug arrive at Ray's motel. The landlady recognises Doug from Ray's description – he often talked about Doug. Sorting through Ray's belongings, Doug discovers photographs and movie reels from his childhood. He also finds Ray's Cadillac outside – Ray crashed Sheri's car in the accident – and decides to take it for a ride. Doug learnt to drive in the Cadillac and remembers Ray always reappearing in it. The car runs out of petrol and they are stranded. They look in the boot but find only toys belonging to Sheri's child – Ray had another son.

Doug and Mark sleep in the Cadillac and are picked up by a truck driver the next morning. Doug decides to attend the funeral service for Pedro Lopez, and to speak to the family. However, the sight of Lopez's bewildered sons is too much and Doug can't think of anything to say. Later, they head to a pawnbrokers and recover Ray's movie projector, rings and Rolex watch. Doug asks for Ray's wedding ring but is told Ray would not pawn it. In the store, Mark buys a cheap necklace for Cynthia.

Mark walks into Doug's room to hear him leaving a message for his girlfriend. Mark wants to know who she is. Doug reluctantly reveals it is Carol. Mark is astonished, especially when Doug admits he loves her.

Later, they watch Ray's home movies. Doug is still bitter that Ray caused such havoc in his life and that of his mother. However, Doug is taken aback to see the movies showing Ray as a doting parent. Mark reveals that his parents barely talk. When Doug realises they live only four hours away in San Diego, he is determined to take Mark to see them.

In San Diego, Mark is greeted excitedly by his mother but finds talking with his father considerably more difficult. Mark's father has emphysema and needs oxygen while his mother is on pills for high blood pressure. Mark tells his mother that he believes his father cares little for him or Rachel. Mrs Greene insists he is wrong and that Mark assumes he knows more than he does.

Doug returns from informing Sheri's family of her death and Mark tells him he didn't miss much by not having a father. Doug is offended and they argue. Doug insists that Mark's father was always there – and that Mark should grow up.

Doug and Mark drive back to Barstow. Mark reflects that he has changed since his assault. He has been acting like a victim; he always wanted to control his life but couldn't. He is unsure who is replacing the old Mark. Arriving at the motel, Doug is pleased to find Carol waiting for him.

The next morning, Mark and Carol join Doug as he scatters his father's ashes in the desert. Doug reflects that he both loved and hated his father. They drink a glass of tequila in Ray's memory.

Fathers and Sons is the first episode to take the ER out of *ER*, but it does it wonderfully well. It's a testament to the quality of the characters of Mark Greene and Doug Ross that the episode hangs together without the familiar tension of the trauma room. Ultimately it's a very clever piece of scripting, moving seamlessly from Doug's story to Mark's and bringing to a head Mark's erratic behaviour.

There are also some landmark events: we get Doug and Carol going semi-public; we put an end to Ray's influence and we are introduced to Mark's father, David, who becomes a bigger character in the sixth season. If *Fathers and Sons* has a fault, it's that it has spawned so many less successful attempts to do the same, notably Season Eight's *Secret and Lies*. Nevertheless, here we have a well-crafted episode, as one would expected from series veteran John Wells.

"Freak Show"

4 – 8: First transmitted 20 November 1997
Written by Neal Baer; Directed by Darnell Martin

Maggie urges Jeanie to fight her redundancy

Maggie believes Jeanie has been sacked because of her HIV status and urges her to fight the decision on the grounds of discrimination. Jeanie is unsure, but reacts bitterly when Kerry tells her she has forwarded a glowing reference to Atlanta Memorial Hospital. Jeanie is also annoyed when she hears Al's job has fallen through and that Kerry has given herself a $25,000 pay increase and hired a new nurse, Yosh Tokada. Resolved, Jeanie claims discrimination before Anspaugh. Weaver objects, but Anspaugh offers to reconsider Jeanie's dismissal.

Benton and Corday are forced to work together

Having heard about Peter's difficulties with Corday, Romano refuses to give Benton a place on his team. However, when a boy with a rare genetic condition requires surgery, Romano reckons it is the perfect chance to show Peter and Elizabeth can work together. The surgery is successful.

Afterwards, Peter discovers that the boy's father, Isaac Price, is an old school friend. Elizabeth believes this will make it easier for the hospital to obtain blood samples for research, but Peter is reluctant to use the boy as a test subject. Eventually, however, he relents and obtains consent from Isaac on the pretext that it will help the boy's treatment.

Suddenly, the boy suffers post-operative problems and dies. Isaac discovers Peter lied and refuses an autopsy. Romano angrily orders Peter to obtain consent, but Peter refuses. Despite this, Romano is impressed and lets Peter join his team.

Mark treats a thrill-seeking attorney

Mark treats Herb Speevak, a lawyer who has been bitten by Flora, a python who ate his neighbour's dog. Herb would rather pursue unusual pastimes than his line of work. He overhears Mark's problems in the Kenny Law case and offers his services. Mark is sure he can't afford Herb's fee but Herb offers a solution – if Mark allows him to perform a few procedures, Herb will make the Law family suit disappear…

Other threads

Mark hands Carol a note addressed to 'CH' from Doug. She puts it behind the reception desk to read later. However, Cynthia Hooper reads it, thinking it is from Mark to her, and they later get to act the fantasy out.

Anna is still frosty with Carter for lying about his background. Meanwhile, George Henry returns to resit his ER rotation after Carter was unable to assess his performance. Henry complains about his allergies and later collapses: he is allergic to the latex gloves. Anna and Carter save Henry, who later claims to have had an out-of-body experience.

Kerry is told she has left her car lights on. Outside, she finds Ellis West waiting with a bouquet of flowers. He thanks her for Synergix winning the ER contract.

"Obstruction of Justice"

4 – 9: First transmitted 11 December 1997
Written by Lance A. Gentile; Directed by Richard Thorpe

Carter is arrested for obstruction of justice

Carter's cousin, Chase, arrives in the ER with a spider bite. Chase insists that their grandfather wants John to succeed him only if he gives up medicine. Carter refuses. Later, Carter treats a police officer who was run down by his wife. The wife has since taken a drugs overdose. Carter is annoyed when the police try to frame the wife. He refuses to provide tissue samples without a warrant and takes the chance to destroy them. Carter is arrested and taken to the station – while the husband and wife repair their differences and make out in the ER! Anna pays Carter's bail, ruefully noting the irony.

Jeanie is reinstated

Kerry is surprised when Jeanie arrives at work, refusing to accept her dismissal. Jeanie has prepared her defence with lawyer friends of Maggie Doyle and accuses Kerry of reacting to Jeanie's breach of her working conditions (4-4). Kerry tells West, who suggests she present at a conference in the Caribbean and get away from it all.

Meanwhile, Jeanie and her attorney speak to Anspaugh and Jeanie is reinstated. Kerry angrily accuses Jeanie of using her condition for her benefit, but Jeanie is convinced Kerry was in the wrong. Jeanie tells Al the good news – but he announces that he has got a job in Atlanta after all. He is leaving that night.

Corday's lust for surgery endangers a patient

The ER staff treat a mother and daughter involved in a car accident. The mother dies while the daughter, Allison, must have her leg amputated. Benton agrees with the diagnosis but Corday and Romano are determined to try a fibula transplant to save the leg. During the surgery, Allison crashes. Corday is momentarily phased and Benton takes over. They stabilise Allison, but she is in a coma. Guilty, Corday wonders if she operated for the challenge rather than for the patient's wellbeing. Benton admits to the same thoughts sometimes.

Other threads

Mark allows Herb (4-8) to shadow him, but soon finds the attorney mistaken for a member of Ellis West's staff and giving out advice! Mark tries to keep Herb under control but the man uses the paddles on a patient. Later, Herb tells Mark that he has got the Law family to drop the case. Mark lets him keep his scrubs!

A young man with sickle cell anaemia arrives in the ER requesting Demerol. Weaver suspects he is an addict and streets him. However, the man later returns to the ER and Doug prescribes the Demerol, to Kerry's disgust.

Mark admits that he is having difficulty keeping up with the racy Cynthia. He leaves Rachel in Cynthia's care during the day. However, when Jen arrives, she and Mark are taken aback to find Rachel in heavy make-up and with purple hair.

"Do You See What I See?"

4 – 10: First transmitted 18 December 1997
Teleplay by Jack Orman; Story by Linda Gase; Directed by Sarah Pia Anderson

Benton discovers he can cure by laying on hands

Christmas Eve 1997. Benton and Anna treat Bart, a homeless blind man who was the victim of a hit and run. Benton is surprised when he restores Bart's sight by touching his forehead! Anna can find no explanation – and Peter later seems to help a janitor by patting him on the shoulder! News soon spreads and Bart's friends arrive in droves asking for Benton to lay his hands on them.

Later, Bart returns after losing his sight. Peter discovers that Bart has a terminal brain tumour that caused the momentary return of sight. Bart, however, is happy that he got to see one last time.

The Kenny Law case is brought to an end

Mark is told to sign a few papers and put the Kenny Law case behind him. Later, he and Carol treat a woman who has "whore" written on her stomach – she has been raped. As Mark and Carol examine her, the woman describes her brutal assault. It is too much for Mark. Afterwards, she tells Mark that she hates her attacker but knows that won't solve anything.

That evening, Mark visits Chris Law and apologises. Chris did not attack Mark but admits he was pleased to hear about the assault. However, he knows hating Mark will not bring Kenny back.

Elizabeth operates on Allison Beaumont a second time

Elizabeth is about to fly to England for the holidays when Romano decides to perform a second operation on Allison Beaumont (4-9). Corday feels guilty but agrees to help. Later, Allison wakes from her coma. Corday tells her that her mother died in the car accident.

She also discovers that Allison's vocal cords were damaged in the accident and calls a head and neck specialist. That night, Corday stays at Allison's side, rather than return home.

Other threads

Weaver chastises Jeanie when she gives needles to a man with hepatitis. Jeanie is indignant but later has to ask Kerry for HIV medication that she has forgotten to take. Kerry provides the medication without hesitation. Jeanie thanks her.

Henry needs to perform a procedure to pass his rotation. Keen to be rid of him, Carter lets Henry intubate a deceased patient. The relatives arrive and they pretend to be trying to help him! Later, Henry and Carter break the news to the family. Henry adds that the man's last words were for Maria – but the wife's name is Angela!

Carol nervously expects a visit from her benefactor, Millicent Carter. Millicent arrives to find Carol putting out a Christmas tree that caught fire! Millicent ominously insists she has seen all she needs to – then gives Carol a new Christmas tree and $150,000! Meanwhile, Carter finds Chase using heroin, but agrees to say nothing.

Carol and Doug announce their relationship to the staff – but they merely divide up their bets! Doug proposes to Carol – and she accepts.

"Think Warm Thoughts"

4 – 11: First transmitted 8 January 1998
Written by David Mills; Directed by Charles Haid

Jeanie takes care of Anspaugh's son, Scott

Anspaugh asks Mark to look after his 13-year-old son, Scott, who has abdominal pain. Donald explains that Scott was treated for cancer ten months previously, but fears it has returned. Scott has a sister but his mother died last year from cancer.

Mark enlists Jeanie's help but Scott is testy with them and resents their tests. He refuses to let Jeanie take a blood sample, but she slowly wins him over, talking about John Woo films. Jeanie is saddened to find Scott is used to the tests and is well aware his tumour may be back. Tests confirm that he is right. Anspaugh is impressed with the way Jeanie handles Scott and thanks her for her help.

Elizabeth arranges neck surgery for Allison Beaumont

Allison Beaumont (4-9) wants an operation to repair her vocal cords but they need to operate on her leg first. Despite this, Corday asks Romano to allow vocal cord surgery but is told that Allison's insurance will not cover it. Corday visits Dr Kotlowitz, a throat specialist, and persuades him to operate on Allison free of charge. Romano is angry that Corday evidently questions his commitment to Allison's care and threatens to pull the operation. Later, he allows it to be scheduled. Corday hopes she and Romano are still on good terms. Robert insincerely remarks that they are "a match made in heaven".

Carter tries to interest prospective students in ER rotations

Carter and Benton are asked to present to second-year medical students on their choice of rotation. The students, however, seem more interested in items retrieved from rectums! One student, Laura Brown, is interested in both surgery and emergency medicine – and asks Carter to dinner. On their way to a restaurant, they find a man in the snow. Carter discovers that the man was simply drunk – but discovers Laura has already taken a greater interest in Peter's gory surgery next door.

Other threads

Doug wants to set the wedding date, but Carol is hesitant. She is irked when her mother says Doug asked her if he could marry Carol. Fuming, Carol makes Doug work in the clinic on his day off to make amends.

Ellis West is concerned that SPG has had little impact at County and that this is set to worsen. Kerry is convinced she or Ellis can win over Anspaugh. Anspaugh is reticent but by the end of the day SPG still have the contract. Weaver and West celebrate.

An elderly woman, Mrs Riley, is brought to the ER by her "meals on wheels" lady. Mrs Riley is forgetful and dehydrated. As she changes into a gown, Carol sees the word "whore" written on her back. She calls the police. Mark reckons Mrs Riley's amnesia is a blessing but the memory of the attack slowly returns...

"Sharp Relief"

4 – 12: First transmitted 15 January 1998
Written by Samantha Howard Corbin; Directed by Christopher Chulack

Carter helps Chase deal with his heroin withdrawal

Chase stopped taking heroin two days ago and is suffering from withdrawal. John offers to help but realises Chase is drug-seeking. They argue and Chase leaves. Anna empathises: she had a friend at med school with a drug problem. Carter is short with her. During the day, Chase repeatedly telephones the ER.

Eventually, John goes to Chase and finds him at breaking point. He makes a call and Anna arrives with some medication to help ease the effects of withdrawal. Anna explains her friend was actually her boyfriend: "I've done the detox dance more times than I can count." Carter is grateful that she has come to help.

Carol has second thoughts about Doug

While Carol is on a ride-along with Doris Pickman and Greg Powell, Doug prepares a surprise wedding just after midnight. Doug tells Mark that Carol is the only woman he has ever felt right with. Meanwhile, Unit 57 finds the latest victim of the serial rapist. Carol rushes her back to the ER but Mark is unable to save her.

Carol and Greg return to the old woman's apartment. Greg reveals he was reminded of when he found his mother after she committed suicide. Carol reveals her own suicide attempt. They kiss. Confused, Carol walks home to think through her day. She arrives late to find Doug frantic. Carol fears they are rushing into things, and admits she kissed Greg. Furious, Doug storms out.

Jeanie is asked to care for Scott Anspaugh

Scott Anspaugh undergoes surgery – the cancer has returned. Afterwards, Jeanie tells Scott, who acts nonplussed. She is able to get through to him by suggesting they go to a hockey game. Anspaugh tells Jeanie that Scott needs chemotherapy and asks her to be Scott's part-time caregiver. Both he and Scott think highly of her. Jeanie readily agrees and stays with Scott.

Other threads

Kerry hears another Chicago ER has been closed and patients are coming to County. The culprit is SPG, which has closed 60 per cent of its ERs in the Midwest. West tries to explain, but Kerry is unconvinced and delays the vote on SPG's takeover until she can enquire further. That night, Ellis tries to sweet-talk Kerry but she wants to do some thinking – about SPG *and* Ellis West.

Elizabeth rearranges her schedule so she can assist Dr Kotlowitz in repairing Allison Beaumont's vocal cords. The surgery is a success and Allison should regain her speech in a few weeks. After, she is able to whisper "thank you" to Elizabeth.

Pleased, Corday invites Benton for a drink at a British bar and teaches him how to play darts. They are still dancing, a little inebriated, when the bar calls last orders. They hesitate as they decide where to go next – but end up taking separate cabs home. Peter admits he enjoyed their evening together.

One to Watch

"Carter's Choice"

4 – 13: First transmitted 29 January 1998
Written and Directed by John Wells

Carter and Anna treat the serial rapist

6am. It is snowing and the forecasters predict three feet of snow later in the day. Carter arrives to find Anna sleeping in Exam Four. She wakes and asks after Chase. Carter says Chase is weak but walking around. They are interrupted when paramedics rush in with a security guard who was shot as he tried to stop the serial rapist from attacking another woman. The rapist is still at large.

The rapist's victim arrives next: she was thrown down some stairs and has a dislocated hip, but was not raped. The word "whore" was carved on her chest with a knife. The woman is stabilised but the security guard dies. "No good deed goes unpunished," remarks Greene acidly.

Soon, the police return with the rapist, Jack Miller, who has been shot and is bleeding badly. He is 19 years old. The nurses seem reluctant to help, and when Mark is called to another patient, Carter has to take over his care. Miller needs a blood transfusion, but County has only four units of O-negative left. Carter is reluctant to use the units on the rapist. Instead, he decides to perform an "auto-transfuse", a risky procedure in which the patient's own blood is used to replace that which he has lost. Anna objects but Carter presses on anyway. Miller survives, but Anna accuses Carter of withholding treatment. Carter is indignant, but later admits that he wanted the rapist to die. Anna comforts him.

Doug and Carol come to an agreement

Ross is angry when he sees Carol talking to Greg Powell in the ER. The irony is not lost on Carol, who notes the list of the times Doug did the same to her. However, Carol becomes emotional as she tells Doug she just needs more time. During the day, Carol helps a mentally challenged couple, Mary and Robert, who are having a baby. Mary fears that social services will take their baby away from them because they can't cope, but Carol reassures them. Once the baby is born, she teaches them some basic parenting skills. Doug joins them and apologises to Carol for pushing her. "Take all the time you need," he says – he will wait for her.

Kerry and Ellis part on bad terms

Anspaugh tells Kerry that the hospital board have acted on her recommendation and will let Synergix take over management of the ER. However, Kerry has changed her mind and wants to speak to the board. She enlists Mark's help. Meanwhile, West arrives, concerned that Kerry is withdrawing her support. He argues that if SPG don't get the contract he has wasted his time. Angry, Kerry accuses Ellis of using their personal relationship for his own ends. West is taken aback. Later, he withdraws the contract, telling Kerry he only wanted it so they could work together.

Other threads

Cynthia tells Mark that her tenancy has expired and her rent is going up. She hints that she could move in with Mark, but he misses the inference and offers to help her pay the increased rent. Doug finds Cynthia upset. She fears that Mark does not think she is good enough for him, or that he cares for her too deeply to admit. Doug can give no honest reply. Later, he tells Mark that he must talk to Cynthia.

Benton is worse for wear after his night out with Corday. She asks him to lunch and abruptly asks if he would like to take their relationship further. Embarrassed, Peter is uncomfortable with the idea but has clearly considered it. During the day, Carla arrives to collect paperwork from Peter to put Reese into daycare. Peter is reticent and has not yet made up his mind. He wants to see Reese and discovers Carla has left him in the care of her new boyfriend, Roger. Later, Peter waits for Corday to finish her shift. He suggests they go out to play darts tonight, but nothing more.

Again we see a darker side to John Carter, but his actions are clearly motivated. Carter's choice is a classic moral dilemma which, in the end, is neatly fudged – Carter risks his patient but the man survives. His confrontation with Anna is good to see, giving some flesh to the relationship that they could have had but sadly never did. It's a wonderfully meaty episode and one that clearly raised more possibilities than it explored – we get a longer replay in Corday's relationship with Dean Rawlins in Season Six.

"Family Practice"

4 – 14: First transmitted 5 February 1998
Written by Carol Flint; Directed by Charles Haid

Greene faces his difficulties with his father

Mark flies to San Diego to see his mother, Ruth, who has broken her leg in a fall. Cynthia also tags along, to Mark's discomfort. David Greene meets them and takes them to a Naval Medical Centre. Ruth is on morphine but acting more strangely than Mark would expect: uninhibited, singing and making unsuitable remarks. Mark suspects a head injury, but there appears to have been none. Ruth undergoes a scan and is disturbed by her own mental state. Mark comforts her. Dr Sayers suggests Ruth's dementia is the result of several small strokes. Mark asks for more tests and a second opinion from a civilian, but David is frustrated.

Concerned, Mark starts to smoke heavily. He is cold with Cynthia, preoccupied with his parents' ill-health and their marriage. Mark discovers that Ruth has been seeing a psychiatrist without David's knowledge. He tells David, who insists that Mark should return to Chicago and mind his own business. As they argue, David has an attack of emphysema. He, too, is admitted to the Naval Medical Centre.

As David recovers, he and Mark agree to hide the attack from Ruth. Meanwhile, Mark speaks to Dr Hemmings, a civilian doctor and school friend, who confirms Sayers' diagnosis: Ruth has suffered minor strokes and will never be the same. Mark returns to the medical centre, where two victims of a helicopter crash are brought in. David asks what is happening and Mark explains. As David tries to comfort one of the victims, the man loses consciousness. David watches as Mark saves the man.

Ruth is discharged from the hospital and brought home in a wheelchair. She talks to Mark and Cynthia about their relationship and tells them they cannot rely on sex to keep them together. After, Cynthia suggests to Mark that he doesn't love her. Mark admits she means a lot to him but agrees, and apologises for leading her on. Cynthia is heartbroken and leaves on the first flight.

Ruth admits that she feels responsible for Mark and David's problems. Mark was conceived by accident: she was too young to have a baby. Her relationship with David was always forced. She tells Mark that David passed up promotion to Admiral because he had to stay at home when Mark was bullied at school. Later, Ruth accidentally starts a fire when she cooks for herself. Mark helps David put the fire out and watches him taking care of Ruth.

The next morning, Mark and David go to the docks as they did years ago. David recalls his time on an aircraft carrier, and the moment when engines would start and they would be answering a distress call. He knows Mark can empathise in his own career. David admits he is proud of Mark. Mark thanks his father for helping him to get there. They return home together.

One to Watch

"Exodus"

4 – 15: First transmitted 26 February 1998
Written by Walon Green & Joe Sachs; Directed by Christopher Chulack

The ER is evacuated

It is Corday's first paramedic ride-along and her unit is called to a chemical plant explosion. Despite being told to observe only, Corday quickly wades in to help Leo Leipziger, an elderly man whose arm is trapped under a collapsed building. Leo's pulse is strong. Corday gives him a morphine drip into his neck to ease the pain. She and Dewey, the paramedic, lubricate Leo's trapped arm with motor oil and try to free him from the rubble. Suddenly, a second explosion rocks the building. Dewey is ordered to pull out but Corday refuses to leave Leo. She uses a car jack to lift the rubble and frees Leo's arm just before the building collapses.

The ER is told to expect six minor casualties but County is soon inundated with many more. Carter treats a retired science teacher with glaucoma who recognises the smell of benzene: it is highly toxic and needs to be contained.

Kerry has a seizure when she tries to treat one of three workers who have arrived covered in the chemical. Randi too succumbs. As more patients arrive, including Leo who Corday rushes to the OR, Carter takes charge. He orders all non-essential patients to be sent home, contaminated patients to the ambulance bay and all others to the cafeteria.

While Benton arranges patients, Kerry is taken to the cafeteria and is filled in by one of her patients, Mr Arteburn. Suddenly, Arteburn crashes. Carter gets some ice-cold water and plunges the man's face into it. The diving reflex slows the heart rate and restores its natural rhythm.

Meanwhile, Doug and Carol are treating Sophie, an eight-year-old who is altered, has respiratory problems and is in renal failure. She has the e-coli infection and needs dialysis urgently. As Doug gets consent from the mother, workers from Hazardous Materials arrive to decontaminate the ER. Carter is chastised for not following the disaster manual (Jerry couldn't find it) but is put in charge.

Doug and Carol take Sophie up to dialysis, but have to put the machine in a separate lift. The fire alarm sounds and the lift stops. Sophie is running short of oxygen and they have no supplies. Doug succeeds in prising the lift door and gets an oxygen tank just in time to save Sophie. Later, Sophie makes a full recovery and tells her mother that Doug and Carol took good care of her.

In OR, Romano is convinced that Leo's arm cannot be saved but Corday is determined to try anyway. They work feverishly but are unable to save Leo's arm. Frustrated, Corday has to amputate. After, Peter checks Corday's eye, which she injured at the scene. She is upset. Peter tells her he is off later and they can meet up.

The decontamination is finished and patients are allowed to return to the ER. Carter is praised, although Kerry is eager to regain command. Carter thanks the Fire Chief, Danniker, for his help. Danniker urges Carter to prepare disaster drills with the fire service in future. Carter points out he is only an intern. Danniker is taken aback, but congratulates John on keeping his head during the crisis. Mark arrives back from San Diego and Carter starts to fill him in.

A hallmark incident episode and one that really builds on the strengths of the ensemble cast. Corday finally comes into her own, showing real determination in her battle to save Leo at the accident site and in the OR. Doug and Carol are shown to work well together, feverishly struggling to save Sophie. But it is Carter who is really a pleasure to watch. Finally we see the man Carter is to become when he takes charge of the ER, even putting Benton to shame.

"My Brother's Keeper"

4 – 16: First transmitted 5 March 1998
Written by Jack Orman; Directed by Jacque Toberen

Chase's attempts to detox have failed

Six drug-users are brought to the ER having taken a new mix of narcotics. Anna recognises Chase and calls for Carter. Chase crashes and is in arrest for a prolonged period of time before Carter regains a pulse. Carol suspects brain damage. Later, Carter's grandparents arrive and are angered to realise John knew about Carter's drug use and was trying to treat him privately. Carter's grandfather, John Carter Sr, berates John and calls for his own doctor. Millicent is more understanding but notes that John and Chase have been given everything in life and "considered it oppression". Dismayed, Carter stays with Chase during the night.

Doug jumps to assumptions at work and in his research

Doug is due to present his research on patient-controlled anaesthesia (PCA) to the hospital that afternoon. Kerry tries to raise a few issues in advance but Doug is called to treat a boy who is seizing. Doug stabilises the boy who suspects that his half-brother, Eric, put photography chemicals in his drink. The father is irate and shakes Eric, but Doug intercedes. Eric shows Doug some cigarette burns on his arms, inflicted by his father. Doug calls the boy's mother and social services before giving his presentation. He comes in for criticism from Kerry and Anspaugh. After, he rounds on Kerry for ambushing him, but Kerry stands her ground. Later, Doug discovers that Eric's burns are self-inflicted and the boy is committed.

Mark tries to repair his recent errors

Mark tries to return Cynthia's luggage, but she has left Chicago and given no forwarding address. Mark is concerned that he acted improperly. During the day, he treats a smoker in the latter stages of lung cancer. The man ruefully notes Mark smoking in the ambulance bay. Later, the man returns in arrest – Corday realises he shot himself. Mark destroys his packet of cigarettes. That evening, Mark gets Cynthia's new address from the telephone company and visits her. Mark tries to make amends but Cynthia acidly notes that he doesn't love her. "I deserve better," she tells him.

Other threads

Romano hands Corday a critical review of her first six months: she has been more concerned with vocal cords and paramedic runs than trauma surgery. As Corday fills Peter in, they bump into Jackie, who is distinctly frosty with Elizabeth.

Scott Anspaugh has his last dose of chemotherapy. He asks Jeanie to go to a movie with him but she is back on duty and does not know her schedule. Scott is put out and leaves, sullen. Later, Jeanie visits Scott and wins him over.

Anna approves the transfer of a motorcyclist to the ER but discovers the other hospital rejected the patient because he has no insurance. Anna complains of gross negligence. Later, she finds the man is undergoing surgery from the negligent doctor who first transferred him.

"A Bloody Mess"

4 – 17: First transmitted 9 April 1998
Written by Linda Gase; Directed by Richard Thorpe

Corday clashes with Romano over a blood study

Without Romano's knowledge, Corday obtains Mark's consent to run a study of artificial blood in the ER. She treats a store owner with gunshot wounds but is later confronted by the man's son who has been tipped off on her use of "haemo-A" by Romano. The patient, however, recovers and thanks Corday. Romano asks Corday to join his own study into artificial blood, but Elizabeth would rather work in the ER.

Meanwhile, Peter hears Reese has a fever and borrows Corday's car to take his son to Carla. En route, Corday suggests that Jackie is uncomfortable with Peter dating a white woman. Peter objects but is distracted and backs into a lawyer! Benton returns Corday and Reese to the ER and tells Carter to take good care of the lawyer. Later, Carter discovers the lawyer had been drinking – and she rapidly drops any charges she was going to file.

Peter is uncomfortable when Carla arrives and talks to Corday. He is testy and Elizabeth snaps at him. Later, Peter apologetically cancels their date. Corday had already assumed as much and breezily asks for her car keys.

Scott Anspaugh suffers a relapse

Jeanie takes Scott rock-climbing but, trying to prove himself, he becomes short of breath and has to be brought back to the ER. Ross thinks the cancer has returned and orders tests. Jeanie objects, hoping Doug is wrong, and is cool when Carol canvasses the staff for bone marrow donors.

Doug is proved right: Scott will need a bone marrow transplant and chemotherapy. Later, Jeanie tells Scott that eight potential donors have been found. Brave, Scott claims eight is his lucky number.

Carol treats a teenager who is having a clandestine affair

Carol treats Natalie, a teenage girl who asks for birth control. Carol wonders if her parents know but Natalie is keen that they do not find out. Carol gives her some condoms and sends her home. Later, Natalie's mother demands to know what happened. Carol discovers Natalie is sleeping with her teacher and files a police report.

Other threads

Morgenstern returns to the ER insisting that his heart attack has given him a new take on life. He sweeps back into work but is rusty and almost kills a patient. Corday is incredulous to discover that this ineffectual surgeon is the ER Chief.

Kerry asks Ross for his fellowship renewal papers, but Doug is not interested. Kerry tells Mark she believes Doug is planning to leave. In fact, Doug is angling for a new post in the ER as a paediatrics attending physician.

Carter is tired at work and falls asleep in the cafeteria. Anna enquires after Chase but Carter is evasive, insisting it is still early days. Later, Carter visits Chase. He has suffered permanent brain damage and is unable to feed or dress himself.

"Gut Reaction"

4–18: First transmitted 16 April 1998
Written by Neal Baer; Directed by T. R. Babu Subramaniam

Benton questions Morgenstern's surgical skill

Corday is delighted to see Allison Beaumont is now a trainee paramedic. She brings in Dr Lars Swanson, Morgenstern's former tutor. Morgenstern performs keyhole surgery, but Benton fears he is making errors. Morgenstern severs the gastric artery and Benton insists they crack Swanson's ribs. David refuses and Peter pushes him away.

Afterwards, Anspaugh wants a formal report. Peter tries to obtain the video of the surgery but finds no tape in the VCR. Morgenstern accuses Peter of causing the error, but Peter insists Morgenstern was at fault. Later, Peter has doubts, but Corday insists he was sure earlier. Now it is a case of Peter's word against Morgenstern's.

Scott Anspaugh consents to more chemotherapy

The bone marrow donors have not matched. Jeanie suggests intensive radiation therapy that will give Scott a slim chance. Catching Jeanie's hope, Scott agrees. However, Doug believes Scott only agreed to please Jeanie – he has a crush on her.

Scott undergoes the treatment but arrests. Jeanie anxiously stands by as the staff struggle to regain his pulse. Once stabilised, Jeanie tells Scott that she will love him no matter what – he does not have to undergo the treatment for her. Scott starts to cry: he doesn't want any more chemotherapy. Jeanie kisses him.

Doug lines himself up for the Paediatrics Attending post

Kerry hears that a Paediatrics Attending may be appointed to the ER and deduces that Doug has spoken to the Dean. She is worried that Doug is the wrong choice but Doug proves his skill when he diagnoses a case of neuroscepsis and saves a six-year-old girl with a new form of intubation. Kerry is adamant that Doug should not be appointed, but Mark is undecided. Later, he tells Doug to go for the job.

Carter makes his move on Anna

Carol sees Carter mooning after Anna and suggests he asks her out. Carter is reluctant to jeopardise their friendship. Nevertheless, he asks and she agrees to join him at the staff banquet. Anna later matches as a bone marrow donor and asks Carter to perform the procedure – he seems more focused on her bottom! At the banquet, Carter asks if she wants a relationship, but Anna is still not over her boyfriend and is reluctant. They agree to stay friends.

Other threads

Jerry and Mark make shambolic preparations for the ER annual banquet. Despite this, the party is a hit. Mark thanks his colleagues: "You stuck by me when I needed you," he says. "Thanks for being my family. I couldn't have made it without you."

Carol discovers that a cheque from the Carter Family Foundation has been stopped and now vital medical supplies are being repossessed. Carter accuses Millicent of retaliating for his treatment of Chase and they argue. However, Carol later announces that the money has come through. She thanks Carter – whatever he said did the trick.

"Shades of Gray"

4–19: First transmitted 23 April 1998
Written by Samantha Howard Corbin; Directed by Lance A. Gentile

Benton is suspended following the Swanson case

The Swanson case (4-18) is due for internal review. Morgenstern and Peter argue bitterly when cross-examined and Peter, accused of letting his emotions get the better of him, is suspended pending further enquiry. However, as Peter is leaving, Mark asks for his help – Peter can still work in the ER. Peter stabilises the patient then takes him upstairs for surgery. Morgenstern takes over and dismisses Peter.

Afterwards, Morgenstern catches up with Peter: David took the tape and, having re-watched it, knows Peter was right. Morgenstern reinstates Peter and resigns. That night, Peter tells Corday he lost his mentor today. He wished he had told Morgenstern how much he respected him. Peter and Corday kiss.

Anna refuses to perform an abortion

Anna and Kerry treat a woman who was undergoing an abortion when the clinic was bombed. The woman starts to bleed out and Kerry orders the abortion to be completed. Anna refuses and leaves. Afterwards, Kerry chastises Anna for taking a moral stance, but Anna lamely refuses to accept she did.

Kerry discovers that this is not the woman's first abortion and suggests contraception. The woman is abusive and leaves. Later, Kerry tells Anna that the patient's wishes are paramount. Anna concurs but can't promise she wouldn't do the same thing again if the situation arose.

Doug treats a pregnant teenager who is brain dead

Doug treats Zoë, a teenager who was at the clinic for a check-up. The baby is fine but Zoë suffers a pulmonary embolism and has to be intubated. Zoë is brain dead but must be kept on the ventilator for the sake of the child. Zoë's parents arrive and are asked to chose between an emergency Caesarean or keeping Zoë intubated and letting the baby reach full term. The parents decide to keep Zoë alive for the sake of the baby, but refuse the boyfriend any part in the baby's life.

Other threads

Scott Anspaugh has died and is to be buried that day. Jeanie practices a hymn she will sing at the service. Later, she speaks to Donald, who gives her a box from Scott: it contains soap opera digest, explaining how Scott could predict the storylines! At the funeral, Jeanie abandons her hymn and sings one of Scott's favourite songs instead.

Carter treats an elderly man with severe bedsores and decides to put him in an extended care facility. The man's son, Newton, objects and calls his lawyer. The old man becomes more coherent and asks to be left to die in his own bed. Carter tries to help but social services take the old man away.

Corday treats a paramedic injured in the clinic explosion: Allison Beaumont. Her injuries are severe and Romano notes their efforts are hopeless. Nevertheless, Elizabeth stabilises Allison. Later, she ruefully notes that she can put people back together but can't keep them that way.

"Of Past Regret and Future Fear"

4-20: First transmitted 30 April 1998
Written by Jack Orman; Directed by Anthony Edwards

Carol treats a dying father

Carol is pensive about lunch with her mother, but is bemused when Helen Hathaway arrives with Javier, her new man. Doug is amused, to Carol's annoyance. During the day, Carol treats Paul Kinturner, who has severe chemical burns. The acid is extracting calcium from his cells and the condition is fatal. Carol discovers Paul has a young daughter, Molly, who he hasn't seen since she was six months old. Carol regrets that she did not see her father before he died. She tries to convince Paul's ex-wife to let Molly see her father, but the woman refuses. Paul is upset and dictates a final letter to Molly. As Carol reads it back, Paul dies.

Later, Carol wonders if her father asked for her and realises she has always taken her mother's advice and not relied on men. She notes the irony that her mother is in a relationship, but Carol is holding back. She tells Doug she is scared of losing him.

Benton and Corday are questioned about their relationship

Benton attends Reese's baptism but gets a cool reception. News that he is dating a white

woman has not gone down well. Meanwhile, Romano invites Corday to lunch. She reveals she is considering staying in the autumn. She is taken aback when Romano asks her out. Covering, Corday claims to have a policy against dating colleagues and turns him down. Romano accepts her excuse, but admits he thought he was competing with Benton! Later, Romano sees Peter and Corday operating on Peter's day off. Romano is pleased Peter also doesn't have a life! Afterwards, Peter invites Elizabeth to Reese's party – he won't be ashamed of her any more.

Carter is asked to take over the family business
Chase's condition continues to deteriorate: he has now lost movement down his left side. Carter refuses to accept the futility of the situation, but seeing Chase confirms the diagnosis. Later, Millicent asks Carter to return home: his grandfather is too proud to ask Carter himself. She asks Carter if he will practice part-time so he can run the family business. Carter refuses: he is a doctor – nothing else will do.

Other threads
Kerry treats Mrs Wynbock, an elderly woman who is suffering a prolonged bout of the flu. A mix-up at the labs reveals she has HIV. The woman's fiancé confides that he has the infection and asks Kerry not to tell Mrs Wynbock. Kerry insists the couple must talk.

Ross treats Josh McNeil, a "crack baby" suffering withdrawal. He discovers that the mother is taking her son's methadone. Doug decides to admit. He is angry when the mother abandons her son in the hospital.

Carter and Anna are surprised when Dr Max Rocher, Anna's boyfriend from Philadelphia, arrives. Anna kisses Max a little uncomfortably as Carter stands by.

"Suffer the Little Children"

4 – 21: First transmitted 7 May 1998
Written by Walon Green; Directed by Christopher Misiano

Doug puts a "crack baby" through a dangerous procedure
Josh McNeil (4-20) is to be placed with a fosterer until he has detoxed. However, Doug later hears that the baby is being returned to his mother. Annoyed, Doug has Josh brought to the ER and admits him for pneumonia. In fact, he sedates the baby and starts a 12- to 18-hour rapid detox programme. Carol is hesitant, but consents to keep the procedure secret. Doug lies to Mark to obtain the necessary medication.

Meanwhile, Kerry is frustrated that Dr Max Rocher (4-20) is assessing the need for a Paediatrics ER. Suspecting that Doug is trying to prove a case for a paediatrics attending, she tries to sidetrack Rocher with charts. Mark, however, disagrees and Kerry quickly accuses him of supporting Doug's application.

Josh McNeil crashes. Mark is furious to discover Doug running the procedure. Kerry admits the baby to NICU and demands Ross explain himself to management. Mark is fuming: "You lied to me, Doug. You looked me right in the face and lied to me."

Carter clashes with Anna's boyfriend

Anna is concerned that Carter will judge Max by his addiction and insists that he is a good guy who is coping well. Carter is concerned Anna and Max are back together but Anna is not sure. Anna treats Tina Marie, a tele-evangelist with kidney problems, who launches a televised prayer vigil from her bed. Tina later worries that her husband is only supportive because it makes him look good.

Meanwhile, Carter is irked to find Max following him for his research. Max is impressed when Carter diagnoses a rare condition in an unconscious 11-year-old. Carter, tells Max he doesn't trust him and doesn't think he is good for Anna.

Corday's relationship with Benton goes public

Peter is reluctant to take Corday to a jazz club. Later, they break from a clinch when Romano arrives. Corday hopes they were not seen but fears they were when Romano hints he may withdraw his sponsorship. Angry, Benton confronts Romano but discovers Romano saw nothing! The truth now out, a bitter Romano congratulates Benton on his "excellent choice".

While Corday is uncomfortable their relationship has gone public, Benton takes strength from it and agrees to take her to the club. He admits he has feelings about her skin colour still, but is working through it.

Other threads

Jeanie wakes with a temperature and a cough and orders a chest film. She takes it to Kerry, not mentioning it is hers, but Kerry notes it is inconclusive and orders a second. This time, Jeanie explains that the film is hers. Kerry assures Jeanie that she will always have a job irrespective of her viral count. They run some blood tests and find Jeanie is OK: she has forgotten some of her medication recently. Kerry offers to listen to Jeanie's concerns, and she readily accepts.

"A Hole in the Heart"

4–22: First transmitted 14 May 1998
Written by Lydia Woodward; Directed by Lesli Linka Glatter

Kerry and Mark are in the minority over Doug's actions

Kerry wants to stop the rapid detoxification of Josh McNeil (4-21) but is told that would endanger the boy's life. Ross doesn't care about the rules and just wants to give the boy a chance. Kerry bitterly tells him not to expect the paediatrics attending position. Meanwhile, Mark encourages Carol to say she was ordered to help Doug, but Carol insists Doug did the right thing. Mark and Kerry close ranks but discover Doug has already admitted his complicity to the senior staff – who have agreed to support his actions.

The rapid detox completed, Doug extubates Josh. The mother asks to have the same

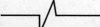

procedure. Doug gives her the names of some physicians who might help, but fears the detox does not overcome psychological addiction.

Kerry arranges for a formal review but Doug is calm. Doug insists he did what was right, but Mark is angry he was not consulted. Doug bitterly suggests their disagreement is down to Mark's inability to see Doug as an equal.

Kerry resigns from the ER

Kerry asks Anspaugh about promotion to ER Chief. She is annoyed when Anspaugh reveals plans for a nationwide search. Already annoyed by Doug, Kerry is soon embroiled in other disagreements. She accuses Mark of being lax on Doug and clashes with an insurance company who refuse to pay medical expenses. Frustrated, Kerry quits as acting chief and storms out – but later takes the budget forms to peruse.

Carol treats a suicidal father

Carol treats Mr Nabel who attempted suicide after arguing with his wife. Carol discovers Nabel has been in three times: it is a cry for help. Later, Nabel returns covered in blood. He hands her a gun and apologises that there weren't enough bullets. Carol races to Nabel's car: Nabel has shot his wife, son and daughter. The daughter is stable but the mother has spinal injuries. The son has a hole in his heart and is rushed to surgery. Nabel lamely tells Jeanie that his wife was going to take his children away from him.

Other threads

Corday is angry to hear Romano has withdrawn his sponsorship and gone on holiday. She asks Anspaugh for a position at County. Anspaugh indicates that she is too late, but Elizabeth is persistent. Peter argues that her persistence was not helpful. Elizabeth is more annoyed that Peter has not leapt on her decision to stay.

Lydia loses some strong painkillers and Carter suspects Max. Anna objects – Max is clean – but Carter recalls that Chase lied to him. Later, Max tells Anna he is recommending a paediatrics unit in the ER and may stay to run it if he and Anna are an item. Anna asks about the painkillers, but Max didn't take them. However, he thinks she was right to be suspicious.

Season Five
1998-9

Themes

Mark's assault comes back to haunt him when he treats a Nigerian immigrant suffering from a post-traumatic stress disorder. Meanwhile, he grows closer to Elizabeth Corday when she breaks up with Peter Benton.

Now a paediatrics attending, Doug thinks he has more control but soon oversteps the mark in his treatment of Ricky Abbott. As Doug takes pity on Ricky's mother, he makes a rash decision that costs him his job and, potentially, his relationship with Carol.

Carol's clinic and her relationship with Doug are on the line after Doug's rash actions in the Ricky Abbott case. Carol discovers she is pregnant, but worries about raising children as a single mother. Buoyed up by the example of a schizophrenic mother, Carol resolves to do her best, but is in for more than she bargained.

Peter discovers that Reese has a hearing impairment and needs greater care. His relationship with Corday falls apart and is soon replaced by competition for a trauma fellowship in the ER. When Benton hears that Carla intends to move to Europe and take Reese with her, he takes drastic action.

Kerry clashes with Romano over sexual harassment claims. Meanwhile, she tries hard to find her birth parents and briefly feels she has found success.

Jeanie starts a new relationship with Reggie the cop, but it is threatened when Jeanie discovers she has contracted a disease from a patient.

Carter finds difficulty teaching new student Lucy Knight. They soon clash when Lucy lets her pride get in the way of patient care. Later, they reveal more personal feelings for each other but are unsure whether to act on them.

Ones to Watch

5 – 8: *The Good Fight* – Carter and Lucy's troubles come to a head when they try to trace a blood match.

5 – 14 & **5 – 15:** *The Storm* – Doug puts his career on the line when he helps a mother grant euthanasia. Meanwhile, Jeanie makes a sad discovery.

5 – 20: *Power* – A manhunt is launched in the ER when a rapist is on the loose. The staff have to contend with a major power cut.

"Day for Knight"

5 – 1: First transmitted 24 September 1998
Written by Lydia Woodward; Directed by Christopher Chulack

Lucy Knight joins the ER

Lucy Knight helps a man who has fainted at the El station. She props up his head, but a bystander thinks she shouldn't have moved him. Mark and Carol take the man and Lucy back to the ER, assuming she is a relative. Lucy explains she is a third-year student and today is the first day of her ER rotation.

Mark gives Lucy a rapid tour of the department. They find Lily, Chuny and Yosh preparing a birthday surprise for Jerry and wake Carter. Lucy meets Maggie and Doug Ross, who quizzes her and discovers she is very bright. Lucy is stunned as she watches Kerry and Benton fail to save a gunshot victim. When the man's cell phone rings, she answers and takes a message!

Lucy takes Kerry's audio tour of the ER, but gets completely lost. Mark suggests she shadow Carter instead. Carter is irked when Lucy uses a portable computer to make a diagnosis. He then tests her on a new patient, Mr Zwicki. They both suspect cancer, but Zwicki doesn't want to stay for tests. Carter tries to convince Zwicki's wife, but is called away. Lucy takes over but uses medical jargon. The Zwickis leave. Carter is annoyed, but Mark reminds him that Lucy shouldn't have been left to talk to the wife at all.

After being left locked out on the helipad, Lucy sees Mark and Carol treating Fernandez, a firefighter who fell 20 feet on to solid concrete. A CT shows his brain has been destroyed. Mark tells Mrs Fernandez. Lucy realises that Fernandez could still hear and encourages Mrs Fernandez to talk to him. She can't bring herself to do so and decides to return tomorrow to discuss her husband's options.

Later, Lucy is dismayed to be assigned to Carter. She is stunned when the staff celebrate Jerry's birthday, despite it being a horrible day. Lucy returns to Fernandez and talks to him.

Other threads

Corday is working hard to stay in Chicago. Benton tells her that Reese has an ear infection and will take a hearing test once it has cleared up. They snatch a moment together in one of the rooms, leaving Lucy to crawl out unnoticed.

Mark mediates between two firefighters who argue about using the helicopter to transport Fernandez. Mark calms them down. Later, a firefighter offers Mark the post of District Medical Director for the emergency services. Mark is politely unenthusiastic about more hours and no pay.

Carter tells Lucy that she has inherited Anna Del Amico's locker, noting ruefully that Anna has returned to Philadelphia to be with her boyfriend.

Doug complains that he must consult Kerry before performing a lumbar puncture. Weaver reminds him that was Anspaugh's decision following Doug's rash rapid detox of baby Josh (4-21).

"Split Second"

5 – 2: First transmitted 1 October 1998
Written by Carol Flint; Directed by Christopher Misiano

Lucy allows Carol to cover for her mistakes

Carter, living as a dorm monitor, has endured a restless night. He is irked to find Lucy arrived for work two hours early. She wants to make a good start in her career and is sure Carter is already working to become Chief Resident. Struck, Carter tells Weaver this is his ambition. Weaver tells him he has plenty of time, adding that good tutoring is the first step towards becoming Chief.

Carter is pleased to hear that he is once more being paid. Later, Carol covers for Lucy during a basic procedure. Lucy is grateful, but Carol won't cover for her again: Lucy shouldn't expect to be perfect.

Corday is offered a job with her father

Corday's father, Charles, arrives in Chicago to recruit her to his practice. Elizabeth is torn, but Kerry suggests she could work as an intern for a year and get her licence to practise. Later, Romano maliciously claims to have considered hiring her, but remembers that the funding is no longer available. Her hopes dashed, Corday relishes pointing out a wound that Romano missed.

Later, Elizabeth tells Charles that she has decided to work as an intern. Charles is supportive, but wonders how much Peter is behind her decision.

Benton discovers that Reese has a hearing deficiency

As they finish surgery, Benton and Anspaugh discuss Reese's upcoming hearing test. Anspaugh asks if Reese was given a potentially harmful drug, but Benton later establishes that the drug amount was within safe limits. Relieved, Benton attends Reese's hearing test but is disbelieving when the test show he is profoundly deaf and only "could" develop language skills. Later that evening, Benton plays some music to Reese but, even as he increases the volume, Reese remains unresponsive.

Other threads

Mark is considering the District Director position (5-1) but paramedic Doris Pickman thinks that the post-holder has never made a difference. Later, Mark discovers that the first-aid kit for Rachel's soccer team is empty and that the fire truck that came to the aid of a karate student was not equipped with a defibrillator. Mark is sure that this is something he could change.

Carol hears that she has got the funding she needs to hire a nurse for the clinic. She meets Lynette Evans, a nurse practitioner who was recommended by Dr Anspaugh. When Lynette reprimands a patient, Carol is impressed and hires her.

Weaver tells Doug that his probationary period is over, but laments the continued public enquiries about the ultra-rapid detox. Doug is flippant, but later has to tell a drug user that he can't perform the detox again. Doug accepts that Weaver made her point but she chastises him for failing to appreciate the impact of his actions or checking up on baby Josh.

"They Treat Horses, Don't They?"

5 − 3: First transmitted 8 October 1998
Written by Walon Green; Directed by T. R. Babu Subramaniam

Weaver will automatically become Morgenstern's replacement

Kerry is stunned when Anspaugh intimates she is not high on his list of candidates for Morgenstern's replacement. Mark has been invited on to the selection board. Kerry fears a conflict of interest and Mark declines the invitation. Mark's day goes from the sublime to the ridiculous: first, treating a bomb-laden patient; then, giving a mineral enema to a horse.

Meanwhile, Kerry's confidence is further knocked when she can't intubate an obese patient and hears that Doug has been made an attending, against her recommendation. Kerry confronts Mark about being left out of the loop. Mark tells Kerry she is obsessing over her title. Later, he agrees to be on the selection committee after all.

Paediatrics attending Doug Ross treats a boy with cancer

Doug discovers that Weaver has recommended he is not promoted to attending due to "ongoing problems with impulse control" ("that's right, Kerry. I'm a psycho"). Nevertheless, Doug is given the post. Later, he treats Dana, a 15-year-old girl with a broken leg. The bone exploded from the inside, potentially due to a cancerous growth. Doug tells Dana they may need to amputate, but adds that the cancer may still spread. Doug stresses that the decision is for Dana and her family, but the parents are annoyed he talked to Dana at all. He is warned to stay away from Dana.

Carter resuscitates a DNR

Carter meets Roxanne (5-1) who invites him to her gym. Carter agrees to come by sometime. During the day, he resuscitates Emily Holmes, an elderly woman found unconscious at home. Emily's neighbour wants to know if Emily is dead, because her sister is waiting for her apartment! Irked, Carter stabilises Emily but later discovers she is a DNR and the hospital will not admit her. Torn, Carter asks Weaver's advice, but she tells him to make his own decisions if he wants to be Chief Resident. Carter extubates Emily and watches her die. Later, he seeks out Roxanne.

Other threads

Reese's doctor confirms that Reese needs a digital hearing aid that costs $5,000. Benton can't afford to pay for it all and Carla agrees to share the costs. They share a warm moment with Reese that Corday observes. Later, Corday testily asks Benton if he is back with Carla. Annoyed, Benton explains about the hearing aid, noting he didn't tell her because "it's private". Corday is chastened.

Lucy helps Mark and Carol treat a patient with a knife embedded in his skull. Lucy is told to restrain the man, but does so incorrectly. Carol chastises her for not listening to the precise instruction. Later Lucy starts an IV on the sedated patient, but goes through the vein. Malik assists and Lucy, hinting at her shortcomings, tells Carter she needed Malik's help. Carter praises Lucy for using the nurses.

"Vanishing Act"

5 – 4: First transmitted 15 October 1998
Written by Jack Orman; Directed by Lesli Linka Glatter

Carol fears she may be pregnant

Carol casually mentions that her period is three days late, sparking panic in Doug. She treats Bo, an 18-year-old who has been stabbed and wants revenge. Lynette suggests sedating him, but Carol angrily insists that is unethical. Bo later escapes security and returns with a gunshot wound.

Meanwhile, Doug hears that Dana (5-3) is to have her leg amputated. He suspects she has phantom limb pain and rewires the motor nerves. Romano is furious as the procedure delays surgery and tells Doug to leave his patients alone.

That night, Carol tells Doug she is not pregnant. A little disappointed, Doug seems to have come round to the idea.

Corday starts over as an intern

Corday has been assigned to Dale Edson, who immediately puts her to scut work. However, Mark appreciates Corday's experience and asks her to look at Mr Darcy's pulseless foot. Dale takes over and insists that Romano sees the case. Edson continues to bully Corday in surgery. Romano tells Corday to scrub out and stall Mark. Corday tells Mark that she still can't admit Darcy, so Greene sends him to Radiology. Later, Romano berates Corday for losing his case. Nevertheless, he admits that he "couldn't handle taking orders from a weasel like Dale".

Lucy tells Carter about her shortcomings

Carter shows Lucy how to run a blood gas. Later, he tells her to start an IV on a four-year-old. Lucy still hasn't done one and asks Carol, who is dismayed. Lucy is saved when Doug makes a policy that interns cannot perform IVs on children. Later, Carter asks Lucy to perform a blood gas, but she fails. He asks her to run an IV instead but she is frustrated and blurts out that she has never done one. Carter finds Lucy upset on the roof. Carter insists her pride has jeopardised lives. He warns Lucy that if she lies to him again she will be looking for another rotation.

Other threads

Jeanie treats a boy called Angel with a heart problem. The mother tries to hide the fact that Angel is an illegal immigrant, but Jeanie assures her that County treats all emergencies. She is frustrated, however, when Kayson insists they can't do thousands of dollars worth of tests on an illegal immigrant.

Jeanie also treats Mr Lipsom who has caused his body to reject a replacement liver by drinking. Lipsom wants Jeanie to keep this from the transplant list, but she refuses. Later, Jeanie finds Doug and asks if she can be his full time PA in the Paediatrics ER. Doug agrees, if Jeanie can sort things out with Anspaugh.

Kerry has "power-dressed" for her interview, but sees another candidate in the same suit. Randi lets Kerry borrow her leather jacket. After the interview, Kerry wonders if the other candidates have used pie-charts. Mark admits she was the first.

"Masquerade"

5 – 5: First transmitted 29 October 1998
Written by Carol Flint; Directed by Christopher Misiano

Mark and Carol treat a pregnant schizophrenic

Mark and Carol treat Coco, a young woman who claims to be in labour but has no sign of pregnancy. Mark orders a psych consult and gives Coco a dose of Haldol to calm her down. Later, Coco reveals she is a schizophrenic and has stopped her medication as it could harm her baby. Carol asks if Mark ran a pregnancy test but he's "starting to wish he had". Coco becomes distressed as Mark explains that the Haldol may result in limb malformation. Carol suspects it may be better if the pregnancy was terminated. Mark adds it would get him off the hook.

Kerry loses out on the ER Chief's post

Kerry is disappointed to see eminent doctor Dan Litvak is being interviewed for the ER Chief's position. She is more unhappy to discover this is his second interview.

Later, Kerry and Peter treat a man with a metal object lodged in his chest. Kerry bemoans not having a sternal saw and Romano suggests a study with Peter. Romano later tells Benton that the study is just to divert Kerry. Later, Mark tells Kerry that Litvak has been given the job. Frustrated, Kerry leaves.

Lucy lets a dorm party get out of hand

Carter breaks a date with Roxanne to chaperone a Hallowe'n dorm party. Meanwhile, Kerry presses Carter to present on an ischemic bowel in his bid to make Chief Resident. Carter leaves the party in Lucy's hands so he can study, but returns to find chaos. Carter ends the party, but Lucy continues drinking with some of the students. Suddenly they notice Willie has passed out. Carter realises they have taken liquid ecstasy and calls the paramedics. Carter yells at Lucy for letting the party get out of control and berates himself for giving Lucy responsibility.

Other threads

It's Hallowe'n dress day and Corday arrives as Heidi. Peter doesn't want to join in and won't let her know who his childhood hero was. They arrange to go out later but Corday is given scut work to do by Dale. Benton has a surprise in store and tells Dale to reassign the work.

They leave for their night out – with Benton dressed as John Shaft.

Doug has decided that he must sign off against all paediatrics cases in the ER. He soon becomes overloaded and has to pass some cases back to the main ER. Kerry compliments Doug on his mature handling of the situation. Meanwhile, Doug and Carol trade Hallowe'n practical jokes.

As Mark's summer with his daughter comes to a close, Rachel lets slip that she and Jen are moving to St Louis. Mark is taken aback but later agrees the move with Jen. Jen is pleased that Mark and Rachel became close over the summer.

"Stuck on You"

5 – 6: First transmitted 5 November 1998
Written by Neal Baer from a story by Linda Gase; Directed by David Nutter

Mark endangers himself on a paramedic ride-along

On a ride-along, Mark puts himself in danger when he helps Kevin, a flirtatious male prostitute who was being attacked. Mark discovers Kevin has a protein "S" deficiency and is prone to blood clots. He suggests an anti-clotting agent, but Kevin fears he could bleed to death if attacked again.

Later, Mark discovers there is a warrant for Kevin's arrest. He fears Kevin could be beaten up in a juvenile detention centre, so sneaks him away with some money and his pager number. Later, Mark apologises to the paramedics for putting himself in danger and is invited to join their poker game.

Carter and Lucy's relationship deteriorates

Carter moans at Lucy for losing his job at the dorm. Benton tells Carter to teach Lucy, not be her friend. Carter and Lucy treat Brad Enloe, a 12-year-old with leukaemia. Carter suggests experimental therapy, but the insurance company won't pay for it. Carter fudges the claim by admitting Brad for dehydration – he can have the treatment on the side. Lucy probes Carter and discovers his lie. Mrs Enloe overhears and is angry that her insurance company will stop her cover. Carter chastises Lucy, but she insists he tell her what he is doing. Later, Carter visits an apartment with a spare room – and discovers his new landlady is Kerry Weaver.

Benton considers treatment for Reese's deafness

Benton considers a cochlear implant for Reese but Kerry suggests he talk to her friend Lisa Parks first. Parks is deaf and argues that the cochlear implant will rob Reese of his identity as a deaf person. Benton insists he is just trying to fix a medical problem. Later, Benton tells Kerry he doesn't want Reese to live with a defect Kerry challenges the word "defect". Meanwhile, Corday becomes Benton's intern.

Other threads

Carol treats Levy, an old man with diabetes, who resists her attempts to put her in a nursing home. Later, she refuses to give a girl an acne drug until she agrees to take birth control. Lynette is annoyed that Carol undermined the girl's right to choose. Carol relents

and arranges for Levy to live with a friend.

Mark tells Kerry that Litvak used the offer of the Chief's position to get a bigger salary in New York. Kerry's is the only other name on the shortlist. However, Anspaugh reveals that the hospital will start their search again – they want a Chief with a national reputation. Kerry angrily decides to stop working as Interim Chief and will not resubmit her name.

Jeanie treats Katie, a girl with a string of old injuries. Jeanie discovers Katie and her father are trying to beat World Records. Jeanie refuses to let Katie try for the trampoline record – but joins Katie's dad to have a go herself.

"Hazed and Confused"

5–7: First transmitted 12 November 1998
Written by David Mills from a story by David Mills & Carol Flint; Directed by Jonathan Kaplan

Corday endangers a patient's life

Corday has been on duty for 24 hours without sleep. Benton tells her to get some rest. However, Anspaugh encourages her to scrub in on a rare case. Corday starts to fall asleep during surgery and Anspaugh apologises for pushing her to join him. Later, Corday treats a patient who has a severe asthma attack. She administers magnesium but misreads the label and administers a near lethal dose. The man is stabilised, but Anspaugh chastises Benton for leaving his intern unsupervised.

Benton sees a surgeon about Reese's deafness

Benton sees Dr Kotlowitz, an ENT surgeon recommended by Corday. Kotlowitz is almost fanatical in his desire to treat deafness and maligns deaf pressure groups. Although Benton is reassured about the implant, he is taken aback by the force of the surgeon's opinions. After Anspaugh's ticking off, Benton is unwilling to talk to Corday about Kotlowitz, but tells Jackie he's not sure which treatment to pursue.

Carter has to evaluate Lucy's performance

Lucy rehearses a speech to Carter about their professional relationship, recording it into her palmtop computer. Carter later stumbles on the recording and angrily tells Lucy to fill in her own evaluation form: "We'll see how fair-minded and objective you can be." Mark confronts Carter about Lucy's evaluation and Carter realises Lucy handed it in. Mark, sick of their bickering, tells them to work out their problems.

Carol treats a pregnant woman with severe abdominal pain

Carol is still not pregnant so Lynette runs some tests through the clinic for privacy. Together they treat Maria Jones, a woman with two sons who has had two abortions. Maria complains of severe abdominal pains but an ultrasound reveals only a healthy baby. Maria reveals she faked the pains to find out the sex of the baby and will now have an abortion as it is not a boy. Carol protests. Later, Carol's tests come back OK: she just needs to give it time.

Other threads

Doug and Jeanie treat baby Sun, who is cared for by six-year-old Sky while their mother works. Sky lets Sun eat honey from a spoon and may have given her botulism. Jeanie is concerned that Sky is not being allowed to grow up a child. Doug thinks this is nothing compared to the cases of neglect he usually sees.

Mark helps the paramedics deal with a case of DIY trepanation, and later intercedes when Morales picks a fight with the nurses. Later, the paramedics try to "initiate" Mark into their group, but as they strap him to a backboard he panics, remembering his assault (3-20).

Kerry watches Anspaugh struggle as Interim Chief. Later, Donald compliments Kerry on a midline thoracotomy. The ice broken, Kerry admits she was resentful about the job, but is grateful to be focusing on medicine now.

One to Watch

"The Good Fight"

5 – 8: First transmitted 19 November 1998
Written by Jack Orman; Directed by Christopher Chulack

Carter and Lucy find some rapprochement over a kidnapped girl

Mr Sawyer and his daughter Corinna are brought in from a car accident. Sawyer needs sutures, but Corinna is bleeding from her spleen and requires surgery. Sawyer tells Lucy to contact his ex-wife for consent and quietly makes his exit.

Talking to the ex-wife, Lucy discovers that Corinna's father is really called Nelson and that he kidnapped Corinna two weeks ago. Meanwhile, Corinna crashes during a blood transfusion. Although B+, she has a one in 50,000,000 blood type that only her father matches. Carter phones blood banks while Lucy tries to find Nelson based on an address he supplied.

His shift over, Carter leaves to go sailing with Roxanne, but he's preoccupied. He decides to pursue Nelson with Lucy, raising Roxanne's suspicions about his relationship with his student. After chasing a lead from a Chicago cop, Carter bumps into Lucy at a hotel and they get another lead to a friend of Nelson's, Toby, who works at a meat packing plant. Frustrated, Carter maligns Lucy for letting Nelson leave. Lucy angrily retorts that she knew he'd blame her.

At the hospital, Benton, Doug and Anspaugh discuss the desperate measure of operating without blood. However, they hear that two units are being flown in from Nashville. Corinna is prepped for the OR.

As they track down Lucy and Carter find a boy with suspected TB. Carter calls an ambulance, but is attacked for entering the house. The man lets Carter go, but expects him to wait for the ambulance. Lucy heads to a convenience store, ignoring Carter's insistence that they should go together, prompting Carter to shout "God forbid you should listen to me and learn something". As they argue, Lucy and Carter spot Nelson at the El station. Jumping over the fare gate, Carter is blocked by a ticket collector Nelson escapes.

Carter and Lucy track down Toby, who tells them to visit Nelson's Uncle Joey at the stadium. Joey tells them Nelson will be at a cockfight on the South Side.

The blood arrives but could be contaminated. Anspaugh, Benton and Babcock operate, but there are complications. Benton expects Corinna to die.

In search of Nelson, Carter dislocates his shoulder. Lucy fixes it, causing him some pain, as he didn't show her shoulder reductions because they weren't talking that day. Both concede they have been stubborn.

After finding Carter's jeep burnt out, Lucy and Carter take a cab to Nelson's. They hear an answerphone message indicating he is at Doc Magoo's.

Finally found, Nelson gives blood but Mark explains it could be too late as Corinna had multi-organ system failure and is now in a coma.

Carter finds Lucy, upset, on the hospital roof. He tells Lucy that some patients get to you more than others but assures her that she fought the good fight and tomorrow they will fight another one.

The Good Fight is in the "ones to watch" list simply for those of us who are Carter and Lucy fans. This bust-up had been a long time coming. Lucy's failure to admit her lack of experience and her pride give way to a realisation that Carter isn't actually that good a teacher. Carter's difficulties stem from his own training under Peter Benton. It's great to see the first season Benton-Carter relationship played out with the roles reversed. *The Good Fight* finally brings things to a head.

It also breaks the show's format, not unlike Season Four's *Fathers and Sons*, and we get to see a fair bit of Chicago. The story itself provides a neutral environment for Lucy and Carter to deal with their issues and, although the sleuthing goes a bit far, the investigation is compelling. On top of this we have some wonderful small moments, notably from Benton and Mark with Corinna.

"Good Luck, Ruth Johnson"

5 – 9: First transmitted 10 December 1998
Written by Lydia Woodward; Directed by Rod Holcomb

Carter takes Ruth Johnson on a 100th birthday tour

In celebration of the hospital's 100th anniversary, new ER Chief Amanda Lee asks Carter to take Ruth Johnson for a birthday tour. Ruth was delivered on the hospital's opening day and is also celebrating her 100th birthday. Ruth is accompanied by her large extended family, but frequently pretends to be asleep to escape the attention. Carter takes Ruth aside and they share family stories. Carter cries a sob story about his privileged upbringing, but Ruth is amusingly critical. Later, Carter finds Ruth sleeping, but she is not playing possum and actually has candy in her windpipe. Carter treats her and tells her anxious family she will be fine.

Carol is perturbed by a young killer

Doug and Carol treat Wilson, an eight-year-old boy who was hit by a car while escaping a man in the park. His friend, Andy, is brought in with a gunshot wound and dies. Wilson gives a description of the man to police, but can't remember much and asks for his mother. Meanwhile, Andy's mother discovers that Andy's boots are missing from his belongings. Carol finds that Wilson was wearing them, and finds some bullets in his belongings. Wilson explains that Andy wouldn't let him wear his boots so he shot him with his father's gun.

Carol is horrified to find that Wilson has no understanding of his guilt. Doug tells her "stuff happens" and that you can only do your best for your children and wish them good luck. Before Doug and Carol can leave, they help Mark deliver Ruth's great granddaughter also called Ruth. Carol wishes the newborn good luck.

Benton and Corday break up

Benton and Corday continue to seem estranged. As Corday prepares for a hearing on the accidental overdose (5-7), Benton watches Kotlowitz perform a cochlear implant on a three-year-old. Benton is unsettled by the procedure and decides to put off surgery. He attends the hearing and defends Corday, but is surprised when she insists she doesn't need his assistance. In fact, Corday launches into an attack on the practice of working interns for 36 hours straight.

Later, Corday tells Benton that Anspaugh concluded she was not at fault. Benton is pleased, but Corday knows he is distracted. She suggests that their relationship has grown stagnant and that they should end it. Benton agrees, determined to devote more time to Reese.

Other threads

Having crashed at Doug and Carol's while his apartment is fumigated, Mark is woken by Doug with an air horn. Mark and Amanda have been on a date, but Doug can't get any more information. Later, Mark and Amanda decide to go out again.

"The Miracle Worker"

5–10: First transmitted 17 December 1998
Written by Paul Manning; Directed by Lesli Linka Glatter

Carter and Lucy perform Christmas miracles

Carter gets a Christmas card from a patient who claims that the doctor is an "instrument of God". Lucy, an agnostic, is bemused that God got the credit. Later, Carter treats Steven Richards, an 18-year-old with a brain haemorrhage. Doug wants to call time of death but Carter, having heard the mother's pleas, saves Steven. Carter is deflated to realise Steven is brain dead. Carter admits he let the "instrument of God" comment go to his head.

Later, a girl arrives in liver failure. Steven has the same rare blood type and Carter takes this as a sign that his efforts were not in vain. However, Mrs Richards refuses to donate. Carter tells Lucy there are no miracles, but is surprised to see Mrs Richards has consented

Absent friends: Anthony Edwards as Mark Greene,
the heart of ER for eight years.

Alex Kingston, alias Elizabeth Corday, who shot to fame in the UK before making her own rapid and successful transplant to the US.

Anthony Edwards during a chance break in the show's
hectic filming schedule.

New blood: Goran Visnjic, ER's Luka Kovac, who
quickly proved to be more than a replacement
for Doug Ross.

Teachers and students: the much-missed Eriq La Salle
with show stalwarts Noah Wyle and Maura Tierney.

Extended family: All the faces during the seventh
season. From left to right: Paul McCrane, Ming-Na,
Alex Kingston, Maura Tierney, Anthony Edwards,
Eriq La Salle, Noah Wyle, Michael Michelle,
Erik Palladino, Laura Innes and Goran Visnjic

Noah Wyle, the longest serving member of cast, now takes centre-stage at the end of the eighth season.

to the transplant. Lucy admits she introduced the two mothers. Pleased, Carter reckons Lucy is an instrument of God too.

Jerry grows suspicious of Amanda Lee's behaviour

Mark is dismissive when Jerry claims Amanda was going through Mark's locker. Later, Jerry shows Kerry a "triple X sex fantasy" written by Amanda about "MG". Amanda explains it was written by a hypersexual patient who fantasises about Merv Griffin! As the day draws to a close, Amanda orders an impromptu staff party. Mark can't find his lab coat but Jerry, suspicious, stays quiet. Later, Amanda wears Mark's lab coat as she puts heart shaped pictures of her and Mark on her Christmas tree…

Benton and Romano come to blows, almost

Benton tries to get away early to be with Reese, but Romano loads him with extra work. Fuming, Benton struggles with a gastroplasty patient who bursts his stomach staple. Romano does not answer his page, so Benton starts without him. Later, Romano arrives drunk. Benton refuses to let him operate. Romano swings a punch, missing Peter and knocking himself out in the process. After, Romano threatens to have Benton sacked but Peter casually reveals proof that Romano's blood alcohol was over the limit. Benton is pleased when Carla arrives with Reese.

Other threads

Corday treats David Gardner, a trumpet soloist with prostate cancer. Corday warms to Gardner as they joke about her taste in music – "I'm going through a disco phase". Gardner hears he may loose sexual function after his operation and fears a sperm donation will be his last sexual experience. Corday escapes a night with Romano and invites David for dinner instead.

Carol insists that Doug attend her family's Christmas party but Doug refuses to go to Mass. They treat Laura, a pregnant 13-year-old. At first she wants an abortion but has second thoughts. Carol persuades Laura to speak to her mother. Doug is annoyed when the mother arrives with a priest. Later he apologises to Carol. Carol accepts, admitting she loves her "pig-headed heathen".

"Nobody Doesn't Like Amanda Lee"

5 – 11: First transmitted 7 January 1999
Written by Linda Gase; Directed by Richard Thorpe

The hospital discovers the truth about Amanda Lee

Mark treats Edie, an agoraphobic, and discovers Amanda wrote a paper on phobias for a medical journal. Interested, Mark finds the article on the Internet but the author, A. W. Lee, is a 40-year-old Asian man. Amanda explains it was a mix-up and a correction was printed next month. Mark tries to get the journals from the library but they are out. Later,

Mark takes Edie to CT, but is followed by Amanda who locks him in. She claims to love Mark "more than any man deserves to be loved". Mark calms Edie as Amanda escapes. Later, Mark discovers Amanda has several aliases. Meanwhile, Edie leaves a cured woman – "If I can survive this hell hole, I can survive anything."

Reggie, a Chicago cop, asks Jeanie out.

Police officer Reggie brings in a boy with a broken arm. Reggie asks Jeanie out, insisting he is not bothered by her HIV status. Angry that he knows, Jeanie tells Reggie not to feel sorry for her. Meanwhile, Kerry and Amanda treat Robin, a 28-year-old in labour following a car crash. Reggie orders an alcohol test on the husband. It is positive. Reggie arrests him while Robin gives birth to their daughter.

Carter is irked when Lucy goes out with Dale

Roxanne persuades Carter to meet her friends, so he cancels tutoring Lucy that evening. Seeing his chance, Dale invites Lucy to a river casino, insisting that he can help her study on the way. Lucy agrees, much to Carter's chagrin. Later, Lucy accidentally sticks herself with a needle. Tests show Lucy hasn't contracted anything. Dale tells Carter he is pleased – he may score that night.

Benton grows more comfortable with Reese's deafness

Benton treats Lisa Parks' granddaughter, who has appendicitis. Benton learns the sign language for "father". Later, as Parks scrubs in for the surgery, Anspaugh talks about her as though she were not there. Benton takes issue with his rudeness and Anspaugh apologises. The surgery is a success and Benton leaves to collect Reese. He shows him the sign for father and is delighted when Reese responds.

Other threads

Doug meets Joi Abbott. Her son, Ricky, has advanced ALD. Joi struggles to care for Ricky and his sister on her own. Ricky will not live past ten years. Carol suggests a home help, but Joi refuses. Later, she has second thoughts and asks for help.

Carter tells Kerry that her mother called the apartment. Kerry is surprised, because both her adoptive parents are dead. She has put her details on the internet and the caller could have been her birth mother.

Mark receives a package from NASA. He was accepted for the space programme years ago and but had to drop out to support Jen and Rachel. An old friend of his is interested in involving him in a new study.

"Double Blind"

5–12: First transmitted 21 January 1999
Written by Carol Flint; Directed by Dave Chameides

Mark helps Doris and decides against the NASA post

Mark is pleased when Anspaugh offers Mark tenure in three years if he doesn't take the

NASA job. Meanwhile, Doris complains about a policy to put paramedics on fire engines. Mark later treats Jim Haggerty, who was brought in by his wife because the paramedics were called to a fire. Mark saves Haggerty by performing a burr hole procedure. While Mark attends a lecture by a NASA representative, Doris tells him she has been suspended: it was her unit that left Jim Haggerty. Mark offers to talk to her chief and Doris is relieved. Later, Doug asks Mark about the NASA job, but the day's events have convinced him to stay in the ER.

Doug prescribes experimental drugs for Ricky Abbott

Ricky Abbott can't talk and has to have his morphine reduced to save an impacted bowel. Joi fears Ricky will not be able to tell her if he is in pain or not. Doug finds out that a pain study run by Mark has spare medicine that Ricky can use safely. Mark is angry when Doug prescribes the drug. Mark and Kerry decide to hush it up, fearing the hospital will lose the research funds. Doug complains about Mark and Kerry, but Carol appreciates their point. Doug is frustrated.

Corday hears of sexual harassment charges against Romano

Lucy wonders whether she should feel special when Romano stares at her breasts. Corday assures her that he only does that to females, as far as she knows! Meanwhile, Kerry tells Corday that she is investigating Romano for sexual harassment and asks if she has been harassed. Corday suggests the complainant is thin-skinned, but is surprised to discover it is Maggie Doyle. Maggie confronted Romano, but he gave her a bad evaluation. Corday fears Maggie will be in trouble but Doyle retorts: "Self-respect's a bitch." Having heard Romano bad-mouth Maggie earlier, Corday offers to talk to Kerry about it the next day.

Other threads

Carol treats Mr Ackerman, who is in the final stages of pancreatic cancer. Ackerman wants to smoke a joint to relieve the pain, but is not allowed. Later, Carol hears Ackerman's son hasn't arrived and he will have to stay the night. Seeing that is in pain and can't inhale, Carol lights the joint and blows smoke in his mouth.

Jeanie takes issue with plastic surgeon Dr Baker when he is curt with a patient. He is shamed into making more of an effort. Later, he invites Jeanie to the Art Institute and, warming, she accepts. Meanwhile, she and Reggie plan their weekend.

Benton treats Charlie Barnes, who claims to be over 140 years old. Benton is reluctant to operate as Charlie is high-risk but Charlie convinces him. He relents but Charlie falls into a coma before the operation.

"Choosing Joi"

5-13: First transmitted 4 February 1999
Written by Lydia Woodward; Directed by Christopher Chulack

Doug prescribes drugs for Ricky Abbott illegally

Perturbed, Doug muses about his present situation: "All this just about helping a kid." At work, Doug is told that Kerry and Mark will co-sign his orders for certain drugs. Doug agrees, but is insistent that he did the right thing for Ricky. Later, Ricky returns. Doug tries to get him a PCA (patient controlled analgesia) machine, but geneticist Roger Julian wants to admit Ricky and can't arrange one in time. Doug wants a PCA from Carol's clinic but needs Mark's signature. Mark refuses – he needs permission from Julian. Doug signs the order himself. Later, Joi has difficulty with the machine. Carol goes round to help and Doug arrives later.

Weaver's inquiry into Romano's conduct collapses

In Doc Magoo's, Corday tells Kerry about Romano's sexual advances. Kerry asks if Romano ever gave a reason for ending her fellowship. Corday reveals he asked her out, but is unsure the two matters are related. They quickly leave when Romano arrives. Later, Romano asks about Kerry. Corday covers, but Romano already knows. He warns that the hospital would be unimpressed if her relationship with Benton, while his student, were to come out. Corday is taken aback by the threat but later retracts her deposition, angering Maggie.

Kerry has to close the enquiry but tells Romano the testimonies are still on file. Hearing Kerry's threat, Romano offers to redraft Maggie's evaluation. However, he gets the upper hand when he offers his services as Acting Chief of Emergency Medicine to a pressured Anspaugh. Romano is unimpressed with the title, but Anspaugh says he can call himself Almighty God if he takes the job!

Mark treats Mobolage Ekabo

Mark offers to treat Mobolage Ekabo, a quiet Nigerian maintenance worker, who has back trouble. As Mark tries to examine him, Mobolage becomes hysterical and leaves. Later, he apologises and says he is impotent and wants Viagra. Mark insists on carrying out the examination and finds large scars on Mobolage's back. He asks about what caused the injuries, but Mobolage doesn't answer. Later, Mobolage struggles to talk to his wife Kubby about his impotence.

Other threads

Carol treats Alice Presley. She has no insurance and radiologist Steve Flint refuses to order an X-ray. Annoyed, Carol offers to pay for the test herself. Meanwhile, Malik and Jerry are roped in to care for Presley's dogs – enough to fill her van!

Carter teaches three students how to perform basic physical examinations. One student finds a problem with Strauss. Carter is dismissive, but then finds a problem with Strauss' lymph nodes. Carter performs a biopsy that reveals Hodgkin's Disease.

Mark tells Kerry and Jerry that Rachel needs glasses and hopes that's the worst thing she has genetically inherited from himself. Jerry jokes that she can't inherit his baldness. Talk of family influences Kerry, who meets Sam Broder, a private investigator, at Doc Magoo's. Broder searches out the parents of adopted children and Kerry hopes he can help find hers.

One to Watch

"The Storm"

5 − 14: First transmitted 11 February 1999
Written and Directed by John Wells

Doug helps Joi to end Ricky Abbott's suffering.

Carol wakes Doug at the Abbotts' house. Ricky is in great pain and Joi asks Doug to end his suffering. Doug knows he can't, but shows Joi how to reconfigure the PCA to administer the drug in greater doses. Later, Ricky is admitted in full arrest by his father, Richard Abbott, who urges the doctors to help his son. It is too late and Ricky dies. Richard Abbott calls in Dan Sullivan, his co-worker at the attorney's office, to investigate. It could be a case of first-degree murder.

Mark discovers that Genetics did not authorise the PCA machine and confronts Doug. He is furious when Doug reveals he gave the access code to Joi so she could change the dosage. Carol is stunned when she hears the same from Sullivan.

Meanwhile, Anspaugh is furious that Carol's clinic provided the PCA and orders Romano to close it immediately. Donald tells Kerry and Mark that they will both face disciplinary action for covering up Doug's actions (5-12). Carol confronts Doug over the closure of her clinic and is derisory of his apology. Chastened, Doug decides to tell Anspaugh he coerced Mark and Kerry but Mark insists he made his own decisions and will face the consequences.

Carter tells Mark that a school bus has been hit by a snowplough leaving several children injured. As Mark prepares to leave with a paramedic, Doug attempts to join him, but is told he is off service. Indignant, Doug decides to go to the accident and Jeanie joins him. On the way, Doug hits a patch of ice and his car skids into a wall.

Carter and Lucy admit their attraction for each other.

Lucy has rented *Titanic* for an evening in with Dale, but he seems unimpressed. Lucy is annoyed when Carter agrees it's a "chick flick". Carter asks Dale if he and Lucy have slept together. They haven't yet, but Dale does know that Lucy wears thongs! Later, as Lucy treats a woman who was kicked in her kickboxing class, Carter seems transfixed by her bottom! Lucy is bemused by Carter's interest. Later, Carter tries to find Lucy, who is absent from rounds, and finds her being taught kickboxing – and is kicked in the chest. Lucy tends to him and they slowly fall into a kiss. Chuny discovers them. Suddenly Malik and Jerry want to know the gossip.

Other threads

Kerry complains to Maggie and Mark that "bullet-head" Romano has taken over as Acting Chief of Emergency Medicine. Romano overhears and can't resist suggesting he start an investigation into misconduct. Later, Kerry is incredulous when Romano divides all his work between her and Mark, saying he intends to "supervise".

Mark sees Mobolage and asks if he has seen the urologist. Mobolage hasn't, as he has not told Kubby the truth. Mark offers to talk to her and later speaks to them both about the possibility of surgery.

Benton discovers that sign language lessons for Reese will cost $150 per week. Romano suggests Benton could earn $10,000 for a short stint at a rural hospital during his vacation.

One to Watch

"The Storm, Part Two"

5 – 15: First transmitted 18 February 1999
Written and Directed by John Wells

Doug Ross leaves the ER

Doug flags down an ambulance to transport him and a concussed and lacerated Jeanie back to County. He gives the lowdown on Jeanie's condition as they rush her in. Kerry immediately takes over and tells Doug he will not be working at County any more. She orders him to see Carol about his own cuts.

On the scene of the school bus accident (5-14), Mark tends to the trapped children. He treats one girl, J. J., whom he promises to see later. In the ER, the team treat the victims and Kerry orders the use of the trauma room where Ricky Abbot died, even though it is now a crime scene. Mark checks on J. J., who is sent to another hospital for amputation.

Carol confronts Anspaugh over his decision to close the clinic, claiming it will put services beyond the reach of the most needy. Anspaugh claims not to respect her judgment any more, arguing that a lawsuit against the hospital will hurt more people than the clinic closure. Carol persuades Anspaugh to let the clinic continue with someone he can trust in charge. Later, she convinces Lynette to run the clinic, for the sake of their patients.

Doug tells Carol he intends to resign. He fears he is losing Carol and Mark and has damaged their careers. Upset, Carol wonders where he will go. Doug reckons the Pacific Northwest, Portland or Seattle. He asks her to come with him. Emotional, Carol insists she loves him but that her life, work, family and friends are in Chicago. They agree to talk about it later.

After being confronted by Richard Abbott, Doug confirms to Carol that he has resigned. However, Dr Julian in Genetics defended Doug and the police will not press charges. Although Carol doesn't want to wake up without Doug tomorrow, he knows she won't come with him. They say their tearful goodbyes and Doug leaves, throwing his hospital ID on the floor. Before he leaves Chicago, Doug and Mark share a beer by the lake, talking about basketball as though nothing has happened.

Other threads

Kerry and Benton notice fluid around Jeanie's liver and order blood tests and a liver biopsy for forms of hepatitis. Later, Kerry warns Jeanie about a possible infection. Jeanie fears it is

AIDS, but Kerry suspects Hepatitis C. Kerry assures Jeanie that no positive diagnosis has been made but Jeanie is sure of Kerry's abilities.

Carter spends much of the day trying to convince Chuny and others that there is nothing between him and Lucy. Chuny insists he and Lucy make a cute couple.

Later, Carter tells Lucy they can't be in a relationship and Lucy offers no-strings sex, which throws him. Lucy laughs that Carter is so gullible. As they describe why they are unsuited, Lucy admits they remind her of her grandparents – married for 56 years and still having great sex.

Mobolage's wife, Kubby, talks to Mark about her husband's operation for erectile dysfunction. She admits they have not had sex partly because she may not be able to. She recounts how in Nigeria Mobolage was a dissident and tortured and she was raped by ten soldiers. Carol urges Kubby to tell Mobolage of the rape but she insists it would kill him and leaves.

Later, Kubby is rushed in, apparently stabbed by her husband. Carol comes across Mobolage who becomes aggressive when he hears Kubby may not survive. As Kerry calls security, Carol explains Mobolage may have post-traumatic stress.

Peter looks into vacation work in Northern Minnesota and North Dakota.

It had to end this way. Doug's final infraction was written on the wall more than four-and-a-half years before the case of Ricky Abbott. It's a harrowing story and one where we feel every inch for the mother, Joi. Doug's betrayal of Mark was equally foreshadowed, but still stings when you see it. The final scene by the lake is a wonderful touch. But, more than anything else, it's Carol's decision to stay that makes the story. Just at the point where she and Doug seem ready to move on together, it all falls apart. *The Storm* also works well in bringing to a climax other story threads, especially Mobolage Ekabo and the Carter-Lucy relationship. Although the car crash at first seems like a moment of false drama, it leads neatly into Jeanie's continuing story. *The Storm* leaves the series looking quite different.

"Middle of Nowhere"

5–16: First transmitted 25 February 1999
Written by Carol Flint & Neal Baer; Directed by Jonathan Kaplan

Peter works his vacation in Mississippi

Benton plans to supplement his income with a stint in Northern Minnesota, but is sent to LaVerne, Mississippi instead. Romano tells Peter he is in line for a cardiothoracic fellowship on his return.

En route, Peter's car overheats and he is ignored by a pickup driver. In LaVerne he finds no hospital, only an ill-equipped clinic in a run-down building. Nurse practitioner Maureen Chapman has neck and leg injuries and requested cover. She sends her boy, Sonny, to pick up Peter's car – he is the pickup driver Peter saw earlier. Maureen leaves Peter to treat Jesse Morgan, an old man with an ulcerous foot. That evening, Peter eats with Maureen before retiring to a cramped trailer. He is woken when Sonny throws a glass bottle at his door and drives away.

The next day, Peter finds his patients do not want to be treated by a black man. Annoyed, he leaves but comes across a tractor accident. He helps the injured and is soon back in LaVerne.

Peter does Maureen's Tuesday rounds. He sees pregnant young Melanie Ebee. Melanie's father refuses to let Peter examine Melanie indoors: she has had enough help from Peter's "kind" already. Peter also treats Adelina, a young diabetic who does not monitor her glucose level. Peter shows Adelina how to administer her insulin and laments the lack of medical education. Maureen wishes they had 100 per cent medical care, but realistically settles for 60 per cent.

Melanie goes into labour and Maureen sends Peter. After several hours, he delivers the breach baby successfully. Mr Ebee is pleased that the baby is white – he would kill it if it wasn't. Peter pretends the mother and baby are jaundiced and takes them to the clinic, aware that the baby's pigment may only appear days later. It doesn't, but Maureen praises Peter's good sense.

Maureen asks Peter to take Adelina and her grandmother for a check-up, and reveals the hospital has a videophone. At the hospital, Adelina is diagnosed with a hole in the heart. She needs an operation, but the grandmother refuses permission. Meanwhile, Peter speaks to Reese and Corday on the videophone and tries out some sign language.

Peter is sad to hear Jesse has died. At the funeral, Adelina is being teased for wanting to become a doctor. She's not so sure she does since Benton missed her diagnosis.

As Peter is about to leave, Sonny takes Peter to a shrimp boat accident in Southport. With Sonny's help, Peter saves the life of one fisherman. Won over, Sonny eagerly shakes hands with Peter.

Peter returns to Chicago with Adelina and her grandmother, having convinced them to go ahead with the surgery. He discovers Jeanie has had a setback – "I can't do this, I can't." Peter says she can't do it alone, but he is there for her.

"Sticks and Stones"

5 – 17: First transmitted 25 March 1999
Written by Joe Sachs; Directed by Felix Enriquez Alcalá

Carter runs over someone while on a ride-along

On a ride-along, Carter's unit is called to an apartment building. The tenants have attacked their landlord when he turned off their heat for non-payment of the rent. The angry tenants turn their attention to the rig, injuring Zadro. Carter breaks policy and drives, running over someone. In the ER, Carter blames the landlord for the angry scenes and is chastised by Kerry.

Doris and Lars bring in Avery, the boy Carter ran over. The father insists that someone will pay for this. Later, Carter apologises to the landlord for blaming him for the riot, but the man shows no remorse and expects his scar will look good before a judge. The man is returned, but the rig's driver, Lars, is shot by the mob. Carter realises it was meant for him. Lars dies and Carter has to break the news to Zadro.

Mark discovers the truth about the Ekabo stabbing

Mobolage is brought in from prison with dehydration. Mark tries to help but Mobolage remains silent. Later, Kubby wakens from her coma and reveals she tried to kill herself. Mark tries to assure Mobolage he was not at fault, but Mobolage explains that Kubby told him about the rape and he was not supportive. "She needed me and I left her." Later, Mark learns that all charges against Mobolage have been dropped. However, he came into the country on a forged visa and will be deported.

Lucy is diplomatic with an elderly patient.

Lucy treats Mrs Fong, an elderly woman who cannot speak English. Lucy discovers Mrs Fong has lung cancer, but that her family have not told her: they fear she will die sooner if she knows. Granddaughter Emily wishes Mrs Fong could know the truth but the son is adamant. Lucy mentions cancer and is horrified when Mrs Fong knows the word and seizes. When Mrs Fong comes round, Lucy tells her she has epilepsy. The son thanks Lucy for hiding the truth.

Other threads

Jeanie is annoyed that Al gave her Hepatitis C as well as HIV. Baker asks her out on a date but she says she is seeing someone else. She gives the same answer to Reggie. Later, Jeanie learns that Al did not give her Hepatitis C and that she must have caught it from a patient.

Malik and Jerry bother a pro-wrestler called Kornberg who has a knee injury. Kerry discovers that Kornberg is not enamoured with fame and tries to shield him from his fans. However, he draws attention to himself when he head-butts a door to rescue a trapped patient. Kornberg's father, a small Jewish man, is eager to publicise the rescue and arrange a photo shoot with sick children. It's clear Kornberg wrestles for his enthusiastic dad. "You know how parents can be," he adds – but of course, Kerry doesn't.

"Point of Origin"

5–18: First transmitted 8 April 1999
Written by Christopher Mack; Directed by Christopher Misiano

Mark helps Mobolage remember his torture

1 April 1999. Mark hears that Mobolage will be discharged then deported. He convinces Corday to admit Mobolage on a false chart so the man can try to get asylum. Mobolage talks to a psychiatrist, but cannot recount the torture. Later, Mark brings Mobolage to the scene of his own assault (3-20). He describes the attack vividly and wonders why he didn't fight back. "You cannot fight back," remembers Mobolage who starts to recall the horrific details of his torture.

Kerry resuscitates a DNR who she believes is her mother

Kerry rushes Mrs Brennan, an elderly DNR in arrest at a nursing home, to the ER. Carol angrily notes that Kerry's "judgement calls" are acceptable, but Doug's weren't. Emotional, Kerry reveals that Brennan is her mother. She hoped they could talk, but when she found her she was dying. Carol is apologetic and helps stabilise Brennan. Later, Sam Broder arrives with more information on Brennan. Kerry, however, has discovered that Brennan cannot be her mother: their blood types do not match. She fires Broder and sits with Mrs Brennan as she dies.

Corday and Benton compete for a trauma research fellowship

Benton is annoyed when his surgery with Weinstein is rescheduled – Peter will miss a school open house and Reese will be stuck in nursery for another month. He's more annoyed when Weinstein reschedules again as he and Romano are scrubbing in. Later, Corday tells Peter she is first in line for a trauma research fellowship she suggested. Benton is interested for himself and offers to co-author a sternal saw study with Weaver to improve his chances. Corday is annoyed that Peter is muscling in but Peter insists he can't serve in cardiothoracic for five years – he needs to spend time with Reese. Corday angrily tells Peter not to use Reese as an excuse. She urges him to apply for the job, confident she will get it.

Other threads

Carol has morning sickness and worries about being a single mother, Later, Coco (5-5) returns to the ER in labour. The baby is delivered safely but Coco, a schizophrenic, becomes agitated and is prescribed Haldol. Calmer, Coco apologises and is determined to return to her medication so she can care for her son. However, she fears she will not be allowed to care for him. Impressed by Coco's determination against the odds, Carol registers with an OB clinic.

It's April Fool's Day and, ironically, Carter is chief resident for the day. Amid Jerry's practical jokes, Carter sees Mrs Leason's four-month-old baby and discovers she has four broken ribs. Carter suspects abuse and calls the police. Later, he checks another X-ray and finds another broken rib. The baby has brittle bones and broke the rib during a check-up. Now Carter has to apologise to the mother and tell her that her the sad news.

"Rites of Spring"

5–19: First transmitted 29 April 1999
Written by David Mills; Directed by Jonathan Kaplan

Mark and Corday grow closer as she competes with Benton

Corday is due to present at a physicians' conference. Mark is also attending. Corday is pleased to discover Peter is not going to the conference, but irked to hear his sternal saw study is being published and may attract the research grants the fellowship post needs. Irritated, Corday bickers with Peter in Trauma. Meanwhile, Benton comes under pressure from Romano to pursue the cardiothoracic and not the trauma fellowship. Later, Corday and Mark share a laugh as they singularly fail to get to the conference on time. It is clear they are growing closer.

Jeanie is buoyed up by a show of faith

Jeanie treats Reverend Matthew Lynn, the preacher at Benton's mother's church. Jeanie

reveals she had her fill of church as a child, but Lynn is convinced he has met Jeanie for a purpose. Lynn needs blood draining from under his thumb but Jeanie cannot perform the procedure for fear of infecting him. Matthew shows faith in Jeanie and asks her to help. Afterwards, he offers healing prayers. Jeanie is touched and later visits his church.

Coco's example provides more solace for Carol

Lynette is annoyed when Coco misses an appointment, and claims she can't look after her child. However, the hospital's record was wrong and Coco arrived early. Coco is keeping a meticulous log of the baby's activity and her own medication. Carol assures Coco that she's doing well. Later, Carol tells Mark she is pregnant and cramping. Mark performs an ultrasound, but they can't find a heartbeat and need a better scan. He asks if Doug knows but Carol won't tell him until after the first trimester. Later, a second ultrasound finds a heartbeat.

Lucy shows promise during her psych rotation

Lucy talks to Sally McKenna, whose husband has glass in his eye after smashing up his car in rage. Lucy is chastised by Myers, her psych resident, for not seeing Michael McKenna instead. However, Mark reminds Lucy she is there to learn about talking to patients, not to chase after her resident. Lucy's next patient is an aggressive foster child named Seth. Lucy manages to break through to Seth and finds he has been overmedicated. She suggests to Myers' boss, DeRaad, that Seth needs psychotherapy as well as rationalised medication. DeRaad is impressed and tells Myers he could learn from his student.

Other threads

Carter mentors Antoine, a local school pupil interested in the ER. Carter is impressed by Antoine's diligence and offers helpful, if stern, advice. Together they look after a baby with lead poisoning and Antoine quickly realises a friend's child has similar symptoms. Carter checks the baby out and Antoine asks if he can stay longer to watch. Carter happily agrees.

Mobolage tells Mark that this is his last day at County. He has been allowed to stay and is going to school to get his civil engineering licence. Mark is pleased.

One to Watch

"Power"

5 – 20: First transmitted 6 May 1999
Written by Carol Flint; Directed by Laura Innes

A manhunt takes place during a power cut in the ER

While Chicago is in the middle of a lightning storm, Romano confronts Mark about trying to steal Corday away from surgery. Meanwhile, Haleh finds a patient, Laurie Heller, who has been beaten and raped in the hospital. Corday saw the patient being pushed by a tech, but can't identify the man and can't be sure he was staff.

As a manhunt is launched, Corday and Romano operate on Laurie but the power goes

out. The surgery is completed but she crashes and when the back-up generator fails, Laurie has to be bagged. At Laurie's bedside, Romano compliments Corday on the surgery and admits he will make himself scarce if she will stay. Later, Corday identifies a man who hanged himself as the tech she saw earlier. Mark encourages her to wind down and takes her to an amusement arcade.

Lucy applies her psych skills when she returns to the ER

Lucy has started a second ER rotation and is again assigned to Carter. She treats Phyllis Farr, who sells pheromone sprays to attract the other sex. Lucy tries one and waves her wrist in front of Carter with no success. Later, Carter drops an entire bottle over himself and is fooled when Mark pretends to be attracted to him! Meanwhile, Carter picks a fight with Roxanne over selling insurance to Farr and they break up.

Carol and Lucy treat Mrs Armstrong, an elderly woman who fell down the stairs and has bed sores. Lucy is concerned about Mr Armstrong's mental state and orders a psych consult. Carter agrees, but reminds her that Mrs Armstrong is the actual patient. On further examination, Lucy discovers one of Mrs Armstrong's bedsores is a bullet wound. Mr Armstrong shot her to get the insurance.

Lucy confides in Carter that she is clueless about long-term relationships and psychoanalyses the cause. Carter jokingly asks how long she was on psych rotation.

Other threads

Corday complains that Peter is determined to go for the trauma fellowship position, but he insists he hasn't made up his mind. During the power cut, Peter has to help Reese, who is scared of the dark. With Reese strapped to his back, Peter treats Mr Joiner who has been struck by lightning. Peter realises his muscle tissue was breaking down from the lightning strike and merely needed fluids. Kerry is impressed.

Carol has decided to write to Doug and asks Mark for comments on the letter. Mark thinks Doug will be on the first plane back once he hears the news. Later, Carol tries to fax the letter but it gets stuck when the power goes out. Jerry rescues the letter and Carol decides to send it later.

A strong regular episode in which the power cut adds that little bit extra. The manhunt in the ER provides a lot of suspense while the power cut works neatly with the Reese story and Carol's decision to write to Doug. But the episode really works because it's a strong character piece. Peter's concern for Reese is wonderful to see. The pheromone strand is very funny, especially Carter's concerned reaction to Mark. And we finally get a sense of the real Romano when he reveals the high regard he has for Corday. There's an unrequited love story brewing.

"Responsible Parties"

5 – 21: First transmitted 13 May 1999
Written by Jack Orman; Directed by Christopher Chulack

The ER deals with a harrowing car accident

Three teenagers are brought in following a car accident on Prom night. The driver, Justin, pulled Travis Mitchell from the back of the car but Travis has third-degree burns over 80 per cent of his body. Travis' sister, Shannon, has a spinal injury. Justin's date, Melissa, is missing. Chicago cop Reggie wants Justin to take a blood alcohol test. Justin breaks down and reveals the accident happened as he changed a CD in the car. Meanwhile, Travis is dying and Carter has to intubate him until the parents arrive. Mr and Mrs Mitchell are told that Shannon may lose function from the waist down and Travis only has a 20 per cent chance of survival.

The trauma fellowship is awarded

It is decision day on the trauma fellowship position. Benton assures Romano that he is still interested in the cardiothoracic fellowship. Romano is unconvinced and encourages a bemused Corday to apply for it. Meanwhile, the decision on the fellowship is divided between three candidates. Anspaugh picks Benton and Mark breaks the news to Corday. Romano confronts Benton for being dishonest. Corday later asks Romano if he was serious about the cardiothoracic fellowship.

Carol tells Doug about the pregnancy

Confident that the pregnancy is going well, Carol decides to fax her letter to Doug with a note asking him to call. During the day she is exposed to a number of risks in the ER: an X-ray and a patient with HIV and CMV. Kerry notes her behaviour and deduces that Carol is pregnant. Kerry is supportive and tells Carol only to do what she is happy with. Carol is grateful. Later she receives her call from Doug and tells Mark that he won't be coming back. Carol jokes this is the first time he has respected her wishes. Mark encourages her to come for a milkshake with him and Corday later. Carol agrees, so long as he's paying – she's eating for two.

Other threads

Carter discovers that Lucy is taking Ritalin and has been on it since the eighth grade. Carter expects her to stop now but she insists her doctor still prescribes it and she is not an addict. Lucy hopes he will respect her decision.

Two FBI agents bring in Amber, a stripper who was shot through her breast implant. The agents ask a lot of questions and are shifty when Mark insists Amber has a chest tube and must stay. Later, a real FBI agent arrives but tells Mark the identity of the others is strictly "need to know". Later, Mark receives $2,000 dollars from a mysterious benefactor. Randi tells him to call the FBI.

"Getting to Know You"

5–22: First transmitted 20 May 1999
Written by Lydia Woodward; Directed by Jonathan Kaplan

Carol has a revealing ultrasound

Kerry finds an abandoned toddler and brings him to the ER. She and Carol discover the boy, whom they call Jack, has a neurological problem and Carol suggests he may have been abandoned for this reason. The implication is not lost on Kerry. Later, the boy's parents are found: the boy was kidnapped by his nanny and her drug addict boyfriend three weeks previously. The police bring Jack's parents in.

Meanwhile, Carol treats Celinda, a woman with appendicitis who claims to have medical empathy. She quickly realises Carol is pregnant, starting rumours, but can't determine the sex. Later, Mark and Elizabeth help Carol with her ultrasound and discover two heartbeats – Carol is having twins. The ER celebrates.

Carter realises the pressure he puts on Lucy and others

Lucy arrives late and gives a poor presentation to Romano. She tells Carter she stopped taking Ritalin two days previously. Carter is supportive but during the day Lucy gets into trouble with Mark and irks Seth (5-19) with her tardiness. Meanwhile, Carter treats Antoine (5-19) who was mugged on his way to an interview that Carter had arranged. Later, Antoine returns again, beaten up after going after the mugger. Carter is angry he lost his chance at summer science lab. Carter is further annoyed to find Lucy taking Ritalin again. Lucy bitterly complains that she has never lived up to his expectations. Carter is struck and apologises to Antoine for putting him under pressure.

Peter takes drastic action to keep Reese

Benton is learning sign language with Reese but is annoyed when Roger, Carla's boyfriend, attends one lesson. Later, Carla reveals that she and Roger were married last week and are moving to Germany. Peter angrily tells her she can't take Reese, but Carla is confident. Later, Peter picks up Reese from the babysitter at Carla's apartment. Carla calls Peter's answerphone, bitter that he has taken Reese without her permission, but Peter doesn't pick up.

Corday and Mark make their feelings clear.

Corday tries to talk to Mark all day but is constantly interrupted. Romano offers Corday the cardiothoracic fellowship during surgery, taunting Peter. Corday takes issue with Romano's behaviour towards Peter and others, and this is vindicated when Anspaugh picks Romano up on a similar issue. Later, Corday finally gets to talk to Mark. She is scared about moving on too soon. Mark assures her they have found something amazing and he doesn't want to miss an opportunity.

Other threads

Reggie talks to Jeanie but is called away to deal with a gun-wielding lunatic. Later, Jeanie

hears that the man has been shot after he injured a police officer. She is relieved to discover that the officer is not Reggie, although Reggie shot the gunman. Jeanie tells Reggie that she broke up with him over her Hepatitis C, but has realised she needs to deal with it. She comforts Reggie over the shooting.

Season Six
1999–2000

Themes

Kerry supports Romano's promotion to Chief of Staff and is made Chief of Emergency Medicine. She appoints her mentor Gabriel Lawrence as an attending but the situation is problematic.

Carol gives birth, but struggles to cope as a single mother. New ER attending Luka Kovac supports her, but their romance is short-lived. While Luka makes a play for Carol, she realises she has only one true soul mate.

Tragedy strikes the ER when a psychotic patient attacks Lucy and Carter. Carter struggles to cope with the consequences and becomes addicted to pain medication. His colleagues discover the truth and issue him with an ultimatum.

Abby Lockhart switches careers from OB nurse to become a medical student and joins the ER for a trauma rotation. She has trouble adjusting to the demands of her new position.

Peter is told he may not be Reese's father but is determined to keep hold of him. After a battle with Carla, he finds romance with the new Paediatrics Attending, Cleo Finch.

Mark's father moves to Chicago and has a brief fling with Elizabeth's mother. Later, Mark receives tragic news about his father's emphysema, and supports him in his declining health.

Corday saves a murderer, but finds a debt of duty in trying to help the families of his victims. She is given an unwelcome promotion to become Associate Chief of Surgery and has several run-ins with Romano.

Ones to Watch

6 – 8: *Great Expectations* – Carol goes into labour but the deliveries are not without their complications.

6–13 & **6–14:** *Be Still My Heart / All in the Family* – a psychotic patient attacks Lucy and Carter. The staff work feverishly to save them.

6–21: *Such Sweet Sorrow* – Carol makes a dying patient comfortable for her last moments with her family and is persuaded to join her soul mate, Doug.

"Leave It to Weaver"

6–1: First transmitted 30 September 1999
Written by Lydia Woodward; Directed by Jonathan Kaplan

Kerry supports Romano as Chief of Staff

Weaver is surprised to hear that Anspaugh is returning to general surgery. She is more anxious to hear Romano is his likely successor as Chief of Staff. Mark and Kerry agree to oppose Romano's appointment. However, a meeting of department heads proves there is wide support for Romano. Mark still objects but Kerry, aware the battle is lost, backs down. Mark is furious: "You hung me out to dry." Kerry reckons she was just politically astute – this is confirmed when Romano appoints her as Chief of Emergency Medicine. Mark takes out his frustration playing baseball: "I thought a Romano-Weaver double homicide was overkill."

The ER deals with the wounded from a coffee shop

Heavily pregnant, Carol narrowly escapes death when a truck crashes into a coffee shop. She treats the wounded, many of whom she had met minutes before. One teenager who was rude to Carol is horrified to find she is to treat him. As the ER stacks up, Kerry is pestered by a man with a migraine. She closes trauma, but Romano later reopens admissions.

Suddenly there is a fire alarm. Randi discovers the migraine man started the alarm to get some attention – and punches him to the floor. Later, Carol discovers that a kind lady she was rude to at the coffee shop has died.

Luka Kovac starts in the ER

Croatian doctor Luka Kovac is filling in at the ER. Against Kerry's wishes, he takes a young girl to her critically ill mother. Carol is quietly impressed but Luka, reduced to suturing, thinks that Mark and Kerry don't rate his abilities. Later, Carter deals with a pregnant women injured in a car accident. Luka performs an emergency Caesarean and has a reluctant Carol help him. After, Carol tells Luka she feels very lucky – and that she thinks he is a good doctor. Luka is grateful.

Jeanie takes care of a baby who may be HIV+

Jeanie and new paediatrics attending Cleo Finch treat a mother with end-stage AIDS. Finch can't order an HIV test on the baby, Carlos, without the mother's consent, but Jeanie does anyway and puts the baby on the triple cocktail. Fostering services tell Jeanie that finding a mother will be difficult. Jeanie tells Reggie she would like to foster but is unmarried. Reggie proposes, but Jeanie is torn.

Other threads

Carter is surprised to treat Elaine Nichols, his cousin's ex-wife. Their attraction is obvious and Carter later meets Elaine at a Carter Family Foundation fundraiser. He invites Elaine for a drink, but she has something else in mind...

Concerned that she can't work with Romano, Elizabeth talks to Rush Hospital about pursuing a cardiothoracic fellowship.

Peter and Carla attend a court-ordered mediation over Reese's future. Peter reveals that he and Reese have moved in with Jackie to give Reese more support.

The ER takes a message for Mark: his mother has died.

"Last Rites"

6 – 2: First transmitted 7 October 1999
Written by Jack Orman; Directed by Felix Enriquez Alcalá

Mark and Kerry disagree over a DNR

Mark returns from his mother's funeral. He is thrown back into work when Carter asks him about Amy, a 20-year-old with end-stage melanoma. Amy is a DNR. Alone, Amy tells Mark that she doesn't want to die today. Mark asks her to confirm that she is revoking her DNR. She does and he intubates her. Amy's father is irate and Kerry argues with Mark when Amy codes. Mark threatens to resign unless he is allowed to save her. Kerry is torn. Mark bitterly tells Kerry to act like an ER Chief. She stands back and lets him try. Mark is unable to save Amy.

"Dr Dave" joins the ER

Second-year resident David "Dr Dave" Malucci joins the ER. His work is distinctly slipshod: he ignores Carter's orders, gives incomplete answers to Lucy and takes Carol's diagnosis rather than see her patient.

Later, Dave hears of an accident at a construction yard and persuades Carter to go with him. They bring the injured man in, but incur the wrath of the paramedics. Kerry is also annoyed and tells them they are not trained or insured to work on the street. Carter is angry that Dave got him into trouble.

Corday is given an unwelcome promotion

Corday is surprised when Romano publicly announces her as the new Associate Chief of Surgery. She confronts Romano, but he knew she'd take it. Corday warms to the idea but Mark notes Romano is untrustworthy. Later, Romano gives Corday his dirty work – stopping Peter's elective surgery and firing some staff.

Jeanie accepts Reggie's proposal

Baby Carlos' mother has died and he is due to be taken into care. Jeanie offers to take Carlos but an official from DCFS says she is not a licensed foster parent. Jeanie persuades him to look into the matter. Later, the official discovers that Jeanie illegally tested Carlos and tells her she won't be permitted to foster without a qualification. Jeanie is disappointed, but realises that marrying Reggie is not just about keeping Carlos any more. She accepts Reggie's proposal.

Other threads

Carla demands to know if Peter has hired a private investigator to follow her. Peter hasn't, but his lawyer may have. An argument ensues and Carla reveals that Rees emay not be his. Momentarily taken aback, Peter recovers and insists Reese *is* his son.

Carol treats Vanessa, an elderly Catholic woman who is dying. Vanessa refuses a priest, but later changes her mind. Carol asks Luka to provide Dopamine, but when she returns finds Luka playing the part of a priest for Vanessa's benefit. He gives her the blessing and she dies peacefully.

Carter sees Elaine in an exam room with Corday. He finds out that Elaine has breast cancer and needs a mastectomy. In bed that night, Elaine realises from Carter's cold behaviour that he knows. She quietly tells him to leave.

"Greene with Envy"

6 – 3: First transmitted 14 October 1999
Written by Patrick Harbinson; Directed by Peter Markle

Mark is irked when Dr Gabriel Lawrence starts in the ER

Kerry has hired her mentor, Gabriel Lawrence, as an attending. Gabe quickly shows his creativity when he uses a blood pressure gauge as a tourniquet. Mark is annoyed that Kerry did not tell him about Gabe. He is peeved when Gabe proves one of Mark's patients has no neurological disorder and discharges him. Mark insists that Gabe should have waited for a CT, but Corday politely agrees with Gabe's diagnosis.

Later, Mark and Corday argue over a reporter in the ER. Out to prove himself, Mark adds extra tests to Gabe's orders and saves a girl's life. Gabe is annoyed that Mark checked up on him. However, Mark sees Gabe's strengths when he saves a patient. That night, Mark apologises to Elizabeth and they end up in bed.

Luka treats a domestic abuse case

Luka treats Loren, who has a broken arm and cuts. Loren is vague about her injuries and Luka, checking records, suspects abuse. He orders Loren's husband, Pauly, be restrained as "a danger to others". When DeRaad refuses to hold Pauly, Luka provokes him into a rage. Pauly throws a punch and is taken away. Carol knows they won't hold him without Loren's statement. Later, Kerry tells Luka that he is not needed now that Gabe has started. Carol gives Luka a lift home.

Carter tries to talk to Elaine before her mastectomy

Carter hears that Elaine is coming in for a mastectomy. She is anxious and doesn't appreciate Carter's concern. Elaine worries about the surgery and tries to leave, but is persuaded by Elizabeth to stay. The surgery is a success and Carter watches Elaine in recovery. A nurse tells him he can go in, but he doesn't.

Jeanie and Reggie get custody of Carlos and are married

The nurses celebrate Jeanie's engagement. As Jeanie and Reggie are about to leave for New Orleans, Kerry and Adele arrive with Carlos. Adele has arranged for Jeanie to take Carlos temporarily and will arrange a permanent settlement when Jeanie becomes a registered fosterer. The couple are thrilled and get married in the city hall, with Randi and a deliveryman as witnesses.

Other threads

Peter's lawyer encourages Peter to take a DNA test if he's "looking for a way out". Later, Cleo looks at Reese for an ear infection and says it could be hereditary. Peter asks Jackie if he had ear infections as a child, but she can't remember.

Carter and Corday treat Joshua, a 16-year-old with a gunshot wound. When they realise the "friend" who came in with Joshua is the shooter, a gunfight ensues. Miraculously, no one is injured.

Romano orders Corday to show a reporter around the ER. The reporter sees Carter working on a critical patient and generally gets in the way. Mark angrily tells Corday she can always refuse Romano's orders.

"Sins of the Fathers"

6 – 4: First transmitted 21 October 1999
Written by Doug Palau; Directed by Ken Kwapis

Gabe jumps to conclusions about a suicidal teenager

Mark and Dave intubate Tommy Stevens, a teenager who has tried to hang himself. Dave reckons Tommy is "veggie burger", but doesn't see Tommy's girlfriend Becky standing behind. Gabe berates Dave for his callousness. Later, Gabe hassles Tommy for his father's details, but Mark tells him to leave matters to the police. Later, Mark intercedes when Gabe accuses Mr Stevens of pushing Tommy to suicide by abandoning him. Tommy later reveals he was depressed about breaking up with Becky. Gabe admits he jumped to conclusions. He tells Mark that he worked too hard and that his son once injured himself just to get to see him.

Corday confronts Romano about her role

Elizabeth is horrified to find her photo in a critical newspaper article about County General (6-3). Romano angrily tells Corday she should protect his interests. He tells her to change Anspaugh's schedules as they interfere with his own.

Corday reluctantly speaks to Anspaugh who says she should refuse Romano's dirty work if she disagrees with it. Later, Corday attacks Romano for trying to push Anspaugh out. Romano insists he just wants Fridays off: "When you assume, you make an ass out of you and me."

Dave's compassion gets the better of him

Dave and Carter toss a coin for Larry, the most injured of two parachutists. Dave wins and stabilises Larry. He then tries to push in on an interesting procedure, but Mark tells him to wait for Larry's CT. Larry is dying. Dave calls Larry's wife who asks Dave to read a message to her husband. Dave is reluctant, but Mark presses him to do so. By the time he has transcribed the message, Larry is dead. Dave leaves, but his compassion gets the better of him and he returns to read the message to the deceased.

Other threads

Cleo and Yosh treat a four-year-old with an upset stomach. Cleo diagnoses food poisoning, but the child is readmitted in full arrest. Cleo is guilty that she missed iron poisoning, but Kerry's investigation shows Cleo did all she could. Kerry helps Cleo by letting her lead a later paediatrics trauma.

Gabe, Lucy and Carter work on Larry's friend. Gabe orders tests but insists he asked for different ones when the results come back. Lucy is positive he gave her wrong instructions. Carter doesn't think Gabe would make that mistake.

Carol meets Meg, a pregnant waitress who is fired from Doc Magoo's. Meg has no OB so Carol arranges an ultrasound. She gets Meg a job interview in the cafeteria on the condition that Meg quits smoking. Meg agrees but misses the interview. Carol tries to sort something out.

Carter hears that Elaine is due in to have her stitches taken out. He talks to her and starts to win her round. They agree to meet later.

"Truth & Consequences"

6 – 5: First transmitted 4 November 1999
Written by R. Scott Gemmill; Directed by Steve De Jarnatt

Gabe goes into "meltdown" during a multi-victim trauma

An explosion in a High School laboratory brings chaos to the ER. The science teacher, Mr Sutherland, is critically ill, but there are many more minor injuries. In the frantic pace, Gabe starts to get his patients mixed up.

Kerry asks Gabe to help out with a peritoneal lavage but, frustrated and confused, Gabe throws the kit across the room. Kerry is concerned but Gabe apologises and partially reassures her. She defends Gabe against Mark's accusations that Gabe went into "meltdown". However, at the end of the day she finds Gabe looking for his car. He refuses her help, but Kerry knows that something is wrong.

Mark injures a relative when Carter is attacked

Mr Perez calls to see his son Nathan, who was in the lab accident. Perez is angry that Nathan may lose the sight in one eye and blames a boy named Howie who Nathan says switched chemicals in the lab, causing the explosion. Howie confesses to Carter, but Perez rushes in, angry. Carter intercedes but is thrown into a glass window.

Mark arrives and manhandles Perez to the floor, crushing Perez's larynx in the

process. Romano is angry at Mark for a potential lawsuit. Carter speaks to Howie, who is racked with guilt.

Lucy and Carol compete over detox beds

Lucy sees Jesse Keenan, a frustrated young artist who ate his paints. He is taking cocaine for inspiration. Lucy persuades him to join a detox programme. Meanwhile, Carol discovers that Meg (6-4) is using heroin and poaches Jesse's bed in rehab. Lucy angrily confronts Carol before trying to convince Jesse to join the outpatient programme. Jesse is unsure and leaves. Later, Carol discovers that Meg left without checking into detox – both patients have missed out.

Other threads

At Doc Magoo's, Elaine tells Carter that she is leaving for Europe. When he hopes to meet up on her return, she avoids his question.

Peter treats Benjamin Hearn, who was hit by a car. Mr Hearn refuses to let his son have anything but his family's blood. However, Benjamin's brother Aaron turns out to have HIV. Peter convinces Aaron to tell his father. Later, Aaron tells Peter he took his advice and his father has disowned him.

Dave spends much of the day asking the staff about Weaver's leg. Weaver finds out and tells him to ask her if he really wants to know. Shamed, Dave suggests it's not really his business. Kerry firmly agrees.

"The Peace of Wild Things"

6 – 6: First transmitted 11 November 1999
Written by John Wells; Directed by Richard Thorpe

Kerry and Mark discover Gabriel Lawrence is ill

Gabe is unsettled when he helps Cleo with an elderly woman with dementia. He is acting a little scatterbrained and Kerry finds his spectacles in the fridge. Concerned, Kerry speaks to Gabe's former employer at New Western, Renee Spielman. Renee reveals she suspected a problem, but Gabe quitted when she asked for a neurological exam. Mark tells Kerry to fire Gabe, but she is not sure she can.

Later, Mark asks Gabe to prescribe medicine for a patient Gabe saw earlier. Gabe does, but is surprised when Mark reveals the patient is actually a member of staff in disguise: Gabe never treated the woman. Humiliated, Gabe storms out. Kerry finds Gabe and he confesses to having Alzheimer's. Cleo's patient confirmed his fears of ending up alone. Kerry sobs that she will visit him but Gabe sadly notes that even if she does, he won't know who she is.

Carol takes drastic action to keep Meg off heroin

Carol tells Meg she needs medicine for a bladder infection and asks about the detox

programme. Meg insists she has been clean for five days. Carol gets Cleo to write a prescription for Meg and takes it to her but finds Meg talking to a dealer.

Carol, determined to keep Meg off heroin, tells Reggie and they arrange a stakeout. Meg and the dealer are caught and arrested. Meg is furious and screams at Carol. Later, Carol regrets her actions and confesses to Mark that she misses Doug.

Carter and Cleo disagree over an obese child with diabetes

Carter treats Eddie Bernero, an obese 12-year-old who is diagnosed with diabetes. Eddie's father has no medical insurance, but is starting a new job and will have benefits soon. He asks Carter to take diabetes off the chart so he can get the insurance to pay for treatment in three months. Cleo lambasts the father for not giving the boy treatment immediately. Carter reasons that without insurance, the child will get no treatment at all, and later agrees to change Eddie's chart.

Other threads

The ER treat the victims of a fire at a nursing home. Carter helps Mrs Connelly find her husband, who is having difficulty breathing. She is scared of being left alone and wants them to intubate. However, tests show that her husband has a progressive heart disorder. Carter persuades her to sign a DNR and stays with her as Mr Connelly dies. He quietly calls the time of death.

Peter tells Jackie about Carla's claim that he may not be Reese's father. He has a DNA test kit, but is not sure whether to use it. Jacky tells him that Reese will find out the truth eventually. At work, Peter decides to perform the test and, when he drops Reese at Carla's, reveals he has decided to get the results. He makes a heart-rending plea to Carla not to take Reese from him.

"Humpty Dumpty"

6−7: First transmitted 18 November 1999
Written by Neal Baer; Directed by Jonathan Kaplan

Corday coerces a rapist before administering aid

On a ride-along, Corday treats a car crash victim. A detective from Violent Crimes reveals that the man is a carjacker and demands to know where the passenger is. Corday tells the detective to back off but he fears the passenger, Sandra Perry, could be in danger. Corday threatens to let the man bleed to death unless he tells her where Sandra is. The man gives the location.

Later, as Benton and Corday work on the carjacker, his victim is brought in. Luka and Kerry identify multiple stab wounds and order a rape kit. The woman is intubated before she can identify her attacker. Her condition worsens and she dies. Meanwhile, Corday saves the carjacker.

Romano tells Corday that someone has complained she coerced her patient. Corday admits she did so for good reason, but Romano points out that confessions given under duress are thrown out.

Cleo deals with an alcoholic mother and son

Mrs Kottmeier brings in her son, Chad, who she believes is taking drugs. Lucy insists Chad doesn't have to undergo a test but Cleo gets Chad to agree, if it will stop his mother's harping. Lucy is angry that Cleo questioned her in front of her patient. Later, the test shows Chad is clean but has liver problems. He is an alcoholic. Chad tells Cleo that his mother also drinks heavily. Cleo confronts the mother, but she is only relieved Chad is not taking hard drugs.

Carol sees Meg's baby taken away from her

Carol feels like an overgrown pumpkin and is reduced to answering the telephones. She has a dizzy spell and is put on a foetal monitor, but everything is fine. Later, Carol hears that Meg has given birth: she is in the jail ward and wants to see Carol. Carol reluctantly visits and Meg begs to keep her baby. Social services take him away. Disturbed, Carol leaves quickly as Meg starts screaming for her baby.

Other threads

Lucy treats a gospel choir involved in a bus accident en route to a competition. Mr Owens, the choirmaster, has congestive heart failure. Lucy persuades him to stay for extra tests but he and his choir are late and leave. Later, Owens is brought in after a heart attack. He is mad because his choir missed the competition!

When Gabe struggles during a neurological exam, Mark calls for his son. Gabe doesn't want to be a burden, but later he agrees to live with his son. As Gabe prepares to leave, Carter has a patient he can't diagnose. He appeals to Gabe who is reluctant. Eventually Gabe intercedes and saves the man's life: "Score one for the absent-minded professor, huh?" Kerry hires Luka to fill Gabe's post.

One to Watch

"Great Expectations"

6 – 8: First transmitted 25 November 1999
Written by Jack Orman; Directed by Christopher Misiano

Carol has twins but the labour is problematic

Carol comes to work on her day off to train Lydia to cover for her but finds Lydia is on a different shift. She heads home but on the El her waters break. Fifteen minutes later, Luka sees Carol sitting at an El station and manages to get her back to the ER. Carol wants to be taken to OB rather than deliver in the ER, but it is too late and Kerry tells Carol she has no choice. She refuses to let Carter get involved! Carol gives birth to a baby girl, Tess, who weighs a healthy six pounds, and is taken up to OB. She is joined by Abby Lockhart, her OB nurse.

Mark arrives and is uncomfortable to find Carol's doctor is unavailable and Janet Coburn is filling in. Carol is prepped for the OR as a precaution. Suddenly, the baby's heartbeat slows. Carol is rushed to surgery and has a crash Caesarean. The second baby is delivered but is blue. After some time, she starts to pink up. However, Carol starts to bleed out. Coburn orders a hysterectomy tray and Carol is dismayed. Mark forcefully objects to Coburn's plans as Carol loses consciousness.

Carol wakes. Both babies are fine and Mark is holding one. Abby confirms that Carol "owes her future children" to Mark, who prevented the hysterectomy. Grateful, Carol wants to name her second daughter after Mark's mother. She is disappointed to hear her name was Ruth! Instead she settles on Mark's mother's middle name, Catherine, and names her second baby Kate.

Corday spends Thanksgiving looking after Rachel and David

Elizabeth hosts Thanksgiving for Rachel and Mark's dad, David, when Mark is called away to help Carol. The meal begins shakily, with David making digs at English food and the British role on D-Day and Rachel explaining how the founders escaped English persecution ("Yes, so they could go about persecuting the Indians," retorts Elizabeth). Nevertheless, David and Elizabeth slowly to warm to each other and discuss the loss of Mark's mother. Rachel is missing for half an hour and Elizabeth finds she has started her first period. She sends David out for sanitary towels, but he slips on the ice and cuts his head. Later, Mark sees David being sutured by Elizabeth in the ER and, when she has gone, David admits he likes her.

Dave makes a surprising diagnosis

Carter struggles to diagnose Shelley Robinson, an 18-year-old with a range of symptoms. Dave asks if Shelley has recently travelled overseas or to Florida and surprised, Carter notes she has. Dave diagnoses Jamaican Vomiting Syndrome (JVS) but Carter is unconvinced. After checking up, Carter discovers Malucci was right. Malucci reluctantly explains he had to settle for a medical school in Grenada after messing up his exams. Carter can't resist a dig, but Malucci points out that his badge still reads MD.

Other threads

A motorist hits an ambulance carrying Mrs Olson, a 78-year-old in chronic renal failure. Olsen now may have chest trauma as well. Luka examines her and finds she missed her dialysis to have her hair done for her birthday. He notes fluid collecting around her heart, but can't determine if this is due to the renal failure or the trauma. Her condition deteriorates and Luka and Carter are unable to save her.

A great all round episode that really shows the show's range. We have tension and tragedy but perhaps the most remarkable thing about *Great Expectations* is the humour. Carol's lumbering trek into work then back home again is followed by her amusing struggle on the El with Luka. After a moment's panic where Carol loses consciousness, we're back into comedy mode with Kerry cheerfully insisting Carol deliver in the ER and Carter being told he can't help out. Then Carol's high after being given pain medication by Babcock – "He'll always be the epidural man to me." It's all a joy to watch – perfectly crafted to lull you into a false idea of what the episode is about before you're hit with the complications. Mark's disagreement with Coburn is a wonderful touch for long-term viewers, harking back to Season One's *Love's Labor Lost*.

"How the Finch Stole Christmas"

6 – 9: First transmitted 16 December 1999
Written by Linda Gase; Directed by Fred Einesman

Lucy arranges an emergency procedure for Valerie Page

Christmas Eve 1999. Lucy treats Valerie Page, a 24-year-old with cardiomyopathy. Valerie will not live unless she has a heart transplant. Benton agrees to move her up the transplant list. Lucy looks into LVAD (Left Ventricular Assist Device) to keep Valerie's heart working. She seconds the equipment from a neighbouring hospital, but discovers the only person who can use it is Romano, now on holiday. Lucy calls Romano, but gets the cold shoulder. Later, she turns up on his doorstep and demands his help. Despite himself, Romano is impressed with Lucy and performs the implant. Lucy will still face a disciplinary hearing though – Romano has his reputation to think about.

Corday convinces the rapist to undergo surgery

Corday's carjacker, Dean Rawlins (6-7), fakes chest pains to talk to her. He gloats that her actions mean his confession is inadmissible. Later, Corday hears that Rawlins has been linked to another crime. Corday talks to Rawlins. He complains of leg pain but Corday suspects he is faking. In fact he has a blood clot and needs surgery. Rawlins refuses consent: he would rather die than face jail. Corday does not want to persuade Rawlins, but Anspaugh reminds her of her duty. Eventually she persuades him to undergo surgery but notes how easily her scalpel could slip.

Cleo decides to take action to protect Chad Kottmeier

Chad Kottmeier (6-7) is brought in after a fall. Chad is drunk and has sustained an ankle fracture and possible head injury. Mrs Kottmeier explains she was having a party and didn't hear Chad fall. She admits she gave Chad one beer, but Cleo insists it was more than one. Cleo has Adele put Chad on an alcohol treatment programme rather that let him go.

Other threads

Carter treats Taylor, a 15-year-old, who has been shot by a gang. Carter confiscates Taylor's gun and gives it to the police. Carter is incredulous when Taylor insists it was a gift for his kid brother. He gives Taylor one of the ER's secret Santa gifts, Malik's GameBoy, as a replacement. Soon, kids wanting to swap guns for GameBoys inundate him! Later, a seven-year-old dies from a shot to the head. The shooter was Taylor. Carter angrily dumps the impounded guns on Taylor's lap.

On a visit to the ER, Carol reveals she is exhausted looking after the twins. The ER staff rally round to give Carol a rest. Later, Luka gives Carol a ride home and she invites him to stay for eggnog.

Kerry helps a group of businessmen dressed as Santas who have come down with food poisoning. One of them helps Kerry fix the ER's Y2K problem – and invites her to Doc Magoo's. Kerry declines, but later accepts his offer.

"Family Matters"

6 – 10: First transmitted 6 January 2000
Written by Patrick Harbinson; Directed by Anthony Edwards

Jing-Mei (Deb) Chen returns to the ER

Carter is surprised when Deb Chen (1-20) returns as a resident: her father has bought her a job. Deb, now preferring to be called Jing-Mei, reveals she regained her faith after helping a man four months after leaving County. Although she claims she was too intent to show others up, Chen has lost none of her ambition and clashes with Carter over two patients.

Later, Chen treats an abandoned girl, Alyssa, and calls her parents. However, Alyssa reveals she ran away when her parents put her in a treatment centre to "cure" her homosexuality. When Dr Ramsey from the centre arrives, Chen says Alyssa is pregnant and can't be released. Carter backs her up, but Ramsey goes for a court order. When the coast is clear, Chen directs Alyssa to a gay and lesbian support centre.

Corday offers euthanasia to Rawlins in return for information

A detective tells Corday that the body of one of Rawlins' victims, Jenny Cordova, is still missing. Corday is not hopeful, but agrees to talk to Rawlins. Rawlins is racked with pain and snaps at her when she offers a small amount of morphine. Romano introduces Corday to the Cordova family and persuades her to try again. Rawlins agrees to talk, but only to Jenny's sister, Lindsey. When they meet, Rawlins is cruel. Corday calls him as bastard as she leads the tearful Lindsey away.

Later, Rawlins is tired of the games and wants to die. Corday offers to give him 100mg of morphine – a fatal dose – if he tells her where Jenny is. Rawlins agrees. As she gives him the dose, Corday asks for his answer…

Cleo treats a high school student under pressure

Cleo treats Tamara, a high school basketball player who drove into a telegraph pole. Cleo deduces that Tamara is stressed and reckons she injured herself to get out of a big game. Tamara denies it. Nevertheless, Cleo decides to buy Tamara some rest time and puts a cast on her wrist, even though one is not needed. Benton makes Cleo remove the cast. Cleo hopes Tamara will take her life more slowly.

Other threads

In between pursuing Chen, Dave treats Jason, an 11-year-old with chest pains. He discover Jason has lymphoma that has spread to his heart. Dave tries to get oncology to tell the boy but Luka insists Dave do it. Dave struggles to tell Jason that his condition is inoperable.

Luka treats Dillon, a teenager, and his mentally disabled brother. Kerry insists they can't care for each other and calls DCFS. Luka objects and arranges a job for Dillon.

However Social Services split up the boys. Luka angrily tells Kerry his wife and children were killed during the war: "You don't break up families."

Mark's father has left his nursing home and returned to the family house. Mark convinces David to move to Chicago with him.

"The Domino Heart"

6 – 11: First transmitted 13 January 2000
Written by Joe Sachs; Directed by Lesli Linka Glatter

A donor is found for Lucy's heart transplant patient

A heart has been found for Valerie Page (6-10) but she has a mild fever. Kerry says Valerie can't undergo surgery but Lucy finds research evidence to the contrary. She persuades Romano to proceed with the transplant ("You're like a crazed Energiser bunny on this one. You keep going and going…"). After the operation, Valerie has a stroke and enters a persistent vegetative state.

Romano now needs consent to perform a "domino heart" procedure – where the transplant heart is taken out and given to another patient. Lucy objects, but Romano insists Valerie is already dead. Lucy gets consent from Valerie's mother. Later, Lucy tells Luka that helping one person can make a day worthwhile – that hasn't happened. Luka sees a new patient arrive and suggests this could be the one.

Chen and Carter disagree over caring for a caregiver

Mrs Duffy, an elderly woman with Parkinson's Disease, is brought in by her exhausted daughter, Louise. Mrs Duffy needs a change of medication, but Louise is dismayed her mother can't be admitted so she can get some rest. Later, Louise returns after she slipped on ice. Mrs Duffy is slightly hypertensive. Carter chastises Chen for not permitting a soft admit to give Louise a rest. He admits Louise, forcing Chen to admit Mrs Duffy as she has no other caregiver.

Mark deals with a domestic abuse case

Mark treats Michael, an injured 28-year-old who is brought in by his partner, Curt. Mark discovers that Curt beats Michael and encourages Michael to press charges. He is unsuccessful and Curt angrily takes Michael home. Later, Curt is brought in after Michael "accidentally" ran him over. Chen and Carter work well to save him. Michael claims it was an accident, but is pleased that he will be safe at home tonight. He thanks Mark for the encouragement.

Other threads

Cleo needs a Spanish speaker and Dave comes to her aid. He discovers her patients have taken illegal medication from a backroom clinic. Angry, Dave goes to the clinic and returns with a black eye – and medication he can use to close the clinic.

Corday didn't give Rawlins the real medication he wanted. She visits him in his jail ward and reveals she enjoyed the power she had over him and knows what a pathetic man he is. Her job "for better of worse, was simply to put [him] back together…" Rawlins screams abuse at Corday as she leaves.

The ER suffers a water shortage all day and elective surgery is cancelled. Peter notes that "some of us" may get away early to get something to eat, hinting that Cleo should join him. Cleo plays dumb until Peter asks her out directly, and then accepts.

"Abby Road"

6 – 12: First transmitted 3 February 2000
Written by R. Scott Gemmill; Directed by Richard Thorpe

Abby Lockhart starts in the ER as a medical student
Carol sees Abby Lockhart (6-8) and assumes she has been sent to cover the busy ER. She is uncomfortable to learn Abby is a third-year student and this is the first day of her ER rotation ("What can I say? I went over to The Dark Side"). Abby's day is difficult: she is bitten by a man on PCP, helps a patient who vomits blood, and is treated coldly by Carol. Eventually, Abby asks Carol if she is uncomfortable with her being a student, but Carol insists she isn't.

Later, Abby treats Mr Spencer, a hypochondriac who complains of chest pains. Abby discharges him, but he has a heart attack. Mark reviews Abby's work and points out her errors. He tells her she has to think like a doctor now.

Carter helps an aggressive boy address his illness
Darnell Smith, an angry teenager with muscular dystrophy, tells Carter he was pushed down the stairs at school in his wheelchair. His attacker, Marty, tells Cleo he acted in self-defence. Cleo notes that Marty has infected sores on his legs. It transpires that he is being bullied at school and has been taking human growth hormones using his grandmother's discarded insulin needles. Carter tries to talk to Darnell and eventually breaks through to him by encouraging him to take out his rage on the room. Darnell finally admits he resents how much help he needs.

Luka, Carol and Abby mount a sting operation
Luka and Carol are friendlier, but she tells Mark nothing is going on. Luka treats Connor Brant, whose mother is well informed about her son's history of bowel obstructions. Luka's tests prove inconclusive, so he recommends exploratory surgery. The mother is hesitant, but agrees. Later, Carol discovers that Connor has a history of such surgery and suspects the mother. Luka agrees. They use Abby to entrap the mother, who they see trying to inject peroxide into her son. The mother is arrested and Luka angrily tells her she needs help.

Other threads
Lucy treats Mr Clayton, a homeless man with frostbite and suspected flu. Clayton has congestive heart failure and needs to be intubated. He politely refuses, admitting he just wants to die in a warm bed with clean sheets. Later, Lucy fulfils his wish to throw his money from the roof for the homeless.

Romano cancels Peter's scheduled cosmetic surgery on the grounds that it is not

hospital core business. Romano later collapses in the OR with a kidney stone. Peter operates and gets Romano to agree to let the cosmetic surgery continue.

Corday's mother, Isabelle, arrives in town unannounced. Mark persuades Elizabeth to talk to her. Later they meet and, though they are a little distant with each other, Elizabeth convinces her mother to stay with her.

One to Watch

"Be Still My Heart"

6 – 13: First transmitted 10 February 2000
Written by Lydia Woodward; Directed by Laura Innes

Carter and Lucy treat a psychotic patient

Valentine's Day 2000. Carter and Lucy treat law student Paul Sobriki, who complains of headaches. She puts her proposed treatment to Carter, who insists he trusts her. However, Carter later finds Sobriki in an altered state. He is concerned about possible meningitis and orders a spinal tap. Sobriki protests loudly as Carter holds him down that Lucy can perform the tap. The fluid is clear. A fellow law student arrives and describes Sobriki's recent odd behaviour. Lucy suspects the problem is psychological.

Later, Mark sees Sobriki confronting his fellow student in the hall and tells Carter to pay more attention to Lucy and her patient. The ER staff start their Valentine's party around the admit desk. Carter realises he hasn't seen Lucy for hours and heads to Curtain Three. As he enters, Sobriki approaches Carter from behind and stabs twice. He collapses to the floor and sees Lucy, barely conscious, in a large pool of blood before he blacks out.

Mark and Elizabeth have their evening hijacked by their parents

Mark is annoyed to be woken by his father singing along to old songs from his wife's record collection. Meanwhile, Corday is frustrated by her mother's sudden interest in a laser angioplasty later that day. Mark and Elizabeth share their woes and look forward to a dinner alone. However, Mark later tells Elizabeth that all four of them are going out tonight. During the meal, David and Isabelle trade compliments about their talented children and later duet at the karaoke to a song from *Gigi*.

Chen and Malucci let competition get in the way of care

Chen and Malucci compete over George Hudson, who has been involved in a motor vehicle accident. Mark apologises to the patient, who turns out to be a doctor, much to the shame of the two residents. Later, Hudson is diagnosed with vena cava syndrome and has a life expectancy of one year. Chen and Malucci discuss radiation and chemotherapy, but fail to ask Hudson. Mark speaks to Hudson who opts for chemo but crashes. They have to pursue radiation therapy instead.

Luka treats two children following a car accident

Luka and the ER staff help Mr and Mrs Eddlestone and their children, Robby and Julia, who have been involved in a car accident. The children are shocked but the parents are seriously injured. The staff fight hard to save the parents, but both die.

Luka breaks the news to the children. Robby insists on seeing them. Julia runs from the room and into Haleh's arms at the sight of her father, but Robby bravely carries on, eventually resting his head on his mother and crying quietly.

Other threads

Mrs Connelly (6-6) arrives in the ER with urosepsis and asks for Carter. Abby treats her and suggests some aggressive treatments she would like to pursue. Carter asks about Mrs Connelly's choice but Abby hasn't asked. Mrs Connelly prefers a low tech approach and slowly deteriorates. Abby seems unsure whether to intubate and Carter tells her to respect Connelly's wishes. The old lady dies. Abby confesses this is the first time she has seen an old person die. Carter says she will never get used to it.

Corday is paged to the OR for an operation – on Romano's dog Gretel. The operation is a success, but Corday's mother is bemused by the choice of patient.

"All in the Family"

6 – 14: First transmitted 17 February 2000
Written by Jack Orman; Directed by Jonathan Kaplan

The ER staff work feverishly to save Carter and Lucy

Kerry arrives in the ER to find the Valentine's party in full swing. Annoyed by the loud music, she lets them have five more minutes before they must get back to work. As she walks through the ER she sees blood under a door. She is horrified to find Lucy and Carter in Curtain Three, both unconscious in a large pool of blood.

Carter is brought into Trauma, barely responsive. Chen and Luka begin work. Next door, Dave sees Lucy has been stabbed four times. Kerry intubates and runs a central line. She is furious that no one realised Carter and Lucy were in trouble.

Hearing the news, Peter races into the ER and immediately works on Carter. He demands a catheter before reluctantly leaving someone else to perform an emergency tracheoscopy on Lucy. In the other room, the catheter reveals that Carter's renal artery has been severed.

Having been paged, Mark, Elizabeth and their parents arrive and break past the police cordon. Corday joins Lucy's team.

While Carter is quickly taken to the OR, Lucy's pulse fades and the team have to open her chest. She is stabilised and also taken to the OR. As Mark tells Luka that Lucy's chances are good, an angry Kerry walks outside and is sick.

Samantha Sobriki, Paul's wife, arrives having received a call from Lucy earlier. She refuses to believe that Paul is psychotic, but Luka convinces her that he is a danger to himself and others.

In the OR, Benton and Anspaugh work on Carter. Benton wants to remove Carter's leaking kidney, but Anspaugh is more cautious. Peter ignores appeals to help one of Cleo's patients, refusing to leave Carter.

In the next room, Romano and Corday work on Lucy. Despite loosing blood, Lucy is stabilised and the wounds repaired. She is taken to recovery.

Paul Sobriki is brought in, having been hit by a car as he left the hospital. He is quickly restrained, but his babbling and violent outbursts disturb Kerry, who asks Mark to take over. After Sobriki has been stabilised, his wife sees him and is horrified by his altered state.

Lucy appears stable and whispers "Thank you" to Corday. Suddenly she suffers a blood clot and is rushed back into surgery. Corday tells Lucy she needs another transfusion and promises to get her through the operation. As she is prepped, Lucy suffers a second clot. Romano cracks her chest for the second time. They work valiantly, but are unsuccessful. Corday calls the time of death.

Meanwhile, Peter and Anspaugh stabilise Carter and he is brought out of surgery, his kidney intact. In recovery, Carter realises that Lucy has died.

In Doc Magoo's, Dave, Chen, Abby, Luka, Lydia and Haleh talk animatedly about Lucy and Carter. Chuny arrives and says simply: "Lucy." They all fall silent. Kerry joins Romano in the OR. He thanks her as they prepare Lucy's body.

Be Still My Heart and *All in the Family* rank as two of the most enthralling and horrific episodes of the series. In the former, Sobriki's symptoms and behaviour are so effectively underplayed that you really have little idea of the potential consequences. Carter's trust in Lucy and supportive attitude is all the more ironic given subsequent events. It's almost impossible to forget the horrific moment when Carter falls to the floor and sees Lucy, barely breathing, unable to speak.

All in the Family seems to start with an almost interminable delay before Kerry finds them. Once we're into the surgery, it's pure adrenalin. Benton's ferocious, even violent attempts to save Carter serve to underscore the strength of their relationship. Equally, Romano's efforts in the OR superbly show the respect he came to have for Lucy over the Valerie Page incident. The 45 minutes seem to fly by – but at the end you are left totally drained.

"Be Patient"

6 – 15: First transmitted 24 February 2000
Written by Sandy Kropf; Directed by Ken Kwapis

Luka helps the victim of a hit-and-run

Luka narrowly avoids driving into a young girl, but she is caught by another car. The driver races off, to Luka's disgust. He waits impatiently for an ambulance, but persuades a man to drive him and the girl, Laura, to County. On the way, he uses a needle but clips a blood vessel when they hit a bump. Luka feels guilty.

In the ER, Laura is stabilised, but has a liver injury and needs surgery. Luka sees the

hit-and-run driver being treated and angrily berates him. The man asks after Laura but Luka insists he has no right to ask. Later, Luka tells Laura's mother that surgery was successful. Peter admits he wouldn't have waited for the ambulance.

Mark receives some sad news about his father

Elizabeth returns home to find Isabelle has spent the night with David Greene! Mark laughs the news off and David, in for a check-up, insists things will be back to normal when Isabelle returns to London. Isabelle moves into the Ritz Carlton to spare Elizabeth's embarrassment and the two argue about Isabelle's suitability as a parent. Later, David mediates and arranges for them all to go out. Meanwhile, David's X-Ray shows he has lung cancer that has spread to his liver. David knew but didn't want to be defined by his illness. He confesses that he is scared.

Carol treats a schoolgirl with an STD

Carol treats Andrea and Terri, two schoolgirls who fear they have syphilis. They try to swear Carol to secrecy. Kerry finds that Andrea may have cervical cancer. The girls tell Carol they have been to sex parties and don't know who is passing on the disease. Carol insists that the school must know so that other girls can be tested, but the girls refuse and leave. Later, Andrea is brought in after taking an overdose. She is saved. Carol tells her that she didn't tell her parents, as Andrea had feared.

Other threads

Abby is annoyed her "soon to be ex-husband" has not paid her student loan fees. She treats Ron Perth, who had surgery on his haemorrhoids but is still bleeding. Abby orders a comprehensive test to rule out internal bleeding. Kerry overrules and orders Perth be discharged. Abby warns him to return if he feels "flu-ish". Later he returns with internal bleeding and is saved. Kerry admits Abby was right.

Chen is pleased Carter is recovering but he hides his discomfort. Later, Lucy's mother arrives to clean out her daughter's locker. She asks Carter how the attack felt. Carter lies that he was too shocked to feel the stabbing.

Peter tells Carter that he and Cleo are off to the jazz club. Carter knows what happens after the jazz club... But that evening, Cleo suggests they get a coffee and talk instead. Peter wryly notes that she will disappoint Carter.

"Under Control"

6–16: First transmitted 23 March 2000
Written by Neal Baer & Joe Sachs; Directed by Christopher Misiano

David Greene refuses chemotherapy

Mark and David view old family slides. Mark has made an appointment for David with an oncologist, but David is annoyed because his cancer is inoperable. Their argument is cut short when the projector breaks. At work, Mark finds he is the only attending and institutes "power rounds" – seeing each patient in rapid succession. His day is frantic. Later, David arrives feeling short of breath and insists on seeing Elizabeth, not Mark. He tells her about his cancer – Mark has not told her. He doesn't want chemotherapy and wants to die in peace, Elizabeth tells Mark. He asks Elizabeth to persuade David to change his mind, but she is reticent. Later, Mark and David view the slides and find a happy picture of the two of them, taken 20 years ago.

Elizabeth's mother leaves

Isabelle indicates that she approves of Mark. Pleased, Elizabeth agrees to meet later for coffee. At work, she treats Robert Jackson, an 18-year-old gunshot victim. Jackson is brain-dead, but Corday is determined to save his organs. She tries several measures to keep Jackson alive, but the police can't find his parents and suspect he is a runaway. As Jackson deteriorates, Mark has to stop Elizabeth saving him. Jackson dies and his organs are not harvested. Later, Elizabeth has to cancel coffee with her mother – but Isabelle has already taken an earlier flight.

Carter has a difficult return to work

Carter returns to work on crutches and in pain. He is frustrated by his lack of mobility. He treats Adam Pullido, who may have taken a Benadryl overdose. Carter suspects renal problems, but has a procedure overruled. When Pullido deteriorates, Carter lies to a dialysis nurse to help him run the procedure. Mark chastises Carter, but the procedure succeeds. Meanwhile, Kerry suggests treatments for Carter's pain and asks if he has been to counselling. Carter is evasive. Later, he tells his grandmother that his first day back was tough. Millicent reckons his persistence proves that medicine is the right career for him. Carter is cheered.

Other threads

Abby treats Mr Tadlock, who has colon cancer. Tadlock needs the fluid drained from his abdomen and Chen agrees to watch Abby perform the procedure. Abby accidentally perforates the colon. Tadlock requires surgery, but refuses and dies. Abby is dismayed and Mark tells her to practise the procedure with Dr Upton in pathology. When she arrives, she is uncomfortable to discover Tadlock is the guinea pig.

Chen treats Frank "Rambo" Bacon, a nurse from ICU, who has fainted. While Chen waits for labs (and ogles Frank), Frank gets involved in the hectic ER and eventually convinces Chen to discharge him to help out. He faints again and is diagnosed with Addison's Disease, but should be better in a couple of days.

Peter and Cleo meet up after work and fall into a passionate kiss.

"Viable Options"

6 – 17: First transmitted 6 April 2000
Written by Patrick Harbinson; Directed by Marita Grabiak

Weaver is suspended after disobeying Romano

Romano decides to work with "the little people" in the ER today. Kerry treats Angie Dwyer, a woman in a vegetative state who will die before she is 20. Kerry sympathises with the foster mother and recommends a central line to stabilise Angie. However, her legal guardian, DCFS, refuses. Kerry tries to get Mark's help, but Romano angrily asserts Angie is a "pet" and forbids the procedure. Kerry performs the central line herself. Angie is stabilised and Romano, suspends Kerry as Chief until further notice. Angry and frustrated, Kerry leaves.

Chen treats a man with a serious hereditary condition

The staff have to pull apart Terry Waters and Randall James who fight in the ER. Jo Waters insists her father is acting out of character. Chen can't make a diagnosis. Mark enquires into the Waters' family history and discovers that Terry's father committed suicide. Mark discovers that Terry has a hereditary neurological disorder and suspect his father killed himself when he was also diagnosed.

Chen confirms there is a 50-50 chance Jo has it too. Terry, like his father before him, decides to keep his illness secret from Jo so she can live an ordinary life. Chen objects, but cannot change his mind.

Eddie Bernero returns to the ER

Eddie Bernero (6-6) returns to the ER, unconscious. Cleo doesn't remember him and suspects diabetes, but this is not on the old chart. Later, Cleo realises the boy is in a diabetic coma and deduces that Carter doctored Eddie's chart at Mr Bernero's request. Carter is annoyed and confronts Mr Bernero for not helping his son as he promised. Bernero gives a lame excuse and Carter is dismissive. Mark promises the insurance company that he will investigate the old chart and talks to Carter. Carter claims a simple misdiagnosis, but Mark is unconvinced.

Other threads

Cleo treats Mr Grunwald, who complains of abdominal and back pain, but Peter rejects surgery and orders medication. Cleo prescribes the drugs, but doesn't check the label. Later, Grunwald returns with critically low blood pressure after taking the wrong medication. Romano berates Peter, who is fiercely critical of Cleo. Later, he apologises to Cleo. She coldly heads for a shower – then invites him to join her.

Corday has a donor kidney but Luka can't find a suitable candidate. His first has angina, the second is pregnant and a third has been using cocaine. He calls for a fourth, but Corday refuses to wait and gives the kidney to the drug user, to Luka's annoyance. The nurses thought he would have to take the kidney home with him!

David complains about Mark's apartment and asks Elizabeth about hospices. Elizabeth approaches the Morgan Centre but Mark is annoyed. When David asks, Mark claims there was a long waiting list and tells David he's stuck with him.

"Match Made in Heaven"

6 – 18: First transmitted 13 April 2000
Written by R. Scott Gemmill; Directed by Jonathan Kaplan

Carter struggles with the effects of his attack

Carter hears that Lucy has matched for a residency at County: administration have made an error. He treats Mr Fazio, who fell off a ladder, and diagnoses the injury as an "MU". Haleh later queries the acronym and Carter explains: "Made up." However, test results show Fazio has leukaemia. Fazio is stunned. Carter later discovers the tests were mixed up and he was right about Fazio.

Next, he treats Pablo, a regular homeless visitor. Pablo accidentally knocks a tray over and Carter, thinking he is violent, gives him Haldol. Carol protests, but realises that Carter is still struggling to come to terms with the attack. He explains that Lucy would have become a psych resident at County. Carol tells Carter that working will be his best coping strategy. That night, Carter can't sleep.

Abby helps a stressed young mother obtain an abortion

Abby treats Lynn Parker, a mother who fainted while struggling with her many children. Abby discovers Lynn is pregnant and hasn't told her husband. Lynn guiltily admits she can't cope with another baby and was starving herself to try to miscarry. Abby confirms this is what Lynn wants and arranges an abortion. Mr Parker arrives and is angry to realise what is going on. He arrives in OB too late. Later, Abby hears that Ken has "forgiven" Lynn for her "moment of weakness" and that she has agreed to try for another baby soon. Abby is stunned.

Carol thinks about her children's futures

A diner at Doc Magoo's reckons Carol, Luka and the twins make a cute family. When Luka asks after the "Hathaway twins", Carol reveals their surname is Ross. Later, Carol worries that her twins need a father. Doug has invited her to join him in Seattle and she thinks he is serious. Later, Luka is uncomfortable when he sees pictures of Carol's twins. Carol asks to see photographs of Luka's children but he only has one of his daughter. To see his son, he has only to close his eyes.

Other threads

Mark arranges for a care nurse, Mrs Fredricsson, to look after David. He is later called home when David insults the nurse. David doesn't want to burden Mark and reacts badly when Mark brings home a portable toilet. That night, Mark is woken by a clatter as David falls trying to get to the bathroom. David sadly notes how helpless he feels and how this is exactly what he didn't want.

Cleo calls for a surgical consult, but Corday refuses to operate. Irked, Cleo calls for Peter and persuades him to perform the exploratory surgery. Corday is annoyed and performs the surgery herself. She tells Cleo not to play on her relationship with Peter and to come to her if she disagrees with her judgement.

"The Fastest Year"

6 – 19: First transmitted 27 April 2000
Written by Lydia Woodward; Directed by Richard Thorpe

Mark arranges a trip for his father

Mark examines David and finds he has pneumonia. David needs an X-ray and is brought in to the ER. Meanwhile, Mark gathers supplies for David and hides his sadness from Elizabeth. Mark hears David talking to Sarah McKenzie, another patient whose husband is also ex-Navy. David describes the soothing calm of the sea. Later, Mark takes David to the lake and David describes how this has been the fastest year. Mark introduces David to Sam McKenzie, Sarah's husband, who has agreed to take David out on his powerboat. David is overjoyed. Mark props up his father as they sail across Lake Michigan.

Carter is plagued by flashbacks to his attack

Carter is suffering from insomnia and starts to have flashbacks to his attack. He placates his grandmother by insisting he will be fine but during the day he is haunted by the spinal tap he and Lucy performed on Sobriki (6-13). Later, when Carter goes for a chart on a patient, he asks to see Sobriki's chart. DeRaad interrupts and, asking after Carter, invites Carter to see him.

Later, Carter admits he keeps thinking about the "accident". DeRaad insists it was no accident but a brutal attack, and advises that Carter's recovery will take time. Later, Carter contacts Sobriki's wife. She too is plagued by thoughts of the attack and doesn't understand how she could have missed signs of Paul's illness.

Abby bridges a family rift

Abby treats Mr Chadsey and his daughter Delia, who have been involved in a car accident. Delia has been in remission from leukaemia for six months but a blood test now shows it has returned. Delia needs a bone marrow transplant but the only good match is Chadsey's other daughter who lives with his ex-wife. Abby visits the mother, Mrs Lomax, who refuses to let her daughter help. Later, the daughter arrives but cannot donate without consent. Mrs Lomax is called and, seeing Delia and her daughter talking, consents to the tests.

Other threads

Kerry returns to the ER after a few weeks' suspension. She has an odd day with Edgar Braxley, a small boy who reacts badly to her and her cane. Throughout the day, Edgar spies on Kerry, apparently hiding, but later they share a smile.

Luka struggles to help Carol buy a second-hand car. They talk about their families. Luka explains how his wife and children were killed when a shell hit their apartment.

Carol's new car gives out on the way home. As they wait for a tow, they kiss.

Benton introduces Cleo to Jackie and the kids. Jackie worries that Peter is serious about Cleo – because she is sure Cleo is not serious about him.

"Loose Ends"

6 – 20: First transmitted 4 May 2000
Written by Neal Baer; Directed by Kevin Hooks

Mark's father dies

David has pleurisy from his pneumonia and is fading fast. Mark cuts himself as he prepares David's medication and Elizabeth arrives to suture his hand. David offers her his wife's pearls. Elizabeth is uncomfortable but accepts them to please David. Elizabeth leaves and Mark gives David a sponge bath.

Disorientated, David admits that Mark is a good doctor and confesses how Mark's graduation was the proudest day of his life. He tells Mark he loves him and Mark emotionally responds. Later, Mark wakes from a nap and finds David has died. He kisses his father goodbye.

In the ER, Kerry tells Elizabeth, who goes to see Mark. He is calmly completing the paperwork, but breaks down when he admits he promised David he would keep the family house but can't see a reason to. Elizabeth comforts him.

Carter shows renewed vigour at work

Millicent Carter is pleased to find John's appetite has returned. At work, Carter also seems to be on top form. He covers for Mark, helps Abby with her first intubation and annoys Dave by taking two of his patients.

Later, Luka stabilises a man with chest pain and falling blood pressure. Carter suspects a hole in the heart and performs a risky procedure without Luka's consent. He is successful, but Luka is annoyed. Kerry tells Carter that attendings are here to supervise. Carter is dismissive.

Carol ends her potential relationship with Luka

Luka gives Carol flowers for her birthday, but she is cold and evasive. At work, she is distracted and Kerry is annoyed when Carol fails to provide information she needed for a meeting. Later, Carol lets an IV run dry and Kerry realises that something is wrong. Emotional, Carol admits she loves her job but can't understand how she is bringing up twins alone. Supportive, Kerry allows Carol to take leave. Later, Luka wants to cook dinner for Carol but she is still quiet. "It's not you, it's me," she explains, leaving Luka disappointed and alone.

Other threads

Corday treats Claire, a young woman with anorexia and bulimia. She hopes for a psych hold, but DeRaad can't help. Corday calls Claire's mother, enraging Claire further. As Claire makes to leave, Corday angrily tells Claire that if she won't care for her health, neither will the hospital.

Chen treats a young boy with a genetic disorder. She is angry when Romano refuses to test for the disorder with all newborns. However, Chen traps Romano into signing a petition for the tests to become standard. Romano grudgingly admires her tactics.

Peter is annoyed when an elderly black man is given limited treatment by Luka and must have his leg amputated. Luka insists he acted within professional limits, but Peter is furious.

Dave treats Shelly, a young girl who has been sexually abused by her father. He attacks the father – and later sutures him with insufficient pain medication.

One to Watch

"Such Sweet Sorrow"

6 – 21: First transmitted 11 May 2000
Written and Directed by John Wells

Carol leaves the ER to be reunited with her soul mate

Mrs O'Brien, a mother with terminal cancer, arrives at the ER with her husband and their two daughters. She is a DNR and will die soon. Carol makes Mrs O'Brien comfortable and hopes to keep her at County, but she wants to die at home. Kerry tells Carol to arrange for transport home. As they wait, Mrs O'Brien stops breathing.

Suddenly, Mr O'Brien wants her resuscitated so she can see her children one last time. Carol lies to Luka to get him to save Mrs O'Brien, later incurring his and Kerry's wrath. The family share her final moments. Later, Mr O'Brien asks Carol if she believes in soul mates. He is convinced he will never love again.

Finally, Carol is decided. She quickly says her goodbyes to Luka, promising him he will find someone, and leaves. In Seattle, she meets Doug – reunited, they kiss.

Carter's behaviour becomes increasingly erratic

Chen and Dave both comment on Carter's drawn appearance. Carter appears tired but later appears suspiciously energetic and treats two patients at once. He gives his orders, but is annoyed when Malik doesn't get round to giving one patient her antibiotics. Carter takes it upon himself to start the IV, but gives her the wrong medication and sends her into shock. He rips out her IV and barely covers his error. He snaps at Chen for her questions then runs to the toilet and cries.

Chen tells Mark that Carter is behaving erratically and asks him to help. Mark later finds Carter in a darkened room and cautiously broaches the subject. Carter reluctantly accepts a referral to a therapist.

Dave and Abby come in for criticism from Corday

Abby performs a pelvic exam on Cathy, a 22-year-old who fears she has syphilis. Abby assures her it is only pelvic inflammatory disease (PID). Confident she knows more than Dave, she asks him to discharge Cathy. He readily complies.

However, Cathy collapses and is soon brought back to the ER. Abby discovers that Cathy has an ovarian abscess. As Cathy is taken to the OR, Corday is given a weak explanation of events. She chastises Abby but saves the worst for Malucci, whose medical professionalism and skill she says is questioned around the hospital.

Other threads

Mark is unsure how to dispose of his father's ashes and Elizabeth suggests he place them with his mother in San Diego. Mark is surprised when Elizabeth returns his mother's pearls. She feels Rachel should have them and insists Mark doesn't read too much into her decision.

Later, Mark explains his decision to take the ashes to San Diego. He gives the pearls to Rachel, echoing his father's words about how beautiful they look on Corday, and hopes she doesn't grow up too fast.

After six years, we finally say goodbye to Carol Hathaway. It's a neat episode, with her thought processes played out through the tragic story of the O'Brien family. One her mind is made up, Carol's exit from the show is whirlwind-quick and builds to a happy conclusion. The almost casual reappearance of Doug Ross, as though he has never been away, is simply the icing on the cake.

On the flipside, we have the story of Carter's self-destruction and a few more clues to what is happening. The moment when his confidence collapses and he realises his error is acted superbly by Noah Wyle. Plus we have Corday's fierce attack on Dave, almost a year in the making. This is one episode where few people come out unscathed.

"May Day"

6 – 22: First transmitted 18 May 2000
Written by Jack Orman; Directed by Jonathan Kaplan

The ER staff confront Carter about his drug abuse

Carter and Abby treat a man with a dislocated hip. Carter gives the patient some pain medication and pockets the rest. Abby catches him injecting the remaining 50mgs into his wrist. She eventually tells Mark, who confronts Carter with Kerry. Although Carter is indignant, Kerry sadly sees he's lying. Later, during a quiet moment, Carter confides to Mark he needs the pain medication to function. Mark is sympathetic, but tells him to stop seeing patients.

Mark and Abby treat Tanner, a rugby player with a broken collarbone. Mark orders a clavicle film. Later, Abby finds Tanner unresponsive. Carter quickly realises Tanner has a rib fracture and starts to insert a chest tube to save Tanner's life. Mark arrives and takes over the procedure, to Carter's annoyance.

Resolved on a course of action, Mark, Chen, Kerry, Peter and Anspaugh face Carter and offer their support. Mark tells Carter he must admit himself into a rehabilitation clinic or he is fired. Carter reacts badly and storms out, but Peter follows. Outside, Peter becomes angry and tells Carter he will end up like his cousin Chase. Carter throws a punch and breaks down. Peter comforts him. Later, we see Carter on the plane to Seattle, Peter at his side.

Luka chooses who to treat, angering Peter

Luka and Peter are flown to a shootout at a school. A police marksman takes down the last shooter and Peter tends to his injuries. He needs immediate transport, but Luka loads a less seriously injured child, Nicholas, on to the chopper. Peter is furious.

At the ER, Corday discovers the bullet has entered Nicholas' blood stream and is heading towards his heart. Peter arrives, but his patient has already died. He confronts Luka for making preferences instead of helping the most serious case. Peter helps Corday with Nicholas and together they make a remarkable save. Cleo watches uncomfortably as Peter and Corday discuss writing up the case.

Luka tries to save an unborn child

Cleo and Luka treat Gloria Milton, an 18-year-old who has been stabbed. Gloria is shocked to discover she is pregnant and, fearing her parents' reaction, refuses to have a Caesarean to save the baby. Angry, Luka tries to persuade Gloria but he, Coburn and DeRaad are unable to alter her opinion. Luka decides to get a court order, but the baby's heart rate becomes critical. He is about to start a C-section against Gloria's wishes when Cleo talks him out of it. The baby dies. Luka is disgusted when the signed court order arrives too late.

Other threads

Dave treats a man who has drilled a wood screw into his leg with a drill. The man refuses pain medication but is heard screaming when Dave uses a screwdriver to get the screw out. Mark asks Dave to keep the noise down.

Season Seven
2000-1

Themes

Mark and Elizabeth get engaged and married. Soon a child is on the way. However, Mark is diagnosed with a brain tumour that is at first thought to be inoperable.

Elizabeth botches an endoscopic procedure and is sued for malpractice. Her ability to work when pregnant is questioned by Mark and Romano.

Kerry meets psych consult Dr Kim Legaspi and starts to explore her sexuality. Their relationship flounders when Kerry insists they meet secretly. However, Kerry becomes annoyed when Romano makes homophobic comments.

Luka comes to terms with the loss of his faith when he treats Bishop Stewart. He starts dating Abby, but their relationship comes under scrutiny from Carter.

Abby returns to nursing. She is annoyed when her bi-polar mother, Maggie, arrives and causes havoc. When Maggie endangers herself, Abby finds more support from Carter than her boyfriend Luka.

Peter is fired by Romano and finds his reputation has been tarnished. Back at County he is given a new job as Director of Diversity. Meanwhile, his relationship with Cleo comes under strain when she injures Reese.

Carter returns from a rehabilitation clinic but finds new constraints put on him. Matters become worse before he can come to terms with his addiction. Later, he discovers he is not being considered for new posts as his residency comes to an end.

Chen is pregnant and has to make hard decisions about her baby. She alleges discrimination when she misses out on the Chief Resident position for taking maternity leave.

Ones to Watch

7 – 6: *The Visit* – Abby's estranged mother, Maggie, unexpectedly arrives in the ER.

7 – 15: *The Crossing* – Luka confronts his loss of faith and family when he attends a train wreck.

7 – 19: *Sailing Away* – Abby hears that Maggie is in trouble. Carter travels with her to bring Maggie back to Chicago.

"Homecoming"

7 – 1: First transmitted 12 October 2000
Written by Jack Orman; Directed by Jonathan Kaplan

Carter returns to Chicago

May: Benton takes Carter to a drug rehabilitation centre in Atlanta. Carter immediately goes to group therapy.

September: Carter has an exit interview with a counsellor. He insists he has taken responsibility for his addiction and won't let it beat him. The counsellor thought the same his first three times.

Carter flies back to Chicago. He expects to be collected by Benton, but he is inundated at the ER and has sent a new medical student to pick up Carter. Carter is withdrawn on the way back. They arrive at County to see the ER in full swing. As the student runs inside, Carter watches briefly then walks away.

Football rivalries spill over in the ER

Mark and Dave treat Mike Palmieri, a 17-year-old injured while playing American football. Mike complains that the other team committed an illegal play. Later, Mike has chest pain and Mark orders more tests. Mark promises Mrs Palmieri that her son will be OK but his condition worsens and he has to ask consent for a procedure. A rival footballer arrives with a tibial fracture, followed by more casualties from a post-game riot.

Mike crashes and has to be intubated. Mark warns Mrs Palmieri that Mike could die, but she insists that he must save him as he promised. One of Mike's team hears the exchange and starts a fight. The ER erupts as the two teams face off. Meanwhile, Mark saves Mike.

Abby is not allowed to work as a med student

Kerry tells Abby that she is not permitted to work in the ER: her tuition fees have not been paid. Furious, Abby confronts her ex-husband, Richard. Richard was meant to pay as part of their divorce settlement, but gives her a sob story. Abby angrily notes that he had enough money to pay for an apartment for his mistress, and leaves.

Other threads

Jing-Mei Chen is pregnant. Coburn performs an ultrasound and reports that the baby boy is fine. She asks if Chen has arranged maternity leave, but Chen admits she hasn't told anyone yet.

County is in the midst of a janitors' strike and laundry is piled high. Luka pretends to help a deceased woman so her elderly husband, Mr Bristo, can prepare himself for the news. Bristo leaves to get his wife's medication. When he returns, Luka tells him that his wife died. Under pressure for rooms, Mr Bristo is left with his wife in the hall. Later, Chen finds Bristo dead: he has taken his wife's medication.

Corday backs Peter for a faculty position with responsibility for resident research.

234

Romano is more interested to know if Peter has applied elsewhere. Peter refuses to say and Romano cuts the interview short. Peter is frustrated and Romano reveals he doubts Peter's loyalty. Peter insists he will be a team player, but later wishes luck to the striking janitors.

"Sand and Water"

7 − 2: First transmitted 19 October 2000
Written by Jack Orman; Directed by Christopher Misiano

Mark proposes to Elizabeth

Elizabeth is annoyed to receiving a parking ticket at Mark's place and launches into a tirade about his living accommodation. The refrigerator is warm, the toilet rocks and there are scurrying noises coming from the walls. Later, Elizabeth apologises for her bad temper. Mark reveals he has plans for them that evening. They drive to a large house that Mark intends to buy. Inside the new fridge is a diamond ring and he asks Elizabeth to marry him. Elizabeth is overwhelmed, but quickly agrees.

Carter returns to work under strict conditions

Before work, Carter attends an AA meeting and is surprised to see Abby there. On his return to the ER, Carter finds new stipulations set against his employment: compulsory AA meetings, random urine tests and drugs to block the euphoric effects of narcotics. He is clearly a little resentful when Kerry and Mark ask him to take one of the pills in front of them. Nevertheless, he thanks them for their help.

Later, Abby tells Carter she is a drunk who has been sober for five years. Carter needs a sponsor and asks Abby. She is reluctant, insisting she has too much to deal with herself at the moment. However, Carter is able to convince her to help him.

Chen is emotional when she delivers a premature baby

Abby and Chen help Regina Morgan, a young woman who has gone into labour at 22 weeks. Chen struggles to deal with the delivery and has to leave Kerry to it. Later, Chen tells a sympathetic Kerry that she is also 22 weeks pregnant. Meanwhile, Abby tries to give the family and baby privacy as the boy struggles to survive. At one point they fear the baby is dead and Luka is about to pronounce when he starts to breathe again. The baby is baptised on the hospital roof and dies later.

Benton treats Mr Fletcher (7-1), who has repeatedly missed his dialysis. However, Conway from finance tells Peter to transfer Fletcher as his insurance company has gone bankrupt and he has $200,000 in unpaid medical bills. Peter is furious and later tries to take Fletcher for surgery but is barred by Romano.

An inspector arrives later following an anonymous tip-off that the hospital is refusing to treat a patient without insurance. Romano denies all knowledge and takes Fletcher up to surgery – but knows Peter is the culprit.

Other threads

Luka treats Glenda Walton, a woman in late middle age who has had a stroke. Her life

235

partner, Judy, explains that Glenda did not want any tubes or machines. However, Kerry sadly explains that Judy does not have power of attorney. Instead, Glenda's absentee brother insists on a respirator. Kerry says "I'm sorry" as Judy watches, powerless to ensure her partner's wishes.

"Mars Attacks"

7–3: First transmitted 29 October 2000
Written by R. Scott Gemmill; Directed by Paris Barclay

Carter has a mixed day on his return to work

Carter is warmly welcomed back to the ER, but Kerry informs him that he is on severely restricted duties: no trauma, needles, narcotics or procedures. Carter is left with a motley crew of patients: a man who pierced his own nipple, a homeless man with crabs and a boy with a bug in his ear. Later, he treats Dennis, a young boy paralysed from the waist down. He builds a good rapport with the boy and is cheered. However, at the end of the day, Carter is asked to take a urine test for Mark.

Peter is fired by Romano

Peter arrives at work to find he can't enter the car park. He soon discovers all his attending privileges have been withdrawn – Romano has sacked him after the incident with Mr Fletcher (7-2). Peter heads home and lies to Jackie about why he is early. He is struck when Reese, playing with toys, prefers the stethoscope. Later, Cleo encourages Peter to fight Romano, but Peter appears defeated.

Mark plays surgical consult for the day

Elizabeth tells Mark that most of the surgeons are at a conference and not to call any unnecessary consults. However, with Benton missing, the ER struggles for surgical cover when an accident at a sci-fi convention results in numerous casualties.

As Elizabeth treats a young man with a pelvic fracture, Mark treats the man's brother Danny. Short-staffed, Mark is instructed how to save Danny's pulseless leg by Corday, who describes the procedure while she works on the brother. Later, Elizabeth congratulates Mark on his handiwork.

Abby returns to nursing in the ER

Abby is working in the ER following Kerry's insistence that the experience will help her when she returns to medical school. She has a busy and successful day, looking after a Trekker who has given himself Mr Spock ears, a trio of Japanese businessmen with food poisoning and a young girl with gonorrhoea.

When treating the sci-fi fan casualties, Luka asks Abby to put in a chest tube. Short of staff, she does, but incurs Kerry's displeasure. Later, Abby confides in Luka that she felt she did everything wrong as a medical student. Luka insists she will be a great doctor. Pleased, she kisses him, much to their mutual surprise.

Other threads

Frank, the desk clerk, spends much of the day checking patients against police records. His actions soon lead to the arrest of a suspected murderer. Later, Kerry hears one of her patients is wanted for bouncing cheques. Aware of how the patient is struggling financially, Kerry helps the woman escape before the police arrive, to Frank's great disappointment.

Kerry treats a man with a history of spontaneous combustion in his family. Though dismissive, she is shocked when the man later catches fire.

"Benton Backwards"

7 – 4: First transmitted 3 November 2000
Written by Dee Johnson; Directed by Richard Thorpe

Peter is unable to find new work in Chicago

Peter tries to get work at another Chicago hospital, but is unsuccessful. Dr Gottschalk inadvertently reveals that Romano has been spreading negative comments about Peter and hints that he may find it difficult to get work locally. Benton confronts Romano, who is dismissive of him. Nevertheless, Romano offers Peter a per diem position with lower salary and stature. Peter tells the "arrogant little prick" he will never work with him again.

Instead, Peter approaches Kerry but she needs Romano to find the money for a post. Corday gets Peter a job offer in Philadelphia but Carla refuses to negotiate visitation rights, recalling Peter's attitude when she wanted to move to Germany. Beaten, Peter heads back to the hospital to grovel to Romano.

Carter's miraculous save comes to nothing

Carter is permitted to treat trauma patients and helps Luka treat a girl who has been shot. Carter finds an exit wound at the back of the heart and miraculously saves the patient. He is roundly congratulated. Later, a young woman arrives asking if the patient is OK. Carter explains she is doing well. Suddenly the woman draws a gun and kills the patient, splattering Carter and room in blood. Carter leaves dismayed and returns to his grandmother's house angry and frustrated. Millicent warns Carter he has had the spirit beaten out of him. Carter denies it and later returns to work.

Abby and Luka are attacked by a mugger

Abby asks Luka out on a date and, bemused, he agrees. After being beaten at table football, Luka suggests a walk. Suddenly, Luka is hit by a mugger who then makes a grab for Abby's bag. Luka grabs the mugger and starts to beat him, repeatedly smashing the man's head into the floor. The man loses consciousness. In the ER, Mark and Elizabeth try to save the man as Luka watches guilty. Abby corroborates his story and the detective assures Luka it was self-defence. The mugger dies and Luka leaves, ignoring Abby's attempts to comfort him.

Other threads

Jing-Mei treats Kenneth Stein, a boy with a terminal disease. Kenneth needs a splenectomy, but Mark advises against it and Romano refuses to operate. Chen breaks the news to the mother who says Jing-Mei will understand when she has her baby. Later, Chen tries to arrange surgery for Kenneth.

Peter's nephew, Jesse, has been injured at school. Jackie is worried that Jesse has a wayward girlfriend. Peter gives Jesse a pep talk and tells him to respect his parents.

Psych consult Dr Kim Legaspi helps Kerry with an old man. She arranges a place for him at the VA's but the man panics. They discover he deserted in 1951 and is still wanted. Kim uses the social security number of a dead man to get him into a shelter. During the day, Kim and Kerry become friendlier.

"Flight of Fancy"

7 – 5: First transmitted 8 November 2000
Written by Joe Sachs and Walon Green; Directed by Lesli Linka Glatter

Mark's helicopter fails on a ride-out

Mark is flown out to bring Tom Coggins to County for a heart transplant. Tom is eager for his fiancée, Janet, to be at the hospital. During the flight, Tom has chest pains and Mark stabilises him. Then, the helicopter's main rotor fails. They make an emergency landing in a junkyard. Paramedics arrive and try to take Tom to Oakdale, but Mark insists that they go to County where Janet is waiting.

Back at the ER, Tom is given an emergency pacemaker. Mark tells Janet that Tom may not live to get the transplant. Janet and Tom wed in the trauma room. Inspired, Corday decides against an elaborate wedding in favour of a simple ceremony.

Luka is plagued by the death of the mugger

Luka does not arrive for work. Instead, he waits at the police station, hoping to find out more about the mugger. The detectives have found nothing more and recommend that Luka forget the incident and move on. Luka makes his own enquiries without success.

After seeing the body of the mugger in the morgue, Luka returns to work. Kerry angrily tells Luka he missed his shift and patients almost died. Luka offers to work the night shift but is not needed. He ignores Abby on his way out, but she later finds him at his hotel room. She insists they don't have to talk and kisses him gently.

Peter is left in charge of the ER

With Luka absent, and the ER short-staffed, Mark leaves Benton in charge of the ER. Cleo is annoyed that Peter considered moving to Philadelphia, aware he wouldn't stay in Chicago for her. Peter's day deteriorates as the patients stack up. After treating a frantic child, a man stabbed with a pencil and a prostitute with a roll of money stuck somewhere, Peter finds a surgical patient, only to have him snatched away by Romano. Under pressure, Peter closes the ER to trauma cases.

Kerry arrives and tells Peter it was unfair of Romano to give him the ER – Peter is untrained in ER management. Later, Peter tells Cleo he was sure he could handle the job, but couldn't. Cleo bitterly observes she is always there to listen to his problems, but he is never there for hers.

Other threads

Carter treats Trent, a young man who has cut his hand during art class. Trent's grandmother reveals that Trent has HIV, but that they have not told him so he can live a normal life. Carter insists that Trent should know and tells Trent the truth. Trent is shocked. Later, he returns with his girlfriend, Emma, who also tests positive for HIV. Carter leaves them alone. Moments later, Trent is rushed back in after being hit by a car while he fought with Emma. Trent dies and Emma blames Carter.

One to Watch

"The Visit"

7 – 6: First transmitted 16 November 2000
Written by John Wells; Directed by Jonathan Kaplan

Abby's mother pays a surprise visit

Kerry finds a middle-aged woman cheerily making bagels for the staff in the lounge. The woman, Maggie, claims to be Abby's mother. Abby is surprised by the news and, seeing the woman from a distance, insists she isn't her mother. However, Abby calls her brother Frank and insists she can't take care of Maggie. Kerry confronts Maggie and the woman becomes hysterical. She is only calmed when Abby arrives and says a simple "Hi Mom," surprising Kerry. Abby is unhappy to see Maggie and annoyed when she realises Maggie has left her job to come to Chicago.

Later, Kerry guesses correctly that Maggie is bi-polar. Abby tells Carter that her mother was often neglectful through her illness and insists she can't go through that again. When psych arrives, Maggie refuses her medication because she claims it inhibits her creativity (she draws fashion designs). Frustrated, Abby tries to buy Maggie off with cash and a plane ticket back to Florida. Angry, Maggie leaves. Later, Abby finds Maggie cold and alone on the El platform and takes her home.

Benton's nephew Jesse is brought in with a gunshot wound

Benton is not amused when Dave jokes about a patient's severed hand and warns him to show more respect. Later, Dave and Elizabeth work on a gunshot victim in a serious condition. Cleo sees Jackie in chairs and realises the boy is Jesse. She quickly grabs Peter, who arrives just in time to hear Malucci thanking the shooter for giving him an interesting case.

While Peter works feverishly, Cleo tells Jackie that Jesse's condition is grave. Jesse's girlfriend Kynesha arrives and Jackie, blaming her wayward friends for the shooting, screams at the girl to leave. Back in trauma, Peter is fighting a losing battle and Elizabeth slowly helps Peter to let go.

As he approaches to tell Jackie that Jesse has died, she sees his face and starts screaming "No!" Later, Dave tries to apologise to Peter for thinking Jesse was just "a banger", but his comment sparks a fight. After they have been separated, Cleo and Peter silently prepare Jesse's body.

Corday botches an endoscopic procedure

Mark and Elizabeth look forward to leaving at 6pm for a weekend break. During the day, Elizabeth sees Al Patterson, a middle-aged man who has hurt his back while surfing. Elizabeth suggests an endoscopic procedure to remove broken disk fragments. She is annoyed when Romano insinuates she chose the less invasive surgery so she can leave early for her holiday.

As Elizabeth performs the procedure, Babcock notes fluid around the disk but Elizabeth reckons it is saline. She closes and leaves for her holiday. Later, Romano is called to Mr Patterson who is in great pain. He realises Patterson has leaking spinal fluid and angrily calls for Corday. Receiving the call, Elizabeth is shocked.

Other threads

Luka treats Teresa Ruiz, a 13-year-old girl who fell at school. Her father is impatient to get back to work. Initial tests show no broken bones or neck injury and she claims not to be pregnant. When Luka checks her back, he finds bruises. Suspecting abuse, he orders a CT to keep the girl in the ER until the police can come. Later, the police arrive and question Ruiz who protests his innocence and claims Teresa falls over a lot. Meanwhile, Luka discovers that Teresa is pregnant and as they talk he realises she is being assaulted by her boyfriend.

Chen has decided to give her child up for adoption, but needs the father's consent. At County, Chen finds a shocked Frank (6-16) and breaks the news. She asks him to sign the necessary papers.

This is a significant episode because it sets up so much to come. Abby's relationship with her mother dominates the rest of the season and returns in Season Nine. It's a magnificent performance from Sally Fields who effortlessly takes over every scene she is in. An equally impressive performance comes from Khandi Alexander as Jackie. If Peter's desperate efforts to save Jesse are heartrending, Jackie's scream when she realises her son is dead is utterly crushing. We also see the start of Corday's malpractice suit and her disagreements with Babcock. All in all, it's one of the quieter "ones to watch" and one that is made by the performances of the supporting cast.

"Rescue Me"

7-7: First transmitted 23 November 2000
Written by Neal Baer; Directed by Christopher Chulack

Abby is unable to get rid of her mother

Thanksgiving 2000. Abby drops Maggie off at the bus station and returns to work relieved. However, it is not long before Maggie returns. Abby angrily tells her to wait in chairs while she treats a cyclist injured in a car crash. As she waits, Maggie comforts the cyclist's wife – but it is actually the motorist. The cyclist dies and Maggie tries to console the driver.

During the day, Maggie pleads with Abby to let her stay, insisting that she never chose to be ill. Abby angrily retorts: "You never tried to get better." Abby's next patient starts smoking and ignites a gas bottle. The room explodes, but Abby escapes with a broken rib. As Abby leaves, she ignores Maggie – then changes her mind and takes her home with her.

Both Mark and Elizabeth receive life-changing news

Romano is furious when Elizabeth is told she is being sued for malpractice. Mark promises to speak to a friend in Risk Management on her behalf. Later, during a trauma, Elizabeth is sick. She is astonished when a pregnancy test proves positive.

Meanwhile, Mark finds himself unable to talk when treating a patient. Anxious, Mark takes an MI scan that reveals a large mass on Mark's frontal cortex. Mark is told to speak to a neurosurgeon immediately. That night, Elizabeth gives Mark her good news. Mark is pleased, but cannot bring himself to tell her about his condition.

Carter assumes a man is drug-seeking

Carter treats Mr Florea who has a cut hand and complains about a sore knee. He asks for lidocaine but Carter, suspecting he is drug-seeking, refuses. Tests show a clot in Florea's knee and Carter realises he was wrong. Florea has left and Carter chases after him. He finds Florea unconscious at the El. Back in the ER, Carter begins tPA. Luka argues about Carter's choice of treatment, but Chuny notices Florea improving.

Other threads

In chairs, Maggie talks to Mrs Chen and congratulates her on Jing-Mei's pregnancy. Mrs Chen is confused until she sees Jing-Mei. She is shocked, but calms down and agrees not to tell her husband. Later, Chen arrives at home. Her mother insists the family will be supportive but Jing-Mei asks if they still will be if the baby is black. Mrs Chen's shocked expression says it all. Chen leaves dismayed.

Cleo is annoyed about the standard of care for Jesse and her breast cancer patient. She assumes both were ill-treated because they were black. Peter snaps that Cleo should stop teaching people to be black. Angry, Cleo refuses to see him later.

Kerry and Kim go to dinner and laughingly share past experiences. Kim wonders if this is a second date. Kerry seems taken aback but admits she knows Kim is gay. Kerry is confused and confides she hadn't expected "this".

"The Dance We Do"

7 – 8: First transmitted 7 December 2000
Written by Jack Orman; Directed by Christopher Misiano

Maggie's behaviour becomes more erratic

Abby has spent the night with Luka but they are distant. She returns to her apartment where Maggie has plans to stay. Abby suspects Maggie has taken anti-depressants and asks her to take a blood test. Maggie claims to have a job interview.

At County, Maggie tries to get out of the test and eventually Abby relents. Later, Abby is called to the store where Maggie has attempted to steal a scarf and smashed a glass door. As Luka sutures Maggie, Abby apologises for her mother.

Maggie becomes aggressive and has to be restrained, but Legaspi says she can only be admitted voluntarily. Seeing Abby's dismay, Maggie offers to admit herself and pleads: "I'll get better." Later, Abby hears that her mother left before a bed was found. She knows Maggie will return. That night, she leaves Luka's bed and sobs.

Peter treats Jesse's ex–girlfriend, Kynesha

Cleo treats Kynesha (7-6) who has been thrown out of her gang. Peter tries to persuade Kynesha to give the police names, but she resists. He blames her for endangering Jesse. Kynesha tells Peter the names. Later, Peter passes the information on to the police, but they can only act on Kynesha's testimony. Kynesha refuses to talk to the police and leaves angry.

That night, Peter is surprised to find Kynesha waiting for him outside Jacky's. Her gang has been arrested, probably on Peter's word, and she fears she will be killed. Peter takes her back to Cleo's, promising to figure something out.

Corday gives a deposition in the Patterson case

Elizabeth is due to give her deposition in the Patterson case. Mark offers to attend, but Elizabeth insists on going alone. The deposition quickly becomes heated when Patterson's attorney mentions Jesse's death and Elizabeth's relationship to Peter. As tensions rise, Elizabeth is baited into stating she wanted to leave by six o'clock on the day of the surgery. Her lawyer orders a break and reminds her to answer only yes or no. When they return, Al Patterson is present, paralysed from the waist down. The questioning continues and Elizabeth lies that she performed a thorough check for spinal fluid before she closed.

Mark hears his prognosis from a neurosurgeon

Mark is devastated when he is told his tumour is inoperable and he could die within eight weeks. Mark is distracted and doesn't pay attention to Carter's compulsory blood test. Carter becomes irate and they argue. Suddenly Mark has a seizure.

He is stabilised and explains about his tumour. Carter asks what Mark will do. "Die, I guess," he says. That night, Corday returns, pained that she lied under oath. Mark insists that God owes them one – and tells her about the tumour.

Other threads
Dave spends his day avoiding a blonde named Stephanie. Cleo jokes it was a different girl the day before. Randi indicates that the same has happened to her.

"The Greatest of Gifts"

7 – 9: First transmitted 14 December 2000
Written by Elizabeth Hunter; Directed by Jonathan Kaplan

Chen gives birth but finds it hard to let go of the baby
Carter gets into bed, but is paged to return to County: Jing-Mei is in labour. Carter speaks to James and Linda, the adoptive parents, but does not let them attend the birth. The delivery is smooth but Chen doesn't want to see the baby. She is upset when the new family and Carter want her to say goodbye to her child.

On seeing her son, Chen is not sure she can live with herself for letting the boy go. Carter tells her she is not abandoning her son, she is making a new family. Chen hands her son over and watches as Linda sings Michael Alexander a lullaby.

Kynesha causes more trouble for Peter and Cleo
Cleo is annoyed that Kynesha, staying at her house, allows her friend Tiny to visit. She gives Peter two days to find a foster carer. Later, Kynesha calls to say Cleo's car has been stolen. It is later found with a burned-out clutch. Cleo suspects Kynesha and threatens to call the police. When she returns home, Kynesha admits she suspects Tiny of stealing the car. Cleo is ready to throw Kynesha out, but the girl begs to stay. She has nowhere else to go.

Carter succumbs to temptation during a difficult shift
Having helped Chen, Carter stays to fills in on a shift. His treats several young children who were hit by a motorcycle. Carter finds drugs in the motorcyclist's pocket and takes two pills. Suddenly, he thinks better of it and makes himself sick in the restroom. He retrieves the two pills intact. Carter tells Abby, who insists he tell Weaver and go home sick.

Mark obtains a second opinion
In New York, Mark waits for a second opinion but Elizabeth struggles to encourage a positive outlook. In the hospital, Mark is scanned before meeting Dr Burke. Elizabeth is saddened to overhear that survival rates are only 12 to 14 months. After, Mark asks if Elizabeth will still have their child if he dies. Elizabeth promises that she will. When they see Dr Burke, he says can remove the tumour and insert chemotherapy wafers. His patients have a survival rate of 24 months and counting.

Other threads

Peter chances upon Taylor, a young girl who complains she is a regular donor for her sister Nicole. Peter tells the mother that Taylor is scared of more procedures. The mother angrily refuses to explain her family's situation to another stranger.

Kerry spends the day suffering from hiccups. Kim tells Kerry that they are not in the same place emotionally. She has been in a similar situation with a straight woman before and it didn't work. She kisses Kerry and Kerry seems flustered. The kiss proves Kim's point and seems to cure Kerry's hiccups.

"Piece of Mind"

7–10: First transmitted 4 January 2001
Written by Tom Garrigus & R. Scott Gemmill; Directed by David Nutter

Mark undergoes neurosurgery

New Year's Eve 2000. As Mark awaits surgery, he admits he has had an operation before. Elizabeth tries to reassure him, but Mark is unconvinced. He asks Elizabeth to sign a power of attorney and order no heroic measures. As he waits, Mark befriends Leo, a young boy scared about having surgery. Mark admits he is scared too.

Mark is taken to the OR. He blacks out and wakes to see Elizabeth and neurologist Dr Malcolm. As Burke presses parts of Mark's brain, Malcolm tests Mark's response. Mark has a seizure. Images flash before his eyes: a birthday cake, a motorcycle, an irate Jen, his mother and father. After a torturous half-hour, Mark regains consciousness and is even able to talk about the baby to Elizabeth. Burke continues and the tumour is removed.

In recovery, Mark suffers post-operative bleeding but is stabilised. Weak, he watches helplessly as Leo suffers complications. Later, Mark hears Leo is touch-and-go. Mark's surgery, however, was successful. Burke tells Mark to mobilise his inner resources and he will survive.

The ER treats a father and son injured in a car accident

As Dan Harris drives his son, Paul, to hockey practice, they argue about the boy's skills. Dan is hopeful Paul can earn a college hockey scholarship. As they reach a crossing, a garbage truck smashes into the side of their car.

Dave Malucci is first on the scene. Dan and Paul are stabilised and taken to County. While Carter gives Dan a chest tube, Paul is treated by Kerry. Abby takes Dan for a CT and tells him they are trying to reach his wife, Debra. Dan worries that Debra will blame him for the accident: their first son, Nathan, died when Dan was looking after him, but there was nothing he could have done.

Paul suffers a relapse but is stabilised. Dan gives a statement to the police, but can't remember the incident. The policeman says witnesses saw Dan running a red light. Dan insists he wouldn't do that, but can't be sure. When Debra arrives, Dan tells her he ran the light. Debra is furious. As Dan tries to explain, he suffers chest pains.

Luka realises Dan is at risk of a heart attack. He suspects Dan blacked out due to his condition and that this caused the accident. Dan is relieved, but his condition worsens. As he is prepped for surgery, Debra arrives apologetic and tells him that Paul is doing well. Debra is rushed out as her husband's condition deteriorates.

The surgery goes well and Dan sits up in recovery. Paul is wheeled past and tells his dad that his leg injury will put him on the bench for the rest of the season. Nevertheless, father and son are both OK.

"Rock, Paper, Scissors"

7 – 11: First transmitted 11 January 2001
Written by Dee Johnson; Directed by Jonathan Kaplan

The malpractice suit takes its toll on Elizabeth
Elizabeth anxiously prepares to see her lawyer but hears the hospital has settled out of court for $1.5 million. Her lawyer suggests the surgical equipment was at fault and the manufacturer is liable. Elizabeth knows the equipment was fine, but Romano tells her this is the right result. Elizabeth is taken aback when Patterson arrives, bitter about the settlement. He hopes she never forgets his face.

The encounter disturbs Elizabeth and she struggles to cope in a trauma and then in the OR. As her patient weakens, Elizabeth panics and calls for help. Romano discovers Elizabeth has missed a basic procedure. To his anger, she leaves.

Luka treats a Catholic bishop
The casualties of a car accident are brought to the ER. Luka and Cleo are unable to save Amy Hembree, but stabilise her mother. Later, Luka treats Kevin Poole, an aggressive drunk. Realising Kevin was the cause of the accident, Luka inserts the nasal tube as roughly as possible without pain medication.

Luka's next patient is a Catholic bishop. The bishop inquires about Luka's religious beliefs and is intrigued that Luka was confirmed a Catholic. Luka is uncomfortable with the line of questioning and is angry when the bishop absolves Kevin Poole shortly before the man dies. Luka bitterly wonders if God was with Amy when she died, as the bishop suggests. Luka discharges the bishop, insisting he walk with a stick in return for the steroids he requested.

Kerry avoids Kim at work
Kerry treats Roger Pilarsky, a regular visitor to the ER, who complains of chest pain. Kerry is dismayed to discover a pair of scissors sticking out of his chest! Kim, hearing about Roger, wonders why she wasn't called and confronts Kerry, insisting that what happened between them should not interfere with patient care. Kerry is defensive and they later clash over Carter's patient. That evening, Kerry admits her confused feelings to Kim, but hopes they will be more than friends.

Other threads

Peter receives a call from Kynesha and rescues her from a fight. Peter discovers Kynesha started a fight at the half-way house. Kynesha wants to stay with Peter, but he arranges for Adele to make Kynesha a ward of the state. Kynesha bitterly blames "that bitch Cleo" and later ransacks Cleo's house. As Peter and Cleo clear up, Peter admits his true feelings for Cleo – theirs in the only relationship he has wanted to work at. Cleo is still upset about Kynesha's behaviour and seems unmoved.

Kerry is pleased with Carter's rehabilitation and asks him if he has anything to add. Carter starts to say something, but is interrupted. Abby asks Carter if he has told Kerry about his relapse. He hasn't. Abby tells him to find another sponsor. Later, Carter tells Kerry the truth. She listens, but reserves judgement until tomorrow.

"Surrender"

7–12: First transmitted 1 February 2001
Teleplay by Jack Orman; Story by R. Scott Gemmill & Joe Sachs;
Directed by Felix Enriquez Alcalá

Kerry has a rough day and returns to Kim

Kerry has spent the night with Kim. She asks that their relationship remain their secret and Kim hesitantly agrees. At work, Kerry is edgy around Kim. Kerry treats a patient who she suspects is an illegal immigrant. Against Luka's advice, Kerry calls a Health and Safety body. Later, she treats workers from a sweatshop: her tip-off led to a raid that caused a fire. Luka watches accusingly as Kerry fails to save a young mother. Kerry guiltily wonders what will happen to the woman's daughter. Kerry heads home but, needing company, decides to go to Kim.

Carter visits Chase

Carter visits Chase in a clinic but Chase reacts badly. At work, Kerry tells Carter his probationary period is starting over and he will not be able to prescribe narcotics. Carter dutifully agrees. Abby is pleased he finally talked to Weaver. Later, Peter asks Carter to give a critical patient drugs and Carter refuses, getting Malucci to help instead. Peter is angry that Carter has not been given more responsibility and accuses Kerry of holding Carter's one mistake against him. Kerry tells Peter that Carter isn't yet clean and Peter is disappointed. Later, Carter returns to Chase and admits he didn't visit because he was afraid to admit he was also a drug addict.

Romano forces Elizabeth to regain her confidence

Her confidence broken, Elizabeth has cancelled some of her surgeries. Annoyed, Romano tells Elizabeth to cover the ER as penance. She and Mark treat a 15-year-old who has shot himself while playing Russian roulette. Elizabeth performs a transfusion, although there is little hope for the boy, and later admits to Mark she was wrong. Her confidence is shaken further when Malik and Mark almost have to tell her to operate on a patient. In the OR, she panics and calls for Romano. Unseen, Romano watches on as Elizabeth becomes more agitated. He is pleased, however, when she regains her senses and saves the patient.

Other threads

Peter is surprised when Romano offers him a raise of $20,000 per year to take on some "administrative" duties. As soon as they shake on the deal, Peter is rushed into a press room and introduced to journalists as County's new Director of Diversity. After some tricky questions, Benton accuses Romano of hiring him just because he is black. Romano admits just that and tells Peter to get over it.

It is Mark's first day back and Kerry is concerned to hear him mixing his pronouns. He also shows a more brusque attitude with patients. When Carter picks Mark up on his speech problems, Mark insists he is just tired.

Abby treats Walter and Earl, two horny old men from the Oakville Retirement Home who got into a fight over a woman resident. She is surprised to find both men have chlamydia!

"Thy Will Be Done"

7 – 13: First transmitted 8 February 2001
*Teleplay by Meredith Stiehm; Story by Meredith Stiehm & Joe Sachs;
Directed by Richard Thorpe*

Mark's cavalier attitude draws criticism

After radiation therapy, Mark arrives at the ER in the midst of the flu season. He is noticeably difficult: he breaks hospital policy, makes little effort to save an 85-year-old woman and urges flu patients to leave by refusing to prescribe antibiotics.

Romano picks up Mark on his behaviour and sees first-hand Mark's difficulty expressing himself. Kerry at first defends Mark, explaining about his mild aphasia, but later sees his dispassionate, almost cruel behaviour first-hand. Concerned, Kerry asks Mark to take time off, but he refuses. Later, she calls a helpline for information about testing Mark for cognitive impairment.

Dave looks after a patient who requires sensitive handling

Carter treats Jeff, a young man who has had unprotected sex with Sean, his HIV+ partner. Carter orders a blood test before leaving and worries about passing the case to Dave. Dave insists he can handle the case sensitively. He tells Jeff he is not infected but the news is not received well. Jeff reveals that he has been trying to get infected to be closer to Sean. Dave is stunned that Jeff is a "bug chaser", and insists that Sean would not want Jeff to be infected if he loved him. He tries to persuade Jeff to use condoms. Jeff admits he probably won't take Dave's advice.

Bishop Stewart returns for more steroids

Bishop Stewart (7-11) asks Luka for more steroids, claiming he can't see his own doctor at weekends. Luka is annoyed to discover the bishop has not told him about his diabetes –

the steriods Luka prescribed have exacerbated a disease called lupus that is slowly killing him. The bishop is dismissive, explaining he needs the steroids to continue his ministry. He probes Luka about his beliefs but Luka remains quiet.

Meanwhile, Luka treats Nick, a young boy who would rather die than go through a third heart transplant. Luka defends the boy's rights against his parents and Romano with no success. Observing, the bishop hopes Nick will fight, and Luka notes the irony that the bishop is not willing to do the same. The bishop observes that Luka respected Nick's wishes and hopes he will respect his too. Luka prescribes the steroids, and lets the bishop leave.

Other threads

Carter's date is unable to go to a Carter Family Foundation charity ball, so he asks Abby. She agrees and during the evening they seem to grow closer. However, Abby is dismayed to meet her ex-husband, Richard, at the party. On their way home, Abby finds Richard's car and lets down a tyre. As they make their getaway in a limousine, Abby apologises for ruining their evening. Carter insists it hasn't been ruined and they agree they've had a good time.

"A Walk in the Woods"

7–14: First transmitted 15 February 2001
Written and Directed by John Wells

Luka helps Bishop Stewart carry out one final duty

Bishop Stewart arrives short of breath and is stabilised. Luka wants to call the bishop's personal physician, but Stewart prefers Luka's care. Test reveals that the lupus is severe and Stewart should be in the ICU. However, he is determined to attend an ordination and leaves.

Later, Luka finds the frail bishop at a Cathedral. Stewart reveals he decided to become a priest after a walk in the woods. He laments that he has not done all he should have. Luka helps the bishop through the ordination. During the ceremony, Luka is reminded of the burial of his wife and children. Afterwards, he treats Bishop Stewart, who is in arrest. Luka sadly tells Abby that the bishop is dying.

Peter takes affirmative action

Romano passes a young black student, William White, on to Peter. White has complained he did not get an interview. Peter check's White's application in the records office and also looks at his own. After, he tells Cleo he found "AA" on his file – affirmative action. His results were low for the year and he got his place because he was black. White's results, by contrast, were much better. When Romano, Coburn and Benton interview candidates, Peter insists that White's case be reconsidered.

Kerry struggles to come to terms with her sexuality

Kerry is perturbed when Kim and her friend Christy invite her to a meal that night. Kerry pretends to be working late, but Kim has checked her schedule and she is free. During the day, Kerry feels uncomfortable as Dave relays gossip about Kim. She is more uneasy during the meal when Christy notes that Kim has slept with all three dinner guests. Unnerved, Kerry makes a hasty exit, and feebly argues she is not interested in "adopting a lifestyle".

Other threads

Carter treats four-year-old Zach, who has a fever and breathing difficulties. The school doesn't have a signed medical consent form for Zach and Carter has to get the chart co-signed to order a spinal tap. Meningitis is ruled out and Carter is surprised to realise that Zach has measles. He is angry to discover that Zach's mother has refused to immunise her children and is not aware of the seriousness of the illness. Later, Zach crashes and dies.

Mark is surprised when Dr Robert Wilson arrives to evaluate his competency to practise medicine. Kerry explains to Mark that he has been argumentative and insensitive and she needs an objective assessment. The news soon reaches Elizabeth who fiercely berates Kerry, going so far as to wish a potentially fatal disease on her. That night, Mark laments he has five days testing ahead of him: "The good times just keep coming," he notes sadly.

One to Watch

"The Crossing"

7–15: First transmitted 22 February 2001
Written by Jack Orman; Directed by Jonathan Kaplan

The ER staff deal with a train derailment

Luka is distracted at the end of a long day in the ER. Kerry tells him they did well – only two casualties out of more than 30 cases. She urges him to leave, but Luka instead heads to the ICU to see Bishop Stewart. Luka notes the bishop will need to a ventilator soon. The bishop refuses, saying his "bags are packed".

Seven hours earlier. A train has derailed after it hits a car stuck on a crossing. As the ER is prepped for mass casualties, Luka and Carter take the chopper to the accident. It is carnage, and for a moment Luka is reminded of his past in Croatia. Luka tends to Shannon, the young driver who was in the car. He then helps a young mother, pinned to her seat, who asks for her seven-year-old son, Miles. The boy is found and again Luka is haunted by memories. The mother makes Luka promise he will help Miles first. Luka takes them back to County and has to let Miles take priority, even though the mother is more seriously injured.

Meanwhile, Carter works on a firefighter whose legs are trapped under a train carriage. Elizabeth is sent to the scene to assist and begins to amputate, but suddenly goes into labour and has to return to County. Carter is left to perform the amputation, under instruction from Peter over a mobile phone, but is frequently left to fend for himself. He succeeds in amputating and brings the firefighter to County. Although Romano is disdainful, Kerry tells Carter he did well.

Corday is flown back to County where Abby takes care of her. Elizabeth is given drugs to stop the contractions and the baby, at only 25 weeks, is saved. Mark insists she must take things easier from now on.

Kerry treats Shannon, who seems morbidly aware of the patients from the accident. Kerry slowly realises that Shannon parked her car on the tracks to commit suicide. She calls Kim to assess the girl.

The trauma is over and Luka is at the bishop's bedside. Bishop Stewart knows why Luka has come – that he is searching for his faith. Luka tells the bishop how his apartment was bombed in Croatia, killing his son and leaving his wife and daughter seriously wounded. Luka fought to save his girl but couldn't leave his wife to die. He prayed but nothing happened and, unable to sacrifice one for the other, he lost both of them. The bishop prays for Luka before he dies.

Other threads

Before the multiple trauma, Carter meets Rena Trujillo, a young woman working as a Child Life Specialist. There is a mutual attraction.

Medical school candidate William White tells Peter he has been given an interview. Peter encourages White to stay and observe, to give him something meaningful to talk about at his interview. It is an extreme day in the ER and William sees a man's chest cut open, a leg bone detached and Peter bore into a man's skull. He even has to hold the phone to Peter's ear as he instructs Carter. At the end of the day William has decided not to apply, afraid he may become used to the horrors of the ER like Peter. Peter hopes William will still go to the interview.

Mark undertakes the competency test. He appears to do well, and is even cocky, but becomes concerned when he gets the next few questions wrong.

The Crossing is one of ER's hallmark single incident episodes but it's here as a "one to watch" for a much smaller part of it. Luka's relationship with Bishop Stewart is one of the most interesting and involving in the show's history, comparing favourably with that of Kerry Weaver and Gabriel Lawrence. The question of Luka's faith is neatly explored in parallel to the unfolding story of the train wreck. The final moments, where Luka returns to the fold, are impressively enacted. By contrast, the train wreck itself is a little overwrought, playing largely through noise and gore. Carter's forced return to surgery makes an interesting aside, showing more than anything that Carter is dealing with his addiction.

"Witch Hunt"

7 – 16: First transmitted 1 March 2001
Written by R. Scott Gemmill; Directed by Guy Norman Bee

Kerry's shame of her sexuality jeopardises Kim's career

Uncomfortable being seen with Kim, Kerry quietly leaves Kim's house when two police detectives arrive. At work, Kim is upset by Kerry's behaviour. She explains that Shannon Wallace, the suicidal girl who caused the train derailment (7-15), has accused her of sexual harassment. Although critical that Kim told Shannon she was gay, Kerry defends Kim to the police.

She later takes issue with Romano, who insinuates that Kim's lesbianism is the problem. Nevertheless, the issue clearly has resonances with Kerry and she decides to keep her sexuality a secret. At Kim's hearing, Kerry's defence is lukewarm, angering Kim. Kerry insists she has fought to be accepted all her life and doesn't want to go through it all again. Kim tells Kerry to get back to her own life.

Abby feels responsible when a baby is snatched from the ER

Dierdre Jeffries brings in her baby daughter May, who is having breathing difficulties. Later, Abby leaves the baby alone in the room and returns to find she has been taken. A frantic search ensues and County is turned upside down without success. The mother is beside herself with worry and makes a TV appeal for May's safe return. Abby blames herself and concentrates only on the search. She is relieved when May is found at an El station and is brought back to County unharmed. Abby arranges for Deirdre to sleep in May's room.

Malucci takes issue with Mark's attitude

Mark is tetchy all day as he awaits his competency test results. He and Malucci treat James, an amateur wrestler who is found to be taking steroids. Malucci sees how scared James is that his father will find out and suspects domestic abuse. Mark is dismissive and Dave angrily remarks on Mark's lack of compassion. When the father arrives, Malucci speaks to him, preventing Mark from relaying the information about steroids. He baits the father who takes a swing at Dave and is carried away. Unimpressed, Mark suspends Malucci for one week. Later, Mark receives his test results. Despite his bad mood, he has passed.

Other threads

Elizabeth is annoyed to find Romano has asked Peter to take over her surgeries while she is on leave. Despite Mark's appeals, Elizabeth insists she is able to return to work. When she tells Romano about a pregnant woman who killed someone because she had a hormone imbalance, Romano relents.

Carter has spent the night at Rena's and seems taken with her. Later, he is shocked to learn that Rena is only 19 years old. He confides in Abby, who is incredulous. Defensive, he insists that Rena is old for her age. Abby jokes that Rena could be Britney Spears' little sister!

"Survival of the Fittest"

7 – 17: First transmitted 29 March 2001
Teleplay by Joe Sachs; Story by Elizabeth Hunter; Directed by Marita Grabiak

Peter is complicit in the death of an elderly patient

1 April 2001. Cleo and Peter treat Mrs Howard, an elderly black woman who recently had surgery. As Mrs Howard waits for her test results, she becomes agitated and altered. She grabs a policeman's gun and waves it, demanding treatment. A policewoman orders her to put the gun down but she isn't listening and is shot twice in the chest. She dies. Peter is furious when he sees the two police officers checking their story. However, he and Cleo discover they both missed that Mrs Howard was dehydrated, which caused her altered state. They too get their stories straight. When Peter talks to the family, he hides the truth.

Elizabeth operates for hours while heavily pregnant

As Elizabeth performs routine surgery, Romano arrives and notes a complication. Already tired, Elizabeth refuses to appear weak before Romano and continues. Later, they discover the patient needs a five-hour procedure. Elizabeth wants a bathroom break but Romano threatens to call Peter. Again, Elizabeth refuses and is ready to ask for a catheter when Romano lets her go to the bathroom.

After several hours, Elizabeth leaves surgery, determined to go on maternity leave. She receives a pizza and ice cream from Romano for her efforts. Mark wonders if someone should taste it first.

The ER staff treat a party of school children

A party of school children complain about fumes on their bus. An obese asthmatic boy, Stuart, is particularly unwell and is teased by three unruly boys. Carter discovers that the boys were sniffing solvents. Mark scares one of the boys, Bo, into telling them which solvent. Later, Mark sadly discovers Bo is in liver failure due to the solvent and will die without a transplant. Meanwhile, Luka treats Emily, who reveals she is pregnant. Luka implies as much to Emily's mother and sparks a fierce slanging match between mother and daughter. Luka calls a social worker. Emily is pleased – she wants to sign up for benefits now.

Other threads

Carter has difficulty with Simon, who refuses to have his blood drawn. Rena manages to calm him, winning Carter's admiration. They arrange to go out again but, seeing Abby's disapproval, Carter asks Rena not to mention it to Abby, implying she is a jealous ex-girlfriend. Rena agrees but later asks if Abby is OK. Abby plays along for Carter's sake – but tells Rena that she dumped him!

Yosh calls Abby and Luka to assist with a violent man who cannot be restrained. Luka grabs a syringe of Haldol and injects in into the patient. The man screams in pain – it is Malucci playing an April Fool's prank. Throughout the day, Malucci suffers the lethargic effects of the drug. Finally, Luka finds Malucci in a deep sleep – and glues his hand to his forehead.

"April Showers"

7–18: First transmitted 19 April 2001
Teleplay by Tom Garrigus; Story by Tom Garrigus & Dee Johnson;
Directed by Christopher Misiano

Mark and Elizabeth's wedding day does not go smoothly

It is the day of the wedding. Chicago is in the midst of a storm, Rachel has to get another flight and Mark has left his wallet at work. As he leaves for County, Mark calms a fretful Elizabeth, insisting: "Everything is going to go like clockwork." While Elizabeth braves her mother and father, Mark's day goes from bad to worse. His car is towed away, then Rachel cancels completely and finally public transport comes to a standstill. Mark gets a lift with Peter, but traffic is stopped by an accident. Amid the torrential downpour, Mark and Peter help the injured and end up back at County. Eventually, Mark makes it to the church and apologises to Elizabeth at the altar: "It was raining," he explains.

Luka and Carter clash in the ER

Multiple victims of a prison van accident are brought to the ER. Carter works on an injured policeman, aware of the man's colleagues looking on. He is annoyed when Luka insists Carter pronounce the man dead. Carter is further irked when Luka passes patients to him as his shift is ending.

Carter treats Veronica, a recovering drug addict with a dislocated shoulder. Veronica refuses morphine, fearing she will become addicted. As Carter tries to reset her shoulder, Luka insists she is given the drug. Abby later chastises Luka for being hard on Carter. Luka insists Carter was disobeying his instructions. At the wedding, Rena asks Carter if Luka is his supervisor. Carter answers: "Technically."

Chen is reminded of the duties of parenthood

Chen treats Sara Morris, one of the female inmates injured in the prison van accident. Sara was on her way to see her daughter for the last time when the accident happened. Later, Sara slips free of her captors, but is quickly recaptured. All the time she screams that she wants to see her child. Chen's second patient is Bryan, a little boy who has hypothermia. His parents forgot to pick him up from soccer practice. Chen is furious with the father for failing to remember about his son. Later, Chen telephones Linda, the new parent of her baby, and asks about the boy's progress.

Other threads

Kerry has not been invited to the wedding and leaves for a conference in Las Vegas. Her flight is grounded and she spends the day talking to a businessman called Mike who is clearly interested in her. Kerry enjoys the company but later leaves the man's business card, deciding against his offer to meet up again.

Peter is suspicious when Cleo makes excuses for not attending the wedding. Cleo explains she is not happy about attending Peter's ex-girlfriend's wedding, nor that he assumed she would go anyway. Peter decides to go alone but finds Cleo waiting for him, all dolled up for the do in a little black dress.

One to Watch

"Sailing Away"

7-19: First transmitted 26 April 2001
Written by Jack Orman & Meredith Stiehm;
Directed by Laura Innes

Abby receives another call to help Maggie

Abby's ex-husband Richard arrives at the ER with news that Maggie is holed up in a motel near Tulsa. She has stopped answering her door. Abby decides to bring Maggie home, but Luka insists she should be admitted in Oklahoma. They clash. Meanwhile Carter offers to keep Abby company. He tells Rena, who is jealous.

The next day, Abby and Carter arrive at the motel. Maggie is quiet and weak, a far cry from her manic persona. The encounter troubles and angers Abby, who gets Maggie ready for the trip home. On the road, Abby apologises for getting Carter involved. She tells Carter about her mother's suicidal episodes. They stop another night at a motel, where both Abby and Carter have troubled telephone calls with their partners. Carter breaks up with Rena. That night, Maggie tells Abby she should give up on her.

The next morning, they stop at a shop before driving on to Chicago. On arrival Abby and Carter find Maggie unresponsive. She has overdosed on sleeping pills from the shop. At County, Maggie has her stomach pumped and is stabilised. Abby tells Luka she should have listened to him – Maggie should have been hospitalised. Luka insists Maggie will be OK. Sadly, Abby knows that will never be the case.

Elizabeth gives birth

Elizabeth feels contractions and is taken to County. She is frustrated to realise she has been taken in by phantom contractions and leaves embarrassed. The next day the couple return for the real delivery and Elizabeth gives birth to a baby girl, Ella. Dave is keen to hold the little "heifer", but Mark refuses. Dave insists Mark owes him $300 for a box of cigars.

It is frat week in Chicago

It is rag week and the ER staff treat a number of casualties. First Luka treats two girls who have been injured while chasing a greased pig. Later, a drunken frat boy is brought in after he failed to jump between two roofs. Peter then treats Adam, a young man who was locked in a car boot as a frat initiation. He is surprised to learn this is Adam's second attempt to get through the ritual. The next day Adam is brought back with "loser" written on his head. He has drunk 40 tequila shots while his big brother watched. Adam dies and Peter angrily tells the brother to clean Adam up.

Other threads

Peter meets Mr Ferris, his High School science teacher, who has left-side weakness following a stroke. Peter tells Cleo how Ferris' tutoring inspired him to take up medicine. Peter is able to arrange a care home for Ferris by agreeing to visit him regularly to take blood tests. Later, Peter is visited by William White, who has been admitted to med school. "Don't thank me," notes Benton. "Just work your ass off."

Another "road trip" episode, not unlike *Fathers and Sons*, but one that pushes the characters forward. Ever since the AA meeting in *Sand and Water*, Carter and Abby have grown closer. When Abby hears about Maggie, both she and Carter are on bad terms with their partners. Suddenly there's motive and opportunity... It's a promising situation for them both, yet they never quite get there. On top of this tension, you have the fantastic Sally Fields making a welcome return as Maggie. The overdose is hardly a surprise but still makes for powerful viewing, especially Abby's realisation that Luka was right all along.

"Fear of Commitment"

7-20: First transmitted 3 May 2001
Written by R. Scott Gemmill; Directed by Anthony Edwards

Maggie appeals against her committal to a psych ward

Abby is surprised to hear that Maggie, on hold for 90 days in the psych ward, is appealing against her committal. Abby wants to go to the court alone. Luka asks if she would prefer Carter's company but Abby resents the implication. In court, Abby testifies to Maggie's suicidal tendencies in the hope she will be committed. Maggie's lawyer tries to make Abby appear selfish and unwilling to care for her mother. Maggie claims she misread the instructions on her sleeping pills to Abby's audible disgust. Eventually, the judge upholds Maggie's appeal.

At County, Abby coldly wishes Maggie luck and tells her she will see her next time. Maggie supposes there won't be one, but Abby is unconvinced. That night, Maggie arrives at Luka's hotel to see Abby.

Kerry has a childhood memory shattered

Kerry is surprised to discover an elderly bag lady was the puppeteer of her favourite

childhood TV show. The woman refuses treatment but gives Kerry Mr Whiskers, one of her puppets, as a gift. Meanwhile, Kerry treats two "furries" – people who are excited by getting dressed up in animal costumes. The kangaroo bemoans how he fought a possum when he put his hand down his pouch! Later, Kerry is horrified to find the possum masturbating with Mr Whiskers!

Peter treats his old teacher for congestive heart failure

Peter discovers Mr Ferris is in congestive heart failure. On the way to County, their ambulance hits a motorcyclist and Peter injures his hand. At the ER, Peter has to work on the more seriously injured motorcyclist. Romano notices Peter is hampered by his injured hand and, diagnosing a small fracture, tells Peter to scrub out. Peter is surprised to find Carla, a little flirty, in the hospital with a broken ankle. He looks after Reese for her and checks on Mr Ferris. The two reminisce. Peter thanks Mr Ferris for inspiring him into medicine. He admits he has found happiness as a doctor and a father.

Other threads

Carter treats Noni, a young woman with abdominal pain. Noni discovered she was pregnant two weeks ago. Later, Noni starts to haemorrhage and is sent to the OR. Her boyfriend, Victor, guiltily admits he gave Noni a root extract to cause a miscarriage. Carter has the boyfriend arrested.

Dave and Chen treat an unconscious young Asian girl with unusual burns on her back. Dave recognises that the girl has been "coined" – the dragging of hot coins over the skin to purify the spirit. They try to talk to the mother, but she does not speak English. Earl, from Mr Ferris' nursing home, was a translator in the army and intercedes. The mother believes the girl is possessed. Suspecting the girl's altered state is psychosomatic, Dave has the priest give a blessing. The girl is miraculously better, to Dave's smug self-congratulation.

"Where the Heart Is"

7 – 21: First transmitted 10 May 2001
Written by Dee Johnson & Meredith Stiehm; Directed by Richard Thorpe

Abby fears to hope for Maggie's rehabilitation

Maggie is improving and invites Abby to join a therapy session. Abby is hesitant but agrees. However, during the session, she derides Maggie's intention to return to Minneapolis. Later, Carter asks if Abby would be happy with anything Maggie plans and she admits not. That night, Abby tells Maggie she is scared to hope too much. Maggie insists she wants to get on with her life, and let Abby get on with hers. Abby breaks down as she tells Maggie that she was once pregnant but aborted the baby fearing it would be bi-polar. Sympathetic, Maggie insists there is always risk in life but you have to embrace it. Together they go to a staff softball game.

Mark treats a domestic abuse case

Mark treats Ben Fosen, an aggressive seven-year-old boy who has burned his hand. A message is left for Ben's father. Mark finds the boy has bruising behind one ear and suspects abuse. When Fosen arrives, Ben becomes quieter. Fosen insists that Ben gets into fights at school. Mark checks old charts and discovers a previous arm fracture. Adele and Mark decide to separate Ben and his father. Fosen is furious and insists he will get a lawyer. Later, Ben confirms that his dad caused his wrist fracture. Ben blames himself for being naughty, but Mark insists the fault is not his.

Kerry is given some relationship advice by Luka

Kerry tries to give a letter to Kim but is surprised when another woman answers Kim's door. At work, Kim asks about the letter but Kerry says it wasn't the right time. Luka interrupts the moment. Later, a sad Kerry tells Luka she and Kim have broken up. Luka asks if Kerry loves Kim. She does. Luka tells her to go forward with her feelings, not back. Later, Kerry hands Kim the letter.

Other threads

Kerry tells Carter that the stress of becoming Chief Resident would jeopardise his recovery and hands back his application. Carter congratulates Chen, expecting she will get the post. However, Chen is not eligible either, because her maternity leave put her behind schedule. Chen alleges discrimination and urges Kerry to take her concerns seriously.

Kerry treats Jim Vogel, who has been run over. His sister, Bonnie, has the mental age of a child. Jim dies and Kerry struggles to explain the news to Bonnie. Kerry watches sadly as Bonnie is taken to a group home.

Peter leaves Reese in Cleo's care while he sees Carla. Carla announces that Roger has left her and tries to get back with Peter, but he is not interested. Peter receives a call from Cleo. As they talk, Reese traps his hand under a piano lid. Carla berates Cleo and Peter intercedes, but is cold with Cleo. Cleo is upset.

"Rampage"

7 – 22: First transmitted 17 May 2001
Teleplay by Jack Orman; Story by Jack Orman & Joe Sachs;
Directed by Jonathan Kaplan

Mark finds his family the target of a ruthless gunman

Mark arrives at County to treat the victims of a shooting at a foster care facility. The gunman became angry with the foster manager and started shooting. The shooter has not been found.

Moments later, a carjack victim of the shooter is brought in, followed by a mother and son. The mother is Ben Fossen's neighbour (7-21) who identifies the shooter as Derek

Fossen: "He said if I was going to take his boy away from him, he was going to take mine away from me." The neighbour dies and Mark has to tell her disbelieving son.

Mark tells the police that Fossen wants his son back. They collect Ben and his foster family for their protection. The police post extra officers at County. The next victim is a police officer who tried to apprehend Fossen. Then comes Adele Neuman. Adele has been shot in the back and can't move her legs. Adele was shot at home and Mark realises Fossen could be after his family too. The police break down Mark's door, but there is no sign of Elizabeth, Ella or Fossen.

Finally, Fossen is found. An armed civilian shot him after he attacked a taxi driver. The taxi was en route to Mark's house. Fossen angrily shouts that Mark is the cause of all this. Elizabeth calls, safe and well, but does not know what is happening.

On the way to the OR, Mark and Fossen are left alone in the lift. Fossen flatlines. Mark prepares to shock him but discharges the paddles into the air. Fossen watches as Mark does this again, and again, aware that this is how he will die...

Other threads

Peter and Cleo treat Mr Jeffries, the carjack victim, who reveals he has AIDS. Peter can't persuade Jeffries to have surgery. Cleo discovers Jeffries will die within a year and refuses to counter-sign the surgery. Peter gets Mark's signature instead. Annoyed, Cleo argues with Peter and breaks a tube of Jeffries' blood, cutting herself. Peter tests Cleo and puts her on the triple cocktail. Cleo is shell-shocked.

Carter is looking elsewhere, now that he is not being considered for Chief Resident or an attending position. Abby tells Carter about her irritation with Luka, who is trying to get her back into med school. Carter is frustrated. He doesn't want to hear about Luka any more – he wants to be more than Abby's friend.

Kim has read Kerry's letter (7-21) but insists nothing has changed to make their relationship work. Later, Romano fires Kim over a minor matter. Kerry objects but Romano insists Kim is a problem, noting "that other matter". Indignant, Kerry lists Romano's history of discrimination. Romano tells Kerry she is the Chief of Emergency Medicine, not County's lesbian advocate. Kerry announces that she is both, and warns Romano to choose his battles wisely.

Season Eight
2001-2

Themes

Rachel Greene stays with Mark and Elizabeth and endangers their daughter Ella. As Mark's marriage breaks apart, he discovers his tumour has returned and is inoperable. He refuses treatment and spends his last days trying to "fix Rachel".

Peter discovers he is not Reese's biological father and fights for custody of his son. He is told his work schedule endangers his chances, but Romano is unwilling to compromise. He looks for alternative employment at Cleo's new hospital.

Carter starts dating Susan Lewis who has returned to County as an attending, but he is still hung up on Abby. Meanwhile, Chen is dismissed as Chief Resident and Carter takes over. When Mark Greene leaves, Carter finds himself setting the tone.

Abby breaks up with Luka but Carter seems disinterested. Abby tries to help her neighbour escape an abusive relationship and is attacked. She finds support from Luka.

Kerry fights to keep her sexuality secret, but faces problems when she starts dating Sandy Lopez, a firefighter. Her difficulties with Dave Malucci and Jing-Mei Chen come to a head and they leave. But Chen threatens to sue the hospital and returns with new privileges.

Luka's relationship with Abby disintegrates. He gets involved with Nicole, a waitress, but their relationship becomes complicated. When Abby is attacked, he offers her support.

Medical student Michael Gallant joins the ER but clashes with arrogant young intern Gregory Pratt.

Ones to Watch

8 – 11: *Beyond Repair* – Abby has a difficult day and starts drinking. Carter meets Sobriki and sparks an argument with his estranged mother.

8 – 14: *A Simple Twist of Fate* – Abby is assaulted by her violent neighbour. Mark receives news that his tumour has returned and is inoperable.

8 – 18: *Orion in the Sky* – Mark spends his last working day in County General. He decides to refuse treatment.

8 – 20: *The Letter* – News of Mark's death reaches the ER and impacts on all the staff. Carter steps into Mark's shoes.

"Four Corners"

8 – 1: First transmitted 27 September 2001
Written by Jack Orman & David Zabel; Directed by Christopher Misiano

Weaver fears that her sexuality has become a topic for gossip
Kerry returns from holiday to a cool reception in the ER. She claims to have visited Nairobi, but bought her souvenir bracelet from a street trader outside. Anxious, Kerry asks Luka if there has been any gossip about her. She treats Peter's psych patient and hears that Kim has yet to be replaced.

Kerry is unsettled when she has to mediate between a homophobic man and a transsexual. She is still distracted during the Fossen enquiry. Afterwards, Kerry asks Romano if he has told anyone about her sexuality. Romano insists it is a personal matter and not for discussion. Kerry is still uneasy.

Peter grows concerned for Jackie
Joanie tells Peter that Jackie has lost her job – Jesse's death is haunting her. Joanie asks after Cleo and Peter says she wants some space at the moment. Peter treats Alice who was injured during a talk show fight. She has just discovered her boyfriend is her half-brother. Peter tells a stunned Alice she is ten weeks pregnant.

Joanie arrives, fearing Jackie is having a breakdown. As Peter assures her, he is paged to the ER: Alice has jumped from the fourth floor. Alice dies. Later, Mark discovers the mother lied to get on television. After work, Peter visits Jackie. She admits she can't deal with Jesse's death. Peter tries to comfort her.

The Carter family attend the funeral of John Carter Sr
Carter returns from his grandfather's funeral with his cold and distant mother, Eleanor. Abby joins the wake and Carter is pleased for the company. Carter admits his parents don't handle loss well, noting the death of his brother, Bobby. Carter urges his father, Richard, to stand up to Eleanor and deal with their loss. Richard won't listen.

Later, Carter finds Millicent trying to escape the wake in a vintage Jaguar. Carter offers a warm eulogy to John Truman Carter Senior as they crack open a bottle of champagne. Millicent puts the Jaguar in gear and they drive away.

Mark is questioned over the Fossen case
Mark has a head CT before starting work. He is due to present the Fossen case (7-21, 7-22) for review that afternoon. Legal are concerned that Mark took 17 minutes to transfer Fossen to the OR. Mark claims it took time to get help. Romano accepts the answer, adding that no one's going to be crying over Fossen. At the review, Elizabeth

discovers that Fossen was conscious when Mark supposedly shocked him. Elizabeth, whom Mark has told, is disturbed by the fact. That night, as Mark cradles Ella, there is an air of disquiet between them.

Other threads

Chen has made Chief Resident and thanks Kerry for her help.

Cleo tells Mark she is sick from the triple cocktail. Mark recommends a change in her medication. Later, a concerned Peter asks Mark if Cleo is OK.

"The Longer You Stay"

8 – 2: First transmitted 4 October 2001
Written by Jack Orman; Directed by Jonathan Kaplan

Carter is "sucked into the ER vortex"

Carter has six weeks to run on his residency, but has heard nothing from County. Abby persuades him to talk to Kerry about attending positions but Kerry wants more experienced candidates. Chen, struggling with her new workload, asks Carter to help out even though his shift is over.

Carter reluctantly treats a roadie with a cut toe, but the man's friend, Vincent, goes into respiratory arrest. Carter tells Vincent's mother who has a cocaine habit and has to be admitted for nasal surgery. Carter then helps a girl with an infection from a genital piercing. Her drug-crazed friend jumps him and Yosh has to make out a chart for her too. Carter finally finds a room and gets some sleep.

Chen shows her weaknesses as Chief Resident

Chen asks Kerry for advice but is told not to check with her all the time. Meanwhile, Dave treats a 27-year-old who has an MI. Dave orders a tox screen but wants to use anti-clotting drugs without seeing the results. Chen is unsure and pages Kerry but she never arrives. Pressured, Chen allows the drugs, but the tox screen comes back negative. Carter arrives and realises the patient has a weak aorta: the drugs have caused him to bleed into his chest. Carter collects Kerry who stops their actions, angrily telling them they have killed the patient. Kerry is disgusted with Chen but saves her ire for Malucci who, she insists, shouldn't be allowed to practise. Chen feels guilty.

Abby and Luka break up

Luka seems more engrossed in his PlayStation than talking to Abby. Abby objects and they decide to go out. At a local bar, Abby is frustrated that Luka knows everyone, including waitress Nicole. She is again abandoned. Upset, she tells Luka she wants to leave. He testily agrees, but chats to a fellow Croatian while paying the bill. They argue. Luka accuses Abby of playing both him and Carter; Abby insists Luka is "married to a ghost". Angry, Luka says Carter can have her.

Other threads

Carla is involved in a car accident. Peter has to tell Roger and Reese that she has died. Roger asks Peter to look after Reese for a few days. Peter already assumed that he would.

Elizabeth is angry when Mark is late to collect Ella. She insists they need more help, but Mark thinks they have too much now. Elizabeth begins surgery but starts to leak breast milk and is contaminated. Romano tells her to scrub out. That night, Elizabeth struggles to cope when Ella starts screaming.

Sam Broder, the investigator who failed to find Kerry's birth mother, thinks he has found her on a database. Kerry and Sam meet in Doc Magoo's. Distracted, Kerry leaves her pager and does not get Chen's urgent plea for help.

"Blood, Sugar, Sex, Magic"

8 – 3: First transmitted 11 October 2001
Written by R. Scott Gemmill & Elizabeth Hunter; Directed by Richard Thorpe

Kerry fires Dave

Dave hits on an attractive female paramedic and follows her into the lift. As they talk, the lift stops. Dave calms the passengers but one man starts to vomit blood. Dave improvises an intubator with a med kit and stabilises the man. The paramedic is impressed, so much so that Kerry finds her and Dave in a compromising position in her rig. Furious, Kerry fires a stunned Dave.

Afterwards, Dave tells Chen that medicine is the only thing he is good at. He resolves to convince Kerry, but she is unrelenting and brands him a cowboy. Dave rails at Kerry and calls her a "Nazi dyke" before he leaves. Kerry is taken aback.

Abby enlists Carter in a sting on Luka's place

As Abby retrieves her belongings from Luka's she accidentally cracks his prized fish tank. At work, Abby tells Carter that she and Luka have split up and ropes him into helping her replace the tank. Later, Carter and Abby break in to Luka's, but are arrested by the police. Luka is called but does not press charges. Abby invites Carter home but he seems uneasy and claims he has to be up early the next day.

Rachel unexpectedly arrives at the ER

Mark is surprised when Rachel arrives. She angrily claims that Jen kicked her out and says her mother needs therapy. Mark calls Jen to Chicago. Jen is tired that Rachel ignores her curfew and doesn't help out. Rachel bitches that Jen thinks only of her career. Mark tries to mediate, but Rachel refuses to go home and storms out. Later, Rachel asks Mark if she can live with him. Elizabeth is a little annoyed when she sees

Rachel in chairs and realises Mark has agreed she can stay without consulting her.

Chen's confidence is knocked

Romano tells Kerry to supervise Chen more closely or become a scapegoat. Later, Kerry passes one of Chen's patients to Carter, annoying Jing-Mei. Chen's confidence is further knocked when she struggles with a newborn baby. Carter runs an umbilical IV, impressing Chen. Carter tries to talk up Chen's diagnosis of the baby, but Kerry seems unimpressed.

Other threads

Jackie is caring for Reese until Peter can find a full-time nanny, but seems lost in thought. Later, she gives Reese back to Peter – the memory of Jesse is too painful. Peter is given time off by Romano, who signs a message to Reese.

Cleo's tests show she does not have HIV. She needs to be checked again later, but the signs are good.

A tired Elizabeth tries to convince Mr Tanzi to consent to his wife's appendectomy. Mrs Tanzi has Alzheimer's and he wonders if it is better for her to die. Later, Mrs Tanzi is more lucid and Mr Tanzi asks for the surgery. By now the appendix has burst. Elizabeth almost falls asleep on her feet in the OR.

"Never Say Never"

8 – 4: First transmitted 18 October 2001
Written by Dee Johnson; Directed by Felix Enriquez Alcalá

Susan Lewis returns

Susan Lewis disembarks the train at Union Station and makes her way to County. She catches up with the nursing staff but is less pleased to discover Weaver is now boss! Susan reveals she is moving back to Chicago and is in town for interviews. Mark is in a trauma with Elizabeth, who is surprised he is taking Susan to lunch. Mark is delayed but they meet up after Susan's interview. She has decided against a job at Northwestern, but has three more interviews. Mark offers her a place at County, but frosty encounters with Kerry and Elizabeth seem to have put her off. Later, he digs out Susan's old white coat. She muses then accepts the position.

Chen quits

Kerry is surprised to discover Chen is seeing Risk Management and tags along "for support". Chen tries to defend herself over her missed diagnosis (8-3). Risk Management are also concerned that Chen had not completed her residency when she signed off Malucci's procedure – Kerry promoted Chen to Chief Resident and ignored her maternity leave. Chen is angry when she realises Kerry is present to cover her own actions, not support Chen.

Realising she is complicit, Kerry asks Romano if the administration will support her. Romano reckons the family will want more than Malucci's dismissal. Later, Kerry tells Chen she is no longer Chief Resident and will be on a year's probation. Chen is angry to discover Kerry is not being punished for her failure and quits. Kerry offers Carter the post of Chief Resident. Chen tells Carter to take the job but to make sure the sacrifices he makes for his career are worth it.

Peter has to rely on Roger's help

Peter treats Mr Warshaw who fell from a roof and was impaled on a fence post. Peter tells Mr Warshaw he will be fine but Warshaw thinks his family need the insurance money more than he does and plunges the fence post into himself further. The surgery takes longer. Peter rings Jackie to collect Reese but she ignores the call. Desperate, he calls Roger who readily helps. Mr Warshaw dies. Later, Peter calls to collect his son but is convinced by Roger to let Reese stay the night.

Other threads

Elizabeth treats Kenny Schudy, a six-year-old with a severe debilitating condition. His parents hope Kenny can be allowed to die in peace, but Elizabeth gently persuades them to consent to surgery. In the OR, Romano takes photographs of the rare case. Later, Romano finds the parents have left and falsified their papers. Sympathetic, Elizabeth suggests they were under great pressure. Romano simply says: "Boo-hoo."

Nicole arrives in the ER with a cut hand. She tells Luka she has been fired and worries about her visa. Luka talks to his immigration lawyers and helps Nicole. She returns to the ER with cookies for Luka. Abby is bemused by Luka's efforts.

"Start All Over Again"

8 – 5: First transmitted 25 October 2001
Written by Joe Sachs; Directed by Vondie Curtis Hall

Susan starts working in the ER

It is Susan's first day back in the ER. She helps Carter with Mr Norden, who lost consciousness. Carter impresses all with obscure facts during his diagnosis. However, Susan realises Norden is faking the coma and tells his brother. She is shocked when the brother starts breaking Norden's legs with a metal stand – he is actually a hired goon.

Next, Susan and Luka treat Mrs Gadasco, who is unreactive. Susan, a Spanish speaker, realises that she has overdosed on her tuberculosis medication: the English label says "once a day", but in Spanish "once" means 11. They fight to save the woman, but she dies. Susan breaks the news to Mr Gadasco.

Susan also treats Amal, a young girl with an ectopic pregnancy. The girl insists on going home and Susan urges her to come back when she can escape her parents. Kerry is angry and Mark urges Susan to call the girl back. Just then, Amal returns. Later, Susan tells Carter her first day was like "an acid flashback, without the good parts". However, the day ends on a happier note when together they deliver a baby while standing on a ladder!

Elizabeth has a hat-trick of post-operative deaths

Elizabeth convinces Mrs Wilson to consent to colon surgery. Later, she hears one of her patients has died of post-operative complications. Romano congratulates her on her "hat-trick" that week. Elizabeth then operates on Mrs Wilson. As she finishes, Carmen Torino from Infection Control tells her that she is suspected of a bacterial infection that has killed her patients. Elizabeth reluctantly consents to several unpleasant tests.

Carter starts as Chief Resident

Chief Resident John Carter shows two med students around the ER. They get in trouble and Abby tells Carter to supervise them more closely. Carter does, but one of them shocks him with paddles. Meanwhile, Carter's grandmother is brought in after she fainted. Carter wants her admitted, but Millicent is reluctant. She admits she misses her late husband. Carter lets Millicent leave but tells her driver to check on her in an hour. Susan assures Carter that Millicent will be fine.

Other threads

Peter hears Reese is missing. Roger arrives in panic and they call the police. To their surprise, Jackie arrives with Reese who got into a fight at nursery. Roger is annoyed that Reese has too many carers and implies that he and Carla took better care of Reese. Jackie protectively defends Peter.

Mark lets Rachel go to a party if she promises to return early. He is annoyed when she arrives back late and was driven home by a boy. Mark insists Rachel call in future. She tries to get Mark to buy her a mobile phone.

Kerry calls a woman she suspects is her mother. The woman is upset by her questions and refuses to talk further. Kerry is left at a dead end.

"Supplies and Demands"

8 – 8: First transmitted 1 November 2001
Written by Meredith Stiehm; Directed by Jonathan Kaplan

Carter warms to Susan and goes cold on Abby

Carter is suffering from back pain. Susan suggests a pain medication, but Carter is evasive. They talk about Abby and Susan realises Carter doesn't want to be "the rebound guy". Susan treats a student, Lara, who has the flu and discharges her. Later, another student, Andy, is brought in with similar symptoms. This time, Abby notices spots on Andy's hands. Susan realises he has a highly contagious and dangerous strain of meningitis. Both students were at the University of Illinois; Lara kissed Andy at a party. Andy dies and Lara has to be intubated. Susan is annoyed she missed the diagnosis, but Carter insists he missed it too. Later, Carter tells Abby she has too much history with Luka for them to get involved.

Elizabeth is accused of mercy killings

Elizabeth is dismayed to find Mrs Wilson has a post-operative infection. Carmen starts shadowing Elizabeth and points out every minor fault to her. Later, Elizabeth hears Mrs Wilson has crashed. Desperate, she tries to resuscitate Mrs Wilson but Peter warns that Wilson is a DNR. Elizabeth is fraught, but Peter assures her he would want her if he or Reese needed an operation. Later, she is incredulous to hear the Health Department suspect her of euthanasia. Annoyed, she returns home and is furious to find Rachel ignoring baby Ella's cries. Elizabeth tells Mark she is not sure she can cope. Mark insists they will work things out.

Luka finds Nicole a job at County

Abby complains that she can't find some equipment. She discovers Nicole distributing the supplies after Luka got her a job. Abby wonders if Nicole is Luka's girlfriend, but he's just helping her out. Later, Abby can't find a catheter and she and Carter become impatient with Nicole. Luka defends her. Later, Luka treats Wes, a young man who has used his chest catheter to shoot Demerol. Luka tells Nicole that Wes will need a new catheter. Later, he finds Wes has gone. Nicole suggests that he didn't want a new catheter, but Luka didn't tell Wes he needed one. Nicole is evasive.

Other threads

Peter tells Jackie that Roger will be collecting Reese today. Jackie questions Roger's continued involvement with the child, but Peter reckons Reese misses him. Later, Roger confronts Peter, claiming that Jackie is preventing him taking Reese. Peter refuses to discuss visitation arrangements. Annoyed, Roger questions whether Peter is Reese's real father. Peter angrily tells Roger to stay away from his family.

Abby treats a fireman who asks her out on a date. Abby lies that she is unavailable. Later, she helps Rick, a young man who tried a self-circumcision to please his girlfriend. Abby talks to the girl and discovers she asked for the circumcision hoping to force them to break up without a confrontation. Abby confesses she appreciates what she was trying to do.

"If I Should Fall From Grace"

8 – 9: First transmitted 8 November 2001
Written by R. Scott Gemmill; Directed by Laura Innes

Michael Gallant joins the ER

New medical student Michael Gallant arrives for his ER rotation. He prescribes a course of pills to an old woman but another patient, Grace, suggests he run a CBC to rule out a platelet problem. Grace reveals she is a second-year med student from a different hospital. Carter examines Grace, who is anaemic and dehydrated. She is stressed as she prepares for medicine and law exams.

Carter notices scars on her arm and Grace admits she used to cut herself. Susan finds new cuts on Grace's thigh. Grace becomes agitated and wants drugs to help her study. Carter has to restrain Grace and calls a psych consult, despite her protests. Later, Gallant sees Grace has calmed and asks to study with her. Grace agrees.

Luka and Gallant treat a mall security guard

Peter operates on Jeremy, a skateboarder who fell in a mall. Meanwhile Luka and Gallant treat Mr Hilliker, the mall security guard who has an injured foot. Jeremy's family accuse Hilliker of throwing his stick at Jeremy. Hilliker has an anxiety attack, which Luka calms. Hilliker confesses he chased Jeremy, who was terrorising the mall. An ex-cop who never used his gun, Hilliker feels guilty. Later, Gallant and Nicole find Hilliker attempting to hang himself. They cut him down. Gallant, an army reservist, feels sorry for Hilliker and tries to persuade Luka to keep the incident from the police, where Hilliker still has friends. Luka refuses.

Elizabeth investigates the post-operative deaths

Elizabeth fears Carmen's investigation is giving her a reputation: Luka seems to doubt her opinion and Romano has kept her off surgical service. Concerned, she investigates the post-operative deaths herself and discovers Babcock attended each surgery. She sneaks into his laboratory, believing he could be infecting his patients deliberately, but is discovered. Babcock complains to Romano and Elizabeth admits her suspicion. Babcock blames Elizabeth's incompetence. Romano suspends both from surgery until the matter is cleared up.

Other threads

Millicent faints again. Carter is dismayed to discover she has a condition that puts her at risk of a heart attack. Millicent spends the day driving. As Carter waits at home for Millicent, he tells Susan about his stabbing and drug addiction. Susan flirtatiously asks to see his scar. They admit they both had crushes on each other. Carter is glad Susan is back.

Peter hears that Roger is suing for custody of Reese. Jackie tells Peter he shouldn't fight the DNA test and Cleo insists that whatever the results, Peter is Reese's father. Later, Peter provides DNA samples.

Rachel is sent home from school after threatening to cut off another girl's hair.

Luka incurs Abby's wrath when he tries to help Nicole train as a Nurse Aide. However, Abby softens when Nicole cries over Hilliker's attempted suicide, explaining that her father hanged himself when she was ten.

"Partly Cloudy, Chance of Rain"

8 – 8: First transmitted 15 November 2001
Written by Jack Orman; Directed by David Nutter

Weaver and Gallant make a daring rescue

Weaver and Gallant race to the scene of an accident: an ambulance carrying a stabbing victim in labour is trapped under active power lines. Firefighter Sandy Lopez refuses to let Kerry get in to treat the patient, Vicki. The power line explodes and Sandy saves Kerry. Gallant saves another firefighter.

Kerry and Gallant dive into the ambulance. They need to deliver the baby to save Vicki. Kerry has only performed one C-section and the mother died, but she gets consent to perform another one now. Gallant helps as much as he can. They successfully deliver the baby boy. Gallant takes the baby and jumps out of the ambulance. There is another explosion and the power lines go out. Vicki crashes and is loaded into an ambulance. Kerry tells Lopez to see a surgeon about a hand injury.

Romano berates Kerry for taking extreme measures. Kerry checks on the baby, who is doing well. Later, Gallant compliments Kerry on her actions. She thanks Gallant for staying focused. Gallant admits he was scared. Kerry tells him some days are good days – he should enjoy them when they come.

Susan and Carter deal with a hit–and–run

Susan and Carter treat the 24-year-old victim of a hit-and-run. Later, Carter is surprised to treat Millicent and realises she was the driver. Millicent thought she had hit a dog and continued driving. Jill arrests and Carter has to stabilise her. Carter takes Millicent for an MRI but she panics and becomes disorientated. She asks for her husband. Carter has to remind her that her husband is dead.

Mark helps a troubled boy

Mark treats Daniel Pendry, a 12-year-old who almost drowned. His little brother Joey is still missing. Mr and Mrs Pendry are furious at Daniel and say he should be the one missing. Daniel is Mrs Pendry's son from a previous marriage. Joey is found, but is critically ill. The parents angrily turn Daniel away. Miraculously, Mark saves Joey. Later, he tells

Daniel to ignore everything his parents have said. He insists that Daniel is just as special as Joey – and one day his parents will see that too.

Other threads

Frank discovers Nicole is stealing from work. She runs away but later returns and tells Luka she is pregnant. Abby wonders if that is why Nicole stole. Luka claims it is a pattern of behaviour after her father abandoned her when she was 16. Recalling Nicole's story after the Hilliker case (8-7), Abby is suspicious.

Peter tells his lawyer he is not Reese's biological father. The case is now more complicated – two stepfathers seeking custody. He urges Peter to grant visitation rights to appear reasonable to the court. However, Peter refuses and tells Roger he is keeping Reese.

Cleo leaves County to head up a new paediatrics unit.

"Quo Vadis?"

8 – 9: First transmitted 29 November 2001
Written by Joe Sachs & David Zabel; Directed by Richard Thorpe

Peter begins his battle to keep custody of Reese

Peter arrives late for the first stage of his custody battle. Roger testifies that he has never had to pass Reese's care on to others as he works from home and has a flexible schedule. When Cleo takes the stand, Roger's lawyer presents her as negligent, recalling the piano incident (7-21).

During recess, Peter is annoyed that Roger is twisting the facts and Jackie confronts Roger. Peter is cross-examined and criticised for his hectic schedule. After the hearing, Peter's attorney warns that Peter's work schedule is hurting them and that he needs to make some tough decisions…

Corday presses for organ donation

Corday tells Mr Pruett that his wife has no meaningful chance of recovery and urges him to permit organ donation. Pruett agrees, but has second thoughts when he discovers his wife will still be alive when the organs are removed. Luka suggests an alternative procedure: the woman dies, then the organs are harvested. Corday is angry at Luka's intervention. In the OR, she extubates Mrs Pruett, but she breathes on her own. Romano is annoyed – they will have to wait until the woman dies.

Mark and Susan treat a brain–damaged teenage boxer

Mr Escalona arrives with Rudy, his younger son who was injured while boxing with his older brother. Rudy deteriorates and Susan realises he has a burst artery in his brain from a pre-existing condition. The boy dies and Rudy's brother bitterly confronts Mr Escalona for putting Rudy under too much pressure: the brain bleed was caused by the "power drinks" Rudy drank to impress his dad. Later, Gallant talks to Rudy's brother and manages to reunite father and son.

Luka discovers the truth about Nicole

Luka tries to have Nicole reinstated but Kerry insists the hospital has a clear policy on theft in the workplace. Meanwhile, Abby asks Nicole about the discrepancy in her stories about her father. Nicole explains her real father hanged himself; she was evicted by her stepfather. Abby is still unconvinced about the pregnancy and warns Nicole that Luka will find out eventually. Later, Nicole tells Luka she lied, explaining she wanted to keep hold of him at all costs.

Other threads

Kerry treats Sandy Lopez, the injured firefighter (8-8), and asks her out on a date. Sandy agrees and Kerry is pleased her instincts were right.

The police bring Rachel's friend Andrew in with breathing difficulties. He and Rachel were stealing street signs and Andrew has been smoking marijuana. Mark insists Rachel takes a drug test. The test is negative, but Rachel is angry with Mark.

Carter deduces that a young woman is allergic to semen – and to prove it, for her to have sex with her partner in an exam room. Carter catches Susan listening in. After he is proved right, Carter kisses Susan and asks if she has any allergies he should know about.

"I'll be Home for Christmas"

8–10: First transmitted 13 December 2001
Written by Dee Johnson & Meredith Stiehm; Directed by Jonathan Kaplan

Peter begins his battle to keep custody of Reese

December 13. Peter tries to arrange more flexible working hours, but Romano is dismissive. Peter is persuaded to scrub in on an unusual surgical case.

17 December: Peter is anxious that Judge Alter wants to speak to Reese, but refuses to do a deal with Roger. The attorney warns that Roger is looking to be the better candidate and arranges a negotiation. Peter balks at 38 days visitation and refuses to talk further. In court, Roger argues he can spend more time with Reese. Peter lies that he has new working hours at County. The judge asks for proof and Peter promises to get it. Roger is furious. Peter asks Romano again but Romano refuses. Peter quits and speaks to the director of surgery at Cleo's new hospital.

19 December: the day of the ruling. Peter gives Judge Alter his new letter of employment but the Judge is angry that Peter lied about working at County. Peter is pensive about the ruling. In court, Alter speaks to Reese in private. On his return, he grants custody to Peter: Reese has always thought of Peter as his father. Roger is granted visitation rights. Cleo and Jackie are overjoyed.

Christmas Eve: Peter tells Cleo that it almost took losing his son to recognise his priorities. He works a final shift at County and performs a miraculous save that astounds even him. Elizabeth insists County will miss him, but Romano is simply disappointed. The two men part in silence.

Later, Peter is jogging when he sees Carter. Carter thanks Peter for being a good influence. "Hey, Peter. I'm a good doctor because of you," says Carter. "No you're not," teases Peter. "But keep trying."

Abby discovers more about Nicole

Luka tells Abby that Nicole has taken some money and left. He admits she was right about Nicole. However, Abby later finds Nicole in the OB ward: Nicole lost her baby after eight weeks. Nicole asks Abby not to tell Luka the truth – she mistook his kindness for love. Meanwhile, Luka considers posting bail for a man who stole Christmas presents for his kids. Abby convinces him there is only so much he can do for people. Sad, Luka agrees.

Carter's parents are divorcing

Carter hears his parents will be home for Christmas, but only his father arrives. Richard explains that he is leaving Eleanor and they are getting a divorce. Dismayed after the news, and treating a mother with lymphoma, Carter tells Susan she is the only thing going right in his life now.

Other threads

Sandy Lopez arrives in the ER and wonders why Kerry didn't call after their first date. Kerry, embarrassed in public, pulls Sandy to one side and offers to have lunch the next day. Their search for a restaurant proves fruitless and Kerry suggests they head back to her house instead.

One to Watch

"Beyond Repair"

8 – 11: First transmitted 10 January 2002
Written by Jack Orman & R. Scott Gemmill; Directed by Alan J. Levi

Abby's birthday puts her in mind of parenthood

It is Abby's birthday, and she is woken by her rowing neighbours, Joyce and Brian. At work, she is upset that Luka doesn't remember her birthday. She is also taken aback when her ex-husband Richard arrives to announce he is marrying a woman with a six-year-old son. At work, Abby treats Merrill Stipes, a young woman who is having an adverse reaction to her fertility treatment. Merrill is worried that she aborted a baby once before and may not be able to conceive again. Abby is struck.

Abby also sees Douglas Leeman, a young boy walking the ER in search of his mother. Abby tries to find the mother, but discovers that she had a brain haemorrhage and died. Abby breaks the news to Douglas, who doesn't believe her. Kerry tells Abby to arrange social services until Douglas' father arrives. Abby is uncomfortable as Douglas is dragged away, demanding to stay with her.

Abby returns home after a long day and sees Joyce sitting on the stairs. She has had another fight with her husband. They crack open some beers and drink to Abby's birthday.

Carter's stabbing comes back to haunt him

Carter and Millicent are surprised when Eleanor arrives in Chicago. Eleanor admits that she and Jack separated and left matters a little open-ended, but is surprised that John already knows this. Carter is nonplussed and heads to work.

Gallant tells Abby that an agitated patient who lost consciousness after a fall is demanding his caseworker. Abby is surprised to see it is Paul Sobriki, the man who stabbed Carter and Lucy (6-14). Sobriki is on conditional release.

Eager to keep Sobriki away from Carter, Abby wants Sobriki transferred, but Susan refuses until they have the results of a head CT. Eventually, Carter stumbles on Sobriki. The man eagerly apologises, insisting he has a disease but is getting better. Carter is disquieted. Later, Abby passes Carter a letter from Mrs Sobriki. He notes that Abby couldn't protect him from her, either.

At home, Carter is annoyed to find Eleanor sent Millicent's private nurse home. Eleanor claims to be looking after Millicent, determined not to let Jack split up the family. Carter scoffs at Eleanor's idea of family. Emotional, he angrily asks where she was when he was stabbed and bitterly notes she was elsewhere, as she always has been with him. "Bobby died and I lost a mother," he angrily notes.

Other threads

Mark tells Elizabeth he has found a cigarette lighter in Rachel's laundry and decides to search his daughter's room. Elizabeth is unsure but Mark proceeds anyway. Rachel catches him just as he finds a packet of cigarettes and a condom. Mark presses for answers but Rachel becomes angry, slamming the door in his face.

Carter meets Chen in a shopping mall. She tells Carter that she went to Doc Magoo's to ask about the night of the Marfan case and that Weaver left her pager in the bathroom. Carter asks what Chen intends to do, but she says nothing...

Sandy ribs Kerry about her snoring when they wake at Kerry's apartment. Later, they go to a hockey game and see Malik and Susan, enjoying tickets they found on "Icicle Andy". Kerry hides her face and Sandy realises Kerry isn't out. Annoyed, she tells Kerry she doesn't have time for this and leaves.

Beyond Repair is a fantastic low-key episode – no major accidents and no messy traumas. It's really an Abby/Carter story. The fact that it works so well is testament to the writers and how quickly and effectively they have integrated Abby into the show. Abby's difficult day is a clever piece of character development – when she cracks open a beer at the end, the significance almost goes over your head. Meanwhile, the chilling reappearance of Sobriki gives way to the more spectacular confrontation between Carter and Eleanor. It's an argument that has been 20 years in the making, and the sheer ferocity of Carter's words mark every day of that long wait. It's a great story about two people who have been changed by their past irreparably.

"A River in Egypt"

8 – 12: First transmitted 17 January 2002
Written by David Zabel; Directed by Jesús Salvador Treviño

Kerry is angry when she is forced to reinstate Jing-Mei Chen

Kerry is called to Romano's office where Chen demands to be reinstated. Chen accuses Kerry of covering herself when she had lost her pager (8-3). Kerry refuses to back down and tells Chen to grow up. However, Romano orders Kerry to reinstate Chen as an attending. Kerry fears she will have no authority over Chen. Her suspicions are confirmed when Chen demands that she will report to senior faculty members but not to Kerry. Kerry accepts she was in the wrong about her pager, but tells Chen that if she was a better doctor, she wouldn't have been needed.

Carter is caught in his parents' divorce

Carter reluctantly meets his father to mediate for Eleanor. Jack is dismissive and warns that Eleanor is "an emotional vampire". Carter returns home to find Eleanor emotional and a little drunk: she is feeling guilty about abandoning John after Bobby's death and has been asked to leave by Millicent. Eleanor meekly asks if Carter wants her to leave. John admits that he doesn't.

Mark and Rachel come to an agreement

Mark discovers Rachel has broken her curfew and they argue. Rachel wants to move back home to Jen. Elizabeth is sceptical of Mark's attempts to solve their difficulties with Rachel. Later, Mark treats Mr Echeveria, who had a heart attack en route to his daughter's wedding. The daughter wants nothing to do with him because he abandoned her as a child. Struck, Mark tells Rachel he won't let her go when things get rough. They agree to be straighter with each other in future.

Abby intercedes between her warring neighbours

Abby hears Joyce cry for help from her apartment and calls the police. When the police arrive, Joyce refuses to press charges. Joyce insists everything is OK, but later arrives at the ER with a sprained ankle. Abby tries to give Joyce an "escape kit" to help her leave Brian. Joyce defends Brian and doesn't take the kit.

Other threads

Kerry asks Sandy to stop leaving messages for her at work. Despite this, Sandy arrives. Kerry tries to keep their conversation quiet, but Sandy is angry and kisses Kerry in front of everyone. Later, Kerry is angry Sandy has made her go public. Sandy bitterly insists she did Kerry a favour, she just doesn't see that yet.

    Carter treats Dimon, a homophobic rapper who has clamydia. Carter suspects Dimon's girlfriend Aisha is the carrier, but it turns out to be Dimon's male friend CC, who is also HIV+. Dimon also tests positive. CC begs Dimon to come clean about his sexuality, but is punched to the floor. Later, Aisha arrives to be tested also.

Susan treats Kinney, a murderer on death row. Kinney does not want heroic measures and attempts to kill himself. Susan is annoyed when Kerry resuscitates him: but death row convicts are not permitted DNRs.

"Damage is Done"

8 – 13: First transmitted 31 January 2002
Written by Dee Johnson; Directed by Nelson McCormick

Ella's life is threatened by Rachel's carelessness

Elizabeth is bed-ridden with a stomach bug and can't care for Ella. Trying to help out, Rachel volunteers and Mark eagerly accepts. Later, Elizabeth is woken when Rachel can't stop Ella crying. Elizabeth realises Ella has taken some pills and Rachel realises with horror that she has ingested two of her ecstasy tablets.

At the ER, Mark and Elizabeth work frantically on Ella. Kerry eventually persuades them to step aside and let her and Chen work. Ella is intubated and stabilised and taken to the PICU. Elizabeth refuses to let Babcock near Ella.

Mark is furious with Rachel and tells her Ella may have learning difficulties from now on. Rachel is mortified and Mark softens as Rachel sobs. Later, Mark tries to console Elizabeth but they know Ella's life still hangs in the balance.

Kerry finds working with Chen is problematic

Romano is concerned that Kerry is falling behind in her administrative duties and has appointed Susan as her assistant. Kerry's confidence is further knocked when Chen and Mark handle a trauma case and reject her help. Susan, too, finds that Kerry only gets in the way. Irked, Kerry later tells Chen that she doesn't want a divisive staff. Chen suggests that Kerry could always quit.

Carter is concerned that Eleanor wants to relive his brother's illness

Eleanor brings Mickey, a young orphan with leukaemia, to the ER and demands John's help. Carter orders some tests and encourages Eleanor to go home, but she is eager to stay. Later, she steals the test results and takes them to Carter, who confirms that Mickey's leukaemia has returned. John wonders why Eleanor has been staying with Mickey and tells her that he does not share her need to relive Bobby's illness. Carter is unsettled that Mickey is boosted by Eleanor's support.

Other threads

Mark and Chen treat Mr Brower and his six-year-old daughter Jessica. Brower opened a letter bomb at home. Mrs Brower, a doctor, arrives to find Jessica is stable but watches as her husband dies. Distraught, she tells Mark that she was working on cloning and should have told her family about the death threats.

Gallant treats Manny Kindlevitch, a blind diabetes sufferer who is accompanied by his 'seeing eye' dog, Stinky. Gallant is allergic to dogs and Stinky takes a liking to Kerry and follows her about. Later, Manny dies and Kerry inherits the dog.

Abby hears a frantic knocking on her door. Joyce is fighting with Brian and, scared by him, asks to hide in Abby's flat. Brian is soon banging on the door as Joyce cowers. He soon stops and Joyce asks if she can stay the night.

One to Watch

"A Simple Twist of Fate"

8 – 14: First transmitted 7 February 2002
Written by Jack Orman; Directed by Christopher Chulack

Elizabeth issues Mark with an ultimatum

Mark and Elizabeth are relieved when Ella is extubated and breathes on her own. Elizabeth asks if the police have charged Rachel with anything, but realises that Mark has not informed them. She is angry when Mark seems to make excuses for Rachel and implies that Mark was to blame for the incident with Ella. Angry, Mark returns to the ER but soon has troubles of his own. He struggles to find a word and then shows signs of neurological dysfunction. Susan tries to reassure Mark, but he clearly fears that his tumour has returned.

Rachel arrives to beg Elizabeth's forgiveness. Unrelenting, Elizabeth demands that Rachel pack her bags and return to Jen. Upset, Rachel tracks down Mark, who insists that she doesn't have to leave. Mark is distracted by his own health concerns and misses his appointment with Elizabeth in the PICU, sparking another row.

Elizabeth refuses to bring Ella home until Rachel is out of the house. Mark insists he can't choose between his daughters – but Elizabeth says she has made the choice for him. Later, Mark tries to calm things with Elizabeth but she is resistant. Instead, he goes to Radiology for a head scan…

Brian attacks Abby

Abby tries to convince Joyce that Brian needs counselling, but Joyce still acts the victim. After leaving Joyce hiding in her apartment, Abby bumps into Brian. She lies that she has not seen Joyce. Later, Abby receives a call from Joyce and returns home to find her bleeding with a broken cheekbone.

She brings Joyce to the ER where Luka, who has just returned from two months working in Bosnia, helps her. Abby keeps Brian away from Joyce by threatening to call the police. Luka watches Brian leave. The police question Joyce, but she again denies abuse. Abby tells them to check the Windbreaker Bar where Brian hangs out. Luka insists they will find a shelter for Joyce.

At home, Abby calls Joyce in the shelter. She is interrupted when Brian arrives, asking to know where Joyce is. Abby refuses to tell him and watches Brian leave. However, seconds later he bursts back into the apartment and viciously knocks Abby to the ground. Regaining consciousness, Abby looks in horror at her bloodied face. She heads to the ER where she is treated by Luka and Susan. Susan tells Abby to stay with her tonight. She slowly agrees.

Luka finds Brian playing pool in the Windbreaker bar. Brian cowers pathetically as Luka beats him. Fierce, Luka threatens to kill Brian if he goes near Abby again.

Susan is swamped in her new managerial role

Susan finds the ER staff tucking into free food from a pharmaceutical company. Kerry chastises Susan for being ready to tuck in, noting that she can't compromise her managerial position by taking gifts. Susan heads to Doc Magoo's instead. She is soon swamped with cases as the staff fall ill with food poisoning – including Kerry, who had a sneaky bagel herself! After dealing with a midget prostitute and an obese asthmatic, Susan gets a quiet moment to catch up with Jerry, temping at the admissions desk. As he tucks into a bagel, she tells him he'd better leave now.

Carter is angry when Eleanor abandons Mickey

Eleanor has stayed with Mickey (8-13) all night. She asks Carter about bone marrow transplants but chemotherapy is the only option. Carter admits it is as much luck as treatment now. He tells Eleanor to get some rest but she insists on staying. Later, Mickey starts vomiting blood and Eleanor panics. She tells John she can't see this sort of pain again and starts to leave. Carter can't believe she is abandoning Mickey after raising the boy's hopes.

That night, Eleanor has packed to leave Chicago. She apologises to John, upset that she gave Mickey the hope that she gave Bobby. Carter reveals that Bobby only pretended to have hope for Eleanor's sake. John promised Bobby that he would help their mother forget the pain, and apologises that he couldn't. Eleanor tells John that she loves him. Later, they both sit with Mickey as he undergoes the chemotherapy.

If *Beyond Repair* is a low-key way to move the characters forward, then *A Simple Twist of Fate* is the exact opposite. Mark's arguments with Elizabeth are hard enough without the awful realisation that Mark's tumour has returned. It's a neatly structured story with revelation after revelation played out in realistic timescales, each making Mark's situation more and more desperate and tragic.

Attached to that, there is the horrific assault on Abby after a few weeks lead-in. Abby's reaction to her bruised and bloodied face is painful to watch. Later, Luka's attack on Brian will have you cheering, for all it will damage any chance of a prosecution. Plus we have Carter and Eleanor, almost as an aside. This is a blockbuster character episode in the finest tradition and just goes to show that single incident episodes aren't automatically the ones the watch.

"It's All in Your Head"

8 – 15: First transmitted 28 February 2002
Written by R. Scott Gemmill; Directed by Vondie Curtis Hall

Mark's worst fears are confirmed

In New York, Dr Burke tells Mark his tumour has returned. It is inoperable: Mark has four to five months to live. Back at County, Mark tells Susan. Upset, Susan asks how Elizabeth has taken the news, but Mark has yet to tell her. Meanwhile, Elizabeth has refused to come home. She is angry when he misses an appointment with their paediatrician, unaware that Mark is undergoing chemotherapy. Elizabeth tells Benton she fears Mark has distanced himself from her and Ella. She worries that she may have found an excuse to leave Mark.

Meanwhile, Mark treats a brain-damaged father whose son takes advantage of him. Struck, Mark decides not to tell Elizabeth or Rachel. He fears they will look on him differently. Susan takes Mark home and looks after him.

Abby learns that Brian will not be put on trial

Abby is working shifts to avoid meeting Brian who is at home awaiting trial. Luka offers to let Abby stay at his place until the trial is over, but Abby is not convinced it is a good idea. Later, Abby hears the trial has been cancelled: Brian has got away with community service as he was beaten shortly after he attacked Abby. Abby returns home but sees Brian and goes to Luka's instead. Luka has a few friends over and invites her to join them.

Mark and Elizabeth treat a burns victim

Mark treats Ian Nevinger, who has 50 per cent burns after a blast in his garage. He doesn't want his wife to see him. Mark speaks to Mrs Nevinger, a nurse at Mercy, who doesn't understand how the incident happened. Mark discovers amphetamines in Nevinger's blood and realises he lit up around paint fumes. Mrs Nevinger is furious and chastises Ian. Later, Elizabeth tells Mrs Nevinger that Ian's condition is grave. She is taken aback by the woman's venomous refusal to speak to him.

Kerry treats Cooper

Kerry treats Dennis Cooper, who has been shot repeatedly. He dies. The police tell Kerry that Cooper was a drug dealer and murder suspect. His eight-year-old daughter, Brianne, could be in danger as the only witness. Kerry gets Brianne to open up and discovers that Brianne shot Cooper because he threatened to shoot her first if she watched television.

Other threads

Chen receives roses from her date. The man, Randall, arrives later, but Chen lets him down gently. She later explains to Carter that "you give a man hand relief during *Harry Potter* and he wants to marry you." Carter chokes on his coffee.

Jerry breaks his retirement to do a little temping at the ER. He soon runs foul of Frank who insists: "It's him or me." Kerry suspends them both for fighting, but they are saved by Chen's excuses.

"Secrets and Lies"

8 – 16: First transmitted 7 March 2002
Written by John Wells; Directed by Richard Thorpe

Carter, Susan, Abby, Luka and Gallant get detention

Carter is jealous to discover Susan has spent the night at Mark's. Susan insists nothing is going on, but Carter doesn't believe her. She accuses Carter of double standards: he is attracted to Abby. Carter protests and now Susan is disbelieving.

At work, they treat an injured dominatrix and her client. Abby and Susan can't resist looking in the dominatrix's bag of toys and Luka, Carter and Gallant join in amused. Kerry finds them all messing with vibrators and blow-up dolls and ticks them off. Later, Susan tries to apologise but Kerry finds a purple strap-on dildo in her own locker! They are all in trouble.

The next day, Carter, Luka, Abby, Susan and Gallant are sent to a sexual harassment seminar. Accusations fly as to who planted the dildo in Kerry's locker. Carter is tetchy and wants to leave, but Gallant doesn't want any more trouble. Abby discovers Carter's mood is over Susan's sleepover at Mark's. Susan tells Abby that Carter is stuck on her and Carter asks to change the subject. Instead, they wonder how much Carter is worth! A woman interrupts them to announce that their tutor is running late.

After another round of accusations, the group talk about their education. Abby defends her decision to stay in nursing. Luka and Susan seem unconvinced, but Abby thinks they can't understand because they made different choices. Meanwhile, Carter finds some fencing epées in a cupboard: Carter was taught to fence and Luka learned for a school play. As he and Luka engage in a mock duel, Abby tells Susan she hasn't slept with Carter. Neither has Susan. Abby is surprised and advises her of the second date rule – sleep with someone early to find out if you share any chemistry. Meanwhile, Luka and Carter become more competitive and a fist-fight erupts. The women break the two up. As she comforts Carter, Susan kisses him. Carter is taken aback. Susan seems a little disappointed.

After yet more accusations, the subject turns to sex and when each lost their virginity. Carter confesses he was 11 when he slept with a 25-year-old maid. After much protesting, Luka reveals he was a virgin on his wedding night – his wife was religious, so they waited. The group quieten. Luka insists it is a good memory. Changing the subject, Susan discovers Luka played Hamlet at school. Competitive, Carter launches into an overblown performance. Luka finishes the speech more sincerely in Croatian. The tutor arrives and they sit for the seminar.

After the seminar, Abby, Gallant and Luka leave. Susan tells Carter he looked foolish trying to impress Abby. She tells Carter that nothing is going on between Abby and Luka. She asks Carter to kiss her, but again there is no chemistry. They agree to be friends. As they leave, Carter admits Kerry used to have his locker and never changed the combination...

"Bygones"

8 – 17: First transmitted 28 March 2002
Written by Elizabeth Hunter & Meredith Stiehm; Directed by Jessica Yu

Elizabeth discovers Mark's tumour has returned

Elizabeth tries to avoid Mark, but is ordered to cover the ER. She is testy with Mark and sees that he has become closer to Susan. Later, Elizabeth tries to talk to Mark, but he is absent. Susan hints at his illness and Elizabeth finds Mark receiving treatment in Radiology. Guilty, she instantly offers support but Mark only wants her back with him for the right reasons.

Reeling from the news, Elizabeth finds a quiet room where Romano finds her in tears. Elizabeth wonders if she should go home and watch Mark die. Romano says she should. He asks if she still loves Mark. Elizabeth confesses that she does.

Meanwhile, Mark has a rough day and ends his shift early. Kerry is annoyed, but Mark casually notes he has just had chemotherapy and is tired. The staff are shell-shocked. That night, Elizabeth returns home. Mark is being sick upstairs and Rachel has guessed the truth. Reunited, Elizabeth comforts Mark.

Kerry hears that Sandy was injured in a fire

Kerry treats the victims of a fire at an elementary school and is concerned to hear that Sandy Lopez is one of three missing firefighters. Meanwhile, Kerry treats Diane Hayes, a 19-year-old with multiple stab wounds who later dies. Diane had defensive wounds but her friend, Shelley, insists she had no enemies. A second woman, Renée Carlson, is brought in with multiple stab wounds. As they work, Renée whispers: "I loved her." Shelley reveals that Diane was Renée's flatmate but was about to move out. Kerry fears that Renée was the assailant, but Mrs Carlson refuses to accept this. Later, Kerry waits at the firehouse for Sandy. She admits she was worried and that Sandy did her a favour by revealing her sexuality. They kiss.

Chen treats a traumatised young man

Chen takes delivery of a parcel for Luka, but the delivery man, Martin, seems intent on staying. He appears mentally disabled and unable to talk. Chen discovers he hasn't eaten for two days. She calls his home but only gets his answerphone. She presses, but Martin becomes upset and indicates his knitted hat and scarf. Later, Adele reveals that Martin's mother, who knitted him the items, was found dead at home. Martin was traumatised by the discovery.

Other threads

The ER staff treat Viktor, an eight-year-old adopted boy who almost drowned during "socialisation" therapy. The aim was to help Viktor bond with his new parents by recreating the womb. When Viktor recovers and cries for his mother, the therapist claims another success. Mark and Adele reckon it was borderline abuse.

Abby has been doing "vampire hours" and finishes her shift. Carter offers rooms at his house but she refuses. When Abby has left, Susan asks if he has had any luck with Abby – Carter tells her to shut up.

One to Watch

"Orion in the Sky"

8 – 18: First transmitted 4 April 2002
Written by David Zabel; Directed by Jonathan Kaplan

Mark works his last day in the ER

Kerry wants to lighten Mark's load, but he insists on seeing patients. He treats Nora Cruz, a 46-year-old with MS in respiratory distress. Her son, Jeffrey, is not sure if Nora is a DNR – his sister Linda would know – and permits a central line. Later Jeffrey allows Mark to intubate her. Mark's vision blurs and Weaver takes over. She asks Mark to take over the induction of intern Gregory Pratt instead. Mark is disappointed, but agrees.

Jen flies in to see Mark. She suggests that Rachel stay with Mark throughout the summer. Jen is sorry their marriage didn't work out. Mark insists he would change none of it. He tries to tell Jen that he has changed his will, but Jen insists they can talk later. Mark is not so sure.

Mark returns to the ER and treats Al Ervin, an ER regular who will only let Mark see him. Pratt wants to order a psych consult but Mark tells him not to be disdainful of their "frequent flyers". He tells Pratt to get Al's old chart. Irked, Mark then helps deliver a baby. Mark realises the mother is a drug user, but she insists she is clean. The tox screen proves otherwise and Mark angrily tells her everything that could be wrong with her child. "Congratulations, you're a mother," he bitterly adds.

Later, Mark heads upstairs for chemotherapy. He is called back to look after Al, and brings his drip with him. Mark discovers Pratt did not check Al's chart and prescribed treatment without realising he was a diabetic. Carter has to save Al. Mark angrily tells Pratt to pay attention or leave. Pratt discovers Mark has a brain tumour and apologetically tries to explain his behaviour. Mark is dismayed that Pratt knows about his illness. Meanwhile, Linda Cruz arrives with her mother's DNR. Mark sadly orders Nora extubated.

Mark tries to finish his chemotherapy in the ER, but sees Al agitated and helps. Having seen so much suffering, Mark has decided to discontinue his chemotherapy. Later, Al tells Mark that he wants to leave the hospital to die outside. Mark lets him go. Elizabeth is upset by Mark's decision, but he wants to die the way he lived. Meanwhile,

Mark and Pratt have to tell a man he has inoperable cancer. Pratt, uncomfortable before Mark, struggles. Mark intercedes and breaks the news. Pratt leaves, upset.

Mark treats Katie, a young girl with a splinter under her nail, and talks to her to distract her from the pain. She tells him the story of Orion's Belt – how Artemis put Orion in the sky where he couldn't be harmed. His mind made up, Mark thanks Katie for being his very last patient. He makes to leave but on his way, Kerry wonders how many shifts to put him down for next week. Thinking a moment, Mark tells Kerry not to let her work become her life. "Live a little."

Outside, Carter asks if Mark is on tomorrow. Evading the subject, Mark tosses Carter his basketball. "You set the tone, Carter," he tells a bemused Carter. "Work on your jump shots," he says as he turns to leave County for the last time.

Other threads

Arrogant young intern Gregory Pratt joins the ER for a three-month internship. He is due to become a resident in July and hopes not to be matched to County. Cocky, Pratt quickly dives into cases, and examines the wrong patient for a penile fracture, to Carter's amusement.

Carter treats Willa Goldman, an Egyptologist from the Art Institute who lost consciousness at work. Her colleague insists she has the curse of the mummy. Later Willa, embarrassed, admits she just works too hard.

Orion In The Sky was the episode where Mark Greene really left the show. It's a wonderfully sad but fulfilling episode. The early indication that Mark's illness will make it impossible for him to treat patients sooner rather than later is almost casually introduced. From then on, Mark is taken down and down as he deals with the DNR, the "crack baby" and Al, a patient he has treated throughout the years. But with Mark's realisation that his time is up we see the old Mark in action. The moment when he breaks the tragic news to the cancer patient is almost too much to bear. Mark's last moments, where he leaves the ER saying barely a word, is heartrending. Only Kerry has the sense that this is really goodbye. Then he passes the chalice to Carter. This is television writing at its best.

"Brothers and Sisters"

8 – 19: First transmitted 25 April 2002
Written by R. Scott Gemmill; Directed by Nelson McCormick

Susan's sister and niece go missing

Susan receives a panicked phone message from her niece Suzie who says that Chloe is ill and she can't wake her up. The call is traced to New York and Susan flies out to scour the city. Officer "Bosco" Boscorelli is dismissive, but Officer Yokas, hearing the taped message, insists on helping. Susan reveals that Chloe had a substance abuse problem five years ago.

The officers track down Daryl, a drug user, and get a lead. Chloe's apartment is empty but there is drug equipment on the bed. They get another lead from a dealer and find Chloe unconscious in an abandoned bus, but Suzie is not with her. In hospital, Chloe regains consciousness but doesn't know where Suzie is. She reveals that Joe, her husband, broke her heart. Chloe apologises that she has screwed up – and Susan can only agree. Upset, Susan determines to find Suzie.

Pratt's arrogance endangers a patient's life

Pratt annoys the ER staff with his arrogance: flirting with Chen, ignoring the advice of nurses and discharging Carter's patient without consent. Later, a gunshot victim is rushed to the ER and Pratt takes charge, pushing Gallant aside and deriding Gallant's skill. As Pratt and Gallant argue, the man crashes and Pratt proceeds to crack the chest without supervision. Gallant objects but is soon roped in to help. Carter is furious and angrily tells both to wait in the lounge, but Pratt returns to work. Carter berates Gallant, who accepts his complicity but asks not to be confused with Pratt. Carter insists that Pratt get in line. Pratt objects but backs down.

Carter discovers Abby has started drinking again

As Luka puts new locks on Abby's door, Carter arrives. He is taken aback to see Abby drinking and makes his excuses. At County, Carter and Luka treat a drunk driver and clash over Abby's drinking. Abby asks Carter not to worry about her, implying that their relationship is a complication. Carter wonders if they have a relationship. Abby is evasive. That night, Abby has second thoughts about her drinking.

Other threads

Elizabeth and Luka treat Alan, a seven-year-old with severe spinal injuries after a fall. Alan's parents agree to disconnect the ventilator, but the scene is too much for Elizabeth. Later, she receives an urgent call from Rachel, who is with Mark in Hawaii. Mark's condition has deteriorated and he won't be able to return home. Unusually sympathetic, Romano offers Elizabeth his support. She asks him to pray for Mark, and Romano agrees. Elizabeth leaves for Hawaii…

Romano lectures Kerry on lesbian health issues – before asking her to be the "poster child" for County's new Centre for Lesbian Excellence. Kerry angrily refuses, but Romano already has a press conference planned! Later, a woman from the Illinois Women's Health Coalition arrives to speak to Kerry.

Brothers and Sisters was a crossover story with *Third Watch*, a show about the emergency services in New York. In the *Third Watch* episode *Unleashed* (broadcast 29 April 2002), Susan, Bosco and Yokas discover that a cop took Suzie. They interrogate Joe, Chloe's husband, but he did not take her. The culprit is a Neighbourhood Watch worker. They find Suzie, but Chloe quickly takes her and leaves.

One to Watch

"The Letter"

8 – 20: First transmitted 2 May 2002
Written and Directed by Jack Orman

The ER receives sad news about Mark

Carter catches up with Susan – Suzie and Chloe turned up in Elmira after three weeks –
before checking on his faxed lab results. The fax is in fact a letter from Mark Greene, which
Carter proceeds to read aloud to the assembled gang. Mark is in Hawaii with his family,
and says how much he misses County. He praises the ER staff for their skill and friendship
and apologises for his sudden departure.

Carter's face darkens as he turns the page and reads a note from Elizabeth. "Mark died
this morning at 6.04am," he reads. "The sun was rising, his favourite time of day. I sent
this on so that you might know that he was thinking of you all and that he appreciated
knowing you would remember him well." The staff stand in stunned silence. Carter tells
Frank to post the letter on the notice board.

Carter sets the tone

Carter is still shaken by the news during a trauma case, and Romano has to act quickly.
Carter hears that Abby and the staff are going for a drink after work to toast Mark. He
attends and tries to take Abby to an AA meeting. Abby refuses and they end up at Doc
Magoo's, talking. Abby explains she started drinking before her assault, on her birthday,
for self-pitying reasons. Carter presses and Abby agrees to go to a meeting before her shift.

Back at work, Chen tells Carter she is having trouble with Al. Carter explains Al is
Mark's "private patient". Al crashes and, thinking Carter is Mark, asks for no tubes or
shocks. Carter tells Chen that Al is now a DNR. Later, Kerry tells John that people will look
to him as the longest serving doctor to step in and fill the void. She tries to clear out Mark's
locker, but is overcome and asks Carter to do it. Packing away the contents, Carter finds
Mark's stethoscope. He pauses, then takes it for his own.

A man is brought in with a gunshot wound to the face. Gallant can barely look to
hold the man's jaw as Carter intubates. The procedure over, Carter tells Gallant to get some
air outside. A little later, he joins the apologetic Gallant, who wonders if he can do this
job. Echoing those words he received from Greene all those years ago (1-0), Carter explains
that there are two kinds of doctors – those who get rid of their feelings, and those who
hold on to them. "Helping is more important than how we feel." Carter heads back inside,
and sits with Al until the man dies.

Kerry lives a little

Kerry is upset to read the letter on the notice board and tries to continue as normal. She
sutures George, a mentally disabled man, but becomes frustrated. As she watches Romano's

283

saddened reaction to the letter, she snaps at George then runs into a treatment room where she breaks down. Later, Kerry tells Sandy she fears she has lost a friend in Mark. Sandy encourages Kerry to go to the bar for drinks with the staff, but she is hesitant. However, Kerry eventually arrives at the bar with Sandy, and they are readily invited to join the group.

Susan finds the news difficult to absorb

Susan treats Melissa, a young girl involved in a car crash who has a lump on her back. As she waits for test results, Susan receives a call from Chloe: Joe has taken her back and will look after Suzie while Chloe is in rehab. Susan is sceptical, but accepts the news. She receives Melissa's test results and discover the girl has a tumour. Susan calms Melissa as Romano inserts a chest tube. Romano operates and is angered by the spread of the cancer, railing against it as an indiscriminate killer.

Later, Susan asks if Romano got it all. He insists he did. The next day, Carter finds Susan crying in the lounge. She explains how she only found Melissa's tumour because of the car accident. Carter realises she is searching for answers for why Mark died so soon. Susan admits that she misses Mark already.

Other threads

Pratt got his third choice in his match: he will be a resident at County. He asks Carter to put in a good word for him at Northwestern. Carter refuses, noting that County needs good doctors: "For better or worse, we drew you."

News of Mark's death reaches County and the effect is absorbing to watch. The Carter story is particularly well handled. Kerry says exactly what we want to hear: he's the longest serving member of staff, he needs to take Mark's place. His exchange with Gallant – a lift of Mark's exchange with Carter in the pilot episode – is the moment of apotheosis. Carter's use of Mark's stethoscope is a lovely little touch. In fact, it's the smaller moments that are worth noting. Romano's railing against cancer, the "indiscriminate killer", is a fantastic glimpse into the hidden respect he has for his colleagues. And, of course, there is Susan's simple bow of the head when she hears the last paragraph of Mark's fax. Of all the strands, perhaps Kerry's story is the most touching. Her desperate flee to an examination room where she breaks down reveals a side to her character that we sometimes forget.

"On the Beach"

8 – 21: First transmitted 9 May 2002
Written and Directed by John Wells

Mark's final days

"You set the tone, Carter. Work on your jump shots," says Mark as he leaves County General for the last time.

At home, Mark can't sleep. Elizabeth finds him making a list of all the things he wanted to do but never found the time. The list becomes progressively sadder: teach Ella to ice skate; teach Rachel to drive; be there at their weddings. Sad, Mark believes he hasn't been a good father and wishes he could do the last item on his list: fix Rachel.

The next day, Mark picks Rachel up from school. They end up in Hawaii, where Mark recounts the story of their family: his angry teenage years, his difficulties with his father. Rachel is surprised they didn't get along. Mark wishes he could take back all the things he said but can't. Mark teaches Rachel to surf. That night, Rachel cries for Mark. Depressed, she takes one of his pills with some alcohol. Mark watches concerned, but says nothing.

Mark and Rachel move to a retreat house. He teaches Rachel to drive, then they go to the beach. Mark asks when Rachel started getting high. She refuses to talk but Mark chases after her. He insists he loves her, but won't be around to stop her killing herself. Mark has a seizure. Rachel panics, unsure what to do.

Elizabeth and Ella arrive. Mark refuses to see a neurologist. Elizabeth is concerned by Rachel's relationship with an older boy, Kai, but Mark thinks it is nice. Back at the house, Rachel finds Mark singing *Somewhere Over the Rainbow* to Ella as he did to Rachel. Rachel snaps that she is fed up with hearing about their past. Elizabeth warns Rachel that Mark does not have long. If she is not careful, she will miss her time with Mark and regret it the rest of her life. Meanwhile, Mark suffers partial paralysis. He becomes angry as the final effects of his tumour take hold.

Mark still refuses to see a doctor. He gets Elizabeth to write down letters for Rachel and Ella to open on special days. Later, Rachel finds Mark in bed. He was dreaming balloons and how Rachel would let them go as soon as he gave them to her. He tells Rachel what he needs to say: "Be generous with your time, with your love, with your life." She promises. Rachel plays *Somewhere Over the Rainbow* to Mark. As he drifts away, he remembers the ER, his wife and daughters. Later, Elizabeth checks his pulse. Mark has died.

The funeral is well attended with faces past and present. After the service, Rachel, Elizabeth and Jen ride back. Rachel asks to see Ella during holidays and Elizabeth readily agrees. Rachel looks out of the window and asks the driver to stop. She finds a blue balloon tangled in a tree. She rescues it, then lets it go. Rachel smiles as she watches the balloon sail into the sky.

"Lockdown"

8 – 22: First transmitted 16 May 2002
Written by Dee Johnson & Joe Sachs; Directed by Jonathan Kaplan

The ER is exposed to a potential smallpox outbreak

The ER treat the elderly victims of a bus crash. The driver had a seizure and plowed into a car. As they contend with the mass of minor injuries, Mr and Mrs Turner arrive with their sick children, Adam and Bree. Gallant suspects chicken-pox but Carter is more concerned. He checks a public health poster then isolates the family. He tells Susan it could be smallpox – the disease is airborne and the ER will have to be locked down.

Susan calls Public Health. Chen realises she treated the children for flu days before and could be infected. Carter isolates her with Stan the Can, a feverish homeless man. Susan announces the lockdown. The patients are understandably fearful and agitated.

Later, David Torres of the Public Health department arrives and takes control of the ER.

Outside, Kerry, Haleh and Lily arrive but are refused access. An ambulance arrives and Kerry has to help the gunshot victim outside. A news crew arrives and asks questions, but Kerry wisely avoids saying anything that would start a panic.

Carter discovers the Turners have recently returned from Africa. Suddenly, Bree crashes. Pratt argues for a course of treatment but Carter insists it won't work. The girl dies and Pratt questions Carter's actions. Carter tells him his suggestion was futile and he should learn. Pratt angrily demands Carter teach him but Carter tells him to shut up and follow his lead. Carter suddenly notices Pratt has a high temperature and isolates him with Chen and Stan.

The patients become agitated and a lawyer starts preparing a class action against the hospital. Luka discovers that the bus driver, Marge, hid her epilepsy to get a driver's licence. Meanwhile, Susan treats the driver of the car Marge hit. The man bleeds out and Gallant loses the pulse. Just then, Adam crashes and Carter can't intubate. Carter has to perform a tracheotomy himself. He barely manages to save Adam in time. Meanwhile, Stan has a seizure. Pratt and Chen manage to stabilise him.

An angry group of patients demand vaccinations from Abby. Torres calms them momentarily but they grab a gurney and use it as a battering ram against the main doors. Carter grabs everyone's attention. He explains that they could be exposed to smallpox and urges everyone to stay at County and not take the disease home to their families. As the crowd come to their senses, the riot squad barricade the doors.

A little later, the Centre for Disease Control confirms that the disease is an orthopox, but can't be sure it is smallpox. Torres congratulates Carter and Abby on stabilising Adam but tells them that they must be quarantined now. Alone, Abby asks Carter if the worst is over. Carter doesn't reply. She asks him to tell her they will be OK. He kisses her, and confirms. Then leans in and kisses her again.